Applications in Basic Marketing
Clippings from the Popular Business Press

2002-2003 Edition

Applications in Basic Marketing
Clippings from the Popular Business Press

2002-2003 Edition

William D. Perreault, Jr.
University of North Carolina

and

E. Jerome McCarthy
Michigan State University

Boston   Burr Ridge, IL   Dubuque, IA   Madison, WI   New York   San Francisco   St. Louis
Bangkok   Bogotá   Caracas   Kuala Lumpur   Lisbon   London   Madrid   Mexico City
Milan   Montreal   New Delhi   Santiago   Seoul   Singapore   Sydney   Taipei   Toronto

McGraw-Hill Higher Education

*A Division of The **McGraw-Hill** Companies*

APPLICATIONS IN BASIC MARKETING:
CLIPPINGS FROM THE POPULAR BUSINESS PRESS 2002-2003 EDITION
Published by McGraw-Hill/Irwin, a business unit of The McGraw-Hill Companies, Inc., 1221 Avenue of the Americas, New York, NY, 10020.

Some ancillaries, including electronic and print components, may not be available to customers outside the United States.

This book is printed on acid-free paper.

1 2 3 4 5 6 7 8 9 0 QPD/QPD 0 9 8 7 6 5 4 3 2

ISBN   0-07-255798-2
ISSN   1099-5579

Publisher: *John E. Biernat*
Executive editor: *Linda Schreiber*
Managing developmental editor: *Nancy Barbour*
Marketing manager: *Kimberly Kanakes*
Media producer: *Craig Atkins*
Project manager: *Destiny Rynne*
Lead production supervisor: *Heather D. Burbridge*
Director of design BR: *Keith J. McPherson*
Supplement producer: *Matthew Perry*
Senior digital content specialist: *Brian Nacik*
Compositor: *Electronic Publishing Services, Inc., TN*
Printer: *Quebecor World Dubuque Inc.*

www.mhhe.com

Preface

This is the thirteenth annual edition of *Applications in Basic Marketing*. We developed this set of marketing "clippings" from popular business publications to accompany our texts—*Basic Marketing* and *Essentials of Marketing*. All of these clippings report interesting case studies and current issues that relate to topics covered in our texts and in the first marketing course. We will continue to publish a new edition of this book *every year.* That means that we can include the most current and interesting clippings. Each new copy of our texts will come shrink-wrapped with a free copy of the newest (annual) edition of this book. However, it can also be ordered from the publisher separately for use in other courses or with other texts.

Our objective is for this book to provide a flexible and helpful set of teaching and learning materials. We have included clippings (articles) on a wide variety of topics. The clippings deal with consumer products and business products, goods and services, new developments in marketing as well as traditional issues, and large well-known companies as well as new, small ones. They cover important issues related to marketing strategy planning for both domestic and global markets. The readings can be used for independent study, as a basis for class assignments, or as a focus of in-class discussions. Some instructors might want to assign all of the clippings, but we have provided an ample selection so that it is easy to focus on a subset which is especially relevant to specific learning/teaching objectives. A separate set of teaching notes discusses points related to each article. We have put special emphasis on selecting short, highly readable articles—ones which can be read and understood in 10 or 15 minutes—so that they can be used in combination with other readings and assignments for the course. For example, they might be used in combination with assignments from *Basic Marketing,* exercises from the *Learning Aid for Use with Basic Marketing,* or *The Marketing Game!* micro-computer strategy simulation.

All of the articles are reproduced here in basically the same style and format as they originally appeared. This gives the reader a better sense of the popular business publications from which they are drawn, and stimulates an interest in ongoing learning beyond the time frame for a specific course.

We have added this component to our complete set of **P**rofessional **L**earning **U**nits **S**ystems (our **P.L.U.S.**) to provide even more alternatives for effective teaching and learning in the first marketing course. It has been an interesting job to research and select the readings for this new book, and we hope that our readers find it of value in developing a better understanding of the opportunities and challenges of marketing in our contemporary society.

William D. Perreault, Jr. and E. Jerome McCarthy

Acknowledgments

We would like to thank all of the publications that have granted us permission to reprint the articles in this book. Similarly, we value and appreciate the work and skill of the many writers who prepared the original materials.

Lin Davis played an important role in this project. She helped us research thousands of different publications to sort down to the final set, and she also contributed many fine ideas on how best to organize the selections that appear here.

The ideas for this book evolved from and built on previous editions of *Readings and Cases in Basic Marketing*. John F. Grashof and Andrew A. Brogowicz were coauthors of that book. We gratefully recognize the expertise and creativity that they shared over the years on that project. Their fine ideas carry forward here and have had a profound effect on our thinking in selecting articles that will meet the needs of marketing instructors and students alike.

We would also like to thank the many marketing professors and students whose input have helped shape the concept of this book. Their ideas—shared in personal conversations, in focus group interviews, and in responses to marketing research surveys—helped us to clearly define the needs that this book should meet.

Finally, we would like to thank the people at McGraw-Hill/Irwin, our publisher, who have helped turn this idea into a reality. We are grateful for their commitment to making these materials widely available.

W.D.P. and E.J.M.

Contents

Getting Information for Marketing Decisions

Product

Place

Promotion

Price

Marketing Strategies: Planning, Implementation and Control

Ethical Marketing in a Consumer-Oriented World: Appraisal and Challenges

Marketing's Role in the Global Economy and in the Firm

Drinks for Developing Countries

Seeing Need and Opportunity, Coke and P&G Formulate Vitamin-Packed Beverages

BY BETSY MCKAY

Staff Reporter of THE WALL STREET JOURNAL

Coca-Cola *is using children in rural Gabarone, Botswana as test subjects for a vitamin-fortified drink the company is developing.*

GABORONE, Botswana—Every morning for eight weeks last spring, a group of local nurses drove into the dusty yards of two primary schools here, mixed bright orange powder with processed water in big metal vats and handed one paper cupful of the drink to each child, 250 in all. The beverage looked and tasted like Coca-Cola Co.'s Hi-C orange-flavored drink, but it contained extra ingredients: 12 vitamins and minerals chronically lacking in the diets of people in developing countries.

The daily ritual, a clinical test, was part of "Project Mission," a continuing Coca-Cola research-and-development effort aimed at creating a drink that could help combat anemia, blindness and other afflictions common in poorer parts of the world. By the end of the eight weeks, levels of iron and zinc in the children's blood had grown, test data show. Some parents said their children, whose diets consist mostly of cornmeal and rice, had more energy and had become more attentive at school. Marvin Viekeman said his eight-year-old daughter, Anah, had gained weight by the end of five weeks. "I was suspicious about it at first," he said, "but it has helped her."

And if all goes as Coke plans, the new drink, to be called Vitango, could help boost sales at a time when growth of carbonated soft drinks is slowing.

After its expected launch in a year or so, Vitango will put the Atlanta beverage company in head-to-head competition with Procter & Gamble Co., which has a similar drink that is already being sold. While the market for such drinks is limited, they're meant to offer Coke and P&G a chance to attempt the role of good corporate citizen at a time when being perceived as such is increasingly important for U.S. multinationals.

A Coke document outlining plans for Project Mission puts it bluntly: The new

Undernourished

The most common micronutrient deficiencies in the developing world:

● **Iodine:** An estimated 43 million people worldwide suffer from varying degrees of brain damage and physical impairment due to iodine deficiencies.

● **Vitamin A:** More than 100 million young children suffer from vitamin A deficiency, which contributes to 2.2 million deaths per year from diarrhea among children under five. Severe deficiency can also lead to partial or total blindness.

● **Iron:** Nearly two billion people are estimated to be anemic worldwide. Iron deficiency anemia lowers resistance to disease and weakens a child's learning ability and physical stamina.

● **Zinc:** Malnourished children with zinc deficiency are more susceptible to growth failure and infections. Zinc deficiency, which is increasingly widespread among women in developing countries, is associated with long labor, which increases the risk of maternal and infant death.

Source: Unicef

drink is meant in part to help the company establish relationships with governments and schools that will "serve as a positive platform for brand Coca-Cola."

"It's the right thing to do," says Steven Heyer, Coke's president and chief operating officer for marketing and noncarbonated-beverage brands. "The marginal cost is low, and the return to society high. It's a way of extending Coke's relationships." Coke has big hopes for Vitango in Africa and Latin America, where its products already reach some of the most remote areas. A second clinical test, to determine how well Vitango's nutrients are absorbed in the blood-

stream, was just finished in Peru.

P&G launched its product, Nutristar, last month in Venezuela after years of research and development and clinical tests. A powdered drink that contains eight vitamins and five minerals, Nutristar is sold at most food stores in flavors like mango and passion fruit and boldly promises "taller, stronger and smarter kids." So far, the drink is "really doing well," says Carmen Silvia Garcia, a P&G food scientist and manager for external relations for the company's operations in Venezuela. Available also at McDonald's, Nutristar is the chosen beverage with about half the Happy Meals the restaurants sell,

Ms. Garcia says. P&G is also offering samples in schools, she says.

Nutristar, selling at about 40 cents for a packet of powder that makes one liter of beverage, is priced at about 25% more than other powdered drinks and 30% below carbonated soft drinks, Ms. Garcia says.

Coke's pricing for Vitango has yet to be determined. The company had planned to test-market the drink in South Africa this month at a price of about 20 cents for an 8-ounce liquid serving but scrapped its plans at the last minute and said it would reformulate the drink. Mr. Heyer says the reformulation will reduce costs—and prices—to make Vitango more affordable to those who need it most.

"Micronutrient" deficiencies, or a lack of vitamins and minerals such as vitamin A, iron and zinc, are believed to afflict about two billion children around the world. Werner Schultink, senior adviser for micronutrient programs for Unicef, says the impact of micronutrient deficiencies "is huge, on learning capabilities, health and mortality."

With vitamin pills costly to distribute and pill-taking regimes hard to enforce, fortification of foods offers the most promising prospects for combating some deficiencies, Mr. Schultink says.

But how much of an impact the companies have will depend how many people they reach, and whether they make their drinks available in school feeding and other public programs in addition to selling them in stores. While not limited to the poorest of the poor, the problem is still most severe among those who can rarely afford a treat like a sweet drink. "It all depends on marketing strategy," Mr. Schultink says. Selling it at a price that makes it affordable only by a smaller part of the population "won't cause a

major shift," he says. Both Coke and P&G are targeting middle- and lower-middle-class families who aren't destitute but who still may not have the healthiest of diets.

Developing a fortified drink that is cheap, effective and doesn't leave an aftertaste is a challenge. Coke made an attempt to develop one in the 1970s, but technology wasn't advanced enough at the time for the idea to work. P&G says it dedicated a "major investment" in the 1990s, including consultations with micronutrient experts, to develop its proprietary iron, vitamin A and iodine fortification technology, which it calls GrowthPlus. An initial "learning market" wasn't an immediate success. An orange-flavored powdered beverage, dubbed Nutride-light and launched in the Philippines in 1999, didn't sell well because its price was too high, at about 50% above other powdered beverages, Ms. Garcia says.

Coke's Project Mission got its start in April 2000, when a group of marketing and innovation executives paid a visit to the company's operations in Ecuador. Local managers there were looking for a less obtrusive way to advance the Coca-Cola name in secondary schools than through bottle-cap contests that promoted sales of cola. With economic conditions in the country deteriorating, children were poorly nourished and inattentive in class, recalls Jay Gould, head of innovation at Coke. "Mothers were very concerned," he says. "Their kids were falling asleep during class."

In developing the beverage, Coke determined that a powdered version of Hi-C sold to restaurants appealed to consumer groups tested in South Africa. With that information in hand, the company enlisted a "world-wide nutrition advisory board" to create a

combination of vitamins and minerals that would be absorbed well and whose taste wouldn't be strong.

A pediatrician at the Houston-based Baylor College of Medicine, Steven Abrams, who has expertise in vitamin and mineral absorption, led the effort. A combination of 12 vitamins and minerals, which like Growth-Plus included iron, vitamin A, and iodine, was formed. The effort involved experimenting with different sources of iron and vitamin A to maximize both taste and effectiveness. Powder, liquid and even carbonated forms were developed. Concerned about water quality in Africa, Coke wants to sell Vitango there in a ready-to-drink form.

By aiming products at the developing world, the companies are treading in an area where others have run afoul, such as Nestle SA and its debacle with infant formula. Both say they aim to meet an existing consumer need. To succeed, they must win the support of nutrition and health experts. While the sugary drinks are packed with vitamins and minerals, they contain no actual juice, and the companies stress that they are intended as supplements.

"We're not marketing this as a one-stop shop for health," says Abby Rodgers, a vice president of Coke's Minute Maid unit who heads Coke's development effort. "We're not saying don't drink milk or juice. This augments a healthy diet."

Emily Nelson contributed to this article.

TESCO BETS SMALL —AND WINS BIG

Britain's top supermarket chain was slammed for its go-slow approach to selling goods over the Net. Now it's the world's largest online grocer

"But oh, ho, ho, who's got the last laugh now?"—IRA GERSHWIN, 1936

John Browett, CEO of British online grocer Tesco.com, isn't smug enough to amble around the company's headquarters singing the old Gershwin tune. But few would begrudge him if he did. Assailed by analysts during the peak of the dot-com boom for its go-slow approach to selling groceries over the Internet, Britain's No. 1 supermarket chain has watched one rival after another put up the white flag. Now, Tesco.com has assumed the mantle of the world's largest and most successful online grocer. "We've been a bit lucky," says Browett, "but we've also been right."

Tesco's big bet was to bet small. In 1996, when the Web was exploding and online groceries seemed like a brilliant idea, Tesco PLC dipped its toe ever-so-gently into the water, outfitting a single store in Osterley, England, to accept orders by phone, fax, and a crude Web site. The idea was to test whether customers would buy groceries without shopping in conventional supermarkets. Equally important, Tesco had to figure out whether it made more sense to pick those groceries off the shelves of its stores or build separate warehouses to fill online orders. By March, 1998, the company had proved there was sufficient demand and that picking from stores worked. But it had to keep tweaking the process to get the economics right. It wasn't until September, 1999, that it rolled service out to 100 stores.

Now, Tesco.com is firing on all cylinders. It has expanded to 250 outlets—more than a third of the chain's 690 British stores—enabling it to deliver to 91% of Britain's population. The business is on track to turn in revenues this year of more than $450 million and boasts a respectable net operating margin from groceries of around 5%, or more than $22 million, analysts estimate. Last year, the dot-com unit lost $13 million due to the cost of expanding into new businesses such as CDs and videos, but it was

profitable on groceries. "They were the only company in the world to really get it," says retail analyst David V. McCarthy of Schroder Salomon Smith Barney.

What Tesco got was that selling groceries over the Net was going to be small potatoes for the foreseeable future. After all, the chain is expected to book sales this year of $30 billion, making its online operation a mere 1.5% of revenues. So instead of spending a fortune to build distribution warehouses outfitted with fancy technology, Tesco chose a decidedly low-tech approach. Fewer than two dozen employees are needed to pull products off the shelves in each store and schlep them in vans to customers in the neighborhood. It's kind of like an electronic version of the 1950s delivery boy. Today, Tesco.com handles more than 3.7 million orders per year—and half of its online customers weren't previous Tesco patrons. Now, the company is building on that foundation to expand into other businesses, such as baby products and wine by the case. "We've got a chance to become the leading 'last mile' delivery service in Britain, because we're taking it very incrementally," Browett says.

"Out on a limb." That's a lesson that failed dot-coms likely wish they had learned. Many Net startups were undone by focusing so much energy on growth that they never knew whether their business models worked until they hit the wall. Says Browett, who at 37 could easily be mistaken for the head of a Web upstart: "You can't make a run for revenues and then work out the cost structure later." Despite that timeless logic, e-commerce gurus from McKinsey & Co. and Andersen Consulting (now Accenture Ltd.) questioned Tesco in 1999 for not building warehouses, prompting the company to recheck its math to make sure it wasn't heading down the wrong path. "We were clearly out on a limb when the hype was at its peak," Browett says.

Staying the course proved even sweeter for Tesco after the ignominious failure of Webvan Group Inc. The Foster City (Calif.)

startup, one of the most richly funded in history, went bankrupt in July. It burned through $1.2 billion in two years trying to establish a purely Web-based grocer in the U.S. Webvan's strategy was vintage dot-com: It shot for the moon, aiming to build two dozen automated warehouses around the country, costing up to $35 million apiece, that were supposed to cut 40% off the labor expense of handling groceries. Each was meant to serve a 60-mile radius encompassing millions of potential customers. But after building only three warehouses—in Oakland, Calif., Atlanta, and Chicago—the numbers got worse and worse.

Webvan's Waterloo: Customer demand wasn't high enough to operate the facilities at anywhere near their capacity, so fixed costs swamped revenues. "The first 10,000 customers were easy to find—San Franciscans sitting on the edge of their couches waiting for Web groceries," says analyst Ken Cassar of Internet researcher Jupiter Media Metrix Inc. "But the rest of the country isn't the same." He and other analysts figure Webvan lost $5 to $30 on an operating basis for every order it delivered. When you crank in depreciation, marketing, and other overhead, the loss jumps to a staggering $132 per order.

Growing competition. By contrast, Tesco's decision to pick groceries out of existing supermarkets kept startup costs low. The company spent just $58 million over four years to launch its online grocery operation, and has since laid out $29 million more to expand into nonfood items. The wisdom of that tortoise-vs.-hare approach has been validated by a host of other companies. "Now that the high-cost wacko Internet business model turns out to have been a disaster, Tesco's store-based picking is the direction everybody's going," says analyst Andrew P. Wolf of BB&T Capital Markets in Richmond, Va.

The prime example: In June, Safeway Inc., the No. 3 supermarket chain in the U.S., said that it would partner with Tesco to deliver groceries to online customers. The British chain is investing $22 million for a 35% stake in GroceryWorks, a money-losing Net start-up half owned by Safeway. The companies already have shuttered three GroceryWorks warehouses in Texas. They plan to begin rolling out the Tesco.com system this fall or early next year in a handful of Safeway's 1,500 U.S. stores. "We liked Tesco's track record," says Safeway spokeswoman Debra Lambert. "They understand how to combine technology with bricks and mortar."

That's not to say there aren't drawbacks to Tesco's approach. Orders are automatically routed from a data-processing facility in Dundee, Scotland, to the nearest store, so customers are limited to buying only what's available there. If it happens to be one of Tesco's smaller outlets, they may have only 20,000 items to choose from, vs. 40,000 at larger stores. Analysts worry, too, that the Tesco.com model won't "scale up" when the business gets bigger. Although its fixed costs are low, Tesco.com has relatively high variable costs because more orders require more labor for picking and delivery. As a result, Tesco.com won't likely be able to reap the economies of scale that Webvan expected from its warehouses—meaning it may never become much more profitable than it is today.

On top of that, Tesco will face growing competition. Despite Browett's claim that the secret of Tesco's success lies in painstakingly tested and refined processes, some analysts think competitors can fairly easily copy or improve upon them. For instance, archrival J Sainsbury PLC, the grande dame of British supermarkets, is belatedly rolling out delivery service at 36 of its stores but will also operate warehouses near London and Manchester. "We think picking centers are the way to go in the long run," says Sainsbury spokesman Matt Samuel, "but we're using stores to get to market faster."

None of this worries Browett. He thinks Tesco.com can hit $4.35 billion in sales—about 10 times today's levels—before running out of headroom in its stores. The biggest concern: Aisles could get clogged with pickers, interfering with everyday shoppers. But long before reaching that point, Browett says, Tesco.com likely will embrace a hybrid approach, using warehouses in dense regions and store-picking for rural customers. As for selection, he says, even Tesco's smallest markets can offer more items than Webvan's warehouses did because human pickers can grab a single jar of capers or sate sauce from a shelf, while Webvan stocked goods by the palette, limiting each warehouse to about 15,000 products.

What really riles Browett, though, is the notion that rivals will have an easy time catching up. "This looks simple on the surface, but the detail underlying it has turned out to be very, very hard," he says. That's where Tesco's by-the-numbers management has proven to be an invaluable asset. Founded in the 1920s by immigrant businessman

Jack Cohen, for decades the company played scrappy second fiddle to Sainsbury's. The turning point came seven years ago, when Tesco marketing execs won an internal power struggle with the traditionally dominant purchasing managers. That resulted in the elevation of then-marketing head Terry Leahy to his current role as CEO of Tesco PLC. From that point, says Richard Hyman, a principal at British retail consultancy Verdict Research Ltd., Tesco has obsessively focused on satisfying customer demand. By the late 1990s, it surged past Sainsbury's in sales and market share, despite its less upscale image. "We think Tesco is the best retailer in Britain, period," Hyman says. In re-

cent years, it has expanded into Central Europe and Asia, where it now gets 12.5% of sales, and has opened catalog and financial-services units.

But the dot-com operation may be Tesco's most unlikely triumph. Launched as a skunkworks project with six mid-level managers reporting directly to Leahy, Tesco.com got off to an inauspicious start. For two-and-a-half years—an eternity in Internet time—the unit's managers tinkered with the formula. "We went down some blind alleys and back," admits Tesco.com Chief Operating Officer Carolyn Bradley. After rejecting phone and fax orders as too expensive and error-prone, Tesco settled three years ago on a sys-

---

Easy Does It: Why is Britain's Tesco.com thriving in the online grocery business when Webvan failed in the U.S.? A comparison of the two companies' strategies and operations reveals crucial differences.

A Boost from Bricks

Tesco: Britain's No. 1 grocer picks and packs its online orders from existing supermarkets, then delivers in nearby neighborhoods using only a few trucks per store. By leveraging its brand, suppliers, and database of 10 million affinity-card holders, Tesco launched online shopping for just $56 million.

Webvan: Startup Webvan spent $1.2 billion to build its business from scratch, including $35 million automated food warehouses. With no existing customers or suppliers, costs soared. A lack of experience hurt, too: None of Webvan board members came from the grocery industry.

One Step at a Time

Tesco: The British giant spent years developing and fine-tuning its online order and delivery systems. After launching with just one store in 1996, Tesco gradually rolled out online service to about one-third of its 690 British outlets today. That puts it within a half-hour of 91% of the British population.

Webvan: Webvan tried to run before it could walk. It aimed to enter 24 U.S. markets within three years, and opened warehouses in the San Francisco Bay area, Atlanta, and Chicago in its first 15 months. Even though none of the warehouses broke even, Webvan kept building facilities in New Jersey and Maryland that never opened.

No Free Lunch

Tesco: E-commerce gurus thought grocery buyers wouldn't pay for delivery. Tesco bucked the trend and charged £5 ($7.25) per order. The chain now gets more than 70,000 online orders weekly and collects $27 million per year for deliveries alone–the difference between profit and loss. Plus, the fee encourages customers to place larger orders.

Webvan: Newcomer Webvan wooed customers with free delivery for orders over $50, adding millions in unrecovered costs. Analysts figure that Webvan lost from $5 to $30 on every order it handled.

The Web's Not Everything

Tesco: Tesco.com doesn't have to prove itself as a stand-alone business to be a win for the grocer. The online operation helps extend the brand: Tesco.com says that half its customers come from rivals' stores. Those customers, Tesco hopes, will start shopping at its supermarkets.

Webvan: The startup had to survive on its Web sales alone. Yet the dot-com meltdown is proving that the Net is less an end than a means. Customers had no connection to Webvan except through their PCs, so the online grocer couldn't profit from a quick stop-in for milk, coffee, or junk food.

(Cont.)

tem that lets customers place orders only over the Web. But the process of picking products off the shelf was punishingly inefficient. In the supermarket business, where margins are thinner than a slice of prosciutto, a few pennies per item can make the difference between profit and loss. And the one thing Tesco wasn't willing to do, Bradley says, was to lose money on its dot-com operation.

When the company retrenched in 1998, it came up with a nifty solution. Rather than having pickers traverse the entire store filling orders for individual customers, each supermarket is divided into six zones—groceries, produce, bakery, chilled foods, frozen foods, and "secure" products such as liquor and cigarettes. Each picker, outfitted with a rolling cart, scours a single zone retrieving products for six customers at a time. To save valuable seconds and improve accuracy, each item is scanned at the moment it's picked. Then, customer shipments are assembled in the back room and stacked in vans for delivery. Tesco.com typically fills two to three waves of orders per day, which allows customers to buy as late as noon and receive a delivery by 10 that night.

It's not just the process but also judicious use of technology that lets Tesco.com keep expenses to a minimum. Each picking cart, for instance, is topped with a wireless touchpad computer that plans the optimal route through the store and tells pickers what to grab, one item at a time. That lets them average just 30 seconds per item, so a typical order of 64 items can be filled in 32 minutes, at a cost of about $8.50, including labor and depreciation, say analysts. Despite Tesco's efficiencies, that's still pretty steep—some 7% of the average $123 order.

The company makes up the difference in several ways. First, it saves about 3% of the order value by not using checkout clerks, Jupiter figures. The real saving grace is that online orders tend to have higher gross margins—more than 30%, vs. Tesco's typical 25%, Schroder Salomon Smith Barney analysis shows. That's because online shoppers are more affluent and buy more profitable products, such as organic vegetables, quality meats, and private-label packaged goods. "Our success is dependent on the fact that Tesco.com's margins tend to be higher," concedes Marketing Vice-President Tim Mason, though the company wouldn't provide figures or comment on analyst estimates.

There's another surprising factor that has spelled the difference between success and failure for Tesco. When the company rolled out Web shopping, it bucked conventional wisdom and imposed a £5 ($7.25) delivery fee per order, an amount it figured the market could bear. By contrast, Webvan offered free delivery for orders over $50, which ended up costing it millions in unrecovered expenses. Tesco.com insists customers are willing to pay for service—and the quadrupling of its orders over the past year seems to bear that out. Customer Krista Levey, 27, an executive assistant at Arthur Andersen who buys from Tesco.com about once a month, says the fee "is nothing" compared to the convenience of not having to lug home cases of bottled water on the London Underground.

Charging for delivery proved to be a masterstroke. First, it largely covers the cost of the vans and drivers who blanket the country. Tesco.com takes in about $27 million per year from the fees, close to the estimated $34 million cost of deliveries, figures Booz, Allen & Hamilton Inc. analyst Timothy Laseter. Imposing a fee also boosts the likelihood that customers will be at home during the two-hour window for their deliveries, since they have to pay again for redelivery. That's a big win for Tesco, given that returning merchandise to the store and restocking it could savage margins.

Even more important, the delivery fee has helped raise the typical order size because customers want to get their money's worth. So the average purchase from Tesco.com is three times a typical $35 supermarket transaction, a vital contributor to the online operation's solid gross margins. Eliminating the fee in an effort to stoke demand "would take away the incentive to spend up," says Schroder's McCarthy. And indeed, Tesco.com has no interest in boosting sales if the result is a loss on operations.

Truth be told, Tesco.com also enjoys advantages Webvan never could have recreated even with another $1 billion in funding. By being a part of the Tesco empire, it can piggyback on the parent company's advertising, branding, and customer database. As one of the best-known and most trusted names in Britain, Tesco confers instant legitimacy on its dot-com unit. Plus, the online operation gets free ads in Tesco's quarterly mailing to its 10 million affinity-card holders and has linked its Web site to store databases so customers can easily reorder products they've previously purchased online or in a supermarket. On top of that, having pickers in Tesco stores provides constant publicity for the Web service—a benefit Webvan could never enjoy because it had no retail presence.

Tangible and intangible advantages such as these have prompted some analysts to

Tesco's Advantage By The Numbers

The secrets to Tesco.com's success are higher margins on groceries, a delivery fee, and lower packing and delivery costs than Webvan.

	TESCO.COM	% OF SALE	TESCO STORE	% OF SALE	WEBVAN	% OF SALE
AVERAGE SALE	$123.25	100%	$34.80	100%	$114.00	100%
MINUS:						
COST OF GROCERIES	$85.66	70%	$26.10	75%	$83.00	73%
CASHIERS IN STORE	–	–	$ .87	3%	–	–
OTHER STORE COSTS	$15.16	12%	$4.28	12%	–	–
MARKETING AND ADMIN.	$5.67	5%	$1.60	5%	$133.04	117%
PICKING AND DELIVERY	$17.80	14%	–	–	$30.00	26%
PLUS:						
DELIVERY FEE	$7.25	6%	–	–	–	–
NET PROFIT (LOSS)*	$6.21	5%	$1.95	6%	($132.04)	NM
* Including delivery fee, before taxes						

Data: *BusinessWeek*, ABN AMRO, Schroder Salomon Smith Barney, Booz, Allen & Hamilton, Jupiter MMXI, company reports

question whether Tesco.com would turn a profit if it were a stand-alone business. ABN Amro's Mark Wasilewski, for one, thinks the parent may not be charging its dot-com unit enough in-store costs—depreciation, utilities, marketing, and so on—as a way of making Tesco.com's books look better. Browett dismisses the charge. "There's no point in fooling yourself," he says. Every unit, whether Tesco's financial-services arm or its dot-com operation, has to carry its own weight, he insists. Besides, he adds, the criticism entirely misses the point: Tesco isn't trying to create a stand-alone business. Tesco.com is merely an additional sales channel that lets the company boost revenues and push more products through its system. As long as it's not leaking red ink, it's a net gain.

So what's next for Tesco.com? Analysts are confident it will keep expanding its business in Britain. By 2004, predicts Wasilewski, it will hit $2.2 billion in revenues—still just 7.5% of Tesco's total—and generate net profits of $181 million. Tesco also has announced the first international expansion of its dot-com business, other than the Safeway deal: By the first quarter of 2002, it aims to launch online shopping in South Korea, where it operates seven supermarkets, with 11 more on the way. Tesco chose South Korea because it has the highest residential penetration of broadband Net connections in the world, offering fertile opportunity for on-line shopping. Meanwhile, at home, Tesco.com is rolling out new services such as its baby center and wine club. These offer not just commerce but also chat areas and simple content—information about, say, infant development or top French vintages. With innovations such as these, Browett may soon start singing the old Gershwin song out loud.

By Andy Reinhardt.

Think Nevada, Think Haven for Daredevils

BY CHRISTINA BINKLEY

Nevada is trying to turn to its advantage one of its less-than-flattering features: thousands of miles of desolate desert.

Figuring that it can't compete with the likes of Colorado and Wyoming when it comes to luring nature lovers, Nevada hopes to entice sand surfers, rock climbers and other diehard adventurers to its arid reaches through a new $1.5 million print-ad campaign. The pitch to potential visitors: "A nice quiet place to get in touch with your inner masochist. . . . Ready to get medieval?"

No false advertising there. Nevada's 70.2 million acres are the driest in the nation and the most rugged, with 314 separate mountain ranges. Most of the state is uninhabited. In decades past, these characteristics allegedly put the state's deserts in competition with New York's East River as the preferred dumping ground for mob corpses. A current federal proposal would make rural Nevada a prime depository for nuclear waste.

The ads, which describe Nevada as "a primal playground with more . . . tear-yourself-to-shreds terrain than any other place in this great nation," feature unshaven, decidedly not pretty men, in a state of howling or panting. Developed for the Nevada Commission on Tourism, the ads are set to begin running in coming weeks in adventure magazines such as Outside, National Geographic Adventurer and Blue. They also will run in Western newspapers to reach nearby drive-in markets.

The tourism commission didn't initially set out to tout Nevada's barrenness. The agency has been running "Discover the other side of Nevada" campaigns for 15 years in its mission to get visitors to look past the glitz of Las Vegas and Reno and move on to the state's rural reaches.

But the panel's ad agency, Las Vegas-based **R&R Partners,** got discouraging news last year when it ran 16 focus groups in places including Phoenix and Portland, Ore. For one thing, plenty of states play up their Old West flavor—and many of those are more visually appealing than Nevada. Few

A hiker howls *in the desert in an ad extolling Nevada's arid ruggedness.*

people gave Nevada credit for its own pristine wilderness. Shown photos of beautiful Nevada scenery, the focus groups insisted the shots were taken in other states like Wyoming and Utah.

Rather than argue that Nevada isn't just a wasteland, the agency settled on an altogether different tactic: It decided to embrace the state's bleakness. "OK, it may not be for everyone," acknowledges Tim O'Brien, R&R's creative director.

What Mr. O'Brien is banking on is that those who do find the message appealing will prove to be big spenders. A 1997 study by the Travel Industry Association found that adventure travelers have average household incomes of $49,000, compared with $42,200 for the population as a whole. The harder core they are, the more they seem to spend. The study reported that "soft adventurers," who favor activities such as camping and skiing, spent an average of $820 per trip, while "hard" adventurers—who hang glide, kayak and rock climb—spent $1,275.

Still, it's a long haul to take public perceptions from total wasteland to daredevil haven. In the focus groups, in fact, "very few people thought of us as an adventure state," says Bruce Bommarito, the tourism commission's executive director. He says hardly anyone knows of areas such as Nevada's Ruby Mountains, which must be reached by foot or horseback, or the Blackrock Desert, where people windsurf on wheeled vehicles.

To shoot ads that would appeal to adventurers, the agency hit the road for nearly a month last September and October. They

hired just one professional model—the only woman who appears in the ads. Mostly, the group grabbed anyone they could persuade to pose.

Thus, R&R's balding Mr. O'Brien makes an appearance as an exhausted mountain biker in one ad. "I'm not a pretty boy," he concedes. Even the photographer's Norwegian assistant is featured. He appears shirtless, clad in a rabbit-fur hat that Mr. O'Brien once bought in Russia, with his head thrown back in mid-howl. "You are not well," the caption reads.

That one went too far for some on the Tourism Commission. The parched terrain and the unshaven visage of the fur-hatted Norwegian reminded several panel members of photos they have seen out of Afghanistan. Concerned it might offend some people, they decided to hold that ad for several months until Americans become less sensitive about the search for terrorists and members of Afghanistan's former Taliban regime. "We're a commission," Mr. Bommarito notes, "and we're subject to some politics."

eBay's Secret Ingredient

If your customers gladly held your inventory, shipped your products, and did all your marketing, you'd make money online too. Only question: Can eBay keep growing and not destroy the social capital that is its unique competitive advantage?

By: Erick Schonfeld

After all these years, Lu Matis, a housewife in Flemington, N.J., has finally figured out how to "monetize eyeballs" on the Internet. Her secret? She sells them on eBay (*EBAY*). Glass eyeballs, that is, handblown and hand-painted by German artisans at the end of the 19th century and kept as prosthetic inventory in doctors' offices. Matis got 700 of them a year and a half ago from a dealer for about $7 a pop, but on eBay they fetch anywhere from $20 for a brown eye to $40 for a blue, gray, or green one. "I pay my son's college this way," Matis says. "They are gory to look at, but once you realize the work involved, it is like having a piece of Tiffany glass." Her customers range from collectors to jewelry makers to a guy who glued them to his steering wheel. "Where else could you possibly sell these?" she asks.

Matis's ocular oddities are proof positive that eBay has come a long way on its quest, as CEO Meg Whitman explains it, "to build the world's largest online trading platform where practically anyone can trade practically anything." eBay has gone well beyond collectible Elvis prints and Beanie Babies—or glass eyeballs, for that matter. A motorcycle is sold on eBay every 18 minutes, a laptop every 30 seconds, and a book every 4 seconds. You can buy time-shares in Hawaii, restaurant equipment, gardening tools, or your pick of goods in 18,000 other categories. eBay traded $9 billion worth of goods in 2001—equivalent to roughly 20 percent of all consumer e-commerce that year. More than $1 billion of that total was estimated to come from autos alone, a category that did not even exist on eBay two years ago.

"If you had asked me in September 1998 [when eBay went public] if eBay would be in the used car business, I would have said no," Whitman observes. Today, eBay is the largest online seller not just of autos and collectibles but also of computers, photo equipment and supplies, and sporting goods. To further promote the brand, it is developing with Sony a TV show profiling eBay users and the items they buy on the site. It is beginning to attract larger corporate sellers such as Disney (*DIS*), IBM (*IBM*), and Home Depot (*HD*). And the company is expanding internationally, with operations in 18 countries. In 1999, for instance, eBay Germany reached only 6 percent of the country's Internet users. Now, one out of every four German Web surfers visits the site. Back when she was gearing up for the IPO, Whitman would tell investors that she was going after a $100 million slice of the U.S. collectibles market. Today she estimates the size of the markets that eBay addresses at $1.7 trillion.

At one level, this success is easily explained. eBay has come closer than any other creation of the Internet boom to realizing the promise of the virtual corporation. With no inventory, no warehouses, and no sales force, eBay's electronic bazaar, run properly, is a profit-spewing machine.

Far less understood, however, is the invisible fuel that powers that machine: eBay's unique ability to attract vast amounts of what economists call social capital. The rest of us might call it trust, or goodwill, or credibility. Whatever you call this resource, eBay, in its vast community of buyers and sellers, deploys more of it than almost any company in memory. Social capital is what enables eBay to harness the creativity of the millions of entrepreneurs on its site striving to meet the most capricious demands of the even more numerous buyers who also congregate there. eBay's own customers do much of the company's work, bringing it countless new products and marketing techniques, picking up shipping costs, handling customer service. The high octane of eBay's social capital explains how, even in a down economy, with its dotcom brethren wounded and dying, eBay nearly doubled its profits in 2001 to $90 million. Revenues—bolstered by healthy online Christmas shopping—were $750 million, or equivalent to about 8 percent of the value of all the goods that were traded on its site. By 2005 the company expects to be raking in $3 billion in revenues and $1 billion in operating profits.

But getting there is far from a sure thing. To reach that goal, the company will have to more than triple the number of its registered buyers and sellers to 150 million. Yet some of the very steps eBay is taking to drive growth and keep its stock at a lofty price/earnings ratio of about 80 (on 2002 estimates) are straining the vital bonds between the company and its core customers. Out in the eBay community, it turns out, it's hard work to keep the social fabric from tearing.

As has been well chronicled, eBay takes advantage of the low communication and transaction costs of the Internet to bring its buyers and sellers together. The company takes a commission—typically 1 to 5 percent—on every trade on its electronic exchange; the rest of its revenues come from listing fees and other charges. eBay is considered the classic example of a company benefiting from so-called network effects. The more buyers who go to eBay, the more sellers they attract, who in turn draw even more buyers as the site becomes a larger source of supply with more competitive prices. This positive feedback loop magnifies the volume of trade on the site, and thus revenues to eBay, while making it increasingly difficult for other auction sites to survive.

But there is more to it than that. "eBay's business is so new that it's not well understood," says Rajiv Dutta, eBay's chief financial officer. "There is an enormous amount of subtlety and complexity underneath." eBay, according to Dutta and other eBay executives, is not so much a conventional company as a self-regulating, complex system. And indeed, eBay has few of the characteristics typical of traditional corporations—especially rival retailers such as Wal-Mart. "We have no real cost of goods, and customer acquisition is largely driven by word of mouth," Dutta says. Wal-Mart has nearly $16 billion in long-term debt; eBay has virtually none. Free of many of the costs that almost every other corporation must bear, eBay's business throws off an increasing amount of cash, reflected in operating margins that have gone from slightly negative in 1999 to 19 percent in 2001. (Wal-Mart's operating margin is about 5 percent.) Dutta expects operating margins to hit 30 to 35 percent by 2005, which is how he gets to that $1 billion operating-profit target.

Such an achievement would be pretty spectacular, but it cannot be reached on the strengths of new-wave financials alone. Social capital is the crucial hidden asset that could make it possible. The forms of capital that most people are familiar with are physical (stores, factories, machinery), human (education, skills, expertise), and financial (cash, debt, equity). Social capital flows from social relationships—things like membership in old boys' networks, trust, reputation, and social norms that allow people to do more work (such as coffee breaks). eBay's network effects are an extremely valuable form of social capital, but there are others. What eBay has figured out how to do is tap into the social capital created on its site by the millions of people who trade there, and convert it into profits.

One source of eBay's social capital is its feedback system, whereby buyers and sellers can rate each other. People need such confidence-building mechanisms to buy stuff from faceless strangers. Negative feedback is posted very rarely (less than 1 percent of the time, according to a study by University of Michigan economist Paul Resnick), but sellers are afraid of getting any negative comments and go to great lengths to avoid them. It's not uncommon for sellers to be brutally honest about their wares, going so far as to describe every nick and scratch. "Every time you get a negative feedback, your sales go down," says Howard Getz, who does 600 auctions a week in collectibles such as Barbie dolls and *Star Wars* figures. Displaying a buyer's negative comment by a seller's name is like letting a disgruntled customer leave a sign in a store for all subsequent customers to see.

Like other kinds of capital, social capital earns a return. One of the unique ways it pays off at eBay is in the thousands of small pricing and product selection innovations its members make that keep eBay's merchandising always in tune with the whims of the economy. "No single company could react as quickly as our millions of users do," Whitman explains. MIT economist Erik Brynjolfsson concurs: "If you had a central purchasing department, you would not have all the creativity that the millions of people have who are posting on eBay trying to meet unmet needs and develop products that might otherwise have gone unnoticed." Glass eyeballs, unused vacation real estate, even packing supplies for other eBay sellers—eBay users create markets where none existed before. They then absorb expenses, such as inventory, marketing, and shipping, that eBay itself would have to eat if it were a conventional company. Users even help out with customer support, as anyone who has ever visited an eBay discussion board knows. "Here you have people who are volunteering their time," notes Dan Ariely, a behavioral economist at MIT. "That is the amazing thing."

To keep the community of users happy, Whitman and her lieutenants spend a lot of time listening to their customers and observing trends on the site. Every morning, for example, Whitman is handed a report excerpting comments posted on eBay's discussion boards. And the company regularly conducts intense all-day focus groups, called Voices, with representative buyers and sellers.

The most important way that eBay manages its marketplace, however, is by organizing itself as a collection of startups. Each major category (books, collectibles, music, real estate, tickets) has its own manager. So does every country (eBay runs the number one auction sites in Australia, Britain, Canada, France, and Germany, among other nations). These managers are the stewards of the social capital on their turf. They must be experts in their particular markets and make sure nothing impedes trade there.

They are also responsible for the growth of their niches. When they notice that activity around certain items, such as tickets or automobiles, is growing organically, they signal up the chain that it's time to carve out a new category. "We decide to expand the trading platform based on where users want to go," Whitman explains.

Sometimes, that is away from auctions. So eBay is adding fixed-price components to its site as well, an unabashed challenge to Amazon's (*AMZN*) business. In 2000, eBay acquired Half.com, a fixed-price online store for discounted commodity goods that is being integrated into the regular eBay site. "Half.com is bringing the Amazon buyer into person-to-person trading," says Jeff Jordan, head of eBay's U.S. operations. And about 45 percent of all eBay auctions now have a "Buy It Now" button that lets the first bidder end the auction by agreeing to a preset price. All told, about 19 percent of sales on eBay are now fixed-price rather than auction.

One of the most promising avenues for future growth hinges on eBay's ability to court a whole new class of customers: big corporations. Disney, IBM, and Home Depot, among others, are dipping their toes into eBay's market for discontinued goods, excess inventory, and returned items. Even Dell (*DELL*), which arguably does not need any help with online commerce, sells refurbished off-lease PCs on eBay. It's just another sales channel. Governments are getting into the act too. Seventeen state governments, up from zero in 1998, are using eBay to liquidate foreclosed assets.

The giant sellers are proceeding cautiously and so far account for less than 3 percent of eBay sales. But eBay is working on them—and urging them to expand their offerings to the types of fixed-price, in-season items that make up the bulk of the economy. In a pitch to the Gap clothing chain, for instance, eBay would say, "We have 10,000 Gap items on eBay right now, so whether you like it or not, we are a channel." Or, as eBay marketing VP Bill Cobb likes to tell reluctant corporate sellers, "We have the

technology, the marketplace, and the buyers. Why are you going to do it on your own? Nobody visits your site."

Disney uses eBay to auction collector's items such as ride vehicles from its theme parks, animation cels, and movie props. Recently a statuette used by animators during the making of the film *Monsters, Inc.* went for $3,556. "We create archival items every time a park or a new movie opens," says George Grobar, the head of auctions for Disney's Internet group. Many of the objects used to end up in landfills, but by using eBay, Grobar says, Disney can sell them cost-effectively—and generate promotional buzz.

IBM has gone further. By selling mainly laptops that are reaching the end of their product cycle for about $1,000 each, Big Blue has become eBay's single largest seller (although it accounts for less than 0.1 percent of the site's total sales). The computer giant is finding that rather than stealing sales from IBM.com or other channels, eBay auctions are bringing new clients into the IBM tent. Some 79 percent of its eBay customers—half of which are small businesses—are new to IBM. "We see eBay as an incredible growth engine for us," says IBM.com auction manager Paul Canham. Indeed. Canham's sales on eBay are growing more than 40 percent per *month*.

But the question remains: Will the forces pulling eBay in so many different directions undermine its social capital? After huge surges in 1999 and 2000, eBay's listings growth (a major contributor to revenues) has slowed dramatically. To meet its dramatic financial goals, eBay must continue to expand aggressively into new categories, geographies, formats, and customer types. But the faster eBay grows, the greater the risk to its social capital.

There are already signs that its expansionary strategies are beginning to alienate existing users. For instance, one of the basic principles that eBay has tried to maintain is neutrality. The company avoids taking sides between buyers and sellers whenever possible. That is what the feedback system is for. But the Switzerland stance increasingly does not wash with the people who are the source of all of eBay's revenues: the sellers. The most vocal are those who sell more than $2,000 a month on eBay, known as Powersellers.

Eric McKenna of Pittsburgh quit his sales job at a paging company about two years ago to sell guitars on eBay for $500 to $3,500 apiece. When he had a problem with a deadbeat buyer and wanted eBay to yank him from the site, customer service reps kept explaining to him that they could not do that, and that eBay was a social phenomenon where different rules applied. "I don't want any of your socialistic b.s.," McKenna would tell supervisor after supervisor. "You are a company. I am a goddamn Powerseller! I am paying you 1,000 bucks a month, and I want service." To eBay's credit, the deadbeat was finally barred from the site. But if McKenna wants preferential treatment from eBay for his BoogieStreet Guitars, imagine what IBM will want.

eBay insists that it will maintain a level playing field. "Our vision of eBay consists of a marketplace where your next-door neighbor can compete side by side with large corporations," Whitman says. Indeed, if you search for IBM laptops, you will see IBM's listings alongside auctions from other sellers. From the prominence of the listings, it's impossible to tell which are the next-door neighbors and which is the $86 billion corporation.

The level playing field approach, however, can create another problem. If customers stop benefiting from the relationships they make through eBay, all of the company's accumulated social capital goes out the window. In the original collectibles and antiques categories, for instance, eBay has created such an efficient market that average selling prices have declined 30 percent during the past year, according to the Internet Antique Shop. Gary Sohmers, an appraiser on *Antiques Road Show* and Boston radio host who has been selling pop culture collectibles online for years, is not happy about this trend. He says of dealers' feelings for eBay: "We all hate it. They leveled the playing field, but unfortunately they leveled it underwater."

Another uproar centered on the controversial checkout feature that eBay introduced last fall, which automatically exchanges information between the buyer and seller after an auction. eBay says it is meant to standardize the old procedure, in which buyers and sellers e-mailed one another after an auction to arrange delivery and payment. But many sellers despised the imposed feature, not only because they felt it was clumsy but also because they thought that eBay was trying to come between them and their customers—a violation of the social compact. "I was mad as a wet hen," says Frances Neale, a seller of used books on eBay. eBay responded to sellers' concerns by making the feature optional, but Neale still sees the new checkout system as symptomatic of eBay's larger push to embrace corporate sellers and to further automate the interaction between customers. "I think they want to be the complete system for the large brick-and-mortar companies that want to be on the Web," she speculates.

eBay would be wise to quash that fear quickly. The company derives much of its social capital from the fact that its site is a place where people transact with people, not with large, impersonal corporations. The irony is that, so far, the corporations on eBay are typically the ones adjusting the way they do business. Buyers are just so much more demanding on eBay. Winning bidders expect an e-mail response the next day, not in six weeks, and shipping had better not cost half as much as the entire product.

Some observers argue that eBay could afford to be at least a little less solicitous of its buyers and sellers (as a recent price hike demonstrates). After all, where else are they going to go? But the company knows deep down that its future hinges on figuring out how to continue to grow and appeal to multiple constituents without depleting its crucial social capital. At one recent Voices focus group attended by people who trade in autographs, car stereos, and Renaissance gowns, Jordan acknowledged that "the challenge is expanding eBay to car stereos and all the other things you sell without leaving behind the core." Indeed, the difficulty of relying on a resource that does not appear on your balance sheet is that you won't know it is missing until it is already gone.

"eBay's Secret Ingredient," *Business 2.0,* March 2002, pp. 52–58.

That *%&#)@*$ Cellphone!

Carriers Install Better Gear, Use Roving Fix-It Vehicles But Quality Is Still an Issue

By Andrea Petersen
Staff Reporter of The Wall Street

NEW YORK—Tooling along the streets of lower Manhattan in a white Ford Taurus station wagon, Faris Howat seems like any other commuter on his way to work—except for the quarter of a million dollars of wireless phone equipment in his car.

Mr. Howat is a foot soldier in the battle for better cellular service.

"I monitor the daily traffic, the lost calls and the fast busy signals on our network," says Mr. Howat, a manager of system performance at Verizon Wireless. "If there's a problem, we relay the information to the engineers and try to fix it."

As anyone who carries a cellphone knows, wireless service, which has been around for almost 20 years, still has its problems. Besides dropped calls and fast busy signals, there are "dead zones" where you can't get service at all. Seduced by plans that offer bigger buckets of calling minutes, customers are chatting more and demanding to use their phones everywhere: at home, inside office buildings, even in tunnels. The number of U.S. subscribers has more than tripled in the past five years to 109.5 million. All that traffic is taxing already-strapped networks.

Reliability—and trust—of the wireless networks is becoming more critical. With six national carriers competing fiercely, it is all too easy for customers to jump to another company. The carriers are pushing data services that let users buy stuff or do banking from their phones. But if subscribers are concerned about their voice calls being cut off, they will likely be very wary of doing financial transactions wirelessly. Yet the growth in network demand is sure to continue since only 40% of Americans have cellphones.

In response, the carriers are spending big bucks to beef up their service. Verizon Wireless, a joint venture of **Verizon Communications** Inc. and **Vodafone Group PLC,** spent $4 billion last year and plans to spend more than that this year on upgrades. Overall, the U.S. industry spent $89.6 billion last year on capital improvements, up from $24.1 billion

in 1995. Last year, **Sprint** Corp.'s Sprint PCS added 3,000 cell sites—the antennas, computers and software that send and receive calls. The company expects to add about the same number this year. In general, the more cell sites, the better the service. The number of U.S. cell sites industrywide jumped to 104,288 in 2000 from 22,663 in 1995.

Carriers are also dispatching people like Verizon's Mr. Howat. A metal box in the trunk of his car contains the guts of cellphones from Verizon and competitors including **AT&T Wireless Group, Nextel Communications** Inc. and Sprint PCS. Software prompts the phones to dial a number and hold the call for two minutes and 15 seconds—the length of an average wireless call, Mr. Howat says. On a laptop computer in the passenger seat Mr. Howat can see which calls don't go through and which ones are dropped in the middle. If calls aren't going through on the Verizon network, Mr. Howat can prompt his engineers to check out the cell site in that area and even amplify the power of the sites adjacent to the problematic one to compensate.

Dropped calls often happen when there is a problem with the "hand off" of a call from one cell site to another. When a user is driving down the highway, for example, he or she will eventually get out of range of one cell site and the call will need to be transferred to the cell site next door. If there are already too many calls being handled by the neighboring cell site, the call will be dropped. A call also can be dropped if a user wanders into a dead zone, where no cell site has been built or the signal is blocked by buildings or other obstructions. The other bane of wireless users—fast busy signals—may occur when a cell site already has as many calls as it can handle.

Other things also can cause calling problems: Signals can be degraded by leaves or by the dark coatings found on some office-building windows to filter sunlight.

Many customers wonder why service in the U.S. isn't as reliable and seamless as in

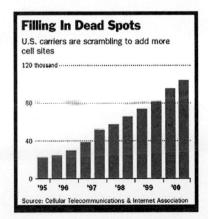

Filling In Dead Spots

U.S. carriers are scrambling to add more cell sites

120 thousand

80

40

0

'95 '96 '97 '98 '99 '00

Source: Cellular Telecommunications & Internet Association

many other countries. One reason is that the U.S. system is a hodgepodge of different technologies and competing carriers. In contrast to the unified technology used in Europe, for instance, U.S. carriers employ several incompatible setups. It stems from the fact that the U.S. government let phone companies go their own ways.

The result is that most phones need to work on two or even three different network systems. A user who places a call on a modern digital signal can end up being flipped to an old-fashioned, scratchy analog signal, or to a different flavor of digital, as he or she moves from one cell site to another. Maintaining so many technologies adds to the complexity and cost of providing adequate calling capacity in each community.

While adding cell towers—which can cost up to $600,000—is the easiest way to improve service, the carriers often face opposition. But they are coming up with creative ways to convince communities to accept the towers. Cingular Wireless added lighting to a Little League ballpark in Evergreen Park, Ill., in exchange for the right to put a cell site next to it. In Palos Hills, Ill., the company gave phone lines to the police department as an inducement.

Cellular coverage at big events such as industry conferences and football games is also improving. COWs—an acronym for cell site on wheels—are rolled in for the event to boost capacity. Service is also becoming available in new places. Verizon Wireless recently installed service in the railway tunnel leading to New York's Pennsylvania Station. In April, AT&T Wireless partnered with telecommunications company Concourse Communications Group to install tiny antennas inside the Newark, N.J., airport to beef up coverage inside terminals.

Big carriers including Verizon Wireless, AT&T Wireless and Cingular also recently paid $17 billion for new spectrum, or airwave capacity. The fate of that spectrum—which was seized by the Federal Communications Commission from bankrupt **NextWave Telecom** Inc.—has been the subject of a court battle, but if it eventually gets into the hands of the auction winners, it will likely help alleviate dropped calls and dead spots.

New technology also may help. Verizon Wireless and Sprint PCS are experimenting with "smart antennas" from **Metawave Communications** Corp. of Redmond, Wash. These antennas boost the number of calls that a cell site can handle. **Conductus** Inc. of Sunnyvale, Calif., is selling a technology that amplifies the signal sent from a cellphone.

The biggest boost to service is likely yet to come—in the form of the high-speed networks most carriers are getting ready to deploy. These networks, dubbed third generation or 2.5 generation (today's networks are considered second generation), are most touted for their ability to allow customers to surf the wireless Web at fast speeds and

(Cont.)

quickly zip off e-mail messages. But they will also, the carriers say, dramatically increase the capacity for standard voice calls.

Yet even after such upgrades are installed, some analysts say wireless service likely will never reach the reliability of a copper phone line. "Dropped calls are a reality of wireless," says Mark Winther, a group vice president at IDC, a Framingham, Mass., research firm. "I don't see it going away."

Ironically, some customers are dreading the day of improved service. Scott Galloway uses his erratic service to politely end annoying or lengthy calls. "Rather than saying, 'I've got to go, Mom,' I just pace over to the more receptively challenged part of my loft," says Mr. Galloway, the chief executive of Internet incubator Brand Farm Inc. in New York. "Then, boom, it cuts off and I can go watch 'The Sopranos.'"

Small Change: Bank That Pioneered Loans for the Poor Hits Repayment Snag

'Microcredit' Icon Grameen Faces Questions as Rate Of Delinquencies Rises

Mrs. Begum's Missing Cow

By Daniel Pearl and Michael M. Phillips
Staff Reporters of The Wall Street Journal

Microcredit is a great idea with a problem: the bank that made it famous.

Grameen Bank, launched in Bangladesh in 1976 by an economics professor named Muhammad Yunus, popularized the idea of giving poor people tiny loans to launch businesses. The bank has helped inspire an estimated 7,000 so-called microlenders with 25 million poor clients worldwide.

To many, Grameen proves that capitalism can work for the poor as well as the rich. It has become an icon for the drive to give needy entrepreneurs a share in economic development. And that iconic status owes a lot to an almost miraculous loan-repayment rate of "over 95%," as the bank's Web site says.

But Grameen's performance in recent years hasn't lived up to the bank's own hype. In two northern districts of Bangladesh that have been used to highlight Grameen's success, half the loan portfolio is overdue by at least a year, according to monthly figures supplied by Grameen. For the whole bank, 19% of loans are one year overdue. Grameen itself defines a loan as delinquent if it still isn't paid off two years after its due date. Under those terms, 10% of all the bank's loans are overdue, giving it a delinquency rate more than twice the often cited level of less than 5%.

Some of Grameen's troubles stem from a 1998 flood, and others from the bank's own success. Imitators have brought more competition, making it harder for Grameen to control its borrowers. The bank's loan portfolio grew rapidly in the early 1990s, but it

has now shrunk to 1996 levels, at $190 million. Profits have declined about 85%, to the equivalent of $189,950 last year from $1.3 million in 1999. The bank, with 1,170 branches, all in Bangladesh, has high operating costs. Grameen would be showing steep losses if the bank followed the accounting practices recommended by institutions that help finance microlenders through low-interest loans and private investments. And the situation may be worse than it appears; the bank is converting many overdue loans into new "flexible" loans that Grameen reports as up-to-date.

Safeguarding an 'Idea'

Microlenders have been reluctant to call attention to Grameen's troubles. "Grameen's repayment rates have never been as good as they've claimed," says Jonathan J. Morduch, associate professor of economics and public policy at New York University. "Because Grameen has been so well-known, nobody has wanted to risk undermining the reputation of the idea."

Microcredit is getting renewed attention as other poverty-fighting tools come under attack. Left-wing protesters accuse the World Bank of selling out the poor to corporate interests. Right-wing U.S. politicians argue that aid to the Third World has been wasted. U.S. lobbies often try to quash efforts to open American markets to imports from poor countries.

But microcredit is an idea everyone can agree on: It uses private enterprise, can be profitable and gets money straight to the poor. Bridging the gap between rich and poor "will help eliminate conditions of despair and hopelessness that breed violence and extremism," declares an electronic-mail message circulated after Sept. 11 by Bill Clapp, the chairman of Global Partnerships, a microcredit support organization based in Seattle.

Alarmed by Rumors

The microcredit industry knows its reputation rides largely on Grameen's. Damian von Stauffenberg, chairman of a Washington-based microcredit rating agency called Microrate, was alarmed by recent rumors of financial weakness at Grameen, even though the agency doesn't rate the bank. "If it's true, it would be a blow to the rest of us, because of the symbol Grameen is," Mr. von Stauffenberg says. He says he repeatedly asked a Grameen affiliate, Grameen Foundation USA, this summer for detailed information on the bank's loan portfolio, but got only a brochure and a 1998 annual report.

"I didn't hear back from him after that, so I assumed he had the information he wanted," says Alex Counts, president of the foundation, which promotes Grameen in the U.S.

Mr. Yunus, a congenial man of 61, acknowledges that Grameen has had some repayment difficulties in the past five years. He blames political upheavals, the 1998 flood and management errors. Told that the Web

site still claimed a 95% recovery rate, Mr. Yunus said it was through "inefficiency" that Grameen hadn't updated some information. Grameen has added a footnote to the Web site saying the information was true as of 1996. But more recent figures still aren't listed.

The repayment troubles are temporary, according to Mr. Yunus. "There is no problem," he said in an August interview in his modest office, which has no air conditioning despite Bangladesh's steamy climate. He says three-fourths of borrowers repay on time every week, and Grameen assumes that the poor will repay even long-delinquent loans. The bank, he says, is stronger than ever.

Mr. Yunus says borrowers have surprised him with their ability to take on new challenges. Borrowers who reach a certain level of savings can buy one share in Grameen, and collectively they own 93%. Mr. Yunus is setting up a mutual fund allowing borrowers to invest in other ventures under the Grameen umbrella: mobile phones, textiles and high-tech office space for rent on the top floors of the Grameen Bank tower.

"We have proved beyond a reasonable doubt that poor people are bankable," Mr. Yunus says. "We are not looking for charity."

Grameen, which means "village" in Bengali, got started after Mr. Yunus visited a village in southern Bangladesh. He met a woman who wove bamboo stools but had to sell them for meager profits to the man providing the materials. As an experiment, Mr. Yunus lent a total of $27 to 42 women in the village. All of them repaid.

When Mr. Yunus approached the Bangladesh government for funds in 1979 to expand his experiment, government bankers were skeptical that poor, landless women would repay. So Mr. Yunus conducted an experiment in Tangail, a fertile district north of Dhaka. His staffers showed up unannounced in villages and recruited groups of women to take loans. Again, all of them repaid.

The 16 'Decisions'

The new bank was a kind of small-business lender, with some unusual policies. It took no deposits at first. It lent only to poor women who had no collateral. Borrowers formed groups of five, each member getting loans only as long as everybody made payments. Borrowers recited Mr. Yunus's "16 decisions" including enforcing loan "discipline" within the group, keeping families small and not giving a dowry for a daughter's wedding a difficult "decision" to follow in this culture.

Grameen, which has provided millions of poor Bangladeshi women with access to credit, became the industry's symbol mostly through Mr. Yunus's personality and proselytizing. He set up the Grameen Trust, which gives loans and holds workshops for start-up lenders who have adopted the Grameen model from Arkansas to Zimbabwe, with mixed results.

Mr. Yunus is also the guiding force behind the industry's main public-relations vehicle, the Microcredit Summit. At the first summit, in Washington in 1997, Mr. Yunus sat at the head table at a private lunch with Queen Sofia of Spain and World Bank President James D. Wolfensohn, who ended the meal by giving Mr. Yunus a big hug. At a regional summit last month, he gave an opening address beside Mexican President Vicente Fox. Friends tout Mr. Yunus for a Nobel Peace Prize.

Mr. Yunus's 1997 autobiography, "Banker to the Poor," gave no hint of doubt in Grameen's future. "All the strength of Grameen comes from its near-perfect recovery performance," he wrote. "It is not merely the money which is reflected through the recovery rate, it is the discipline."

Even then, however, Grameen's recovery rate was slipping. In 1997, 4.6% of Grameen's loans were more than two years overdue, up from 0.7% a couple of years earlier. And Tangail has now become Grameen's worst region, with 32.1% of loans two-years overdue as of August.

One reason is that microlending has lost its novelty. In Tangail, signboards for rival microlenders dot a landscape of gravel roads, jute fields and ponds with simple fishing nets. Shopkeepers playing cards in the village of Bagil Bazar can cite from memory the terms being offered by seven competing microlenders a typical repayment plan for a 1,000-taka ($17) loan is 25 taka a week for 46 weeks. At an annualized rate, that works out to 30% in interest. Surveys have estimated that 23% to 40% of families borrowing from microlenders in Tangail borrow from more than one.

Rebellious Borrowers

Borrowers have also become more rebellious. "The experience was good in the beginning," says Munjurani Sharkan, who became leader of a Grameen group in Tangail's Khatuajugnie village in 1986. To put pressure on "lazy" group members who were slow making payments, she says she used to start removing the tin roofs of their homes. But one day, the whole group decided to stop making payments.

They were protesting Grameen's handling of a fund it created for each group, using 5% of each loan and additional mandatory deposits. The "group fund" was meant for emergencies, but many borrowers wanted to withdraw money from the group fund. After a protest movement, complete with placards and amplified speeches, Grameen finally agreed to give borrowers easier access to the fund.

Borrower groups had become lobbying groups, and Mr. Yunus hadn't noticed the change, says Muhammad Yahiyeh, former director of Grameen Trust. "An entire group would say, 'Unless you pay this person 5,000 taka, we will all stop paying,'" says Mr. Yahiyeh, who now runs a small microlender.

Mr. Yunus says he still thinks groups are good for loan discipline. Grameen just didn't explain the group fund properly, he says, and politicians stirred up the borrowers.

The typical Grameen success story features a woman who turns a small loan into a successful shop or craft business. But Grameen also has customers such as Belatun Begum, a borrower in Khatuajugnie since the late 1980s. She took one loan in three installments, totaling 30,000 taka (about $525). She says the original loan was to buy a cow, but she actually gave some money to her husband, a well-digger, and used the rest to improve her house. She confesses to borrowing a neighbor's cow to show Grameen at meetings. One recent study found one-fourth of microcredit loan money in Bangladesh is used for household consumption.

Mr. Yunus says that doesn't bother him as long as borrowers repay. Grameen tells women to think of a loan as a mango tree and to eat only the fruits, he says, not the tree itself.

But Grameen introduced so many loan options in the early 1990s housing loans, student loans, seasonal loans that borrowers were often paying off one with another, says Aminur Rahman, an anthropologist based in Ottawa, Canada, who studied Grameen borrowers in a Tangail village six years ago. Returning earlier this year, he found only six of 120 borrowers were getting income from Grameen-funded investments.

Massive floods in 1998 hit Grameen's borrowers hard. The bank let borrowers skip several payments. Grameen borrowed $80 million from Bangladesh's government banks, with a sovereign guarantee, and used the money to make new loans to borrowers. Informally, it forgave the old loans.

A 'Flexible Loan'

Grameen also bailed out borrowers whose problems had nothing to do with the flood. Ms. Begum, for instance, stopped paying when she had to provide dowries for two daughters. She skipped group meetings, but Grameen workers came to her door asking for her 200-taka weekly payment, she says. "Let us make some income and we'll pay you," she told them.

Earlier this year, Grameen came up with a proposal: pay just 50 taka a week for six months, and then take a new Grameen loan for twice the amount she repaid. Ms. Begum accepted. Grameen calls the program a "flexible loan," and treats the old, delinquent loans as back on schedule, as long as some regular payment is being made.

At a Grameen branch near Khatuajugnie, manager Mohammed Imam Modem shows his computer-printed ledger, full of cross marks to indicate missed payments. The rescheduling program and Grameen's personal visits to husbands as well as wives are improving the picture: The branch had 1,510 defaulters before; now it has 846. Attendance

at weekly meetings is up to 66%, from 47% before.

"Grameen Bank's philosophy is not to abandon but to rehabilitate," says Muzzamal Huq, a Grameen general manager.

But Grameen may simply be delaying inevitable defaults and hiding problem loans. One paper produced by the Consultative Group to Assist the Poorest, or CGAP, a donor group that sets industry standards, warns that heavy use of refinancing "can cloud the ability to judge its loan-loss rate." CGAP is a collective of 27 public and private donors, including the World Bank, the U.S. Agency for International Development and several U.N. agencies, that account for the vast majority of aid to microcredit institutions around the world.

CGAP says refinanced loans should at least be listed separately. Grameen doesn't do so. It says refinanced loans are one-fifth of its portfolio.

CGAP recommends that microlenders report as at risk the entire remaining balance of any loan with a payment more than 90 days overdue. The Palli Karma-Sahayak Foundation (PKSF), which Mr. Yunus helped set up in 1991 to distribute foreign funds to other Bangladesh microlenders, requires its microlenders to report as overdue any loan that is one week late. The average overdue rate among the foundation's lenders is 2%. It's impossible to know Grameen's overdue rate by that standard, since it reports only loans that are one year and two years overdue.

PKSF also says it requires borrowers to make a 50% provision against potential loan losses for any loan overdue by a year. Grameen made a 15% provision for such loans in 1999, and none last year. Following PKSF guidelines would have produced a loss of more than $7.5 million for 2000 instead of Grameen's reported profit of less than $200,000.

In early 1998, Grameen approached the International Finance Corp., the business-finance arm of the World Bank, about turning some of Grameen's portfolio into securities. The IFC declined to proceed, in part because Grameen "didn't provide all the account information the IFC requested," an IFC official said. The official requested anonymity because the IFC is reticent about discussing its negotiations with clients.

Mr. Yunus denied the IFC official's claims. He said Grameen is "generously covered" against loan defaults.

Other microlenders have become much more stringent. Accion International, a U.S.-based network of microfinance institutions, requires its affiliates in Africa and Latin America to list as "at risk" any loan overdue by 30 days or more. Asked about Grameen's two-years standard, Accion Chief Executive Maria Otero says, "I don't think any [bank] superintendency in a million years would agree to something like that."

Grameen Bank isn't under any formal

(Cont.)

supervision. "They are regulated, but they are regulated by themselves," says Akhtaruz Zaman, director of the Financial Institution Department for the Bangladesh Bank, the country's central bank. He means the board of directors, which is led by borrowers. Mr. Zaman says Grameen's deposits are "well-protected " and the bank is "doing fine."

Harder-headed microlenders are stealing the spotlight, though. One rising star is the Association for Social Advancement (ASA), a Bangladesh charity, which boasts 1.5 million borrowers and just 0.7% of loans overdue, even by a week. Dispensing with borrower groups, ASA leans on borrowers' husbands and relatives if payments are missed, says the managing director, Shafiqual Haque Choudhury. To him, Grameen's approach is an ingenious idea that didn't stand the test of time.

"If we manage our operation in the Grameen way," says Mr. Choudhury, "we'll never be able to cover our costs."

All Of Your People Are Salesmen: Do They Know? Are They Ready?

By KIRK SHINKLE
Investor's Business Daily

Forget automated voice systems and customer relationship software. Real ties are built face to face—on telephones and at the checkout lines.

Keeping that bond means making sure every member of the team, especially those on the front lines, are up to the task.

That means hiring right, training right and checking performance. It also means keeping people motivated and informed.

Two companies that stand out are The Container Store, a private Dallas-based retailer, and Harrah's Entertainment, in gaming.

The Container Store, with $225 million in sales, peddles the do-it-yourself shelves that organize closets. Each store has 10 to 12 full-time workers on the floor.

New workers get 235 hours of training a year, and veterans 162. Retailing averages seven to 10.

Much of that goes to product training and making sure workers know how to group bins and boxes to fit customer needs.

The firm's chairman and co-founder, Garrett Boone, cites a salesman managing the register at the firm's Rockwall, Md., store.

Training Pays

"He's talking to a woman who's buying moving boxes. He finds out that her new house is neat, but the closets are a mess. He shuts down the register and plans her new closets," Boone said.

"In the process of doing something simple, asking questions and getting to know that person, we could help that woman in a way that really delighted her," he said.

Boone keeps up on service firsthand, visiting each of the firm's 25 stores at least once a year. He also works the sales floor and meets with store staff one day a week.

Conflicts do arise. But Boone says well-trained workers have the freedom to solve problems.

Several years ago, a saleswoman in Illinois, now a manager, agreed to pick up the tab for a torn headliner in a shopper's car. It ripped as shelves were loaded into her car.

Betting On Training

"We just say, 'Use your good judgment,'" Boone said.

The chain shuns commissions. Instead, it pays wages 50% to 100% higher than most of its rivals for salaried work, around $25,000 and $28,000 a year.

Its average is more than $36,000. The firm also goes above and beyond for benefits.

In September, it added vision coverage for part-timers, in addition to medical and dental.

In the 24-7 world of casinos, John Bruns, who manages customer satisfaction at Harrah's Entertainment, knows making players happy can mean the difference between cashing in or going bust. With tens of thousands of workers, monitoring results in a meaningful way counts big.

Bruns joined Harrah's three years ago from Ritz-Carlton.

He's helped strengthen data on things like crowd flow and wait times. Harrah's has also instituted what it calls "buzz sessions."

Before or during a shift, small groups of dealers, cashiers and beverage servers meet in groups.

They're updated on any changes and how the rest of the casino is doing. Senior managers make sure everyone attends. They're issued three-by-five cards to keep track of when sessions are scheduled.

"If I'm a general manager, I go for lunch, I drop in on one, I go for coffee, I drop in on one," Bruns said. At the Lake Tahoe casino, senior leaders dropped by 274 buzz sessions in one week.

Harrah's also uses "mystery shoppers." They look for good attitudes as well as competence. Mystery shoppers hit eight departments in every casino eight times a month. Findings are analyzed in days.

For instance, mystery shoppers found cashiers were efficient, but a bit on the surly side.

Managers made sure this was outlined in buzz sessions, and followed up with individuals.

Subtle management pressure helps. At Harrah's in Laughlin, Nev., the general manager found long lines at cashier cages.

The manager sent his cell phone number to employees with this edict: If lines get longer than our set goals, call at any time. That spurred his people to solve the problem themselves.

"We're realistic," Bruns said. "From time to time, we'll disappoint a customer. We train employees to handle service failures."

They're trained to hear out players—and respond.

Employees give away "service recovery certificates" such as free buffet tickets. "It isn't just the pit boss, it is every employee," Bruns said. "It's incredibly important."

Also, the company pays quarterly dividends for improved performance. This year, hourly employees will get an estimated $13 million, or $50 to $200 per quarter.

"How many companies pay for improved customer satisfaction?" Bruns asks. "That's cutting edge."

Overall, Bruns looks for small victories.

"Every day, we want to hit singles," he said. "This isn't a race. It's a journey. Most of the time, it's getting 1% better on 100 things as opposed to 100% better on one thing."

Finding Target Market Opportunities

Reading, Writing and...Retailing

Students Spend More Than Ever "Redecorating' Dorm Rooms; $500 on Daisy-Print Sheets

BY POOJA BHATIA

Staff Reporter of THE WALL STREET JOURNAL

Kate Dworkosky can't count how many hours she's spent in furniture stores this summer or the number of shelter magazines she's thumbed through. And still, the dilemma is unresolved. Should her new sofa be light blue, to match the rugs, curtains and the framed Matisse? Or should she go for cream—a nice, classy counterpoint to it all?

No, this isn't a summer house. It's a college dorm room. "That futon has got to go," says Ms. Dworkosky, soon to be a senior at American University, in Washington, D.C.

Exactly when did student housing become enviable? Despite the slow economy, college kids across the country are taking dorm decor to a new level. Students are cramming their rooms with ottomans, leather recliners and velvet pillows. Thread counts are pushing 500. And while Sub-Zero hasn't launched a dorm line (yet), Samsung has—in snazzy silver and blue. Mattress pads? Try a featherbed.

In all, the National Retail Federation estimates college students (or the Bank of Mom and Dad) will spend a record $5 billion to outfit dorm rooms this year, not even including computers. And more retailers are jumping in, hoping to counter slow sales elsewhere in the decorating world: Upscale catalog Garnet Hill and designer Mitchell Gold are targeting the dormitory set for the first time this year, as is Ikea, which just sent out more 500,000 e-mails touting its hot-pink armchairs. A supplier to Target and Wal-Mart says college furniture sales are growing as much as 10% a year now, twice as fast as sales of regular furniture.

All of which is a shock for a lot of parents, especially when their kids' dorm living rooms rival their own. Cindy McGranagh says the dorm she lived in, circa 1972, was so bland the "nicest thing was the drapes my mother made." But at Grinnell College in Iowa, her son Devan is bringing everything

from an overstuffed velour armchair to a 40-gallon aquarium to his dorm room, enough stuff for two SUV loads. And Devan's digs don't even compare to some of the other rooms she's seen. "Frankly, I was a little jealous," she says.

For Tulane junior Kim McGeever, last year was her daisy period. She spent at least $500 on daisy-patterned linens—a duvet, throw pillows, sheets and towels—then added a daisy-covered inflatable chair, photo frames and a lamp. All topped off by a pair of butterfly chairs and an ample though daisy-less supply of appliances. What would Martha Stewart say? Ms. McGeever isn't quite sure, but she does say her parents had a reaction: "They thought it was a little ridiculous."

Putting on the Brakes

So why aren't parents putting their feet down? Some experts say snazzier dorm rooms are just another byproduct of the '90s boom years. With competition for top students so fierce, colleges themselves have been jazzing up student life with everything from movie theaters to beauty salons. Besides, after spending as much as $30,000 a year for tuition, what's a few extra thousand for an Eames lounge chair?

Of course, if you thought roommate situations were touchy, just try picking out curtains together. Senior Nicole Kaspari at Amercian University returned from a semester abroad last year, only to find that her suitemates had redecorated in a style she abhorred. "How could they?" she remembers wailing upon inspecting the place—everything, the walls, the couch, the tablecloth, was cream.

And wicker, to boot. So she spent $300 jazzing things up with red chairs, a black lacquer coffee table and leopard-print pillows. She wound up satisfied with the decor—but not with her roommates. She's found new ones this year.

Nedim Agalar hadn't even thought about dorm fashion until he arrived at Colgate University, in Hamilton, N.Y., from Turkey last year. His two duffel bags seemed paltry compared with the U-Haul parade arriving on campus. So what did he do? Took out his credit card and bought a modernist, metallic couch; a computer; CD burner; speakers and a DVD player. Then he rented not one, but two fridges. (One for beer, the other for food.) Now, Mr. Agalar boasts, his room looks "like a skyscraper apartment, like you'd see in the movies."

Some colleges are already thinking about putting on the brakes. Fancy dorm rooms are causing everything from blown fuses—thanks to gizmo overload, one dorm at the University of Michigan saw 200 power outages in one month last year—to social strains between campus haves and have-nots. Pepperdine University recently refurnished its Malibu, Calif., dorms in order to encourage freshman fashionistas to leave the Persian rugs at home.

Swarthmore College in Pennsylvania has gone a step further: requiring students to stick with college-issued furniture. "We're a Quaker school, founded on egalitarian principles," says Myrt Westphal, dean of housing. "Our residence halls are part of that."

Still, with retailers pushing dorm fashion so hard, it's going to be an uphill battle. Bed,

---

Dorm Room Décor

Think all you need to go back to college is a couple of milk crates and a Picasso poster? Yeah, right. Today's dorm rooms are stuffed with everything from refrigerators to armchairs. Here, some of the popular items students are taking back to school:

Item/Store/Web Site	Description	Comments
Mitchell Gold down floor pillows $300 each, 800-789-5401	The new beanbag—thick, felt-covered pillows stuffed with down. Scatter a bunch on your floor.	This upscale furniture company even signed on a college spokesman this year, and will decorate his George Washington University dorm room.
Mesh storage cubes $29.99 for three, www.bedbathandbeyond.com	Made of metal, with wheels so you can move them around.	These replace the plastic Yaffa block, which in turn replaced the milk crate as the dorm-room storage basic.
Ralph Lauren Classic featherbed $119.99, www.macys.com	Filled with down and bearing the Polo crest, this comes in the all-important twin XL.	Sleep on a lumpy dorm mattress? Never. A featherbed supplies the cushioning students need to get their rest.
George Foreman Champ Grill with Bun Warmer $24.99, www.bluelight.com	The latest take on the hotplate; comes in an array of iMac-inspired colors.	Dorm-room chefs use the "lean mean fat grilling machine" for burgers, sandwiches and even vegetable stir-fry.
Striped jersey knit linens $130 for an extra-long twin set, www.garnethill.com	Made of soft T-shirt-like material; there are 13 other styles of sheets for students, too.	This is the first time upscale catalog company Garnet Hill has marketed to the dorm set. It recommends a "Flokati Wool Shag Rug" to match.
Tullsta armchair $129, Ikea, 800-434-4532	Comes in this season's "fun" color, hot pink, as well as white and green for the more sedate.	After Ikea sent out half a million e-mails to college-age kids, sales of dorm furniture shot up 20-35%.

(Cont.)

Bath & Beyond, for example, went all out this year, with a Web site that sells 130 items marked as dormitory "essentials," like 440-thread-count sheets and heat-sensitive pillows that change color when you touch them; it also has an e-mail feature that lets you coordinate decor with your roommate-to-be. Pier 1 Imports this summer initiated a 15% discount for shoppers who carry a college ID. And then there's design company Mitchell Gold, which hired a student at George Washington University to convert his dorm space into a showroom. (The company plans to promote it in ads and lifestyle publications.)

For retailers, back-to-school time has a special bonus: Given that dorm furnishings are often as permanent as a college romance, many of these kids will be shopping for new stuff next year. "It's disposable product," says Matt Murphy, a trend manager at Target, which recently overhauled its college line to include artistic lighting and fancy door beads instead of the traditional dense curtains.

Indeed, maybe the most amazing thing at campuses these days isn't how much stuff kids are taking with them—but how much they leave behind when summer comes. Just ask senior Amara Murray, who, with her friends, scored lots of swank gear for their rooms at Harvard this year, including a mahogany-framed futon, a couch, eight inkjet printers, five TVs and a satellite dish.

Their secret? They work on the school's end-of-the-year cleanup crew, and found tons of stuff other classmates had abandoned in their dorm rooms. "The very best thing I got was an Aiwa seven-CD stereo, with an automatic disc changer," says Ms. Murray.

7-Eleven Cracks the Code on Elusive Sugar-Free Slurpee

Breakthrough by Kraft Scientists Allows Broadening of Convenience Store's Brand

BY ANN ZIMMERMAN

Staff Reporter of THE WALL STREET JOURNAL

Since 1965, when a broken soda-fountain machine in Kansas was refined with the help of an automobile air conditioner, a semi-frozen, carbonated concoction called Slurpee has been a huge hit at 7-Eleven.

But the sugar-free version has been elusive. The sugar crystal itself gives Slurpees the consistency of sherbet but also allows it to be sipped through a straw. And everything sugar-free that food scientists tried seemed to turn the drink into a big block of ice. Says Nancy Smith, 7-Eleven Inc.'s vice president of field merchandise, "We just couldn't crack the code."

A few months ago, however, scientists at **Kraft Foods** Inc., which had worked with 7-Eleven on developing other products, had a breakthrough. After working feverishly for a year, they created a sugar-free syrup that could make a drink with just the right consistency. This month, Dallas-based 7-Eleven introduced the fruit of the scientists' labor: a Crystal Light Lemonade Slurpee that contains only eight calories for eight ounces, compared with 118 calories for a traditional Slurpee.

"When they brought it to us to taste, I was so excited I rushed right to [Chief Executive] Jim Keyes' office, because he's been asking for this for years," says John Ryckevic, 7-Eleven's U.S. category manager for Slurpees and Big Gulps.

Kraft isn't divulging any secrets. "The recipe is confidential for competitive reasons," says Mike Murname, director of channel marketing for Kraft, who added that the Northfield, Ill., company is attempting to patent its "invention." Now that the code has been cracked, though, Kraft has additional sugar-free Slurpee flavors in the pipeline, including passion kiwi fruit, raspberry iced tea and peach tea.

The product is being tested by 7-Eleven in 106 stores in Detroit, which buys more Slurpees than any other city, and 35 stores in Kansas City, before rolling it out to the rest of the country in the summer.

Customers like Julie Lippe can't wait. A 26-year-old Arlington, Texas, mother of a six-year-old and a three-year-old, Ms. Lippe got hooked on Slurpees when she was pregnant, downing one or two a day of the 40-ounce size—at 600 calories a pop. She had to quit after her doctor encouraged her to lose some weight.

"I'm very excited about diet Slurpees," she says. "I'll probably go back to having three or four a week—of the big ones. And they'll be a fun treat for the kids, too."

Sugar-free Slurpees are among the products that 7-Eleven customers have requested most frequently. Many inquiries come from aging baby boomers, who are cutting down on sugar for weight or health reasons. Others come from parents of diabetic children, Mr. Ryckevic says.

Slurpees account for just $150 million in sales a year at 7-Eleven, a small portion of the company's merchandise revenue of about $6.6 billion last year. Still, the product, whose sales increase each year, is an important part of its stable of proprietary items, which account for 30% of sales and help differentiate 7-Eleven from other convenience stores. To keep the brand growing, 7-Eleven is investing $40 million in Slurpee machines, updating and increasing the number that stores have so each store can serve more flavors at a time.

The expansion is part of a longtime effort to capitalize on the well-known brand. In addition to developing new and unusual flavors each year—peanut-butter-and-jelly and buttered popcorn are the next new flavors— 7-Eleven also sells Slurpee bubble gum and Slurpee lip balm.

But the sugar-free version has been the toughest to develop. The company first attempted it in the mid-1980s, but the best it could come up with was a Slurpee Light, which cut the amount of sugar in half. It was dropped in the early 1990s.

In August 2000, Kraft decided to try its hand at creating a sugar-free version after hearing 7-Eleven's Mr. Keyes talk about his mission to broaden the company's customer base beyond the beer, cigarette and beef-jerky crowd. Kraft previously worked with 7-Eleven to develop new foods, including Snack Sticks and pizza sticks that could be eaten with one hand while driving. Kraft figured a sugar-free Slurpee would be particularly appealing to women, and a four-member beverage team got busy in its Rye Brook, N.Y., laboratory.

First, they studied the Slurpee machine, a contraption that mixes air with flavored syrup and serves the drink at 28 degrees, four degrees below freezing. With a sugar-filled syrup, this temperature allows the drink to be creamy but not melt too quickly.

Crystal Light is sweetened with sucralose. The challenge to the scientists was to add an additional element that would act like sugar in the freezing process, but not change the taste or the calorie content. Kraft's Mr. Murname says they scrapped three different attempts before getting it right. "We wanted that right mixture of airy and icy, the fine texture Slurpee is known for," Mr. Murname says.

Mr. Keyes, the 7-Eleven CEO, thinks diet Slurpees are just the first step in broadening the brand. He hopes to capitalize on the popularity of energy-enhancing drinks such as Red Bull. A Gatorade Slurpee is also in the works, but in a semifrozen state, the electrolyte-delivery system of Gatorade isn't yet as efficient as it is in liquid form, Mr. Keyes says.

Auto Makers Now 'Slam' Cars Right in the Factory

Souped-Up Engines, Big Tires Are Aimed at Young Buyers Who Used to Do Customizing

BY JONATHAN WELSH

Staff Reporter of THE WALL STREET JOURNAL

Car companies have a new offer for their young buyers: Leave the "slamming" to us.

For years, many drivers of cheap, entry-level compacts like the Honda Civic and Ford Focus have been retooling their cars to make them fast and flashy. Called slamming, the process usually involves such things as boosting engine horsepower, adding racing wheels or showy body panels and installing high-power stereos. But now, auto makers are releasing economy cars in versions that come "preslammed" from the factory.

When **Mitsubishi Motor** Corp. rolled out its new $14,000 Lancer sedan in August, it also released a modified version with spoilers and attention-getting colors such as "lightning yellow." That followed **Mazda Motor** Corp.'s May release of two flashy upgrades to its entry-level Protege sedan, including the $18,000 MP3, which has a faster engine, lowered suspension and a 280-watt sound system that plays MP3 music files.

By the end of the winter, look for race-inspired versions of such workaday compacts as the Civic and the Focus. **Toyota Motor** Corp. will have a hotrod based on its plain-vanilla Corolla, and even usually conservative **General Motors** Corp. is expected to release an entry-level racer. All will sell for under $20,000.

For auto makers, these cars look like a bright spot in an otherwise difficult year. U.S. car sales are expected to fall about 4% in 2001, the first decline since 1995. But thanks to these models' relatively low prices, high fuel efficiency and attention-grabbing looks, they have been strong sellers even during the downturn. Although U.S. auto sales fell 11% in September, Mazda's Protege posted a 54% increase, which it attributed in part to its sportier models. Subaru said sales of its entry-level Impreza line doubled in September, spurred by the souped-up WRX model, which the company, a unit of **Fuji Heavy Industries** Ltd., says accounts for about half of more than 25,000 Imprezas sold so far this year.

That auto makers are customizing such cars in the factory is a sign of their growing cooperation with the $25 billion specialty auto-parts industry. At the annual Specialty Equipment Marketing Association trade show opening today in Las Vegas, GM is expected to announce an agreement called Tek-Connect, under which it will share once-secret design information with makers of after-market components. The deal, similar to one made by **Ford Motor** Co. two years ago, will make it easier for custom-parts makers to design pieces that fit precisely on factory-built cars.

The preslammed trend also shows how car makers have become more aggressive in pursuing young drivers. For decades, buyers under 30 have accounted for a shrinking share of sales—about 9% last year from about 14% in the late 1970s, says CNW Marketing/Research in Bandon, Ore. But now, a larger group of potential new buyers, the children of baby boomers, are entering their car-buying years. Unlike their parents, who may have modified muscle cars like the Chevrolet Camaro or Ford Mustang, they are focusing on economy cars.

While the youth market looks promising, analysts caution that manufacturers are channeling a large number of models toward a sector that is not only relatively small, but notoriously fickle. "There's always a fad element to it, especially with highly styled cars that are anything but basic transportation," says David Healy, an analyst with Burnham Securities.

Yet more such cars are in the pipeline. Ford is preparing the SVT Focus for next spring, featuring more horsepower, huge brakes, oversize wheels and a stiff suspension. Its estimated $18,000 base price is well above the Focus's $12,445 base, but Ford says the modified version will sprint to 60 mph in about seven seconds—comparable to a $40,000 Porsche Boxster.

Toyota is coming out in December with the Matrix, a little hatchback built on the same chassis as its aging Corolla sedan. The Matrix's features include muscular-looking molding on its lower edges and a European-style radio antenna on the roof. **Nissan Motor** Co. released a youth-friendly version of its Sentra earlier this month, the Sentra SE-R, with a 170-horsepower engine, roughly equivalent to those found in competing versions from Ford and Honda. An even hotter version called the "Spec. V," with 180 horsepower, is expected a few months later. Both fall in the $16,000 to $17,000 range.

Honda Motor Co. will counter with a revved-up version of the Civic expected this spring. The Civic Si, a two-door hatchback based on the same chassis as other Civics, will feature higher horsepower, racing-style seats and bulging body panels. "We needed a performance model with European flair to keep younger buyers in the fold," says Peter Rech, assistant product-planning manager for Honda. One such touch: a five-speed shift lever mounted on the dashboard.

Indeed, one of the big influences in these cars is European-style rally racing, in which drivers and navigators compete on rough terrain. Rally racing is gaining popularity in the U.S., thanks to real races—there are about 75 pro and amateur rally races scheduled for the U.S. in 2002, nearly double the number held in 1998. Partly because of that increased popularity here, Subaru is bringing to the U.S. the European rally version of its Impreza, the $23,995 Impreza WRX.

The most extreme preslammed economy car, however, may be a version of the Vibe hatchback from GM's Pontiac division. The Vibe GT will feature a more-powerful engine and pavement-scraping suspension. With prices peaking at about $18,000, the line is "aimed directly at the Ford Focus," says Jon Moss, GM's manager of special vehicles.

NOTE: Toyota Motor Corp.'s new Matrix hatchback will be based on a new 2002 Corolla chassis, not on the Corolla chassis currently in use as reported in a Marketplace article in the Oct. 30 edition. (WSJ Nov. 13, 2001)

Super Bowl XXXVI: The NFL Tackles Mom

Super Bowl soup recipes? Football ads on soap operas? With season ratings at a 10-year low, the league is making a big push for female fans. Sam Walker on the NFL's risky new playbook.

By Sam Walker

Staff Reporter of The Wall Street Journal

When the St. Louis Rams and New England Patriots square off in Sunday's Super Bowl, 84 million people will watch big galoots in body armor bang into each other.

But first, how about a pregame serenade by Paul McCartney? Or an hour-long NFL special on Lifetime (airing tonight) where players cook bouillabaisse and watch game films with their wives? And if you can't decide what cheese to serve with that Shiraz, the league Web site has a few suggestions in a special section for women (think gouda).

If it seems like the National Football League is trying to get in touch with its sensitive side, it's no accident. After decades of pandering to tough guys, the nation's biggest sports empire is making a pass at a historically elusive pool of fans: women. In a marketing blitz remarkable for a sport that is almost a pure expression of guyness (70% of all viewers are men), the NFL is trying everything from running ads on daytime soap operas to partnering with a breast-cancer charity to hosting seminars for women on the rules of the sport called "Football 101." There's even a new line of women's clothes coming out next year. The highlight: lambskin jackets with "subtle" team logos for $350.

The league says it's going after a group that, surprisingly enough, is a bigger player in NFL dollars than you might think—

women spent $1.5 billion last year and made almost half of all purchases of official merchandise. But the idea of the macho NFL giving itself an image makeover strikes some fans as a bit fanciful. After all, the networks that broadcast games are going in the opposite direction—openly courting men with big doses of babes, beer ads and sophomoric humor. And does it make sense to lure women to a sport where cheerleaders still roam the sidelines in hotpants? "We haven't figured that out yet," says NFL marketing chief John Collins.

Given football's recent history with women, the NFL has plenty of convincing to do. More than any other league, its players have been in the news in recent years for charges of crimes against women, some of them grisly and some of them downright adolescent. Just last month, dozens of Philadelphia Eagles cheerleaders joined a suit charging that players on NFL teams spied on them for years at Veterans Stadium using peepholes drilled into the walls of their dressing room.

The Gatekeepers

Meanwhile, the NFL is trying to keep its balance in a growing sports recession. Regular-season ratings fell again this year to another record low, while the price of a Super Bowl commercial dropped about 15% this year. And if you're wondering why the NFL is concerned about women, know this: According to Nielsen Media Research, the number of women between 18 and 34 who watch pro football has dropped 15% since 1999—that's almost twice the rate at which young men have been tuning out. That's all the more alarming given women's role in everything from buying season tickets to letting kids play football in the first place. "Women are the gatekeepers," says the league's Mr. Collins.

Arguably the NFL's first push for women began with former MTV executive Sara Levinson, who ran the league's image machine until leaving for an Internet company in 2000. Among her initiatives: hosting a luncheon for women's magazine editors. Lately the league has stepped up the effort, hiring Marjorie Rodgers, a former executive at Oxygen Media, and running new "image ads" on daytime soaps and talk shows. Unlike the edgier "Feel the Power" spots they replaced, these ads focus on family themes—a father playing catch with his daughter, for instance, and a teenage boy watching football with his grandmother.

And how's this for pandering to women? Last year, NFL marketing officials approached comedian Joan Rivers about doing a "red carpet special" at the Super Bowl. (She said no.)

Betty Touchdown

Switch on Lifetime tonight, and you'll see the slickest ploy of all: an hour-long program for women produced by the league. Hosted by actress Marg Helgenberger, who sits on a couch in dewy light wearing a pair of Oak-

land Raiders slippers, it shows the softer side of NFL players. In one segment, San Francisco safety Ronnie Heard puts on a cooking demonstration ("Today, we're going to be doing a bouillabaisse," he says). And later, Tampa Bay quarterback Brad Johnson watches game films with his wife, Nikki. When the phrase "play action" comes up, an animated character named Betty Touchdown pops on the screen with an explanation.

To be sure, the Super Bowl is the broadcast that counts most when it comes to females: During Sunday's game, about 30 million women will be watching, and they'll make up about 36% of the audience, a slightly higher share than usual. Not only will you see more ads for movies and fewer pitches for motor oil, but a patriotic theme should keep things more subdued, too. Remember when KISS was one of the warm-up bands a few years ago? This Sunday's lineup includes singer Mariah Carey, the Boston Pops and a reading from the Declaration of Independence.

But if there's a problem with the NFL's new marketing plan, it's the networks—whose football coverage (if you haven't noticed) only seems to get raunchier and more sophomoric every year. Take Sunday's game: A few channels over at halftime, NBC will try to steal viewers with a reality game show starring six Playboy centerfolds. Before kickoff on Fox, meteorologist Jillian Barberie, described on the network's own Web site as a "fine weather vixen," will file a report on Super Bowl parties, possibly while baring her navel. And if the past is any guide, Fox commentator Jimmy Kimmel may put on a wig and kiss studio analyst Howie Long. (Surprise! The NFL sometimes complains about the show.) Says coordinating producer Scott Ackerson: "I'd be shocked if the typical 'Golden Girls' viewer got a kick out of it."

If you're wondering why the NFL and the networks are sending wildly different messages, blame it on Madison Avenue. While networks say women are their prime audience for practically everything on television, sports is the one reliable place to find young males. So networks say it's their job to reel in the men and keep them entertained between ads for beer, pickup trucks and the armed forces. "I go with what the sales department tells me," says Fox's Mr. Ackerson. The result: Longtime fan Mary Billard of New York is so fed up that she watches football games with the sound off. "It's been co-opted by frat boys," she says.

Regardless, the NFL is pressing ahead with a plan to remake itself as an entertainment conglomerate along the lines of Disney. The idea, executives say, is to find ways to position the league as something that unites families on Sundays (rather than something that swallows dad for hours and returns him in a psychotic lather). "We have a vision of the NFL as a social connector," says league

(Cont.)

marketing vice president Jesse Ewing.

Does the NFL run any risk of alienating males? Probably not. Come Sunday, they'll still have the Rams cheerleaders, stars of a $10 swimsuit calendar. But in today's sports economy (sorry, guys) it doesn't matter much. With the average cost of four season tickets pushing $2,000, football can be a big household expense. Says University of Oregon sports marketing expert Rick Burton, "most men can't spend that much without getting their wife involved."

Escalade scores with athletes, rappers
SUV's popularity surprises and pleases Cadillac

By Earle Eldridge
USA TODAY

How did Cadillac, which usually attracts 62-year-old white guys, create a truck that almost every black rap artist and rookie professional athlete wants to buy?

It appears to be pure luck, and it took Cadillac by surprise.

But the facts are stunning:

▶ So many twentysomething African-American men have bought the 2002 Cadillac Escalade sport-utility vehicle that the age of the typical Escalade owner is 12 years younger than the average Cadillac buyer's age, 62. Because of the rappers and professional athletes who have bought the SUV, the average family income for Escalade owners is $150,000, about $30,000 more than the typical Cadillac buyer.

▶ About 6.5% of Cadillac buyers are black, but 19% of Escalade buyers are black.

▶ Six players on the Golden State Warriors professional basketball team have an Escalade. Of the six top draft picks for the Green Bay Packers and Denver Broncos football teams, five bought Escalades with their new riches.

▶ At least 10 rap songs, including one by Jennifer Lopez, mention Escalade. In music videos and live performances, rappers often drive Escalades.

▶ Cadillac dealers say they sometimes toss teenagers out of showrooms because they spend too much time fawning over Escalades after school.

So what's the appeal? It's hard to pinpoint.

Escalade, which sells for about $54,000, has a 345-horsepower engine, making it the most powerful SUV.

But basketball and football players say their large body frames need the roominess of the big Escalade.

And then there's copycat cool, of course. Once the athletes and entertainers start driving it, their fans want one, too.

Chris Mills, a forward for the Golden State Warriors and avid car nut, likes Escalade's design. "The truck is awesome looking."

Mills owns 310 Motoring, an auto-customizing shop in Los Angeles that has done $10,000 to $40,000 custom jobs on many of the Escalades bought by NBA players, including teammates such as Jason Richardson.

Richardson initially thought Escalade was ugly. "I was like, 'Man, I don't want that,'" he says. "But it rides just like a Cadillac." So he spent thousands installing big wheels, five TVs, a backup camera on the rear end and a PlayStation video-game system.

A HIP-HOP FAVE

But hip-hop music may be a bigger influence on Escalade's popularity than athletics.

Some rap videos look like an Escalade commercial. A video for the song Southern Hospitality by Ludacris, a popular rapper from Atlanta, uses slow camera pans along the side of the Escalade. The nameplate shows prominently. The camera also shows the rear tailgate, focusing on the Cadillac emblem.

During the MTV Video Music Award show in August, Ludacris opened his performance by driving an Escalade onto the stage.

Ludacris peppers one of his songs with the word Cadillac as in: "Cadillac grills, Cadillac mills, Cadillac fills."

The rapper also owns a custom Escalade. "My family has been driving Cadillacs all my life," he says. "I have a custom grille, 22-inch (wheel) rims and a wood-grain kit inside."

Tyrese, a Los Angeles rapper who owns a custom Escalade, says the SUV has a strong, luxurious and wealthy image that is popular with rappers.

Female entertainers—including Pink and Brandy—have been buying Escalades, too.

"I'm short, so I need trucks to make me look tall," says rapper Missy Elliott of Portsmouth, Va. "I rap about the Escalade because it's a hot car and everyone has one, so I knew they could relate."

Cadillac officials first noticed the Escalade's popularity in February when dealers kept calling to report back orders for athletes and entertainers. After the NBA draft in June, many of the players who were picked told reporters they were going to buy an Escalade with their first paycheck. That's also about the time Escalade began appearing in rap songs and videos.

GOOD NEWS OR BAD NEWS?

All this created a rich opportunity and—because of the content of some of the lyrics and videos, including a simulated drive-by shooting—a potential dilemma for Cadillac. Should it exploit the sudden hipness of the SUV or downplay it?

(Cont.)

Cadillac decided to play it low-key on Escalade. "It is OK for rappers and athletes to call us cool, but the moment we start calling us cool, we are done," says Susan Docherty, Escalade brand manager, who concedes, "You can't buy this kind of buzz."

Cadillac has tracked the use of Escalade in rap songs and videos and has asked dealers to call when they sell one to a celebrity or athlete. Docherty says Cadillac needs to know the thinking of hip-hop buyers to make sure the company doesn't do any advertising that doesn't connect with them or that offends them.

"One of the things I learned is they like really big wheels," she says. "We know that 17- or 18-inch wheels isn't cutting it with them."

Cadillac has quietly put together a 2-minute internal video for its staff on Escalade's new kind of customer. It includes high-energy snippets from rap videos that show the Escalade.

Howard Drake of Casa De Cadillac in Sherman Oaks, Calif., near Beverly Hills, says he sells about 60 Escalades a month, many to rappers and athletes.

Perhaps surprisingly, Rich Willis, owner of Betts Cadillac in Des Moines suburb Clive, Iowa, says he has been seeing a different type of buyer in his showroom, too, because of Escalade. "We don't have many NBA stars or rappers, but we do have some successful NCAA basketball players coming through," Willis says.

Escalade is one of the few luxury SUVs showing a sales increase. And its fortune has likely hurt the older Lincoln Navigator SUV, which also has been popular with entertainers and athletes.

"Everyone wants to have the hottest truck," Mills says. "If Lincoln does a hot redesign of the Navigator, I'm sure it will be the new hot truck."

'Got Milk?' Ad Campaign to Take On a Tough Target: Hispanic Teens

After First Attempt Failed, A Mythical Latin Woman Will Star in New TV Spot

BY EDUARDO PORTER
Staff Reporter of THE WALL STREET JOURNAL

Next month, California TV audiences will meet a phantom of a woman, wailing inconsolably as she wanders through a middle-class home. Many people in the audience are unlikely to recognize her. She is "La Llorona"—the Crying One—a well-known character in Hispanic myth who murders her children, commits suicide and roams for all eternity looking for her lost brood.

She also is the California Milk Processor Board's new pitchwoman in the group's latest attempt to sell milk to Hispanic teenagers.

Best known for its "Got Milk?" ad campaign, which has since been used nationwide, the milk board has been trying to boost consumption among Latino teens, one of the fastest-growing slices of the population. The effort shows how difficult it can be to market to this lucrative group without alienating other consumers.

Hoping to entice young Latinos, an often-bilingual segment of the population, the milk board held focus groups and brainstormed with Hispanic advertising experts back in 1999 to come up with what it believed was a bold approach. The board took the famous "Got Milk?" ads and aired them, unchanged, on Spanish-language TV.

Two years later, milk board officials acknowledge the plan didn't work. "They love 'Got Milk?,' they recall 'Got Milk?'— and they are drinking less milk," says Jeff Manning, executive director of the board. In fact, according to the board's latest tracking study, prepared this March, California teenagers—both Hispanic and non-Hispanic—were downing 12% less of the stuff than they were in 1999.

So now, the milk board is doing a U-turn: Instead of placing off-the-shelf "Got Milk?" commercials designed for the general market on Spanish-language TV, it is spending $2 million to produce and air a custom-made ad about a Latino legend on English-language stations. In the spot, the phantom La Llorona—pronounced "Yoh-ROH-nah"—floats through a house and up to the fridge—only to find an empty milk carton. There's no dialogue, except for a voice at the end that still says, in English, "Got Milk?" The spot is set to air at first in California. It may be picked up later in other heavily Hispanic areas around the country.

Bicultural advertising isn't exactly uncharted territory. Last year, **Ford Motor** Co. aired a spot during the National Basketball Association finals in which El Zorro commanded his Mustang in Spanish. For the past year, **CEC Entertainment** Inc.'s Chuck E. Cheese restaurant chain has run a bilingual commercial aimed at Hispanic kids on the cable network Nickelodeon.

Nonetheless, La Llorona has her work cut out for her in getting Latino teens to raid the milk aisle. Teenagers are famously fickle to start with. Hispanic teens, usually hybrid products of Hispanic and Anglo language and culture, are especially tricky advertising targets. Advertising is all about pushing cultural buttons. With bicultural teens, advertisers must decide which set to push. Each choice risks alienating those who identify with, or simply prefer, the other set.

In 1999, the milk board chose to address Hispanic teens the same way it does other teens. This time, it has taken pains to make an authentically Latino commercial. Its flagship advertising agency, **Omnicom Group** Inc.'s Goodby, Silverstein & Partners of San Francisco, and its Hispanic agency, **Anita Santiago Advertising** of Santa Monica, Calif., drafted a team of four Hispanic students and graduates from the Art Center College of Design in Pasadena, Calif., to devise a message that wouldn't ring false or fall into stereotype.

"Hispanics will appreciate that we have understood and celebrated a story from their culture," says Jeff Goodby, co-chairman of the ad agency. At the same time, English-language television is a surprisingly natural place to air such a tale: Hispanic teens spend more than 75% of their television time watching English-language channels, according to Nielsen Media Research. To pitch their parents, Mr. Manning plans eventually to run the La Llorona ad on Spanish-language TV.

Yet broadcasting the spot on English-language TV risks alienating Anglos who are unfamiliar with the ghost. Two years ago, Chevron Corp. (now ChevronTexaco) tested a Spanish-language spot with English subtitles for one week on English-language stations in Los Angeles. The ad drew angry responses from some viewers, who complained it was un-American.

Aware of the risks, Mr. Manning made sure the spot wasn't so steeped in the Latino legend that Anglo viewers wouldn't recognize it as "Got Milk?"

Indeed, as a rough-cut of the spot was presented to focus groups of Hispanics and non-Hispanics, some of Mr. Manning's fears were born out. "If she was a crying bride, why did she have a cookie in her hand?" asked Candice Schwalm, a non-Hispanic mother of a young child who was befuddled by the concha, a Mexican pastry that La Llorona lugs around to eat with her milk.

The spot ran into further trouble with non-Hispanic teenage boys, who didn't find it humorous. "Even when it was explained I didn't think it was funny," said 15-year-old David Ashkenazi, who suggested an improvement: having La Llorona bump her head as she floats through the wall between the bedroom and kitchen.

Yet, most important to Mr. Manning, Hispanics at the focus groups liked the spot. Adults were pleased to see a commercial addressed specifically at them. Most of the Latino teens thought it was plenty funny. Ana Valdez, 17, liked the way La Llorona's quest was changed—from looking for her children to looking for milk—so much that she gave the ad the ultimate teen compliment: It's "pretty cool."

Upper Crust

Fast-Food Chains Vie To Carve Out Empire In Pricey Sandwiches

Mr. Lynch Likes the Bread At Panera, While Zell And Kravis Back Cosi

Starbucks as a Role Model

BY SHIRLEY LEUNG
Staff Reporter of THE WALL STREET JOURNAL

For years, growth-obsessed fast-food chains expanded around the world without noticing the potential of a 75-cent item on their own menus. Only after that item—the humble cup of coffee—became the high-priced beverage behind Starbucks Corp. did fast-food executives search their kitchens for other undiscovered stars.

Now they think they've found one: the sandwich.

Lately, small restaurant chains with big ambitions have been racking up impressive sales by offering Americans upscale sandwiches as an alternative to burgers and fries. Some of those outlets, such as Cosi and Briazz, have names designed to convey European sophistication. Others, such as Corner Bakery Cafe and Panera Bread Co., have names that emphasize their use of fresh bread. All of them hope to win a big following among the nation's aging and increasingly health-conscious baby boomers.

Their success so far, especially during the current recession, has captured the attention of many on Wall Street, who see an opportunity for at least one such chain to grow into a national brand, pioneering a mass market for made-to-order sandwiches much the same way that Starbucks did for premium coffee.

Above 99 Cents

Though overall fast-food sales growth has been waning for years, growing numbers of American consumers have proved willing to pay as much for a sandwich as for the $4 cappuccino to go with it. That's big news in an industry long accustomed to promoting 99-cent hamburgers or chicken nuggets. And it is making even some fast-food veterans rethink their marketing strategies. For example, roast-beef specialist Arby's Inc., a unit of Triarc Cos., has launched a new line of Market Fresh sandwiches, which are served on thick slices of bread, instead of a bun, and cost about $4 apiece, about 50% more than its average fare.

Already such financial heavyweights as deal maker Henry Kravis, market guru Peter Lynch, real-estate baron Sam Zell and hamburger giant McDonald's Corp. have invested in the sandwich-shop concept. "There's an opportunity . . . to elevate the experience" of eating a sandwich, says Starbucks founder and Chairman Howard Schultz, who also is backing two fledgling sandwich chains.

Nor is the enthusiasm limited to the U.S. A popular new sandwich chain in London, for example, is named for the owner's 18th-century ancestor, the Earl of Sandwich, who is credited with having first stuck meat between bread. "We have a brand that already has 250 years of heritage and literally global recognition," says company founder Orlando Montagu, whose father is the 11th Earl of Sandwich.

Rising Sales

In the U.S., sales of custom-made sandwiches are rising 15% a year, much faster than the 3% growth rate for hamburgers and steaks, says Technomic Inc., a Chicago food-consulting firm. That helps explain why Panera Bread Co., the largest player in the premium-priced sandwich category, has seen its share price nearly triple in the past year.

Panera, which is based outside St. Louis, rang up sales of $529.4 million for 2001, up 50% from the previous year, and it is expected to report an about 80% increase in net income for 2001. The company had average sales per store of $1.75 million in 2001, compared with McDonald's $1.6 million. In 4 p.m. trading on the Nasdaq Stock Market yesterday, Panera's shares rose $3.28, or 5.3%, to $64.65 on volume of 758,500 shares, more than double its average daily volume for the past three months.

Panera and some other high-end sandwich chains also sell gourmet coffee, meaning that success on a national scale could steal sales from their role model, Starbucks. But the chains vying to carve out an empire based on sandwiches face a challenge that Starbucks never did—a field of well-funded competitors. Starbucks, which expanded to roughly 4,100 stores in North America in little more than a decade, was helped by a dearth of big-chain competition. Even today, its largest U.S. competitor, Diedrich Coffee Inc., based in Irvine, Calif., has a total of only 380 outlets.

"The probability of any of these sandwich chains becoming a Starbucks is a major question," says Dennis Lombardi, Technomic's executive vice president. "It is going to be very difficult."

Yet the prospect of spinning prosperity out of a commodity long taken for granted, of dotting the landscape with a recognizable logo, of becoming synonymous with a particular product, is proving seductive. After investing in one sandwich chain that is struggling, Starbucks's Mr. Schultz recently put "several million" dollars into another: Potbelly Sandwich Works Inc.

Until recently, the sandwich was hardly considered cuisine. According to popular lore, it was invented solely to allow the Earl of Sandwich to eat without leaving the gaming table. Its culinary status sank even further when the fast-food industry began to tout it as a low-cost meal, available at most big purveyors for as little as 99 cents.

By contrast, the new sandwich shops treat sandwich-making as an art. Fresh-baked bread is the basis of their strategy for improving the sandwich's image. Sure, the tomato slices are fresh, and the meat is carved off homestyle roasts. But the big difference is what some of the chains call "artisan bread."

Panera employs professional bakers at $13 an hour to make bread from scratch throughout the day. Together, Panera and Smyrna, Ga.-based Atlanta Bread Co. offer more than two dozen kinds of bread, including asiago cheese, nine grain, kalamata olive and sundried tomato. At New York-based Cosi Inc.'s restaurants, bread that's been out of the oven for 30 minutes or more is tossed away unused.

The finished products feature names as fancy as the coffee specialties at Starbucks. The menu blurb describes Panera's Frontega Chicken Panini as: "Smoked and pulled white-meat chicken, red onion, mozzarella, tomato, chopped basil, and our chipotle mayo, on our rosemary focaccia." Compare that with the Big Mac: "Two 100%-beef patties, sesame-seed bun, American-cheese slice, Big Mac sauce, lettuce, pickles, onions, salt and pepper."

Demographic Shift

Of course, the price of the Frontega is $5.75, about $3 more than for the typical Big Mac. The average check is $6.25 at Panera and $8 at Cosi, more than twice that at most burger joints. But the chains can make these prices stick because of a major shift in the demographics of fast-food customers.

The industry's traditional diner is male, between five and 24 years old, and typically short on cash. But now that youthful segment of the population is expected to grow by only 5% over the next decade, while the 45- to 64-year-old population will grow about 30%, according to the U.S. Census Bureau. And compared with previous generations in their current age group, baby boomers are less likely to eat at home. Pressed for time, they want food fast. Moreover, the growing availability of healthier and higher-quality sandwiches has eroded their loyalty to fast-food burgers.

"If the value is there, I'll certainly pay the price," says Karen Davis, a 45-year-old Chicago real-estate developer and self-described former burger fan who says she, her husband and nine-year-old daughter visit Panera about five times a week.

Subway Restaurants still dominates the sandwich arena, with more than 13,200 U.S. outlets. Until lately, the privately held chain competed with other fast-food purveyors on price, charging about $3 a sandwich. But 18 months ago it, too, started going after more affluent consumers. The chain now offers as many as five different breads, including Asiago Caesar and Sourdough. "We made the food more interesting," says founder Fred DeLuca.

Likewise, some of the nation's other fast-food chains are seeking to rev up their sales growth by adding gourmet sandwiches or premium breads to their menus. But some of them are finding that many of the new sandwich diners also want atmosphere, something that Subway and many other more traditional fast-food chains may be ill-equipped to provide.

Some sandwich chains have learned the hard way about the importance of ambience. Boston-based Au Bon Pain was among the first bakery-style chains to offer high-quality meat on fresh-made bread. But its sales growth faltered, and the company sold its namesake division in 1999 in order to focus on Panera, whose predecessor it acquired in 1993. Former Au Bon Pain Chief Executive Ron Shaich blames the chain's minimalist decor. "We thought the paradigm was to be like McDonald's," recalls Mr. Shaich, who is now Panera's chairman and chief executive.

McDonald's itself has joined the contest to attract the high-end sandwich eater. Last year, it paid an undisclosed sum for a 33% stake in Pret A Manger, an upscale British chain now embarked on a massive invasion of New York City. A typical Pret A Manger offering is the Coronation Chicken, a $5.25 chicken-breast sandwich with curry dressing and mango chutney on malted-grain bread.

Custom-Made vs. Prepackaged

But Pret A Manger, which makes its sandwiches fresh each morning, may be learning a different lesson—that its U.S. growth potential is limited by its strategy of selling its sandwiches prepackaged in cellophane and cardboard, not made to order. Consider the fate of Briazz Inc., a Howard Schultz-backed competitor whose sales growth has sputtered and whose stock price has collapsed to $1.50 a share from $8 last May. One problem, competitors say: Many of its stores continue to sell only prepackaged sandwiches.

In other stores, to pump up sales, Seattle-based Briazz has begun offering pricier hot, custom-made sandwiches—and the harried office workers it caters to are eating them up. As much as 35% of some stores' sales now come from the grilled sandwiches. "We have found that many of our guests want hot food and are willing to wait five or six minutes for a prepared hot item," says Chairman and Chief Executive Victor Alhadeff.

Starbucks also found that high-quality sandwiches packaged fresh each morning didn't meet customer expectations. After launching a much-publicized effort to sell prepackaged sandwiches in 1999, Mr. Schultz says that Starbucks, whose stores aren't equipped to prepare sandwiches on site, doesn't plan to emphasize food. "We recognize more than ever our core competency is roasting and selling the best coffee in the world," he says.

Mr. Schultz's latest bet is on Chicago-based Potbelly Sandwich Works, whose custom-made sandwiches are so popular that devoted customers often have to stand outside in the cold waiting to get inside the company's nine stores.

But many other investors regard the field of possible sandwich all-stars as narrowed to a field of two, Panera and Cosi.

Panera's robust net income, sales and market-value growth may qualify it as the restaurant industry's hottest company. And that growth is only expected to accelerate this year, because Panera, which hoarded cash during the boom years in anticipation of a downturn, plans to take advantage of lower commercial rents to add 100 stores to its current 369. Former Fidelity fund manager Peter Lynch, a longtime investor in Panera, says he is also a loyal customer. "Nobody had done bread," he says, "I thought there was a market for it."

Panera serves its sandwiches on real plates and with real flatware in rooms furnished with fireplaces and upholstered couches. Its locations include suburban strip malls that feature discount stores such as Wal-Mart. Mr. Shaich, Panera's CEO, says the chain, originally conceived for neighborhoods with average household incomes above $50,000, also is thriving in blue-collar neighborhoods.

Cosi's chairman and co-chief executive, Andy Stenzler, believes that his will be the more famous sandwich chain. Similar to Panera in its gourmet sandwiches and decor, Cosi offers one twist of its own. It sells alcohol in the evening, which helps in attracting dinner customers. "Our vision is to define what an American cafe is," says Mr. Stenzler.

Cosi now has 66 stores. But this year, it plans to add 40 more. Among the privately held chain's investors are Messrs. Kravis and Zell, as well as Terry Diamond, whose Chicago venture-capital firm made a fortune as an early investor in Starbucks. Recalling how Starbucks became "part of the landscape of America," Mr. Diamond says: "I think Cosi can do the same thing."

Bottom Line

Diaper Sales Sagging, P&G Thinks Young To Reposition Pampers

How to Sell Premium Brand In Penny-Pinching Times? Casting It as a Lifestyle

'Actually a Piece of Clothing'

BY EMILY NELSON
Staff Reporter of THE WALL STREET JOURNAL

CINCINNATI—Deb Henretta, Procter & Gamble Co.'s president of global baby care, put on a pair of thick glasses and checked to make sure her eyesight was blurry. Her legs dangling from a giant cherry-red chair, she peered out at a group of colleagues. An oversized crib and a six-foot-tall changing table sat in the corner.

Ms. Henretta watched as her marketing director put on some gardening gloves and attempted to tie the laces on a tiny pair of Keds sneakers. Her advertising manager has been known to crawl on hands and knees across the floor at shin level. Other managers have struggled to eat spaghetti with big wooden serving spoons or sit through meetings gnawing on huge, specially baked eight-inch-wide bagels.

These executives hope that in mimicking the infant experience they will come up with a new way to sell Pampers disposable diapers. They also hope to crack a larger riddle now facing consumer-products companies: how to continue to command premium prices for household staples during a recession.

In the past decade, through the longest U.S. economic expansion on record, companies could rely on making small changes in their products—adding aloe to tissues, baking soda to toothpaste or calcium to orange juice—as a way to justify charging higher prices. But in a tight economy, shoppers won't readily pay more even for "new and improved" versions of their favorite brands.

Pampers' parent company, P&G, thrived for decades by launching mass-market products—fluoride toothpaste, heavy-duty laundry detergent, fabric softeners and diapers—that became fixtures in most American homes. But the company, which owns such brands as Crest and Tide, stalled in the late 1990s. Discount chains were demanding lower prices, there were more brands on the market, and smaller competitors had become increasingly nimble.

P&G's annual sales increase has been just 2.5% on average for the past five years, a slowdown from growth of between 6% and 8% in the mid-1990s. P&G tried to pep up its marketing arm, a pioneer of brand advertising that had begun to seem bulky and slow, by reassigning executives in the late 1990s.

Now, P&G's profits, which are being hurt by big charges from that corporate restructuring, are about where they were in 1996. The company's former chief executive, Durk Jager, was forced out after just 17 months when his acquisition attempts and plan to boost sales by inventing niche products—such as a vegetable wash and a home dry-cleaning kit—produced disappointing results. The company's new CEO, A.G. Lafley, is hoping instead for even a small percentage increase in sales of the company's large, core brands.

'Contemporizing'

Pampers is P&G's biggest global brand, generating about $5 billion in annual sales, or roughly 13% of P&G's yearly total of about $39 billion. That's why the 40-year-old Ms. Henretta recently looked on blurrily at an important meeting in a room full of outsized furniture. A P&G veteran who was brought in to revive Pampers in late 1999, Ms. Henretta felt the company badly needed to, as she put it, "contemporize" Pampers' marketing.

The brand's advertising talked down to mothers, she concluded, admonishing them to "pamper" their babies, through ads and packaging that came across as dated. Indeed, the image of the world's first mass-market disposable diaper had changed little since the brand was introduced in 1961. Ms. Henretta's alternative: a campaign to present diapering as part of a lifestyle choice, turning Pampers into a brand that moved beyond diapers—into all aspects of baby care.

"The diaper is actually a piece of clothing," Ms. Henretta says. "It's not just a poop catcher. It's a point of interaction between mom and baby."

Ms. Henretta revived Pampers Bibsters, disposable bibs that P&G researchers had periodically considered. She launched the product in the U.S. a few months ago hoping to extend the Pampers name from the nursery to kitchens and restaurants. Pampers Wipesters, packaged face-and-hand wipes, is another new product, aimed at getting Pampers onto more supermarket shelves. In Europe, P&G is testing Pampers Sunnies—sunscreen lotion on a wipe—a product made at the suggestion of a secretary in the baby-care division.

Ms. Henretta recently struck a licensing deal to make Pampers Clean 'n Play, a cleanser parents can spray on toys or other surfaces. She also has licensed the Pampers name to a clothing company to make baby sleepwear, receiving blankets and onesies.

Last winter, Pampers managers began a loyalty program called Pampers Perks, which encourages parents to collect proofs of purchase and to redeem them for toys. A new Pampers Web site features product information, chat rooms and parenting advice, with cartoons depicting a baby's-eye-view of the world.

Ms. Henretta's approach poses some thorny problems. Some parents may balk at dressing their children with a name inextricably linked to a malodorous mess. A larger issue is that Pampers, like many P&G products and competing brands, is priced at a premium. Pampers Premium diapers generally cost about 50% more than their store-brand rivals; standard Pampers, called Pampers Baby-Dry, cost about 30% more, and Luvs, a lower-end P&G brand, a bit less.

The competition among such branded staples is cutthroat because the U.S. market isn't growing. Marketing can't make Americans brush their teeth, shampoo their hair, and wash their dishes more frequently than they already do. For diapers, the U.S. market is even bleaker. Improved diapers last longer, so parents change their babies less often. Years ago, diaper makers could win over parents used to cloth diapers but now, nearly all parents use disposable.

P&G already cut the price of its Luvs diapers by 10% in October. And executives of Kimberly-Clark Corp., maker of the competing Huggies brand, recently blamed the weak launch of Cottonelle Rollwipes, basically a roll of wet baby wipes, partly on shoppers' current reluctance to pay $8.99 to try a new product.

At a P&G board meeting in October, directors questioned executives about their pricing, and managers promised to watch sales data from retailers for early signs that shoppers might be switching to lower-priced competition.

Often, manufacturers cut prices by upping a product's size but leaving the price unchanged, just as Kimberly-Clark did this fall when it added several pull-up diapers to its packs. Generally, diapers are the most expensive baby-care item. Parents typically spend about $2,000 on diapers in the course of raising a baby, says Rich Meelia, president of Tyco Healthcare, a unit of Tyco International Ltd., which oversees the company's diaper operations. About two-thirds of parents buy either Huggies or Pampers. The remaining one-third buy either Luvs or store brands, such as Wal-Mart's store brand, which is manufactured by Paragon Trade Brands Inc., which Tyco recently agreed to acquire. Pampers Premium can cost roughly $496 a year.

P&G's biggest planned product launch in coming months—a new version of premium Pampers called Pampers Baby Stages of

(Cont.)

Development—is expected to cost about the same as the current Pampers Premium when it hits store shelves starting in February. Baby Stages, which replaces the Pampers Premium sold in purple packages, is a line of diapers designed for a baby's specific stage: extra absorbency for newborns, stretchy sides for crawling children, and pull-on pants for older toddlers.

To prepare the launch, Ms. Henretta is encouraging managers to think of Pampers more broadly. So, she holds meetings in a conference room at Pampers headquarters that is decorated like an outsized nursery. When managers put on the thick eyeglasses, they have the vision of a baby, Ms. Henretta says. When they fumble tying shoelaces with gardening gloves, they have the coordination of a toddler. (Ms. Henretta herself has done the shoe test so many times she can actually tie the laces.) Ms. Henretta wants her team to "mimic the experience of a child."

When Ms. Henretta, who had spent 14 years marketing huge brands like Tide and Cheer, was transferred to Pampers in 1999, she thought the move took her away from where the action was. For years, P&G had lumped diapers with its Bounty paper towel and Charmin toilet-paper operations. "They're sending me out to this paper business," she recalls thinking.

Ms. Henretta spent her first month on the job talking with new mothers in focus groups, in visits to their homes and in individual interviews. One mother said, " 'I just want to smile. I want to feel a little less tired,'" says Ms. Henretta, a mother of three who drives a minivan with crumbs from kids' snacks between the seats and a box of tissues on the car floor. "I came back to the organization and said 'our advertising has to make a tired mom smile.'"

With those orders, Saatchi & Saatchi, which designs Pampers' European advertising, came up with TV ads showing a living room from a child's perspective. Furniture and mom float in and out of focus, as with Ms. Henretta's glasses. The camera zooms around, showing how fast a toddler moves. Advertising Pampers is "about parenting, not changing diapers," says John Murphy, a senior vice president who handles Pampers' U.S. advertising at Bcom3 Group's D'Arcy Masius Benton & Bowles.

'Forever Young'

Pampers' TV ad, which began running last year in the U.S., shows bear cubs, baby elephants and penguins snuggling with their mothers to the strains of the Rod Stewart song "Forever Young." The ad doesn't show a diaper or mention product benefits—violating a basic tenet of all P&G advertising, which is to explain a product's value. Even P&G's Pantene shampoo ads show a sexy model flipping her hair with the promise, "hair will be 65% smoother in 10 days." By contrast, the only mention of Pampers comes at the end, with the new Pampers slogan: "We're right behind you. Every step of the way."

Ms. Henretta says the slogan is broad enough to cover products besides diapers. The animals also provided a new image for Pampers. Rival Huggies, made by Kimberly-Clark, is the best-selling diaper in the U.S., even though it came on the market 17 years after Pampers. Kimberly-Clark kept its lead with a double-punch of shipping more efficiently, so that more stores sold its diapers, and making diapers for older toddlers, creating a new and lucrative market for its product.

Pampers has about a 24% share of the about $4.3 billion of diapers sold in the U.S. a year, behind Huggies' 42%, according to data at mass-market stores tracked by market-research firm Information Resources Inc. A P&G spokeswoman says P&G's market share is actually higher than that because IRI doesn't track wholesale-club stores, in which P&G's presence is growing. The data also includes pull-up diapers, she says, which Pampers won't sell until its premium Baby Stages diapers reach stores.

During a recent afternoon, 400 toddlers and their parents arrived at Pampers headquarters, a warehouse-like building about 20 minutes from downtown Cincinnati. A group of eight played in a room, wearing just T-shirts and diapers, as two P&G researchers in white lab coats took notes. In the sample-making room, half a dozen P&G workers constructed diapers with scissors, using premade component parts so that employees can instantly test ideas.

Last year, Ms. Henretta took home a Pampers diaper with a picture of a bear's face on the front and a bear's rump on the back. Her youngest daughter Shannon, now four, wasn't impressed by the two-sided bear. But, Ms. Henretta says, her daughter did like the bear's face and the other animals featured on Pampers' fronts, and liked to sort her diapers by animal. After consumer testing, Pampers decided the extra printing costs for the front-and-back design weren't worth it, but that children enjoyed the various animal images on the diapers' fronts.

A New Package

To prepare for its Baby Stages line, Pampers gradually changed its package design. Last year, Pampers shed the infant's picture that—P&G research showed—made parents shopping for larger sizes, the priciest diapers, think Pampers wasn't for them. P&G also switched the Pampers type font and logo to look like crayon writing, with a heart on top. With its new premium line, Baby Stages, P&G is adding a photo of a baby that is indicative of the diaper's size so parents can more easily spot the size they need. P&G executives say Baby Stages increased Pampers sales and market share in Europe in a test last summer.

But Wal-Mart Stores Inc. also plans to add age-appropriate pictures to its store-brand diaper packages in January. Wal-Mart, in fact, could emerge as P&G's biggest threat in a recession. During the last recession, in the early 1990s, store-brand diapers weren't as much of a threat. Store-brand diapers came in drab packages and were noticeably poorer in quality, while patents protected most Pampers and Huggies features. Now, the quality of store-brand diapers is much improved; they account for 21.5% of the diaper market and are growing faster than premium brands thanks in part to Wal-Mart's introduction of White Cloud diapers in late 1999.

All the marketing could be for naught if consumers focus on price. At Wegmans Food Markets Inc., the chain of upscale supermarkets in upstate New York, about half of all diapers sold are on sale or go to customers using coupons, says Dave D'Arezzo, a senior vice president. Nationwide, shoppers redeem only about 1% of all coupons printed. By contrast, about 20% of all diaper coupons are redeemed, according to Mr. D'Arezzo.

"Huggies or Pampers, there's really not a huge difference for me," says Janet Mednik, the mother of a two-year-old in Silver Spring, Md. But Anthony Sackes, a New York City father, recently started driving to a Costco warehouse store every few weeks to stock up on Pampers Baby-Dry diapers for his one-year-old daughter, Samantha. He used to buy either Huggies or Pampers, depending on the coupons his wife Myriam had clipped from parenting magazines. They switched to Pampers a few months ago when, as their daughter grew, Huggies didn't fit as well.

"I personally have not noticed" Pampers advertising, Mr. Sackes says. "I have to watch cost. I want to get as much as I can get for my money."

SOMETHING STYLISH, SOMETHING BLUE

JetBlue's sleek, sophisticated look, on everything from its advertising to its uniforms, sends a message that low fares don't preclude high style.

By: Amy Goldwasser

In late 1998, when Amy Curtis-McIntyre joined the founding team of JetBlue Airways as vice president for marketing, she knew she had her work cut out for her. "We had a list of the 10 most hated industries in the United States," she recalls, "and sure enough, airlines were up there." That JetBlue intended to be a low-fare, all-coach carrier made it even more challenging. Most people associate such brands with inept customer service, dingy waiting areas, and cramped seats upholstered in leftover 1970s fabric.

Not anymore. As JetBlue turns two this month, flying coach has never been more hip. *Vanity Fair* named JetBlue the "It" airline of 2000, and readers of Conde *Nast Traveler* and *Zagat* rated it the number two domestic airline of 2001, behind Midwest Express, an all-business-class carrier that charges far more. (The cheapest Newark-San Francisco round trip, for example, is $437 on Midwest; New York-Oakland is $298 on JetBlue.) The airline's 42-year-old CEO, David Neeleman, has succeeded Southwest's (*LUV*) Herb Kelleher as the industry's celebrity executive, and no wonder: Despite the triple whammy of simultaneous recession, terrorism, and war, JetBlue reported profits of $10.5 million on $82.6 million in revenues for the third quarter of 2001.

Innovative positioning has been crucial to the company's success, and the carrier's distinctive style—what Curtis-McIntyre dubs "cheap-clever"—is at the heart of it. From the beginning, says the 35-year-old New York City native, the brand has combined low fares with high style and high-touch service. Its strategy has been to excel at the things that can really distinguish the brand but cost relatively little—such as comfort, punctuality, and courtesy—while dispensing entirely with things that can't, like airline grub.

What travelers resent most about airlines, JetBlue realized, is being treated like cattle: packed in, kept in the dark, denied real choice—what Curtis-McIntyre refers to diplomatically as "issues of communication and control." JetBlue addressed the problem, in part, by gambling on a hub at JFK Airport, even though most New Yorkers fly out of LaGuardia or Newark for travel within the United States. The upside was that JFK is far less congested for domestic routes. "We knew it was our opportunity to have phenomenal on-time performance," Curtis-McIntyre says. So far it has paid off: JetBlue's on-time record of 83 percent tops the industry. When delays do happen, moreover, JetBlue goes out of its way to keep passengers informed. By company policy, no more than 15 minutes can pass between updates on a flight's status, and if the delay stretches to more than four hours for any reason other than crummy weather, passengers get credit for a free flight.

Another part of the brand's positioning is an air of sophistication that carries over even to the flight attendants' uniforms. For these, Curtis-McIntyre sought out fashion designer Stan Herman—known for FedEx's uniforms, among other things—and asked for what she called "classic New York black." After Herman gently reminded her that her company, after all, was named Jet*Blue*, they settled on tailored almost-black navy-blue attire that is functional at 30,000 feet but chic enough to fit in at a Soho bar. "People don't necessarily point to one thing—'I'm flying JetBlue because the uniforms look good,'" Curtis-McIntyre admits. "But it's all part of the effort to make everything feel sort of generous and interesting and valuable."

JetBlue's decision to buy brand-new Airbus A320 planes was another inspired trade-off. The jets are more expensive up front than used models, but they require substantially less maintenance over the years. The A320s also have the added benefit of being 8 inches wider than comparable Boeing 737s, meaning that aisles can be roomier and all seats can be 18.5 inches wide, just a half inch shy of standard business class. Adding to the all-business-class feel of the cabin, the airline upholstered the seats in leather and gave each one its own video screen with access to as many as 24 channels of live TV, beamed in by satellite.

JetBlue looked to the Internet as another way to offer high-touch service at bargain costs. Hip New York advertising agency Merkley Newman Harty translated the brand's clean, blue line over to JetBlue.com. "We really wanted to make something that didn't look or feel like any

(Cont.)

other airline's [website] and that [visitors would find] utterly simple and user-friendly," Curtis-McIntyre says. The site is spare, with just a few navigational options, but the customers use it. While the major carriers sell an average of 10 percent of their tickets online, JetBlue books fully half of its fares on the Web and saves about $5 in transaction costs for each ticket booked online.

In getting the advertising message out, Curtis-McIntyre again looked for something "very un-airline." In this case, that meant losing the standard it's-a-small-world sap and introducing some big-city swagger and wit. Last summer, the airline's cheeky slogan was "Somebody up there likes you." The message changed after Sept. 11, to address people's anxieties about flying, but Curtis-McIntyre was careful to maintain JetBlue's distinctive voice. Less than 24 hours after the terrorist attacks, she had met with the Ad Store, a New York agency, and written the "Reasons to Fly" TV and radio campaign, which featured individuals sharing motivations sentimental and unsentimental for continuing to fly. "Because I want to see my family," one says. "Because I want to get away from my family," another retorts. Says Curtis-McIntyre, "I felt that it would be untrue to our brand to deny our sense of humor or personality."

Future campaigns will continue to reach out and reassure customers. Ads will dwell less on amenities like roomy seats and more on punctual arrival times and safety. (JetBlue was the first national carrier to install bulletproof, dead-bolted cockpit doors after Sept. 11.) After all, that's what travelers are interested in these days, and as a result, that's what interests Curtis-McIntyre. "The day I stop viewing the business as a consumer does is a bad day."

Evaluating Opportunities
in the Changing Marketing
Environment

Sony defends top spot
GameCube, Xbox and PS2 fight for supremacy

by Steven Kent
SPECIAL FOR USA TODAY

Nintendo has the plan, Microsoft has the momentum. But by sheer numbers, Sony is still the company to beat when it comes to video games.

Almost three months after the mid-November launches of Microsoft's Xbox and Nintendo's GameCube, the Xbox—which launches in Japan later this month—has established itself among the hard-core gaming community as both the most savvy and the most powerful game console on the market.

"It's hard to complain," says John O'Rourke, director of Xbox sales and marketing. "Sales remain strong."

In fact, the video game industry is booming, with a record $9.4 billion in sales last year, says the NPD group, which tracks retail sales. That's higher than box office receipts, which were $8.35 billion in 2001.

Microsoft sold 1.5 million Xbox consoles through December, while Nintendo sold 1.3 million GameCubes, NPD says—almost all the units available in stores. While Sony sold nearly 2.8 million over the holidays, PlayStation 2 was launched in October 2000 and more units were in stores.

Another indication of consumer satisfaction is the amount of software purchased for every console sold. At the 90-day mark for PlayStation 2, the ratio was 2.3 games per console, vs. 2.7 games for every GameCube sold, and 3.3 for each Xbox, NPD says.

Retailers and industry analysts expected veteran Nintendo to sell well, but Microsoft's numbers took many people by surprise.

"Microsoft is a big company, but it is new to the video games business, and they outplayed Nintendo and sold a more expensive machine," says Matt Casamassina of the popular IGN games Web site.

Price did not seem to be an issue. GameCube sold for a relatively modest $199, compared with $299 for PlayStation 2 and Xbox.

But having been on the market a year longer, PlayStation 2 has 150 games, vs. approximately 40 for Xbox and 23 for GameCube. So Sony has the biggest

list of must-haves, but what has surprised both consumers and retailers is the strength of the Xbox library.

Halo, the lead title for Xbox, has received glowing reviews and has remained on the best-seller list since its release. *Dead or Alive 3*, an Xbox exclusive from Tecmo, has been hailed as one of the best fighting games of all time. *NFL Fever* and *Project Gotham Racing*, published by Microsoft, also have received strong reviews.

More important, several games released for multiple systems, including *Max Payne* and *NASCAR Heat*, are said to play best on Xbox.

"There's no arguing technical specs," concedes Greg Off of *PS Extreme*, a PlayStation magazine. "The PlayStation 2 is a different beast and has its limitations. But it also has a lot of potential, as you can see from second-generation software."

Though PlayStation 2, with its custom-designed 128-bit chip, has the biggest processor, both Microsoft and Nintendo have made their systems more powerful by adding more memory and using significantly more powerful graphics chips.

Designers have complained about the difficulty of programming for the Sony console, but after a year, many game makers have learned ways around those problems.

Rez, a futuristic game from Sega in which players control an evolving spaceman flying through a techno-industrial cyberspace, has brought the PlayStation 2 library to spectacular new levels in visuals and sound design. But other top PS2 titles, such as Rockstar's *Grand Theft Auto III* and Capcom Entertainment's *Maximo*, have been hailed as creative, not technological, breakthroughs.

"We have not been enamored with the problems of creating games for PlayStation 2," says Capcom president Bill Gardner.

Others have been even less complimentary. Tecmo's Tomonobu Itagaki has publicly referred to PS2 as a "last-generation machine"—he says his visually stunning *Dead or Alive 3*, published exclusively for Xbox, could not have run on Sony's console.

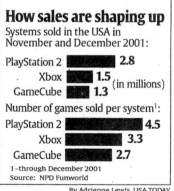

How sales are shaping up
Systems sold in the USA in November and December 2001:

PlayStation 2	2.8
Xbox	1.5 (in millions)
GameCube	1.3

Number of games sold per system[1]:

PlayStation 2	4.5
Xbox	3.3
GameCube	2.7

1–through December 2001
Source: NPD Funworld

By Adrienne Lewis, USA TODAY

(Cont.)

Even so, Sony has shipped more than 20 million PlayStation 2 systems since its Japanese launch in March 2000.

"Sony seems to do no wrong, even when it is quite obviously very wrong," Casamassina says. "It has hardware that is widely accepted as inferior, and still people are snapping it up and going crazy about it."

Having launched GameCube in Japan in September, Nintendo is in second place behind Sony on a worldwide basis. To date, Xbox is only available in North America, but Microsoft plans to release it in Japan on Feb. 22 and in Europe on March 14.

GameCube got off to a slow start in Japan, though sales improved with the November releases of the games *Super Smash Bros. Melee* and *Pikmin.* But with only 1.3 million systems sold in Japan by the end of December, Nintendo could be vulnerable to a well-orchestrated international Xbox launch.

Surveys taken during the Tokyo Game Show last fall suggest that Japanese gamers are curious about Xbox.

"I think Microsoft is quietly confident," says Sega president Peter Moore. "They realize that they need to reach out to the Japanese gaming community, as well as the publishing and retail" communities.

Sega has straddled fences: For PlayStation 2, the console with the biggest audience, Sega offered exclusive first rights to *Virtua Fighter 4,* its most anticipated title. Microsoft got an exclusive on *Jet Set Radio Future* and Nintendo got an exclusive on *Sonic the Hedgehog,* Sega's mascot.

But Nintendo holds an incredible mind-share in Japan, and Microsoft's success is not guaranteed. As *Game Informer Magazine's* Andy McNamara puts it, "You don't see a lot of Cadillacs around Tokyo."

Then again, Starbucks, another Seattle-based sensation, is a major Tokyo success.

"Sony Defends Top Spot," *USA Today*, February 11, 2002, p. 14B. Reprinted with permission.

Adobe had a popular product. Making it profitable took some work

BY MELINDA PATTERSON GRENIER

At a big computer-industry trade show in November 1992, Adobe Systems Inc. demonstrated new software that performed an amazing trick.

The San Jose, Calif., company's soon-to-be-released Acrobat program allowed a document created on one computer to be opened, read, annotated, saved and printed by another computer, even if the second computer used a completely different operating system and applications.

At a time when the World Wide Web and graphical Internet browsers were still works in progress and most people were struggling to send plain-text e-mails, Acrobat made it possible for computer users who didn't have layout or graphics programs to see printed materials such as newsletters and annual reports with all the original pictures, typefaces and formatting preserved electronically.

Acrobat was the hit of the Comdex conference, taking top honors for "Most Significant Technology" and "Best of Show." One financial analyst boosted his rating on Adobe stock, saying the company's new document-sharing software was intriguing for longer-term investors.

He didn't know how right he was.

Setting the Standard

Acrobat is now the de facto standard for viewing documents on the Internet. More than 320 million copies of the software that reads Acrobat files have been distributed world-wide since 1993. But Reader software is free, and in the eight years since Acrobat's introduction, analysts estimate that Adobe has sold fewer than six million copies of the full program, which creates the electronic documents and currently retails for about $250.

Only a relatively small portion of these sales has gone to the business customers Adobe originally intended as the target market for Acrobat. Many of the buyers have been graphic designers who create Web sites or who develop promotional materials such as magazine advertisements. As recently as the first quarter of 1999, Acrobat accounted for less than 10% of Adobe's total sales.

With Acrobat, Adobe has faced a basic business challenge that resonates often in the Internet Age: How do you transform a popular product into a profitable one? It's a problem that almost every free Web site is familiar with.

Here's the story of how Adobe has worked to turn Acrobat's promise into profits.

From the very beginning, Adobe promoted Acrobat as a tool to help all sorts of businesses improve communication, cut down on paperwork and increase productivity.

"Acrobat will fundamentally change the economics of information by removing the critical barriers that have kept electronic documents from moving between computers," said John E. Warnock, one of Adobe's founders, in a June 1993 press release. "Acrobat technology liberates information and the flow of ideas and allows it to enter the electronic age."

Acrobat used Adobe's new Portable Document Format, or PDF, which was based on PostScript, Adobe's very first software program. Mr. Warnock and co-founder Charles M. Geschke had resigned from Xerox Corp.'s Palo Alto Research Center in 1982 and started Adobe, where they developed and licensed the use of PostScript. The program soon became the standard for translating images on a computer screen into printed documents.

Over the years, other Adobe products had come to dominate their market segments: Illustrator for creating charts and graphics, Photoshop for editing images. With Acrobat, Adobe set out to create another dominant brand that would set the standard in its segment—this time for electronic-document distribution.

But in the early 1990s, the concept of electronic documents didn't resonate with too many businesses. A few companies saw the benefits of Acrobat: J.P. Morgan & Co., for example, used the program to create and send reports with detailed graphics to its sales staff.

Most firms, however, just didn't get it. Many companies were only starting to set up computer networks or were struggling to get existing—and widely disparate—networks to talk to each other. In this environment, the idea of turning vast paper files into documents that could be shared electronically seemed, if not frivolous, at least premature.

Even Robert Kleiber, the Piper Jaffray analyst who raised his rating on Adobe stock to "accumulate" from "reasonably priced" following the Comdex announcement, had reservations about corporate acceptance of Acrobat in the short term.

He believed most companies would use the software initially for very technical in-house publishing projects. Then, if they saw its value, they might later begin to convert existing documents to PDF files and exchange them electronically, which could eventually lead to a huge corporate market.

A crack marketing team might have developed campaigns to break through corporate resistance, selling potential customers on benefits such as increased productivity and lower costs. But after a decade in business, Adobe was still primarily focused on technology. It didn't have much experience marketing products to corporate clients, it didn't do much advertising, and it tended to rely on trade shows and word-of-mouth in the graphic-design community to promote its new software programs.

For the fourth quarter of fiscal 1994, which ended Nov. 25, Acrobat accounted for only $1.3 million, or less than 1%, of Adobe's total $165.5 million in revenue.

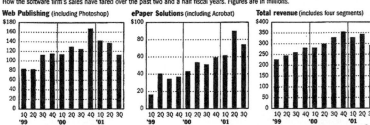

Adobe's Progress
How the software firm's sales have fared over the past two and a half fiscal years. Figures are in millions.

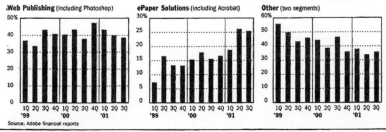

Fancy Acrobatics
Acrobat has become a bigger part of Adobe's business in recent years. Figures represent what percentage of revenue came from each business segment.

Source: Adobe financial reports

But by late 1994 and early 1995, the introduction of the World Wide Web was turning the Internet into a visual medium that computer users could navigate by clicking on special links instead of typing in complicated codes. A new concept—Web publishing—emerged. And the move to put newsletters and other documents online while retaining their original appearance played right to Acrobat's strengths.

For the fiscal quarter that ended March 3, 1995, Adobe proudly reported that Acrobat sales more than doubled to $3.5 million, but the number was still only a tiny 2% of the company's total $168.6 million in revenue for the period.

Adobe also announced a deal with **International Business Machines** Corp. to ship Reader with its business computers. (**Apple Computer** Inc. had begun shipping Reader with certain of its Macintosh computers starting in late 1994.)

Reader, one of several Acrobat products, allowed users to open, look at, explore and print PDF files. Originally Adobe sold Reader in bulk, starting at $50 a copy, but the company stopped charging for it in October 1994, partly because the decoding software for competitors' products was free and partly because Adobe believed companies would be encouraged to create more PDF documents if more people could read them.

With this goal in mind, Adobe made Reader available for downloading from more than 100 online services and Internet servers, including the software company's own new Web site. And Acrobat Reader 3.0, introduced in June 1996, allowed users to view, search and download PDF files while surfing the Internet.

Success and Problems

Gradually, the number of people using Acrobat Reader began to grow. From 11.7 million copies distributed as of December 1997, the total jumped to 57.4 million by the end of 1998.

But the success was illusory. Most people didn't realize that Reader was only one program among several in the Acrobat family, and Adobe made money only when it sold the programs used to create PDF files, not browse them. Acrobat's greatest successes had been with Adobe's traditional graphic-designer customers and with government agencies such as the Internal Revenue Service, which began posting PDF-based tax forms on its Web site in early 1997. The software still hadn't caught on with most businesses. Analysts estimated that despite the big jump in downloads of Reader, Acrobat represented less than 7%, or roughly $60 million, of Adobe's $894.8 million revenue in fiscal 1998.

So starting with Acrobat 4.0, introduced in February 1999, and continuing with Acrobat 5.0, which the company launched earlier this year, Adobe ramped up its effort to finally push the product into high gear.

To tackle the awareness problem, Young & Rubicam designed a series of slick advertisements for Acrobat 4.0. showing a gem in an avocado and pearls in a peapod under the headline, "A fabulous surprise in every pack." The ads emphasized that Acrobat is "a small part" of a "more dynamic" or "more powerful" program.

The campaign ran in publications such as New Yorker magazine—a far cry from the trade journals Adobe typically used to promote its software. The focus in ads for Acrobat 5.0 shifted to the benefits of the full program. One ad, which is running in magazines for lawyers, shows a window for filing court documents that has closed at the end of the day, and says this wouldn't be a problem if the paperwork had been sent electronically as PDF files.

New Features

Each new version of Acrobat has contained additional features designed to appeal to potential corporate clients. Acrobat 2.0 offered the security of password protection. Version 4.0 added digital-signature technology. Acrobat 5.0 allows users to create forms and link them to a Web server so customers or clients can fill them out and sign them electronically from within their browser.

"Historically, we've talked a lot about features or technology, and now we're getting smarter," says Sarah Rosenbaum, director, Acrobat product management. "We're reaching [customers] in a better way by talking about the benefits."

To help get the word out, Adobe is building up its alliances with systems integrators for specific types of businesses or groups. One target: governments world-wide that must comply with new regulations requiring that certain documents and processes be available online within the next few years.

Adobe also has increased the number of account managers internally who focus on Acrobat. It is sending out direct-mail pieces and sponsoring seminars—in person and on the Web—to educate current and future customers about product benefits and features.

The result of all this effort? Sales for Adobe's ePaper Solutions business segment—more than 90% of which is Acrobat—more than doubled in fiscal 1999 to $129.3 million from $61.3 million a year earlier, then jumped again in fiscal 2000 to $207.8 million.

This fiscal year, revenue set a quarterly record of $90 million in the second period, when Acrobat 5.0 was launched, before falling back to $74.3 million in the third quarter. Even after slipping, however, this was a 45% improvement from the year-earlier quarter.

Large new licensees of Acrobat this year include defense contractor Lockheed Martin Corp., the U.S. Department of Commerce, pharmaceutical companies Schering-Plough Corp. and Pfizer Inc., the International Monetary Fund and Wells Fargo & Co.

Acrobat is poised to become Adobe's best-selling product, and represents "a multibillion-dollar opportunity" for the company, President and Chief Executive Bruce Chizen told analysts during a conference call last month. Acrobat now accounts for a quarter of Adobe's business, Mr. Chizen noted.

"Translated," he said, "that could be $300 million [in fiscal 2001]. To have a $300 million business that's potentially growing at 45% or greater is something that we're very excited about."

ON TO THE LIVING ROOM!
Can Microsoft control the digital home?

Meander through the corridors of Building 50 on Microsoft Corp.'s campus and you might, for just one mind-bending moment, feel as if you're in the bowels of consumer-electronics powerhouse Sony Corp. In one room, engineers are ginning up a way to record TV programs on a PC so they can be watched at any hour. Around the corner, workers are noodling over software that makes it a snap to edit home movies and copy them onto a DVD. Still others are figuring out better methods for managing thousands of digital music files. And in the main conference room, rather than the typical corporate white boards, there is a wall-size viewing screen and a sound system that would make the neighbors call the cops—if you dared to have one in your home.

Is Microsoft, the no-nonsense king of PC software, having a midlife crisis? Not at all. The software giant is trying on a new persona for a new environment. With PC sales expected to decline for the second straight year as corporate spending withers, Microsoft is aiming its big guns on entertainment goodies for the home. It's spending more than $2 billion building and marketing its new Xbox game console. And it's sure to spend millions more on everything from its UltimateTV video-recording service to an online subscription music service to a handy wireless electronic tablet for the home, codenamed Mira. On Jan. 7, at the Consumer Electronics Show in Las Vegas, Chairman William H. Gates III revealed Microsoft's next-generation technologies aimed at making the PC the electronic hub of the digital home. They'll route music, movies, TV programming, e-mail, and news between the Web and PCs, TV set-top boxes, gadgets, and stereo speakers. "Everything in the home will be connected," predicts Gates. And if he gets his way, most of the gizmos will use Microsoft software.

That's why Building 50, brand-spanking new, is the digs for the software maker's eHome division, a skunk works of more than 200 engineers responsible for turning Microsoft into the Sony of the 21st century. The digital home is the biggest market push by Microsoft since it launched its assault on server computing a decade ago, and the front-line troops are stoked. Says J. Allard, one of the architects of the company's Internet strategy and now the lead technologist on the Xbox: "This is a way to build a whole new Microsoft."

And perhaps a whole new industry. In the next half-decade, Microsoft hopes to spark a revolution in consumer technology that transforms people's home lives every bit as much as the PC has changed their work lives. The concept is far from new, but Gates and other tech execs say the timing is right now that the Internet has made many consumers more tech-savvy. Indeed, other computer companies are doing the same—from Seagate Technology, which is making storage devices for consumer electronics products, to Apple Computer Inc., which debuted its new iMac for the home on Jan. 7. Says Gates lieutenant Robert J. Bach, who oversees the Xbox group: "The technology revolution has changed the way people do business. The next 5 to 10 years will be the digital entertainment revolution."

Microsoft is banking on its consumer business, along with server sales, to help revive growth, which was stuck at about 10% for much of last year. Morgan Stanley Dean Witter & Co. estimates that Microsoft will earn $9.3 billion in the fiscal year that ends on June 30, on revenue of $28.8 billion. In fiscal 2003, it expects Microsoft's earnings to climb to $11.7 billion on sales of $32.7 billion. Much of that growth will be driven by consumer sales, which include the MSN online service, Xbox, and games. This year, sales from the consumer group will account for 12% of Microsoft's total business. In fiscal 2003, that will jump to 18%—just shy of the 21% that's expected from server products. That's one reason why Microsoft's stock is up more than 50% in the past year, to $70. "This is a large market," says CEO Steven A. Ballmer. "There's a great chance to add value. And anytime there's a great chance to add value, there's also a great chance to make money."

The consumer push comes at a time when the company seems to be coming out from under the cloud of its antitrust woes. Unless nine dissenting state attorneys general succeed in beefing up the remedies, a settlement with the Justice Dept. and nine other states will do

---

Microsoft Hits Home

With its software entrenched in home offices, Microsoft is aggressively reaching into the living room. Here's how its strategy stacks up:

GAME CONSOLES

Microsoft leapt into this $20 billion market in a big way with its Xbox launch in November. The company hopes to leapfrog rivals with online gaming that lets players compete from anywhere.

OUTLOOK FAIR Xbox is off to a glitchless start, but Microsoft hopes to capture 40% of the market in five years—a tall order, since Sony is No. 1. Analysts expect Microsoft to grab less than 25% of the market.

ONLINE SERVICES

The company is aggressively developing paid subscription services on MSN that will let users do everything from downloading music to synchronizing their banking and investment accounts.

OUTLOOK FAIR Microsoft is the innovator in the consumer Web services world today. But with its 33 million online access subscribers to Microsoft's 7 million, AOL has a firmer hand on the consumer's wallet.

HOME NETWORKING

Microsoft is building links in every piece of its software in order to make PCs, set-top boxes, stereos, and handheld devices work better together.

OUTLOOK GOOD Reliable networking requires software, and that's Microsoft's strength. Moreover, Microsoft is the only company that has both the software expertise and the lineup of devices to make home networking prolific.

(Cont.)

PCs

Microsoft has combined ever-more consumer offerings into the newly minted Windows XP. That has made it easier to do everything from organizing music files to gathering digital photos.

OUTLOOK GOOD Microsoft's strength on the PC is insurmountable. Windows ships on 95% of all PCs sold. That gives Microsoft a huge entree into consumers' homes, where it can pitch its other products and services.

INTERACTIVE TV

Microsoft is aggressively hawking its set-top box software to cable operators, hoping to put its technology at a crucial gateway to the Web.

OUTLOOK POOR Microsoft is still losing ground to its chief rival, Liberate Technologies, in the market for software for TV set-top boxes. Several cable companies that Microsoft invested in chose rival software rather than waiting for Microsoft to get it right.

little to prevent Microsoft from using the power of its Windows desktop monopoly to help it win new battles in the consumer realm.

For all of Microsoft's power and ambitions, though, the digital home may turn out to be the toughest market it has ever tried to crack. At best, Microsoft will be one of several top players, but it will never dominate digital entertainment the way it does PC software. Analysts expect the markets for video games, consumer online services, home networking, and interactive TV software to collectively top $63 billion in 2005. Microsoft could win in areas such as home networking, where its PC hegemony gives it an advantage. But it will lap in markets such as video game consoles and online services, where entrenched rivals rule.

Indeed, AOL Time Warner Inc. has a huge lead in the online service business with 33 million subscribers to Microsoft's 7 million. And Sony may be even harder to beat. The world's leading consumer-electronics brand, Sony makes every key piece of hardware—from PCs to set-top boxes to game consoles—Microsoft's focus is primarily the software that goes inside the machines, and so its success depends, in part, on the smarts of its hardware partners. "Ultimately, it's the hardware that provides the great consumer experience," says Sony President Kunitake Ando.

Moreover, Microsoft has been missing the consumer gene for years. All of its major consumer-electronics gambits so far have ended up as disappointments. Its WebTV Internet-access service stalled at 1 million subscribers, and its interactive-TV technologies have gone nowhere. The company's digital stereo speakers and PC-connected telephones were introduced in 1998 only to be abandoned a year later. And the gee-whiz technology in Gates's suburban Seattle mansion—which includes electronic pins that each person wears to signal a preference in digital art, music, and temperature—has required as many as 50 servers, not the stuff of a simple consumer experience. Says Minoru Arakawa, who retired on Jan. 8 as the president of Nintendo of America Inc.: "Microsoft is spending a lot of money, but they are beginners."

Even Microsoft's allies are tinkering with rival software, not convinced that Microsoft will be the end-all in the digital home. Microsoft buddy Intel Corp. has used non-Microsoft software in some of its Web appliances. "There will be a lot of experimentation," says Intel CEO Craig R. Barrett. While he thinks the PC can be a hub for home networking, in some cases it will be on the periphery. One alternative to the PC emerged on Jan. 7 when startup Moxi Digital Inc. debuted a system for managing home entertainment via a set-top box.

Microsoft is playing to win, though. It's going about this with the patient, war-of-attrition approach that has been so successful in the past. The seeds of this assault were planted in March, 1999, when Microsoft execs gathered at a retreat on the shores of Puget Sound to ponder their strategy for the home. Gates, Ballmer, and Bach wondered if they could build a new generation of consumer devices based on PC technologies.

Around the same time, a handful of engineers deep inside the company wanted to build the hottest-ever game console. Nat Brown, one of the ringleaders, recruited Allard to get behind the project during a day they spent together playing video games at Allard's cabin in the Cascades. "The heart and soul of this thing came from the garage—5 to 10 dreamers who wanted to take Microsoft into a new space," says Allard.

Microsoft's brass decided to attack on all fronts. Microsoft seemed to turn the corner at the 2000 Consumer Electronics Show when it abandoned its tradition of setting up a series of booths to market its products. Instead, it created a model home on the showroom floor—complete with Jetson-like gadgets and a family of actors—to show people how digital technologies might shape their future. "That's when the whole company got the 'aha!'" says Microsoft consumer products strategist Craig J. Mundie.

Microsoft decided it would build off what it sees as its "three pillars" for the digital home: MSN, Xbox, and Windows XP, which includes home networking technology. That

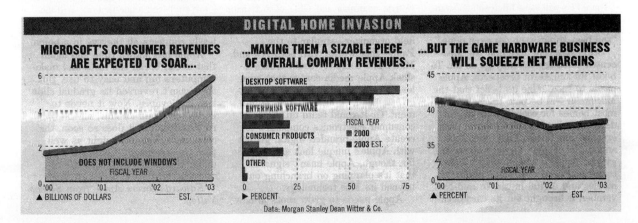

DIGITAL HOME INVASION

MICROSOFT'S CONSUMER REVENUES ARE EXPECTED TO SOAR...
DOES NOT INCLUDE WINDOWS
FISCAL YEAR
6
4
2
0 '00 '01 '02 '03
▲ BILLIONS OF DOLLARS — EST.

...MAKING THEM A SIZABLE PIECE OF OVERALL COMPANY REVENUES...
DESKTOP SOFTWARE
ENTERPRISE SOFTWARE
CONSUMER PRODUCTS
OTHER
FISCAL YEAR
■ 2000
■ 2003 EST.
0 25 50 75
► PERCENT

...BUT THE GAME HARDWARE BUSINESS WILL SQUEEZE NET MARGINS
FISCAL YEAR
45
40
35
0 '00 '01 '02 '03
▲ PERCENT — EST.

Data: Morgan Stanley Dean Witter & Co.

(Cont.)

way the software giant can leverage its strengths into new home entertainment categories such as online music. The plan now is to create specialized products in a wide range of markets rather than try to build an uber-box that would handle every function from gaming to spreadsheets. So, Microsoft teams are pursuing separate tacks on game consoles, consumer PCs, interactive TV, digital home appliances, handheld gizmos, and online services. "The way you get to our vision is by building individual products that are the best in their own categories," says Gates. "It's like Microsoft Office. We built that with Word being the best, Excel being the best. They all had to be the best before the whole integration thing came together."

Although Gates says no detailed plan exists for integrating all these home products, Windows and the PC are central to the strategy. That's why Windows XP, the newest version of the company's operating system, is so important. After years of producing crash-prone software, Microsoft finally delivered an operating system that is more like a consumer appliance. Launched on Oct. 25, XP seldom crashes and is easy to use. With XP, it's a snap to edit home movies or burn CDs, programs that are likely to greatly expand the use of the PC in the home. And Windows XP'S home networking technology lets the PC automatically discover and connect such networked devices as digital audio receivers. "We're moving Windows to the living room," crows James E. Allchin, group vice-president in charge of Microsoft's operating systems.

Microsoft also is taking a page from its past playbook: It's creating an ecosystem in which hardware makers and software developers can create products based on Microsoft technology. "We have partners who are doing cameras and screens and lots of peripherals that will let you reach out to all the different things around the home," Gates says. Already signed up: Samsung, Hewlett-Packard, and NEC, all of which are developing media center PCs that use eHome technology.

Those PCs will use a Microsoft software code-named Freestyle. In addition to peripherals such as a mouse and keyboard, PCs loaded with Freestyle would include a TV tuner card to connect to a cable service and a remote control to navigate the system from a couch. That way, consumers could organize their music files or home movies while they're sitting at a desk and later, use the remote control to select tunes or videos from anywhere in the room. The first-generation, all-in-one Freestyle PCs will have all the functionality of a TV and a stereo. The target market: college students and apartment dwellers who might not have the space or budget for a PC, a TV, and a stereo. The

second-generation Freestyle PCs will focus on the broad consumer market, selling boxes that sit next to TVs around the house and connect back to the main PC.

The first major connected-home product from Microsoft will be a gizmo code-named Mira. By next Christmas, consumers will be able to buy a flat-panel monitor that detaches from its stand and continues to connect wirelessly to the PC from anywhere in the house. With a stylus tapping icons or scrawling letters on a touch screen, Mom can check e-mail from the kitchen, the kids can chat with online buddies from the couch while watching MTV, and Dad can shop at Amazon.com from the back porch. ViewSonic Corp. and Wyse Technology Inc. will make the devices for as little as $500.

Microsoft is counting on Xbox to jumpstart its digital home initiative. Already, Xbox sales are hitting the high end of analysts' expectations. Since the launch on Nov. 15, about 1.5 million consoles have been sold. That beats Nintendo's GameCube, which has sold 1.2 million units since its Nov. 18 launch. Meanwhile, Sony's PlayStation2, out since Oct. 25, 2000, rang up 2.5 million unit sales in North America this Christmas season.

Even the bookish Gates has been sucked in by Xbox. Although he was never much of a gamer before, he took a test version on his vacation in October. Each night, after putting their two children to bed, Gates and wife Melinda plopped down on the couch and found themselves absorbed by Fuzion Frenzy, a collection of 45 arcade-style games. "We played four hours straight the first day, since it was so cool," says Gates.

While Xbox is designed first and foremost to best PlayStation 2 and GameCube, the connected-home vision is a constant undercurrent. Microsoft built networking technology into the Xbox that will let gamers compete against one another from across the street or around the world. The company plans to launch its Xbox online gaming service by the middle of this year. Robert A. Kotick, chairman and CEO of Activision Inc., the No. 2 game publisher, believes online tournaments will be immensely popular. "It's a lot of fun to waste time playing video games. It would be a lot more fun wasting time playing video games and winning a trip to Hawaii as well," Kotick says.

For all the nifty technology, Xbox still needs killer games. And analysts don't count any sure blockbusters in the initial bunch of 20. "What's the must-have game that's going to get people to pay $300 to buy this console? I just haven't seen it," says analyst Edward Williams of Gerard Klauer Mattison & Co. He expects Xbox to capture about 10% of the game console market during the

five-year life cycle of game consoles that's just beginning. So, while Xbox could become a sizable business for Microsoft, it's only a piece of the puzzle.

The companies that win biggest in the home will likely be the ones with the most direct ongoing relationships with customers. Right now, that's AOL Time Warner, which touches 46 million subscribers with its online and cable businesses. "The value is in the consumer relationships, not the technology. It's about subscriptions," says AOL Time Warner Co-Chief Operating Officer Robert W. Pittman. AOL is collecting $24 a month from most of the 33 million consumers who connect to its online service. And its Time Warner Cable unit gets another $54 per month, on average, from its 12.7 million homes. Microsoft can't touch that. It's lucky if it sells a home PC user a $90 operating-system upgrade every three or four years.

And when it comes to mastering consumer technology, Microsoft sucks Sony's exhaust. As cool as Microsoft's Freestyle sounds, Sony already has introduced its Vaio MX media center PC, which does everything that Freestyle aspires to. Microsoft's Mira is nearly a year away. But more than a year ago, Sony introduced its Airboard in Japan, a flat-panel screen that can be used to check e-mail, surf the Web, and play video games. And Sony is developing networking technology, dubbed Feel, that will make it easy to connect all of its devices to one home network.

Still, no company is better fixed than Microsoft to make long-term investments in the digital home. With $36 billion in cash, it can afford to invest heavily, experiment broadly, and wait patiently for the payoff. Microsoft's history is loaded with examples of perseverance. MSN foundered for years before Microsoft figured out how to turn it into one of the top destinations on the Web. For most of a decade, its server software was the laughingstock of corporate computing. This year, it's expected to claim 47% of the market.

So it's not surprising that Microsoft is confident it will win in the home. "A lot of this stuff isn't a question of, 'Will the dogs eat the dog food?' It's 'When?'" says Microsoft's Mundie. Maybe so, but competitors such as Sony have thrived by offering customers steak rather than dog chow. If Microsoft can't match Sony, it will end up on the outside of the digital home, looking in.

By Jay Greene in Seattle, with Steve Hamm in New York, Catherine Yang in Washington, and Irene M. Kunii in Tokyo

"On to the Living Room," pp. 68–72. Reprinted from the January 21, 2002 issue of *Business Week* by special permission, copyright © 2002 by The McGraw-Hill Companies, Inc.

SMART GLOBALIZATION

Being first and biggest in an emerging market isn't always the best way to conquer it. A better tactic: Learn local cultures—and build a presence carefully

A television ad running these days in India shows a mother lapsing into a daydream: Her young daughter is in a beauty contest dressed as Snow White, dancing on a stage. Her flowing gown is an immaculate white. The garments of other contestants, who dance in the background, are a tad gray. Snow White, no surprise, wins the blue ribbon. The mother awakes to the laughter of her adoring family—and glances proudly at her Whirlpool White Magic washing machine.

The TV spot is the product of 14 months of research by Whirlpool Corp. into the psyche of the Indian consumer. Among other things, the Benton Harbor (Mich.) company learned Indian homemakers prize hygiene and purity, which they associate with white. The trouble is, white garments often get discolored after frequent machine washing in local water. Besides appealing to this love of purity in its ads, Whirlpool custom-designed machines that are especially good with white fabrics.

Whirlpool hasn't stopped there. It uses generous incentives to get thousands of Indian retailers to stock its goods. To reach every cranny of the vast nation, it uses local contractors conversant in India's 18 languages to collect payments in cash and deliver appliances by truck, bicycles, even oxcart. Since 1996, Whirlpool's sales in India have leapt 80%—and should hit $200 million this year. Whirlpool now is the leading brand in India's fast-growing market for fully automatic washing machines.

Whirlpool's success story stands out in a time when Corporate America doesn't talk much about emerging markets. Things were different a decade ago. That's when Western economies had stalled, so expanding operations into the fast-growing, heavily populated lands of Asia, Latin America, and the old Soviet bloc was a top priority. The approach to globalization then was brutally simple: get in fast, strike megadeals with top officials, and watch the profits roll in. Multinationals figured local consumers would snap up their products at a premium. Thus AT&T promised some 20 ventures in China, from state-of-the-art telecom factories to research labs. Enron Corp. negotiated giant power plants and pipeline projects in India, Indonesia, and Bolivia. General Motors Corp. envisioned an Asiawide network of car plants, led by its $1.2 billion facility in Shanghai. **SENSE AND SENSIBILITY.** Many of these bets fizzled or disappointed. Enron's $4 billion Indian power plant is a debacle. Other multinationals saw that local competitors can catch up fast—and beat them in price and marketing. Tumbling trade barriers are making local production less essential. Meanwhile, a globalization backlash has forced companies to view their activities in poor nations in a different light. Exxon Mobil, Cargill, Freeport-McMoRan, and Royal Dutch/Shell became targets of local uprisings over oil, mining, and other projects in Indonesia, India, and Nigeria. McDonald's, KFC, and Philip Morris have endured withering criticism at home and abroad for aggressively pushing inappropriate products and ignoring local sensibilities.

The financial crises that ravaged nations like Mexico, Thailand, Russia, Brazil, and Turkey didn't help. Suddenly, "emerging markets" connoted excessive risk. Indeed, compared to the booming U.S. of the late '90s and a unifying Western Europe, emerging markets looked irrelevant to many execs. After explosive growth in the early 1990s, foreign direct investment by U.S. companies in East Asia, excluding Japan, plunged by 74% to $1.33 billion from 1997 to 2000, estimates the U.S. Commerce Dept. The drops have been nearly as dramatic in Latin America and Eastern Europe.

But as Whirlpool and other savvy U.S. companies such as Kodak, Citigroup, and Hewlett-Packard are proving, investing time and energy to understand societies in developing nations can pay rich returns. Rather than swinging for the fences with megaprojects or costly takeovers, the smarter approach is to methodically build a presence from the ground up. Some of the best investments are the most economical—small corner kiosks instead of full-blown stores or bank branches, say, or a tie-up with a savvy local player who owns a factory. Says Bain & Co. global strategist Chris Zook: "Companies are trying to figure out how to build on their strengths, as opposed to throwing a bunch of Hail Mary passes in the hope they connect."

Above all, smart globalization requires extensive homework. Companies are starting to work closely with bureaucrats, entrepreneurs, and social groups at the grass roots. Not only is it easier to head off a local political backlash by cooperating with local players early; multinationals are also finding they can save enormous resources—and develop products local consumers really need.

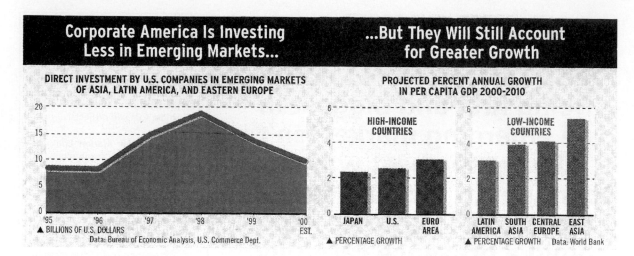

Corporate America Is Investing Less in Emerging Markets...

DIRECT INVESTMENT BY U.S. COMPANIES IN EMERGING MARKETS OF ASIA, LATIN AMERICA, AND EASTERN EUROPE

▲ BILLIONS OF U.S. DOLLARS

Data: Bureau of Economic Analysis, U.S. Commerce Dept.

...But They Will Still Account for Greater Growth

PROJECTED PERCENT ANNUAL GROWTH IN PER CAPITA GDP 2000-2010

HIGH-INCOME COUNTRIES

▲ PERCENTAGE GROWTH

LOW-INCOME COUNTRIES

▲ PERCENTAGE GROWTH   Data: World Bank

Whirlpool has learned many of these lessons. Eight years after launching its global blitz in 1989, it took a $294 million writedown to shed two of the four appliance plants it built in China. "What we absolutely missed was how fast these markets would become saturated," concedes CEO David R. Whitwam. "We could build plants around the world, but where you fail is in the marketplace."

Now, Whitwam believes Whirlpool is on track. Besides its sophisticated marketing and inroads with local distributors, the company reorganized its global factory network. For all appliances, it devises basic models that use about 70% of the same parts. Then it modifies its machines for local tastes. Whirlpool has an incentive to get it right: Through 2009, it expects demand for big appliances in the U.S. to remain flat, while it projects demand overseas will grow 17%, to 293 million units.

Similar dynamics are pushing other companies to renew their global focus. Developing nations are still likely to grow much faster than the industrial West for at least a decade (see chart above). What's more, most multinationals today target mainly the richest 10% of the global population. They've yet to reach the 4 billion who earn the equivalent of $1,500 or less annually. Few can afford a PC, car, or mortgage now. But many experts argue they will be the greatest source of future global growth. That's why Hewlett-Packard Co. has launched a drive to help stimulate computer use in villages from Central America to Africa. The HP program also is politically shrewd: It promotes the beneficial aspect of globalization to the neediest.

Citibank's new campaign to broaden its traditional base of rich clients exemplifies the new approach to emerging markets. In Bangalore, India, it launched a program called Suvidha—Hindi for "ease." It persuaded midsized companies to set up retail bank accounts for their entire staffs, from janitors to top managers. To open accounts, customers need just $22. They get a card they can use to get cash, take out loans, pay bills at local ATMs, and buy groceries. In three years, Citi has gained 200,000 retail clients, doubling its base in India, for about $10 million.

In corporate banking, Citi is targeting companies with revenues of $50 million or less. India's trucking business has been one priority. By opening offices in 23 cities offering credit, savings, and checking accounts, Citi now finances 10,000 truckers—most with fewer than 30 vehicles. It also is gearing up in Poland, Brazil, and the Philippines. Since 1997, small-business clients in emerging markets have risen sixfold, to 8.7 million. "The lower segments of these markets is where the growth is," says Citibank CEO Victor J. Menezes. Such markets earned Citigroup $2.7 billion in net profits last year.

Other U.S. companies are finding they can get ahead working with small entrepreneurs eager for new ways to make money. That's one reason emerging markets are a bright spot for Eastman Kodak Co. While Kodak has struggled in the U.S., in Asia, sales were up 9% last year. Much of this is because of Kodak Express photo supply and development shops, often owned by entrepreneurs such as Qiu Xing, 28. The Shanghai native, who says he had "always been a photography buff," invested $48,000 to open his shop in January. In a deal with a Chinese bank, Kodak lets Qiu use his developing equipment as loan collateral even though he hasn't fully paid for it. Kodak also supplies monthly staff training. Qiu takes in $5,000 a month and makes a 25% profit.

Kodak has 6,000 Expresses across China and expects 10,000 by yearend. Its market share in China has doubled since 1995, to 60%. "We moved so fast, our competitors didn't have time to act," boasts John Tseng, a Kodak general manager for Asia.

In these turbulent times, when political and currency crises rock governments from Jakarta to Buenos Aires, it's hard to tell when emerging markets will be the predictable lands of opportunity CEOs once foresaw. But that was always an illusion—and it's time Corporate America figures out what really works. "The next round of global expansion is as much about imagination as about resources," says University of Michigan management guru C.K. Prahalad: "Putting a billion dollars down does not involve imagination." With the mistakes of the '90s behind them, the winners will approach the world in a smarter way.

By Pete Engardio
With Manjeet Kripalani and Alysha Webb in Shanghai

21

Crossover Success

How Nafta Helped Wal-Mart Reshape The Mexican Market

Lower Tariffs, Retail Muscle Translate Into Big Sales; Middlemen Are Squeezed

'Like Shopping in the U.S.'

BY DAVID LUHNOW

Staff Reporter of THE WALL STREET JOURNAL

MEXICO CITY—Shopkeeper Carlos Huerta recently walked into a Sam's Club warehouse store here and bought $6,000 of Act II brand microwave popcorn. Then he trundled across the street to resell it at his stall in Latin America's biggest wholesale market.

Mr. Huerta used to buy the U.S.-made popcorn direct from the manufacturer's distributor here. But with the U.S.-Mexican border growing increasingly porous, Wal-Mart Stores Inc. now can deliver Act II to its Mexican Sam's Club outlets for only a few cents more than to its U.S. stores, undercutting the product's Mexican distributor.

"I've lost a lot of business," says Mr. Huerta, who sells mostly to small corner grocers. "Now, a lot of people just go directly to Sam's."

Retail Conquistador

Squeezing out middlemen such as Mr. Huerta is just one of the ways in which Wal-Mart is changing the way Mexico does business. By seizing upon the new opportunities offered by free trade and exploiting its massive buying power and distribution network, Wal-Mart, Middle America's most popular merchant, is replicating its U.S. success south of the Rio Grande. Today, barely a decade after it entered Mexico in anticipation of the North American Free Trade Agreement, Wal-Mart dominates this country's retail sector.

Wal-Mart's local unit, Wal-Mart de Mexico SA, has annual sales of nearly $9 billion and rings up about a third of its parent's $1.1 billion in annual overseas operating profits. It also serves as a proving ground for talent and a crucible for ideas to help Wal-Mart translate "the Wal-Mart way" to other foreign nations, such as Germany, where the retailer has stumbled.

Today, Wal-Mart operates 520 stores in Mexico, ranging from Sam's Clubs to Wal-Mart Supercenters to cafes where tired shoppers can pause to grab a quick taco or burger. But Wal-Mart's success here owes to more than just opening cavernous discount stores. It also stems from Nafta, which has turned the U.S., Mexico and Canada into a single trading zone.

Demand Unleashed

After Nafta took effect in 1994, tariffs tumbled, unleashing pent-up Mexican demand for U.S.-made goods. The trade treaty helped eliminate some of the transportation headaches and government red tape that had kept Wal-Mart from fully realizing its competitive advantages here. And it sent European and Asian manufacturers racing to build new plants in the Nafta zone, giving Wal-Mart cheaper access to more foreign brands.

Consider Sony Corp.'s Wega line of flat-screen television sets. In 1998, Ricardo Perera, Sam's Club's electronics buyer in Mexico City, imported a handful of Wegas from Japan. Wal-Mart offered the 29-inch Wegas for sale at about $1,600. The high price reflected a 23% import duty and the cost of shipping the sets across the Pacific. That year, Mexican Sam's Clubs sold just five of the TVs.

The following year, Sony built a giant Wega factory in the border town of Mexicali in order to take advantage of Nafta. Locating the plant in Mexico allowed Sony to ship the plant's TVs anywhere in the Nafta zone duty free. Though Sony's primary target was the U.S. market, Mr. Perera spotted an opportunity.

Passing Along Savings

The Mexican-made sets saved Sam's Club a bundle in shipping costs, and it passed those savings on to consumers. Today, Sam's Club sells the 29-inch Wega sets in Mexico for about $600, roughly what they fetch in the U.S. The Wega line now accounts for about a third of Sam's Mexican electronics sales. Other Nafta-inspired plants have made it possible for Wal-Mart Mexico to offer similar savings on products ranging from underwear to digital cameras.

Things didn't always go so smoothly for Wal-Mart here. Back in the early 1990s, even bringing in Act II popcorn used to be a complicated affair. On top of steep import duties, retailers had to use costly middlemen to obtain hard-to-get import permits. Goods often took a month to clear customs, and Mexican officials sometimes demanded bribes. The paperwork alone was "torture," says Jose Angel Gallegos, a Wal-Mart distribution executive.

Now, thanks to Nafta, Wal-Mart can buy Act II directly from U.S.-based ConAgra Foods Inc., which manufactures the product and even slaps on a Spanish-language label at Wal-Mart's behest. Wal-Mart delivers the popcorn to a distribution center it built in Laredo, Texas, months before the Nafta

treaty. There, a truck hired by Wal-Mart Mexico picks it up, and the next day the popcorn is on the shelf at a Mexican Sam's Club. Its rivals, meanwhile, continue to buy their popcorn from local distributors at higher prices.

Wal-Mart's legendary founder, the late Sam Walton, apparently saw all this coming. In 1990, Mr. Walton met Jeronimo Arango, one of three brothers who pioneered the discount-store format in Mexico. Mr. Arango's company, Cifra SA, had grown to become Mexico's leading retailer. He and Mr. Walton hit it off, agreeing that the free-trade deal then taking shape between the U.S. and Mexico made the time ripe for them to join forces.

There seemed little doubt that Mexicans were hungry for U.S. goods. In the late 1980s, as Mexico emerged from decades of protectionism, Cifra's Superama grocery-store chain did a brisk business selling U.S.-made powerboats and motorcycles from its parking lots.

So, in early 1991, Wal-Mart stepped outside the U.S. for the first time, launching Mexican Sam's Clubs in 50-50 partnership with Cifra. Within months, the first Sam's in Mexico City—a bare-bones outlet that sold bulk items at prices just above wholesale—was smashing Wal-Mart sales records. The joint venture grew to include every new store opened by either company. Though tariffs still made imported goods pricey, Mexicans marveled as "Made in the U.S.A." merchandise began to crop up on local store shelves.

Discounting Clay Pigeons

Not surprisingly, since Mexico was Wal-Mart's first foray abroad, the retailer made some blunders. Its first Mexican stores carried many items Mexicans rarely used: ice skates, riding lawn mowers, fishing tackle—even clay pigeons for skeet shooting. Hapless local managers would radically discount the pigeons to get rid of them, only to have automated inventory systems linked to Wal-Mart's corporate headquarters in Bentonville, Ark., order a fresh batch. Wal-Mart also failed to share its technological know-how and global buying power with new partner Cifra, which it at times treated like an unwanted appendage.

Wal-Mart learned quickly from such missteps, says former Cifra executive Gilberto Perezalonso. It ultimately replaced slow-moving items such as leaf blowers with such local best sellers as maid's uniforms and self-service bakery goods.

But, in late 1994, just as Wal-Mart was getting it right, Mexico devalued its currency, sending the economy into a prolonged tailspin. The company froze its expansion plans in Mexico, where its stores suddenly looked way too big to wrest a profit from the country's cash-strapped consumers. Other U.S. retailers, such as Kmart Corp. and Sears, Roebuck & Co., pulled out of Mexico entirely. But Cifra remained profitable. That fact encouraged Wal-Mart to acquire control of Cifra in 1997 by buying an additional 12% stake in the retailer for $1.2 billion.

The merged company has had its share of culture clashes. Cifra executives, accustomed to a formal business culture, were put off by Wal-Mart's informal pow-wows in Bentonville, where they were handed baseball hats and whistles for use on motivational field trips. They politely declined invitations from top Wal-Mart brass to come to rural Arkansas to go hunting, a pastime many Mexicans find distasteful.

But such awkward moments grew fewer after June 1999, when new Wal-Mart International Chief Executive John Menzer gave local operations more autonomy. Mexican employees who initially groaned at reciting Wal-Mart's obligatory morning cheer ("Give me a W . . .") let it rip after Mr. Menzer approved a local alternative ("Chee-kee-tee-boom-a-la-beem-boom-bah, Wal-Mart, Wal-Mart, rah-rah-rah").

Initially, Wal-Mart faced some logisitical nightmares in Mexico, but it ultimately found an ally in local trucking company Transportes EASO SA. The country's ramshackle roads made delivery schedules dicey. But Nafta encouraged Mexico to invest in improving its transportation infrastructure. And it inspired EASO to ally with MS Carriers Corp. of Memphis, Tenn., which agreed to share a fleet of modern trucks with EASO as well as satellite systems designed to help plan delivery times. That helped EASO cut costs by 25%, savings it passed on to Wal-Mart, which now employs 200 EASO trucks.

Wal-Mart also took advantage of Mexico's cheap labor to hold down costs. It replaced the robots used in U.S. distribution centers with Mexicans earning $5 a day. As a result, Wal-Mart's Mexico City distribution center is the company's most efficient one anywhere in the world, its officials say.

By 1999, Wal-Mart Mexico had lowered its costs enough to toy with the idea of passing those savings on to shoppers in a more systematic way. That August, it closed a single Supercenter in central Mexico for a day to mark down prices there by as much as 14% on 6,000 items. The experiment was such a success that every Supercenter in the country cut prices by a similar amount a

month or so later. Other Mexican Wal-Mart stores followed suit by March 2000.

Wal-Mart's enormous buying power has kept it a leap ahead of Mexican competitors who are likewise seeking to cash in on shrinking tariffs. Because Wal-Mart consolidates its orders for all the goods it sells outside the U.S., it can wring deeper discounts from suppliers than can its smaller local competitors. "I buy 20,000 plastic toys, and Wal-Mart buys 20 million. Who do you think gets them cheaper?" asks Francisco Martinez, chief financial officer of Comercial Mexicana SA, Wal-Mart's biggest Mexican rival.

Wal-Mart Mexico has repeatedly exploited Nafta and other economic forces to trigger price wars. For example, rather than pocket the windfall that resulted when tariffs on Lasko brand floor fans steadily fell from 20% in 1993 to 2% today, Sam's Club executive Jose Luis Laparte ordered price cuts equal to the tariff reductions. And when currency fluctuations earlier this year made Sportsman's Choice, Wal-Mart's private dog-food brand, cheaper in peso terms, Mr. Laparte slashed the product's price.

Such aggressive tactics, unorthodox by local standards, have set off near panic among Mexico's mostly family-run retail chains, whose cost structures make it impossible for them to compete on Wal-Mart's terms. "In the long run, the rest of us will have to merge with local or foreign partners to keep up," says Comercial Mexicana's Mr. Martinez.

Investors seem to agree. Wal-Mart Mexico has a local stock-market value of more than $11 billion, nearly triple that of its top three rivals combined.

Behind much of Wal-Mart's recent success are Mexico's increasingly cost-conscious consumers. The greater economic security that Nafta has brought the country has helped tame Mexico's once-fierce inflation. The resulting price stability has made it easier for Mexicans to recognize a bargain when they see one.

To persuade wary Mexicans that its prices are hard to beat, Wal-Mart does a lot of shopping of its own and posts signs on its shelves comparing its prices with competitors'. Wal-Mart's role as price hawk seems to be playing well here. In the first half of the

year, sales at Wal-Mart's Mexican stores that had been open a year or more rose 5.6% while most competitors' sales fell slightly.

'Like Shopping in the U.S.'

Another big drawing point for local consumers: "It's like shopping in the U.S.—until you get back out to the parking lot," says Mexican army Sgt. Jose Sanchez as he pushes a cart around a Wal-Mart Supercenter in Mexico City.

To a growing number of Mexicans, Wal-Mart stores, with their clean, brightly lit interiors, orderly, well-stocked aisles and consistent pricing policies, are a relief from the chaotic atmosphere that prevails in many Mexican stores. Instead of hiring mariachi bands to trumpet each sale or using miniskirt-clad saleswomen to attract customers, as do some of its rivals here, Wal-Mart lets its prices speak for themselves.

Nor do most Mexicans seem to resent the company's gringo roots. "Why should I care where they're from?" asks Luis de Anda, a 31-year-old plumber who visits Sam's once a month to stock up on staples such as diapers and toilet paper for himself and his entire apartment building. "With the money I save, I take my family to the movies," he says.

Wal-Mart hopes to win hearts and minds elsewhere as its U.S. growth slows. The company's Mr. Menzer says the success of Wal-Mart Mexico's Bodegas stores—a low-price, no-frills and limited-choice chain of neighborhood-based warehouse outlets designed for the lowest-income customers—has inspired Wal-Mart to open a Brazilian clone called Todo Dia. It may also test that format in the U.S. Wal-Mart executives from China are also scouring the Mexican operations for ideas.

Ann Zimmerman in Dallas contributed to this article.

22

Marketers Tread Precarious Terrain

Ads Alluding to Sept. 11 Risk Taint of Commercializing Tragedy to Push Products

BY GWENDOLYN BOUNDS
Staff Reporter of THE WALL STREET JOURNAL

For all the talk about the country moving on from Sept. 11, one group isn't quite ready, and that's the nation's marketers.

During Sunday's Super Bowl, **Anheuser-Busch** Cos. aired an ad showing its Clydesdale horses trekking to ground zero and bowing their heads in respect. Siebel Systems Inc. is selling software it dubs "**Siebel Solutions** for Homeland Security." One recent ad pairs a fuzzy security camera image of two dark-haired men in an airport with the stark question: "Who are the Mohamed Attas of tomorrow?" And this past weekend, designer **Kenneth Cole** published a newspaper insert with text including: "On September 12, people who don't speak to their parents forgot why . . ." The ad, which promotes items including $98 sateen pants, concluded: "Today is not a dress rehearsal."

Marketing after a tragedy is tricky business. Allude to it, and risk alienating those who think the promotion capitalizes on misfortune. Ignore it, and there's a danger of seeming out of touch. "In one sense I don't want anyone to forget what happened on that day," says Jennie Farrell who lost her brother in the World Trade Center attack and has co-founded Give Your Voice for families of victims. "But it's also an open wound for us. You can't watch the Super Bowl without it being right there. And I would hope and pray that everyone's intentions are honorable and for the greater good and not to commercialize it for one reason or another."

And that's the conundrum for marketers. In recent years, branding has evolved from promoting specific products—which bleach washes whiter?—to advocating causes, but often the message gets lost along the way. "I have generally told my clients, and they don't always follow the advice, that unless it

fits into your long-term brand identity to do this, don't," says Erich Joachimsthaler, chief executive officer of **Brand Leadership** Co., which advises Bertelsmann AG among others. "If you try to exploit events on people's minds for commercial purposes, it's a short-term effect."

What's more, the tie-in-to-tragedy technique works only as long as consumers feel directly connected to the event, says Alan Brew, an owner of Addison Branding & Communications in San Francisco. And, he warns, "they are feeling that less and less and less." With Siebel's Mohamed Atta reference, for example, he notes: "You are dragging people back to that event when they want to put distance between that and their lives." A Siebel spokesman declined to comment on the ad's strategy.

Those experimenting with these ads, including Kenneth Cole, say they believe that despite the passage of time the subject is still very top of mind. Mr. Cole's dress rehearsal ads "hit a nerve," says Lori Wagner, the company's senior vice president of marketing. "But they hit a positive nerve."

Not surprisingly, firefighters and police have become popular pitchmen. VMS LP, a New York-based media-monitoring firm, has counted nearly 100 different local and national ads featuring firemen and policemen since the start of December. The New York Stock Exchange has aired two spots showing these officers and espousing the strength of American business; one commercial featured several ringing the NYSE's bell. "What we are doing in the ads is talking about the strength of the market," says Robert T. Zito, the NYSE's executive vice president for communications. "There has been no suggestion in any of our consumer tracking that we tried to capitalize on them."

Consumer marketing was muted during World War II, says George Rosenbaum, chairman of Leo J. Shapiro & Associates a Chicago-based survey-research firm. "The goal was to encourage people to save and support rationing. It's just the opposite thrust now. Here the patriotic thing is to spend."

This time around, marketers with scant connection to Sept. 11 are trying to tap into the nation's reflective mood. Last month, a full-page ad for the movie "The Lord of the Rings," featured the following snippet of dialogue:

Frodo: "I wish none of this had happened."

Gandalf: "So do all who live to see such times, but that is not for them to decide. All we have to decide is what to do with the time that is given us."

The ad doesn't mention Sept. 11, but you can feel it close by—which is what the

movie's marketer intended. "That line had always resonated with me, and now, it seemed to hit just the right note," says Russell Schwartz, president of domestic marketing for New Line Cinema, a division of **AOL Time Warner** Inc.

Even those with seemingly little to gain from reminding consumers of Sept. 11 are addressing the day. Seattle's **Boeing** Co. immediately halted most advertising after the attacks; the four planes that struck the World Trade Center towers, Pentagon and crashed in Pennsylvania on Sept. 11 were Boeing aircraft. But by November, with the busy holiday travel season approaching, Boeing reversed course and launched a rare consumer campaign, which will run at least through April. One print ad reads like just-say-no to terrorism: "The freedom to go where you want to go, when you want to go, is a precious liberty. And . . . the nation's skyways are once again ready to help you make the most of that freedom."

Says Susan Bradley, Boeing's director of advertising and brand management for commercial airplanes: "We had a very important travel season coming up, and we wanted to remind people that through travel, that's how they get to see their first grandchild or parents."

Rob Britton took his job overseeing advertising and marketing planning for **AMR** Corp.'s American Airlines on Oct. 3—mere weeks after two of the airline's planes slammed into a Trade Center tower and the Pentagon. The airline ultimately parried with a campaign that like Boeing's efforts, reminds consumers that they need planes to get to the people they love. The current TV ad, running in various markets this month, shows kids wheeling suitcases and New York tourist icons that are still standing, including the Statue of Liberty.

One thing the commercial doesn't show: planes. "You can guess why not," Mr. Britton says. "The imagery is something we've always used, the silver birds were a point of distinction and pride. But the image that flowed from the misappropriation of those vehicles was pretty powerful."

Suzanne Vranica contributed to this article.

With Islamic Dress, Out Goes the Guy Who Sold Burkhas

As Oppressed Afghan Women Shed the Look, Mr. Islamadin Gets Into the Glassware Biz

By Andrew Higgins
Staff Reporter of The Wall Street Journal

KABUL, Afghanistan—When Taliban soldiers swarmed into Kabul five years ago, Muhammed Ibrahim Islamadin spotted profit in puritanical tyranny.

He sold his battered taxicab, bought a shipping container marooned on the side of the road and set up shop sewing and selling burkhas, the tent-like garment mandatory for all women under the new regime's draconian dress code. "It was a wonderful business," recalls Mr. Islamadin, "Everyone was buying."

He didn't worry about marketing. The Taliban's religious police took care of that: "Women who didn't buy got hit with cables," says Mr. Islamadin. It was the start of Kabul's great burkha bonanza,

A burkha

when teachers, doctors, telephone operators and thousands of other working women in the Afghan capital lost both their jobs and their right to show their faces or any other part of the anatomy besides hands in public.

"This was very bad for them, but it was good for me," he says.

A meshing of medieval morality with modern markets made it profitable for many others, too. South Korean and Chinese fabric companies, Pakistani traders, Kabul bazaar merchants, and small-time hucksters like Mr. Islamadin jumped on the burkha bandwagon. The smothering of Afghan women, undertaken in the name of a prophet, Mohammed, who died in A.D. 632, became a late-20th-century global enterprise.

The Taliban didn't invent the burkha, a crinkly, head-to-toe shroud with an embroidered mesh over the eyes. Women in the Afghan countryside have been wearing burkhas for centuries, believe in them, and probably wouldn't give them up. In Kabul, though, the Taliban did invent a new class of first-time buyers. Through terror, they created the ultimate captive market: Not buying became a criminal act.

In their zeal to erase women from all public life and seal Afghanistan from the modern world, however, the Taliban wrapped themselves in contradiction. Nearly all the fabric had to be imported, and carried brazenly un-Islamic brand names like Mercedes 2001, a baby-blue polyester cloth manufactured by Myunhwa Industries, a textile company in Seoul. Stitching that into burkhas also violated Taliban doctrine: Mr. Islamadin and others hired women to do most of the work.

Today, like nearly every aspect of life here, the status of the burkha is in limbo. The Taliban are gone, the sartorial enforcers of the Department for the Promotion of Virtue and Prevention of Vice driven from the derelict capital by the Northern Alliance. A new interim government due to take office on Saturday includes two women but, aside from the appearance of burkha-free newsreaders on recently revived state television, women's liberation in Kabul so far has freed just a few ankles. And even the risque newsreaders still don shrouds before leaving the studio.

"God willing, we can soon stop hiding," says Samira Rahima, a 24-year-old TV presenter who wears a chic silk headscarf at work but, just in case, always carries a plastic bag stuffed with a dowdy blue burkha. She never goes outside without a full-body polyester carapace. "We're still not sure yet what is going to happen," she says.

The Islamic canon, embraced by the country's old and new leaders alike, offers little clear guidance. The Quran instructs pious women to "display of their adornment only that which is apparent and draw veils over their bosoms." Interpretations of just what that means vary widely.

For those who profited from the Taliban's brutal exuberance, however, the message from the market is clear: It's time to bail out of burkhas. "The future is not good," complains Mr. Islamadin, surveying unsold shrouds hanging like limp Halloween ghosts on the sides of his container. After a long discussion with his father and with his brother, who is also a burkha merchant, he decided to get out of Islamic women's wear and move into glassware instead. Whatever happens next in Afghanistan, he calculates, there will always be customers for glass teacups.

With Kabul now free of Taliban zealots scouring the streets for exposed female flesh, few women worry anymore about skin-revealing rips. The occasional tear was just about the only reason anybody ever replaced one of these durable garments. Indeed, instead of rushing to buy a new burkha, some are flaunting the wear and tear as they probe the limits of their new, relative liberty. Others have started gingerly hoisting fabric from their shins and showing off their eyes.

Desperate to keep up sales, Mr. Islamadin tried offering discounts. Burkhas had recently ranged in price from 300,000 afghanis to 1.2 million, at 22,000 afghanis to the dollar. Prices depend on the fabric and whether it is from Korea (pricey) or Pakistan (cheap). Today, you can buy a million-afghani burkha for 800,000.

Mr. Islamadin installed a curtain at the back of his container so clients could be fitted there. The Taliban never would have tolerated that. On a recent morning, only two stopped at Mr. Islamadin's stall. Both were visiting the capital from the countryside. They tried on a few polyester covers but didn't like the cut. They left without buying. Since the Taliban fled, says Mr. Islamadin, daily sales have fallen 50%. He's now running down his stock and, after an Islamic holiday this week, he plans to give what's left to his brother, whose burkha business is located far from Kabul and, he hopes, is less susceptible to change. Mr. Islamadin has also fired his seamstresses.

Anxiety is rippling through the industry. In Kabul's central bazaar, Sadar Nuri, a fabric wholesaler, points to bolts of Mercedes 2001 cloth gathering dust in the corner of his shop. Under the Taliban, he used to place a bulk order every four months with his supplier in Pakistan, trucking in 8,000 yards of South Korean burkha material for sale to retailers like Mr. Islamadin.

Mr. Nuri's last consignment arrived three months before the Taliban fled. He has sold all but 2,500 yards but hasn't moved an inch since Kabul changed hands. He's now stocking up instead on a more versatile brown cloth from China. He expects it to be a big seller as women trickle back to work and, he hopes, start copying the TV newsreaders, who wear dark shawls and jackets. Blue polyester, he says, has had it.

Park Kyung Hyun, a manager at Seoul-based fabric-maker Myunhwa Industries, is confident that demand for veils in other, far richer Islamic countries can more than take up any slack in Kabul. "The Quran says that they all have to wear it," says Mr. Park. Burkhas and other forms of Islamic garb for women, he says, are a boon for fabric salesmen: They require a lot of material.

No one expects the Afghan burkha to disappear. While Kabul's male residents have mostly trimmed their Taliban-decreed beards, women still hide their faces. "Men rushed to shave on the first day, but women take decisions more seriously," says Suhaila Seddiqi, a feisty, Soviet-trained surgeon and health minister-designate. Women, she says, are less fickle and stronger than men. Uniquely among Kabul's women, Ms. Seddiqi managed to defy the Taliban dress code and a ban on women working: She went to

(Cont.)

work in a car with tinted windows to avoid causing a stir. The Taliban, she says, "needed me to treat their wives and daughters."

A few dozen yards from Mr. Islamadin's burkha stall, an elementary school that once provided some of his best customers is now a source of woe. When the Taliban took power, Rahima Nasir lost her job as a teacher and was in such a hurry to buy a burkha she bought the wrong size and returned a few weeks later to buy a second one. "I was so frightened," she says. Disoriented by the unfamiliar garment, she stumbled into traffic and nearly got run over.

Last week, Ms. Nasir and a group of other teachers gathered at the school to demand their jobs back. The school's principal, a holdover from the Taliban era, stared at the ground as they marched into his office with uncovered heads. They still wear burkhas on the streets out of habit, fear of insults and embarrassment at their threadbare clothes underneath. Ms. Nasir says they hope to shed their burkhas once they recover their jobs.

Meeyoung Song in Seoul contributed to this article.

"With Islamic Dress, Out Goes the Guy Who Sold Burkhas," *The Wall Street Journal*, December 19, 2001, p. A1ff. Copyright 2001 by Dow Jones & Co Inc. Reproduced with permission of Dow Jones & Co Inc. in the format Textbook via Copyright Clearance Center.

24

Brand Builders

Cutting edge. (Gillette's Mach3 and Venus razors reach top of category)

By Christine Bittar

Gillette's Mach3 triple blade razor, introduced in 1998, was the category's biggest news in years. The company had spent six years in stealth-like research and development, and nearly $1 billion bringing the product to market. Despite initial sticker shock of $8 for the razor and nearly $2 per refill blade, Mach3 became the top-selling men's razor in its first year. Logically the next step for the brand was a women's version.

"Wall Street analysts and trade partners were asking us when it was coming," said Mary Ann Pesce, vp of new products-razors/blades at Gillette, Boston.

Launching a new razor for women presented its own set of challenges. Whereas shaving for most men is "life affirming and masculine," said Pesce, most women don't talk about the act openly and there's no gratification in the process.

Enter Venus. Launched in early 2001, the product lived up to its goddess-inspired name, designed in a feminine ocean blue color with an unusual-looking T-shaped handle for comfort. Its only obvious connection to the Mach3 was its triple blade. The cartridges had evolved from a square to a rounded shape with rubbery oval cushions meant to stretch and smooth the skin. The razor was packaged in a convenient shower dispenser, with individually packed and sealed blades to protect them from moisture.

Priced about the same as Mach3, Venus likewise shot up to the No. 1 non-disposable razor slot in less than a year with sales of $45 million through Oct. 7, per Information Resources Inc. Its refill blade sales of $35 million far exceeded those of its biggest competitor, Pfizer's Schick Silk Effects Plus, with $19 million in refill sales for a full 52 weeks. Initial Venus sales surpassed other Gillette female brands as well as competitors', including Schick. "We sold more than 11,000 pieces in six months, compared to about 6,000 refills of [Schick] Silk Effects," said a beauty aids buyer at one drug chain.

Retailers generally were pleased with Venus' eye-catching POP displays and wide media support. Gillette put $150 million into global advertising for the launch, almost $40 million in the U.S. Marketers timed the introduction to the arrival of spring and summer, when more women go bare-legged in skirts and bathing suits.

Despite Gillette's overall disappointing sales in other categories the last two years, demand for its premium razor brands has remained strong. The company's fourth-

> ## "It wasn't about shaving. We were looking for an image of beauty and power."—Al Merrin, BBDO

quarter sales fell 3% to $2.7 billion, but solid performance of its Mach3 and Venus razors led Gillette to its highest share of the U.S. shaving market—over 80% in both blades and handles—in 40 years.

To counter the notion of Venus as a male version of Mach3, marketers even spoofed the brand's own TV ads during a video presentation to the sales team. The Mach3 spots had featured jets, so the video showed a woman flying a pink fighter jet ("Machette") with her scarf blowing in her face. In the end, she gets approval from a male pilot who says, "Super shave fly girl."

"For a moment, no one knew what to make of it. Then one person started laughing and suddenly the whole room was laughing uproariously," Pesce recalled.

When Gillette launched Sensor for Women back in 1992, its product and ads were meant to be pretty. Venus, on the other hand, was seen as promoting skincare. That "aha" moment came during a briefing session with BBDO, said Pesce. "When the first round of story boards didn't cut it, I casually said, 'Guys, this is not just about shaving, it's skincare', and they quickly realized that was it."

The baton was then tossed to Al Merrin, vice chairman and executive creative director at BBDO, New York. "[Gillette] wanted a big idea immediately, and that gave us a big advantage creatively," Merrin said. "We knew from the start shaving is an afterthought and we wanted to elevate it. So that led to a name with a broader appeal."

Gillette marketers also looked for a campaign with a universal and emotional appeal. TV spots showed a cadre of suntanned women laying on the beach with legs crossed and their backs to the camera, tapping their toes to Bananarama's lively version of the song "Venus." The tagline: "Reveal the goddess in you."

Print ads, meanwhile, ran in women's beauty and fashion magazines, including *Cosmopolitan* and *Glamour*. Creative involved closeup product shots and copy highlighting core attributes: a longer lasting shave, three blades, protective cushions, the pivoting head and individually sealed blade refills. "Changing blades, made easy," one ad declared. "Now in one stroke, your skin stays smoother, longer," claimed another.

Marketers wanted the campaign to steer clear of images of primping females or a woman getting ready for a date. "It wasn't about shaving:" said Merrin. "We were looking for an image of beauty and power."

"Brand Builders: Cutting Edge," *Brandweek*, February 4, 2002, pp. 16–18. © 2002 VNU Business Media, Inc. Used with permission.

25

THE ENVIRONMENT WAS RIPE FOR ABUSE

Enron's unrelenting stress on growth and its absence of controls helped push execs into unethical behavior

At Enron Corp., they called her "the Weather Babe." Lynda R. Clemmons, a French and history major from Southern Methodist University, was supposed to be emblematic of the rebels in Enron's freewheeling culture. In 1997, as a 27-year-old gas-and-power trader, she launched an esoteric enterprise in weather derivatives. Within two years, her startup had written $1 billion in weather hedges to protect companies against short-term spikes in the price of power during heat waves and cold snaps.

Clemmons' story made the rounds, from a favorable Harvard Business School case study to *The New York Times* business section, where she was pictured in black leather on a Harley-Davidson. She was, after all, a product of what Enron's culture was supposed to be all about: smart, sassy, creative, and risk-taking. And Enron made the most of her business, trumpeting weather derivatives as yet another high-potential deregulated market.

Like other Enron initiatives, this one never lived up to the hype. "It was such a flaky business," says John Olson, an analyst at Sanders Harris Morris in Houston. "They got more mileage out of the public relations than they actually made in earnings." Not exactly the way Enron's "cultural revolution" was supposed to play out. But as everyone knows, with Enron, nothing was quite as it appeared.

For most of the 1990s, CEOs at Old Economy companies struggled to turn slow-moving organizations into nimbler, more flexible outfits. Failure cost chieftains their jobs at General Motors, Eastman Kodak, Westinghouse, and a host of other behemoths. Truth is, real transformations are the exception rather than the rule. Changing the core values, the attitudes, the fundamental relationships of a vast organization is overwhelmingly difficult. General Electric Co.'s John F. Welch and IBM's Louis V. Gerstner Jr. have been lionized for having led two of the very few successful makeovers.

That's why an army of academics and consultants descended on Enron in the late 1990s and held it up as a paragon of management virtue. Enron seemed to have transformed itself from a stodgy regulated utility to a fast-moving enterprise where performance was paramount. The Harvard case study put it simply enough: "Enron's transformation: From gas pipelines to New Economy powerhouse."

> **SKILLING** Many say the CEO was encouraging all the risk-taking at Enron

If only that were true. Many of the same academics are now scurrying to distill the cultural and leadership lessons from the debacle. Their conclusion so far: Enron didn't fail just because of improper accounting or alleged corruption at the top. It also failed because of its entrepreneurial culture—the very reason Enron attracted so much attention and acclaim. The unrelenting emphasis on earnings growth and individual initiative, coupled with a shocking absence of the usual corporate checks and balances, tipped the culture from one that rewarded aggressive strategy to one that increasingly relied on unethical corner-cutting. In the end, too much leeway was given to young, inexperienced managers without the necessary controls to minimize failures. This was a company that simply placed a lot of bad bets on businesses that weren't so promising to begin with.

Before 1990, Enron was a sleepy, regulated natural-gas company dominated by engineers and hard assets. But that year, Enron Chairman Kenneth L. Lay hired McKinsey & Co. partner Jeffrey K. Skilling, who had been advising Lay as a consultant. Skilling's mandate was to build Enron Finance Corp. into an asset-light laboratory for financially linked products and services. Skilling expanded the unit into a model of what all of Enron would become. Its success led to his promotion to president in 1997 and to CEO in early 2001.

Skilling's recipe for changing the company was right out of the New Economy playbook. Layers of management were wiped out. Hundreds of outsiders were recruited and encouraged to bring new thinking to a tradition-bound business. The company abolished seniority-based salaries in favor of more highly leveraged compensation that offered huge cash bonuses and stock option grants to top performers. Young people, many just out of undergraduate or MBA programs, were handed extraordinary authority, able to make $5 million decisions without higher approval.

HOW A NEW ECONOMY CORPORATE CULTURE WENT AWRY

TYPE OF CULTURE	EMPLOYEE EXPECTATIONS	REWARDS	LEADERSHIP
Old Economy	Security	Salary	Top-down
New Economy	Personal growth	Stock options	Inspirational
The Enron Twist	Personal wealth	A stake in the business	Know-it-all arrogant

In the new culture, success or failure came remarkably fast. "One potential flaw in the model was that Enron managers tended to move relatively quickly, not within businesses but between businesses," says Jay Conger, a management professor at London Business School who studied Enron. "If you move young people fast in senior-level positions without industry experience and then allow them to make large trading decisions, that is a risky strategy."

It was not unusual for execs to change jobs two or three times in as many years. Indeed, turnover from promotions alone was almost 20%. Clemmons, for example, went from analyst, to associate, to manager, then director, and finally to vice-president running her own business, all in seven years.

> **FASTOW** Did he exploit performance reviews to get back at those who opposed him?

"In larger companies like IBM and GE, even though there is a movement toward youth, there are still enough older people around to mentor them," says James O'Toole, professor at the Center for Effective Organizations at the University of Southern California. "At Enron, you had a bunch of kids running loose without adult supervision."

In theory, of course, the kids were closely supervised. Skilling often described the new culture as "loose and tight," one of the eight attributes of the successful companies profiled by McKinsey consultants Thomas J. Peters and Robert H. Waterman Jr. in their best-selling book, **In Search of Excellence.** The idea is to combine tight controls with maximum individual authority to allow entrepreneurship to flourish without the culture edging into chaos.

At Enron, however, the pressure to make the numbers often overwhelmed the pretext of "tight" controls. "The environment was ripe for abuse," says a former manager in Enron's energy services unit. "Nobody at corporate was asking the right questions. It was completely hands-off management. A situation like that requires tight controls. Instead, it was a runaway train."

The train was supposed to be kept on the tracks partly by an internal risk-management group with a staff of 180 employees to screen proposals and review deals. Many of

the unit's employees were MBAs with little perspective and every reason to sign off on deals: Their own performance reviews were partially done by the people whose deals they were approving. The process made honest evaluations virtually impossible. "If your boss was [fudging], and you have never worked anywhere else, you just assume that everybody fudges earnings," says one young Enron control person. "Once you get there and you realized how it was, do you stand up and lose your job? It was scary. It was easy to get into 'Well, everybody else is doing it, so maybe it isn't so bad.'"

It didn't help that Enron's Risk Assessment & Control group was answerable not to the board of directors but to Skilling, who was encouraging all the risk-taking. Another essential "check and balance" in the culture—Enron's in-house legal staff—was also compromised because of its reporting relationships. Instead of being centralized at headquarters, it was spread throughout the business units, where it could more easily be co-opted by hard-driving executives. "The business people didn't want to slow down for much," says one former in-house lawyer.

Central to forging a new Enron culture was an unusual performance review system that Skilling adapted from his days at McKinsey. Under this peer-review process, a select group of 20 people were named to a performance review committee (PRC) to rank more than 400 vice-presidents, then all the direc-

> **LAY** The chairman hired Skilling in 1990 with a mandate to build Enron Finance Corp. into an asset-light laboratory for financially linked products and services

tors, and finally all of Enron's managers. The stakes were high because all the rewards were linked to ranking decisions by the PRC which had to unanimously agree on each person. Managers judged "superior"—the top 5%—got bonuses 66% higher than those who got an "excellent" rating, the next 30%. They also got much larger stock option grants.

Although Skilling told Harvard researchers that the system "stopped most of the game playing since it was impossible to kiss 20 asses," other Enron managers say it had the opposite effect. In practice, the system bred a culture in which people were afraid to get crossways with someone who

could screw up their reviews. How did managers ensure they passed muster? "You don't object to anything," says one former Enron executive. "The whole culture at the vice-president level and above just became a yes-man culture."

Several former and current Enron execs say that Andrew S. Fastow, the ex-chief financial officer who is at the center of Enron's partnership controversy, had a reputation for exploiting the review system to get back at people who expressed disagreement or criticism. "Andy was such a cutthroat bastard that he would use it against you in the

> **CLEMMONS** Her weather biz epitomized Enron pizzazz

PRC," says one manager. He could filibuster and hold up the group for days, the exec adds, because every decision had to be unanimous. A spokesman for Fastow declined comment.

Although managers were supposed to be graded on teamwork, Enron was actually far more reflective of a survival-of-the-fittest mind-set. The culture was heavily built around star players, such as Clemmons, with little value attached to team-building. The upshot: The organization rewarded highly competitive people who were less likely to share power, authority, or information.

Indeed, some believe the extreme focus on individual ambition undermined any teamwork or institutional commitment. At other companies, by contrast, an emphasis on individual achievement is balanced by a strong focus on process and metrics or a set of guiding values. "In the Enron culture, there was no significant counterbalance," says Jon R. Katzenbach, a consultant and former McKinsey colleague of Skilling who has studied the company. "The lesson is you cannot rely solely on individual achievement to drive your performance over time. Companies with only that one path overemphasize it and run into trouble, switching over to vanity and greed."

That emphasis on the individual instead of the enterprise may have pushed many to cross the line into unethical behavior. The flaw only grew more pronounced as Enron struggled to meet the wildly optimistic expectations for growth it had set for itself. "You've got someone at the top saying the stock price is the most important thing,

ORGANIZATION	CORPORATE GOAL	BOARD	APPROACH TO REGS
Hierarchy	Steady growth	Rubber stamp	Aim to meet regulations
Network	Fast growth	Independent	Push the limits
Individual fiefdoms	Appearing to grow fast	Rubber stamp	Circumvent the rules

(Cont.)

which is driven by earnings," says one insider. "Whoever could provide earnings quickly would be promoted."

The employee adds that anyone who questioned suspect deals quickly learned to accept assurances of outside lawyers and accountants. She says there was little scrutiny of whether the earnings were real or how they were booked. The more people pushed the envelope with aggressive accounting, she says, the harder they would have to push the next year. "It's like being a heroin junkie," she says. "How do you go cold turkey?"

The problem is, you can't. "For almost every model or system, there are certain limits," says USC's O'Toole. "It's harder to keep the growth growing and to keep coming up with new ideas. That kind of culture has a subtle encouragement to cut corners and to cheat. You can see everyone else moving forward, and you have to keep up."

Clemmons, who left Enron in March of 2000, isn't so sure. "It's quite clear that there were some accounting issues and bad decisions that had nothing to do with the trading side of the business," she says. "To

distill it all down to the culture is utter bulls—."

As academics do their revisionist thing, they're not likely to agree.

By John A. Byrne, with Mike France, in New York and with Wendy Zellner in Dallas

Buyer Behavior

Living Alone in America

Singleness not the same as not settled; Divorce, late marriages and longevity figure in

By Craig Wilson
USA TODAY

ATLANTA—Years ago, Kris Osborn's father, a psychiatrist, gave him a bit of advice:

"If you go and chase after women, you'll never meet quality women. You only find quality women if you excel in your own life."

At 32, Osborn is working hard at excelling in his own life. One of the newest faces at CNN Headline News here, he became a general-assignment anchor back in July. He's still single, however. Can a quality woman be far behind? Well, there's a new love interest in Boston, but it's too early to tell.

At the moment, Osborn is leading the single man's good life in trendy Buckhead, his treadmill in front of the TV for those Sunday afternoons of football, nothing but bottled water in the fridge. He shares the apartment that faces west over the treetops—a requirement he gave his real estate agent—with a shelter cat named Byron.

While he lives alone, Osborn is not alone. The 2000 Census shows that more than 27 million Americans live by themselves, about one-fourth of all households, nearly 10% of the population. For the first time, one-person households outnumber married couples with children (fewer than 25 million).

"With the increase in the divorce rate, the increase in the age at which people first get married, and with our increasing longevity, the experience of being single is now one of the most widely shared experiences of adulthood," says Bella DePaulo, visiting professor of psychology at the University of California-Santa Barbara.

And when you add in the single people who are living together but not married—everyone from college kids in dorms to young singles sharing apartments to unmarried couples—the number of singles in America soars. Their ranks increased from 38 million in 1970 to 82 million in 2000. Single people now account for more than 40% of the adult population, up from 28% of all adults in the USA three decades ago, according to DePaulo, who cites Census statistics.

"These findings are not surprising. They reflect a 30-year trend in America to marry later in life, divorce or never get married at all," says Xavier Amador, co-author of *Being Single in a Couples' World: How to be Happily Single While Looking for Love* and director of psychology at New York State Psychiatric Institute in New York. "Being single is no longer synonymous with being immature, unsettled in life and irresponsible. Questions such as 'When are you going to get married and settle down?' belong to the past, not the reality of America today."

Zoe Woodland, a 27-year-old computer network manager at Hill Air Force Base near Salt Lake City, has heard the question before. Her response?

"Oh, when I'm 55. That's my standard answer," she says. "Actually, I imagine myself still single at 88. Playing bridge. And riding my mountain bike."

San Francisco retiree Harry Rudnick is 88 and agrees that single life suits him just fine. "If I go out with a lady friend, I take her to dinner and that satisfies me," he says.

According to the American Association for Single People (AASP), an "unmarried majority" has emerged in most major cities, as well as six states, facts the association disseminated on Capitol Hill last month during National Singles Week.

"And within a few years, the majority of households in the nation will be headed by unmarried adults," says AASP executive director Tom Coleman.

Up until a few years ago when the AASP was formed, virtually all singles groups were for dating and matchmaking, focused on social and recreational activities for lonely hearts. But singles today are looking for more, much healthier in their outlook on life. As Woodland says, "I think I'm different only because I'm told I am."

Now, more and more groups are formed for support, even political reasons.

"As single people begin to wake up and realize that we are being cheated—sometimes to the tune of thousands of dollars per year in higher taxes, higher insurance rates, fewer employee benefits and smaller Social Security benefits—more of their attention and support will shift toward organizations fighting for legal and economic reform," Coleman says.

Conservative groups have expressed concern

Living alone in America

The 2000 Census found more than 27 million Americans living alone, about one-fourth of all households and nearly 10% of the population. A look at the numbers that describe who and where they are:

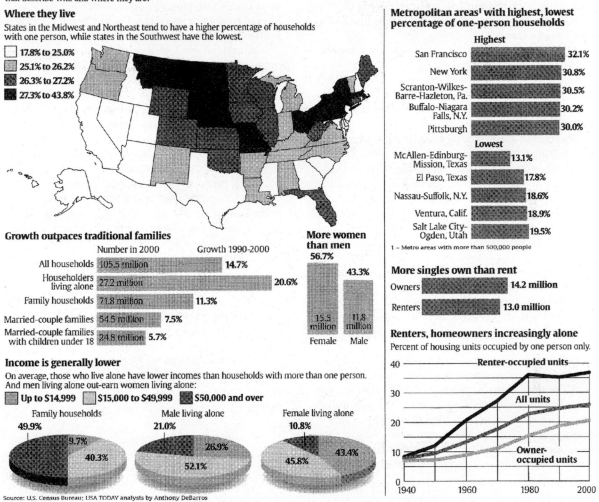

Where they live

States in the Midwest and Northeast tend to have a higher percentage of households with one person, while states in the Southwest have the lowest.

- 17.8% to 25.0%
- 25.1% to 26.2%
- 26.3% to 27.2%
- 27.3% to 43.8%

Growth outpaces traditional families

	Number in 2000	Growth 1990-2000
All households	105.5 million	14.7%
Householders living alone	27.2 million	20.6%
Family households	71.8 million	11.3%
Married-couple families	54.5 million	7.5%
Married-couple families with children under 18	24.8 million	5.7%

More women than men
- Female: 56.7% — 15.5 million
- Male: 43.3% — 11.8 million

Income is generally lower

On average, those who live alone have lower incomes than households with more than one person. And men living alone out-earn women living alone:

- Up to $14,999
- $15,000 to $49,999
- $50,000 and over

Family households
- 49.9%
- 40.3%
- 9.7%

Male living alone
- 21.0%
- 52.1%
- 26.9%

Female living alone
- 10.8%
- 45.8%
- 43.4%

Source: U.S. Census Bureau; USA TODAY analysis by Anthony DeBarros

Metropolitan areas[1] with highest, lowest percentage of one-person households

Highest
San Francisco	32.1%
New York	30.8%
Scranton-Wilkes-Barre-Hazleton, Pa.	30.5%
Buffalo-Niagara Falls, N.Y.	30.2%
Pittsburgh	30.0%

Lowest
McAllen-Edinburg-Mission, Texas	13.1%
El Paso, Texas	17.8%
Nassau-Suffolk, N.Y.	18.6%
Ventura, Calif.	18.9%
Salt Lake City-Ogden, Utah	19.5%

1 – Metro areas with more than 500,000 people

More singles own than rent

- Owners: 14.2 million
- Renters: 13.0 million

Renters, homeowners increasingly alone

Percent of housing units occupied by one person only.

- Renter-occupied units
- All units
- Owner-occupied units

(1940, 1960, 1980, 2000)

By Marcy E. Mullins, USA TODAY

over the "single and alone" trend, calling it a troubling indicator of deeper societal problems. But demographers say what the trend truly reveals is that adults just prefer their own company, living near their families, but not with them. In fact, it's very American.

"Americans are individualists, and unless we're married and raising children, we tend to want to live alone, rather than impose on relatives," says Andrew Cherlin, a Johns Hopkins University sociology professor. "Plus, we like our privacy. So, those of us with more money tend to use it to live alone."

Cherlin says some people are worried that it makes for "a more detached society, but most people who live alone live near friends and family. Americans want intimacy at a distance. That's the highest good."

Demographers, however, point out that the "single" trend will have a profound effect on American institutions. With fewer households having children, for example, public schools will face a more difficult time gathering support for building programs and educational programs.

It also could have a negative effect on Americans' health. Linda Waite, a University of Chicago sociologist and author of *The Case for Marriage*, says several studies show that married people tend to live healthier and happier lives.

"There's evidence that our systems work better when there's someone around that we care about, and care about us. The stress goes down," she says. "Also, we get a lot of the meaning of our life by doing for others, taking care of other people. So if you live alone, that's just not there."

The recent terrorist attacks are sending some singles back into relationships.

"One of my girlfriends broke up with her boyfriend but went back to him on Sept. 11," says Gloria Olson, a single grandmother in Bismarck, N.D. "She said she realized life was too short."

Maybe, but the troubling times and health studies aren't scaring CNN's Osborn to the altar. With a swimmer's body and model-material looks, Osborn could marry just about anyone he wanted. Many a young woman has noticed his arrival at CNN headquarters, more than a few volunteering to help him out in any way he might need.

But at the moment, like many single men his age, he's devoted to his profession. "A huge amount of my time is my job now," he confesses. "Mainly because it's new and I like it so much."

Osborn is typical of many young bachelors in America today. He drives a nice car (a black Lincoln Town Car), wears designer suits from Calvin Klein, eats out more than in.

"If I fit any stereotype, it's that of the bachelor," he says. "Interior decorating is not my thing."

Although Osborn says he has dated often over the years—he had a four-year relationship in California—his professional life keeps getting in the way.

"I went to 10 different countries for Channel One News," he says. "I'm afraid that kind of travel schedule isn't compatible with a serious relationship."

Does he mind still being single?

"No, I like it," he says without hesitation.

"You don't have to worry about commitments to your career (affecting) your commitment to a family. I'm not ruling out marriage. I'm just being very specific about doing it once. There's no rush."

Woodland isn't in any rush, either, playing the field by her own rules, saying she's not obsessed with finding the right guy.

"I don't think that way. It's not one of those things that's necessary for my happiness. The men I date find out quickly that I don't need them as an accessory. If I like them, I'll let them hang out with me for a while."

Being in family-friendly Utah makes some singles more defiant than even Woodland.

"The pressure to marry here is incredible," says Woodland's pal Megan Walsh, 24, a graduate student at the University of Utah. "But I'm not going to settle. I don't care if I'm 65 and single. Yes, it gets old being alone, but there's a difference between being alone and being lonely. I have made the decision to be alone."

Stan Charnofsky, author of *Surfing the Single Life: A Memoir for Women and Men Making It Alone,* thinks all these singles are doing it right.

"Not everybody is paired off or familied up," he says. "Some are singles living marvelous, bountiful, contributory lives."

Contributing: Anthony DeBarros

"Living Alone in America: Singleness Not the Same as Not Settled," *USA Today*, October 23, 2001, p. 1Dff. Reprinted with permission.

In Europe, Hot New Fashion for Urban Hipsters Comes From Peoria

The $500 Jacket, $80 Jeans In Caterpillar's 'Cat' Line Borrow Bulldozers' Allure

BY CECILIE ROHWEDDER AND JOSEPH T. HALLINAN
Staff Reporter of THE WALL STREET JOURNAL

Fritz Rychly, a 25-year-old tattoo artist in Berlin, doesn't look as if he's ever set foot on a construction site, much less picked up a shovel. But in Europe, he's a more typical buyer of Caterpillar-brand clothing than the building crews that normally wear the U.S. construction company's heavy boots and rugged shirts.

Most Americans associate **Caterpillar** Inc., with heavy machinery, which it has made for more than a century. But in Europe, the brand is now a fashion statement. After backpacks and sport utility vehicles, international urbanites have latched onto "Cat" gear as the new symbol of American outdoor culture, with an air of durability and honest hard work.

"The boots look tougher than all that other trendy stuff," says Mr. Rychly, browsing the Caterpillar boutique in Berlin's upscale KaDeWe department store. He fingered an $80 pair of five-pocket jeans with a yellow patch on the back. Caterpillar has bigger plans, including a $285 pair of limited-edition jeans and opening stores in London and New York.

Mary Elizabeth Mastrantonio wore a Cat hat in "The Perfect Storm." Arnold Schwarzenegger

wears Cat shoes, the company says. Some U.S. stores, such as Urban Outfitters Inc. and Nordstrom Inc., carry Cat merchandise. Still, this is one fashion craze that hasn't yet hit full force in the U.S. While trendsetters have discovered the black-and-yellow Cat label on boots, sandals, handbags, and watches, safety wear for real construction workers still makes up most of the company's U.S. apparel business.

Indeed, Caterpillar says it is branching out into casual wear mainly to boost its image among people who drive its trucks and tractors. "In order to expand our share in the work shoe market, we have to be in the growing casual business," says Bill Brown, president of Cat footwear at **Wolverine World Wide** Inc., a Rockford, Mich., company that holds the global license to make Cat shoes and boots.

In Europe, the situation is reversed. Cat gets a high reading on the hip meter but wants more customers who wear its construction gear at work to buttress its industrial image. Europe contributed more than half of Caterpillar's $900 million in world-wide sales of licensed merchandise last year. "Even if people here don't know the brand, they have a feeling that they know it," says Stephen Palmer, whose London company, **Overland Ltd.**, is the world-wide license holder for Cat apparel. "They have seen Caterpillar tractors from an early age. It's subliminal, and that's why it's working."

There aren't any dump trucks or forklifts

in sight in the Cat showroom at Overland's London headquarters. But there are sneakers and sandals, flip-flops and pink baby shoes, nylon handbags, college-style sweatshirts and pastel sun hats. The closest most of these items will ever come to a construction site is the jackhammer-like music at the Bootstore, whose stores on Kings Road, Notting Hill Gate and other London shopping streets sell Cat footwear.

So far, there is just one free-standing Caterpillar store—a 5,000-square-foot shop across the street from Cat's headquarters in Peoria, Ill. It's a pretty hip place, for Peoria. The interior is bright Caterpillar yellow and dominated by a life-size replica of a Cat-sponsored racing car. Whenever someone approaches a display, motion sensors trigger heavy machine noises, like the beep-beep-beep of a truck backing up. Part of the floor is made of wood blocks, just like Cat's factory floors.

In addition to a $500 Cat racing jacket, there's a $289.95 Coach leather bag with "Cat" stamped on it and a Tiffany bracelet for $300 with a sterling silver Cat charm. Cat says it is using such products mainly as advertising—"to get our brand to people who wouldn't normally come in contact with us," says Kimberly S. Neible, the head of Caterpillar's global brand management group.

Next year, Cat plans to extend its line into "fashion forward" accessories like sunglasses and sandals, much of it aimed at 18- to 24-year-olds. Also in the works: a line of children's clothing. For now, though, 64-year old Bob Hodel, who spent 41 years as a Cat employee, is a more typical customer. "Anything that has 'Cat' on it, I have," said Mr. Hodel, shopping in the Peoria store. Eventually, he found something new for his collection: a $7.99 model of a Cat-sponsored Nascar race car.

'Cat' *brand items are catching on in Europe*

Low-fat industry loses out as consumers favor flavor

By Bruce Horovitz
USA TODAY

How quickly the nation has forgotten its fanatical fear of fat.

One minute, we're in a tizzy about all things with one extra molecule of fat. Or cholesterol. Or calories. And the next thing you know, fat is back. Way back.

And low fat is out. Way out.

Just 5 years ago, nearly one in three new food products made a low-fat claim. Today, only one in 10 so much as mentions low fat. The multibillion-dollar low-fat and no-fat food sectors that seemed to amass overnight have mostly thinned to grocery store light-weights.

Instead of looking to save a few calories and a few grams of fat, Americans are pigging out like never before. We want more flavor. We want more taste. We want more fat. Experts say this urge for indulgence in fat-filled foods—and the emotional comfort they can bring—began long before terrorists turned our lives inside out. For the fourth consecutive year, sales of low-fat products are falling.

"In the 21st century, you can't drink, smoke, take drugs or have sex," says futurist Watts Wacker. "There's only one thing left to do: Eat."

It took them awhile, but the giant foodmakers finally are figuring that out. Throughout much of the 1990s, they kept pushing low-fat and no-fat products upon us as if these things were a panacea for the Calorie-Challenged Generation. New products are the lifeblood of the food industry. But sales of fat-free ice cream are down nearly 17% this year, reports Nielsen. Sales of low-fat cookies are down 10.8%. And sales of low-fat sausage are off 8.6%.

Responding to the consumer backlash, foodmakers are back to dishing out the fat. Ben & Jerry's is now mixing two kinds of its decadent ice creams into its 2-Twisted line. Frito-Lay is pushing new gourmet chips. And fast-food chain Carl's Jr. has just introduced its biggest-ever burger.

Obviously, this is what consumers want. Consider: More than one in four potatoes eaten at home is consumed in the form of chips, reports NPD Group, a research firm. The $20 billion snack food industry

> **No fat, no way:** "The more fat they take out of something, the worse it tastes, and the more it costs," says cook Andrea Ratliff. She's tried Wow chips, no-fat yogurt and ice cream.

expects sales to rise 6.4% this year. The number of individual "snacking occasions" is up 33% since 1988, reports the Snack Food Association. And when the snacking trade group surveyed kids about their favorite pastime during road trips, "playing games" barely beat out—you guessed it—"snacking." And you can bet it's not on apples.

We may talk the lean talk. But we are walking—make that waddling—the fat walk. The days of "reduced-fat" snacking aren't dead, but they're in intensive care.

Perhaps no one knows that better than Andrea Ratliff. She can't stomach low-fat anything. She recently bought some Yoplait no-fat yogurt—and chucked it before finishing the container. She bought some fat-substitute Wow potato chips—and never finished the bag. She's even got a half-gallon of Edy's Vanilla fat-free ice cream sitting in her freezer—with just one spoonful eaten out of it. It's been there for a month.

"All you're doing is paying a lot of money for stuff that tastes lousy," says Ratliff, who works as a cook at the Children's Place day-care center in Lincoln, Neb. "The more fat they take out of something, the worse it tastes, and the more it costs."

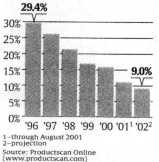

Low interest in low fat

Introduction of products that claim to be "low fat" or "no fat" have declined dramatically in the past few years. Percentage of new products that have made "low fat" or "no fat" claims since the trend peaked in 1996:

29.4%

9.0%

'96 '97 '98 '99 '00 '01¹ '02²

1–through August 2001
2–projection
Source: Productscan Online
(www.productscan.com)

By Sam Ward, USA TODAY

(Cont.)

She's got company. When the Mintel Group research firm asked consumers what they care most about when buying a cookie, 95% said that taste ranked tops, while only 37% factored in low fat.

At issue: Many consumers have figured out "that low-fat products don't taste very good," says Lynn Dornblaser, editorial director at Mintel's Global New Products Database.

GOING ON FINANCIAL DIETS

Corporate victims are piling up:

▶ **SnackWell's.** The division of Nabisco, which made household words of low fat, is but a shell of its former self. Gobs of its products have been dumped, from cheese snacks to pretzels.

SnackWell's revolutionized the low-fat snacking category in 1992 by making low-fat cookies and crackers marketed for their better taste than many similar products.

People ate SnackWell's by the box, ignoring the fact that low-fat goods can still have calories. They thought they could eat as much as they wanted without gaining weight, says Marion Nestle, chairman of the department of nutrition at New York University. "But people are much better off eating a few Oreos than a box of SnackWell's," she says.

Near its peak in 1995, SnackWell's annual sales exceeded $603 million. But for the 52 weeks ending Aug. 12, 2001, sales slid to a comparatively paltry $134 million, reports Information Resources, a research firm that tracks consumer product sales.

So desperate is the brand to find a niche that it recently began marketing sugarless versions of SnackWell's, targeted at people with diabetes.

Nabisco executives declined interviews. In a statement, company spokesman Larry Baumann said, "While the consumer mind-set regarding fat in one's diet has shifted recently, a significant portion of the population is still interested in fat-free dietary choices."

▶ **Guiltless Gourmet.** The tortilla chip and dip maker, founded in 1989, was on a tear by the mid-1990s. In 1994, annual sales rocketed to $24 million. By last year, annual sales had slipped to under $6 million.

What happened? "Consumers are fickle," says Michael Schall, president and CEO of Manischewitz, which bought the brand a year ago.

But Schall still thinks there's an upscale niche for the brand. To improve taste, the chips have evolved from fat free to low fat. Several years ago, the brand started using only organic ingredients. And the company is looking into making chips from sweet potatoes.

▶ **Frito-Lay.** Sales of the snack giant's once high-flying line of Wow Chips, made with a fat substitute, have tumbled since they were introduced in 1997. Sales peaked in 1998 at about $318 million. But annualized sales fell to about $163 million for the 52 weeks ending Aug. 12, 2001, reports Information Resources.

Analysts once projected Wow brand's annual sales would top $500 million. While sales are down nearly 20% over the past year, the steady decline stopped about 3 months ago, says Stephen Quinn, general manager in charge of snack foods at Frito-Lay.

This new world of fat has as many winners as losers. In some cases, companies are winning and losing.

Take Frito-Lay. It's making waves at the indulgent end of the fat spectrum. Sales of its Lay's Bistro Gourmet chips are expected to top $100 million this

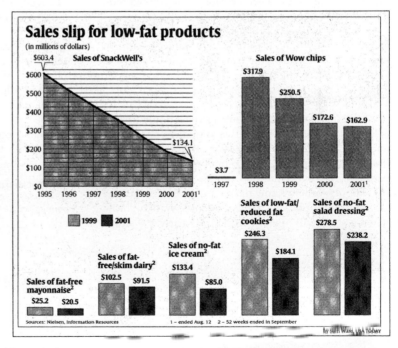

Sales slip for low-fat products
(in millions of dollars)

Sales of SnackWell's: $603.4 (1995) declining to $134.1 (2001[1])

Sales of Wow chips: $3.7 (1997), $317.9 (1998), $250.5 (1999), $172.6 (2000), $162.9 (2001[1])

1999 ▮ 2001

Sales of fat-free mayonnaise[2]: $25.2, $20.5
Sales of fat-free/skim dairy[2]: $102.5, $91.5
Sales of no-fat ice cream[2]: $133.4, $85.0
Sales of low-fat/reduced fat cookies[2]: $246.3, $184.1
Sales of no-fat salad dressing[2]: $278.5, $238.2

Sources: Nielsen, Information Resources
1 – ended Aug. 12   2 – 52 weeks ended in September
By Suh Wah, USA TODAY

year, says Quinn. And executives are expecting big things for the just-introduced Doritos Extremes—thicker, crunchier, more highly seasoned chips. Never mind that more flavor often—but not always—means more fat and calories.

Ben & Jerry's may have the most convincing fat-is-back story of all.

Five years ago, a fat-free line of sorbet accounted for 12% of Ben & Jerry's sales. But sorbet sales fell so quickly that last year the chain dropped the laggard line from grocery stores—although it's still sold at some Ben & Jerry's outlets.

For grocers, "It went from being a priority to get," says brand manager David Stever, "to being a priority to get it out (of the store)."

So why are company executives laughing? Its fatter-than-fat line of premium ice cream is on a tear.

Sales are up 21% this year, says Walt Freeze, chief marketing officer. "It's been years since we've seen anything like this."

Leading the charge: the 2-Twisted line, which combines two Ben & Jerry's ice creams in a single carton. Among them is Half Baked, a mixture of Chocolate Fudge Brownie and Chocolate Chip Cookie Dough, and Monkey Wrench: banana meets peanut butter cup.

Sam Lu is a Ben & Jerry's junkie. The computer programmer from San Dimas, Calif., figures he puts down about a pint a week of Aloha Macadamia Nut. Eats it right out of the carton, too.

Lu, who works out three times weekly, can't stomach low-fat anything, least of all, low-fat ice cream. "If you want ice cream, you want ice cream," says Lu, "not some pasty yogurt taste."

Hot doughnuts now

Executives at Krispy Kreme have no doubt that fat is king. It's not just because the company expects revenue to jump nearly 50% this year compared with last. It's also because of the 6,000 e-mail messages the company receives every month from its "fans."

People want to know the recipe for the best-selling glazed doughnuts. (It's a secret.) People want to know when a store will open near them. (Nearly 200 stores now—and 40 more next year.) But almost no one asks how many calories are in the doughnuts. (Fudge- iced, cream-filled doughnut: 340 calories; 160 from fat).

The typical customer rarely buys one doughnut. Instead, a customer often buys a dozen and takes the box to the office.

"You can become the office hero for about $5,"

> **Mmm, mmm, fat: Sam Lu works out three times a week but can't shake his craving for Ben & Jerry's Aloha Macadamia Ice Cream. He scarfs a pint a week. If you want ice cream, you want ice cream."**

says Stanley Parker, senior vice president of marketing.

If not for the nation's souring on all things low fat, there probably would be no Six Dollar Burger.

That's what the Carl's Jr. fast-food chain is calling its newest, sloppiest-ever burger. It's got a half-pound of beef and two slices of cheese. Never mind that one Six Dollar Burger comes loaded with 949 calories—and 64 grams of fat.

Americans are sick and tired of depriving themselves of good things, says Bob Wisely, executive vice president of marketing at the burger chain. "It's all about indulgence," he says.

Is it ever. In just 6 months, the Six Dollar Burger has become the chain's top-selling burger. One in five customers buys it. But besides its hefty size and gooey ingredients, the Six Dollar Burger has another strategic selling point: It goes for $3.95.

"Low-Fat Industry Loses Out as Consumers Favor Flavor," *USA Today*, October 15, 2001, p. 1Bff. Reprinted with permission.

When Free Samples Become Saviors

Point-of-Sweat, Point-of-Thirst Marketing Offers Freebies When They Are Most Needed

BY GEOFFREY A. FOWLER
Staff Reporter of THE WALL STREET JOURNAL

Unilever is hitting the gym with a new marketing strategy: point-of-sweat sampling.

Starting next month, aerobics instructors at Bally's Fitness Clubs nationwide will hand out Dove body wash, deodorant and face cloths to their perspiring students at the end of class. The idea is to dispense the personal-hygiene freebies at a point when consumers might actually use them.

It is the same concept as point-of-thirst sampling, increasingly used by beverage companies who dole out cold drinks to parched pedestrians on hot streets. Now there is point-of-dirt sampling, used by makers of stain removers and hand cleansers to snare consumers at mall food courts. Coming soon: point-of-relief sampling, when Dr. Scholl's, made by **Schering-Plough** Corp., will bestow blister treatment cushions on runners at the Chicago Marathon in October.

Marketers say the strategy solves a classic problem: You can place a sample in a shopper's hands, but you can't make her use it. In point-of-use sampling, "the product is thought of as a savior—a white knight given to me exactly at the point where I really need

to wash my hands," says Tom Libonate, president and chief operating officer of the Ryan Partnership, a promotional marketing firm. **Unilever,** the Anglo-Dutch consumer-products company, has hired Ryan to give away its Lever2000 hand wipes in food courts and petting zoos.

On a recent 98-degree afternoon, a **Starbucks** Corp. "chill patrol" doled out frozen Frappuccino samples and two-for-one coupons to the sweaty masses passing through Manhattan's Union Square during rush hour. "On a hot day like today, it's like manna on the sidewalks of New York," said Judy Yaskin, 59 years old, gratefully sipping her icy 3-ounce chocolate confection.

Sampling has become a \$1.2 billion industry, a steadily growing portion of the \$249 billion spent annually on consumer promotions, says Claire Rosenzweig, executive director of Promotion Marketing Association Inc. Now, as consumer demand slows and corporate advertising budgets become pinched, marketers are trying to perfect the practice, and they are finding that shrewd targeting can increase potential conversion to brand loyalty.

"We're getting smarter," says Michael Murphy, Unilever's director of home and personal-care promotions. "You must be much more precise in what, where and how you deliver samples."

Instead of just setting up supermarket displays, Pierce Promotions & Event Management Inc., an events-marketing agency based in Portland, Maine, scouts for ideal sampling sites by tapping into a computer database of America's 300 most-popular street corners, plus 10,000 festivals and sporting events called "intercept locations." Nabisco Biscuit, a division of **Kraft Foods** Inc., has hired Pierce to give away a million Milk-Bone Soft 'N Chewy treats in dog parks to pooches out for a stroll. Last year, Life Savers, another Kraft product, had the Ryan Partnership ship two million of its Creme Savers candies to office buildings, with instructions that the treats be placed in employee kitchenettes, ready for when the munchies hit.

While many companies won't detail how sampling programs translate into long-term sales, many say they often see a short-term boost on a new product. When **H.J. Heinz** Co. cooked lunch for 10,000 people in Jacksonville and Orlando, Fla., to introduce 7-ounce packets of StarKist tuna in a pouch, sales jumped 20% in a month. A study by ACNielsen, Brand Marketing Magazine and the Promotion Marketing Association last year found that sampling events produced an average 36% spike in sales in the near term. Sunflower Group, Inc., a promotional services firm in Overland Park, Kan., finds that 80% of targeted consumers happily accept a sample from its "product ambassadors," and 10% to 15% also ask followup questions about the product.

The cost of producing the giveaways can make sampling the most expensive per-capita form of marketing. But advocates of the point-of-use approach say it is more cost-efficient and can save money overall. Doling out 530,000 packets of Cremora Royale, a powdered coffee creamer, by gluing the samples on coffee-cup sleeves in September will cost Eagle Family Foods about \$80,000. But the promotion, organized by BriteVision Media of San Francisco, will better target Cremora's "upscale" brand to \$3-a-latte shoppers, and cost considerably less than a standard Sunday-newspaper insert that might run half a million dollars, says Christy Gilmartin, senior brand manager for Cremora.

"The traditional delivery vehicles are becoming passe," says Steve Sickinger, senior vice president of sales at Sunflower. "The more you want to reach a specific target, the more clever you have to become."

Safe at home and all plugged in

Electronics grow more elaborate as we embrace 'local area nesting'

By Mike Snider
USA TODAY

For Todd Skelton, there's no place like home.

The 37-year-old automotive executive has gone to extremes in outfitting his Palm Beach, Fla., home with a full complement of entertainment gadgets, including an automation and security system, and a theater with three rows of seats for him and his wife, relatives and friends to watch DVD movies on a 12-foot screen.

Although the work was finished in July, Skelton says, the home theater has been a particular source of comfort for his family—including stepchildren and their kids—since the Sept. 11 attacks. "It seems to me that there's a big shift toward spending more time at home and families' homes," he says.

Some trend spotters call it "cocooning," others call it "nesting." But the movement toward spending more time at home—and feathering our nests with more elaborate and entertaining diversions—may be more than a fad.

That, at least, is the hope of the makers and sellers of digital entertainment gadgets. Even though overall electronics sales dipped slightly in 2001, according to numbers to be released today at the annual Consumer Electronics Show in Las Vegas, sales of DVD players, digital TVs and home theater packages spiked significantly—and are predicted to continue their rise this year.

Consumers "want to stay in contact with loved ones. They want to be entertained. They want to have an escape, a diversion through home entertainment," says Jeff Joseph of the Consumer Electronics Association, which runs the CES show, expected to draw about 100,000 industry and media representatives.

The terrorist attacks may not have started the trend toward cocooning, but the events of the past few months have given it added momentum. "People were looking to balance their lives more coming out of the late '90s into the new century as the dot-com economy started to crash," says Cary Silvers of consumer research firm RoperASW. "People were starting to spend more time with family, usually at home."

But since the attacks, people "are keeping to their safe havens," Silvers says. Roper even has coined a term for the trend: "local area nesting."

A Roper phone survey over the weekend found that nearly one in four people intend to spend more on entertainment for the home this year—"a significant number," says Silvers, "and it has already been on an upward trend." More than 25% intend to rent more movies.

About 30% say they'll spend more on technology to keep them connected to family and friends. And in other surveys since Sept. 11, 29% of people said they were more likely to spend even more time at home and 27% were more likely to attend church or synagogue. That suggests nesting doesn't mean simply hunkering down and shunning the world.

"People are rediscovering their local community," Silvers says. "But the home becomes the center, almost like nuclei. . . . The home is the comfort zone."

Family therapist Evan Imber-Black isn't convinced cocooning will become instilled as long-term behavior. "At the beginning, people were staying put and investing in things they could do at home," says Imber-Black, of the Ackerman Institute for the Family in New York. "But it seems that was a more temporary thing. People are out again."

On the other hand, Imber-Black and her husband did buy a DVD player over the holidays—and a second one for their son. "We were looking into that way before 9/11 and just decided this year's Christmas was the time to get it."

As for "local area nesting," she says, "I think it remains to be seen. We are very early in the process. What we have seen in many families is a desire to connect with extended family to do work to repair certain relationships."

However, at Scottsdale, Ariz.-based market research firm Cahners In-Stat, tech analyst Neil Strother thinks the plugged-in nest may prove to have staying power. Consumers have decided to "stay home a little more and are doing more low-end purchases, maybe getting a (Nintendo) GameCube or (Microsoft) Xbox instead of a PC," he says. "Watching a movie or playing a game together is maybe more important than running off to Europe or taking vacations."

And after several years of increased importance

for personal computers and home information, "the television is becoming more important in the home again," says Dave Arland of Thomson Consumer Electronics, which makes RCA products. "People are spending more time in front of the tube."

That may or may not be a healthy development, says Shirley Glass, a Baltimore-area psychologist and marital therapist. "If people are buying more equipment for home entertainment, does that result in family

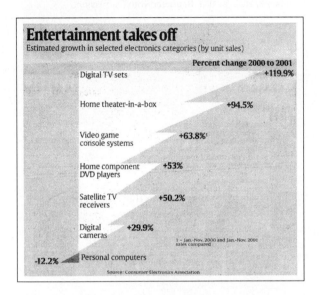

Entertainment takes off

Estimated growth in selected electronics categories (by unit sales)

Percent change 2000 to 2001

Digital TV sets	+119.9%
Home theater-in-a-box	+94.5%
Video game console systems	+63.8%¹
Home component DVD players	+53%
Satellite TV receivers	+50.2%
Digital cameras	+29.9%
Personal computers	-12.2%

1 – Jan.-Nov. 2000 and Jan.-Nov. 2001 sales compared

Source: Consumer Electronics Association

time, or is it creating something where each person is more in their own hives within the cocoon?"

She has childhood memories of a neighbor who had the first TV on the block, who hooked the set to an extension cord and put it on the lawn. Neighbors brought out chairs and watched a Joe Louis boxing match. "Maybe this is the 21st-century version," she says. "People who have huge home entertainment systems often share them with friends and neighbors. Then it becomes a very nice social thing."

For much of the past decade, home PCs and other information appliances helped propel sales of electronics. But in 2001, PC sales dropped about 13% and are expected to decline again this year, according to factory sales figures to be released today at the show.

"Entertainment was the winner in 2001," Strother says.

Holiday sales at Denver-based Ultimate Electronics suggest that buyers are still focusing on the home. "People are a little more selective about their purchases, and I think we are in favor with the consumers now," says Dave Workman, president of the 36-store chain.

The low-priced DVD players that appeared over the holidays—some selling for less than $100—helped fuel consumer interest. DVD movies not only deliver video twice the quality of VHS, but also CD-quality surround sound.

Entry-level home theater surround-sound packages dropped to as little as $300, while systems complete with DVD players are being introduced at the show for as little as $350. Big-screen digital TVs, including sets that can display the high-definition broadcasts slowly being rolled out by the networks, have slid from $3,000-plus to less than $1,800.

"Three or four years ago, home theater was thought of as something rich people went out and bought. Now more people look at it as a way to expand on their television," Workman says.

With more than 25 million DVD players sold in less than five years, the product has become the most successful consumer electronics product ever, adopted more quickly than TVs, CD players or satellite TV systems. "That is obviously having a spillover effect to better televisions and better sound systems."

The industry would like to reach a similar critical mass soon in digital TV. Already about 225 broadcast stations are transmitting DTV signals, some in the high-definition format that offers far more clarity than current broadcasts, in a cinema-like widescreen format. Satellite TV services DirecTV and the Dish Network also offer high-definition movies and programming. But copy-protection issues in Hollywood and compatibility battles with the cable TV industry have slowed the rollout.

Nonetheless, consumers are moving to the new high-tech sets in anticipation of the future. Sales of regular, non-digital TV sets have decreased for two years in a row, while sales of digital sets nearly doubled last year. (Sales of non-digital sets still outnumber sales of digital models 15 to 1.) And digital sets are designed to improve the viewing of DVD movies and standard broadcasts.

The promise of a better picture recently drew Larry Baker, 66, of Rancho Palos Verdes, Calif., to invest in a high-definition TV set. "Prices have started to come down, and we're getting a fair bandwidth," says Baker, who is retired.

As a result, he is considering buying a second digital TV to replace the 60-inch projection model in his den. "I certainly go to the theater a lot less. I wait for movies to come out on DVD," he says.

Installers of custom home theaters, security and other electronics systems are getting similar signals. In a survey to be released today, installers say they expect business to increase 25% to 30% next year, compared with the 15% to 20% increase that has been standard over the past five years, according to the Custom Electronics Design & Installation Association.

After the Sept. 11 attacks, there was an immediate uptick in custom installation requests, says CEDIA president Jeff Hoover, president of the West Palm Beach, Fla., firm Audio Advisors, which installed Todd Skelton's system.

"A large number of people had been putting off their (projects) and decided it was time to go ahead," he says. "People are designing their homes so they don't really need to leave all that often."

That's certainly true at Skelton's home, where his next project involves remodeling the kitchen and adding to the master bedroom. "There's a certain level of comfort in your home," he says. "It's always been difficult to get me out of the house, but I used to feel like I needed to get out of the house. Now, I want to do everything to avoid getting out of the house."

"Safe at Home and All Plugged In: Electronics Grow More Elaborate as We Embrace 'Local Area Nesting,'" *USA Today*, January 8, 2002, p. 1Dff. Reprinted with permission.

31

Exchanges

Making It Work

Meet Aaron Gillum: the face of one online exchange

BY PETER LOFTUS

If you think customer-service work for a retail Web site sounds tough, imagine being responsible for a $10 million order for car-axle assemblies.

That's the kind of high-octane duty Aaron Gillum is charged with every day. He's what's known as an auction engineer for **Covisint** LLC, a business-to-business online exchange created jointly in February 2000 by the Big Three auto makers, **DaimlerChrysler** AG, **Ford Motor** Co., Dearborn, Mich., and Detroit-based **General Motors** Corp., in order to move more parts purchasing online to save costs and speed up buying cycles. Other companies that have since bought smaller stakes in the venture are Japan's **Nissan Motor** Co., French auto makers **Renault SA** and **PSA Peugeot Citroen,** and software makers **Oracle** Corp., Redwood Shores, Calif., and **Commerce One** Inc., Pleasanton, Calif. The Big Three are both owners and customers of Covisint, which gets a percentage of the value of all auctions. A total of 11 auto makers worldwide are Covisint customers. And some 5,000 suppliers are registered to participate in Covisint auctions.

Auction engineers set up auctions after purchasing managers at auto makers contact them with parts orders. A group of auction engineers works full-time on behalf of a certain auto maker. For instance, Mr. Gillum, who joined Covisint in October 2000, and a dozen others work exclusively with Daimler-Chrysler. Auction engineers helped Covisint handle more than $50 billion in auto-parts orders last year. In its biggest auction ever, the Southfield, Mich., company conducted a four-day auction last May in which Daimler-Chrysler purchased about $2.6 billion in auto parts. Compare that with eBay Inc., the top consumer auction Web site, which reported fourth-quarter gross merchandise sales of almost $2.4 billion.

"These auctions are for millions of dollars," says Mr. Gillum, 24 years old. "We're not messing around here with $10 at a time. You're not buying a digital camera or something like that."

Key to making such megadeals run more efficiently—and faster—is the Internet. In the old days, when fax machines were at the cutting edge of communications, auto-supply auctions could take several days or weeks. An auto maker would invite several suppliers to bid for a product order. The suppliers would mail or fax in their bids, with no way of knowing what others were bidding. Purchasing managers at the auto maker would sometimes ask for a new round of bidding in an effort to get a lower price. Or the purchasing manager would call a supplier and ask for a lower bid, but wouldn't say exactly how low.

Now, an auction can be wrapped up in as little as 10 minutes online—Covisint schedules auctions to run at least that long but the average auction lasts about 45 minutes. Once the auction starts, suppliers can place their bids and instantly see what others are bidding so they know how much to adjust their own price.

Prep Work

To DaimlerChrysler and many of its suppliers, Mr. Gillum is the face of Covisint. A DaimlerChrysler purchasing manager usually gives Mr. Gillum at least two weeks to set up an auction. When first notified, he asks the buyer for important details: date and time of the auction, parts numbers, a "quick-and-dirty" description of the parts needed, volume of parts and the opening price or the maximum amount the buyer is willing to pay.

Then the buyer must give Mr. Gillum a list of specific suppliers to invite to bid at the auction. Covisint recommends that the buyer invite at least three suppliers in order to get competitive bids. Some auctions end up with as many as 20 suppliers, Mr. Gillum says. Suppliers range in size from $50 million in annual revenue to more than $1 billion. Only the buyer and the invited suppliers can gain access to the online auction using a secret password on the Covisint Web site.

After getting the basics from the buyer, Mr. Gillum notifies the suppliers that they've been invited, and he provides details of what the auto maker wants to buy. The suppliers also can find this information on Covisint's Web site.

A few days before a scheduled auction, Mr. Gillum runs a trial auction with the suppliers to ensure that suppliers know what to expect and what to do. He types in "Part X" and enters an opening bid of $3 million and the suppliers enter their dummy bids. During the trial and real auctions, he can communicate with the suppliers by an instant-messaging system to answer questions and give live updates.

When auction day rolls around, he likes to visit the DaimlerChrysler purchasing manager's office to watch the auction unfold, especially if the manager is new to online parts auctions.

Others engineers also like to be with the buyers during auctions because a lot of money is riding on the outcomes, says auction engineer Aaron Parsons. In mid-January, he helped Covisint conduct a 13-hour auction for DaimlerChrysler. For some items,

Chrysler saved 40% of the opening price, he says. And an engineer was with the buyer at that event.

"Because it's real time, there's not a lot of margin for error," Mr. Parsons says. But he isn't overwhelmed by all those zeros behind the dollar signs. "We're putting the same effort into a hundred-million-dollar event as we put into a small event."

When there is a problem, Mr. Gillum and the other auction engineers are the ones both sides turn to. If a supplier is having technical difficulties placing a bid online, he calls Mr. Gillum.

"Some people ask if they can make bids from home," Mr. Gillum says. "I say, 'You can do it from home, but you shouldn't. You probably want to do it from a place with a high-speed Internet connection.'" He says the problem is that some suppliers merely shell out $1,000 for a personal computer and use a dial-up Internet connection, which can have access problems, to participate in Covisint auctions.

If a DaimlerChrysler purchasing manager doesn't know how to run an online auction, Mr. Gillum drives 15 miles north to the auto maker's North American headquarters in Auburn Hills, Mich.

One morning late last year, he was about to run a DaimlerChrysler auction with a half-dozen suppliers. (Because of Covisint's confidentiality policy, Mr. Gillum says he can't disclose details about the suppliers or the Chrysler parts being ordered.) At the last minute, a supplier called Mr. Gillum to say a storm had knocked out his power supply, so he couldn't gain access to the online auction. The supplier was calling on his cellphone.

Mr. Gillum immediately notified Daimler-Chrysler and the other suppliers that the auction would be postponed until the afternoon, hoping power would be restored by then. As a backup plan, if power was still out, he arranged for the supplier to phone in a bid to Covisint technicians, who would then enter the bid on the supplier's behalf.

"About 10 minutes before the auction started, the power came back on and the guy's computer came back on," Mr. Gillum says.

Luckily, most glitches aren't that complicated. "The biggest problem is [that suppliers have] lost their password," he says. When some suppliers worry that everyone in the industry will be able to see how much they're bidding, Mr. Gillum tells them that only the auction participants can see bids, and even then, the Covisint Web site only lists the lead bids and doesn't identify who made them.

Be Prepared

Most important, Mr. Gillum tells suppliers to know what their lowest possible bid will be before an auction. Some auctions are over in 10 minutes, which is hardly enough time to crunch the numbers if the prep work hasn't been done.

If a bidder places a bid within the last minute of the auction, it goes into "overtime"

(Cont.)

and is extended three minutes. During those three minutes, if a new low bid is placed, the auction's extended for another three minutes, and so on.

"Even if you get beat, at least you have a parameter for market pricing," Mr. Gillum says. "You always know what the lead bid is. You always have a chance to counter the lead bid."

Mr. Loftus is a special writer for Dow Jones Newswires in New York.

32

B2B Recipe Eludes Grocers

By Murray Coleman
Investor's Business Daily

A food fight is taking place. But it's not the sort seen in movies like "Animal House."

Companies are battling to be the e-marketplace of choice for the consumer packaged goods industry, a potentially huge market.

A feeding frenzy is raging as a host of online marketplaces have sprung up. They all want to be the preferred online conduit between packaged goods makers, retailers and suppliers.

The problems that have risen in the disappointing online business-to-business arena are magnified in the consumer goods field. This has led to a hodgepodge of e-marketplaces, with none doing great.

"It's a comedy," said Robert Rubin, a Forrester Research Inc. analyst. "The retailers don't trust the manufacturers, and the manufacturers don't trust the retailers."

A Year Later

As a result, many e-marketplaces have sprung up. Many are small niche players. But three large ones emerged last year:

▌ **Transora.** It's the brainchild of the Grocery Manufacturers of America. Founders include Coca-Cola Co., Procter & Gamble Co. and Sara Lee Corp. Its 57 initial members invested a total of $250 million to get the online marketplace running.

▌ **WorldWide Retail Exchange.** Where product makers formed Transora, retailers formed this exchange. Its 53 founders include Albertson's, Safeway Inc., Kmart Corp. and Target Corp.

▌ **GlobalNetXchange.** Retailers formed this exchange as well. Major backers include Kroger Co., Sears, Roebuck and Co. and J. Sainsbury PLC. These three alone spend $175 billion a year on supplies from more than 50,000 suppliers.

All three of these big exchanges have had rough sailing. Few suppliers, retailers or consumer product makers have wanted to align exclusively with any of these exchanges, says Gale Daikoku, an analyst with market research firm Gartner Inc.

"Even some of the founders of these exchanges are hedging their bets until they know which ones will turn out to be profitable and which won't," she said.

Where GNX and WWRE might compete somewhat with Transora, they compete directly with one another. Transora also has a big rival. The European-based CPG eMarketplace also focuses on makers of consumer goods.

"At first, Transora focused on North America and CPG concentrated on Europe,"

Uncrowded E-Marketplace

The vast consumer packaged goods industry is slowly moving more transactions to big, public Internet e-marketplaces. It's estimated that most electronic transaction will be on private Internet marketplaces or with an earlier type of private system called an electronic data interchange

Transaction value, in billions

Exchange	2001e	2002e	2003e	2004e	2005e
Private	$0.5	$9	$20	$35	$63
Public	0.5	1	5	17	25
EDI	235.0	240	237	225	203
Total	236.0	250	262	277	291

Makers of consumer packaged goods are ahead of retailers in using e-commerce systems

% of businesses using, 2000

Type	Manufacturers	Retailers
EDI	71%	52%
Exchanges	12	12
No electronic systems	17	36

Estimated % of businesses using, 2003

Type	Manufacturers	Retailers
EDI	32%	48%
Exchanges	68	22
No electronic systems	0	20

(Cont.)

said Daikoku. "Now they're both trying to get into each other's core markets."

These online battles hardly resemble a clash of Titans. Gartner and Forrester doubt that any of these four big exchanges handle more than 1% to 2% of the total buying of any of the big companies that founded them. And no exchange has distinguished itself from the others.

"All of these exchange have similar technologies and appear to be providing similar services," Daikoku said.

One hurdle for the big, public consumer goods e-marketplaces is that the industry already has so many private exchanges. And these exchanges still do a lot of the business, says Jim Balderston, an analyst with market research firm Sageza Group.

"There's been a lot of smoke blown around this whole concept of public exchanges backed by large players," he said. "But everyone's drowning in all of the hype. The pressure is building for consolidation."

Communication A Must

Even the big e-marketplaces agree. "Is there going to be a shakeout? Yes, that's definitely going to happen," said Joe Laughlin, chief executive of GNX. "But there will be survivors."

Earlier this year, Transora and GNX talked about working together on a project. Transora opted not to go ahead with it, says Laughlin. "But we continue to keep in contact with all of our peers," he said.

The online exchanges must keep in touch with one another whether there's consolidation or not, says Transora spokesman Jeffrey Smith. That's because no consumer goods maker or retailer wants to be shut off from any other.

For now, it matters little. Most consumer packaged goods sales and supply purchase are done via phone or fax. Forrester predicts that consumer packaged goods makers will sell $1 billion worth of product online this year. That would be a mere 0.2% of this market's total sales.

That'll rise to $88 billion in 2005, still a small percentage. In contrast, the industry will do $200 billion in sales in 2005 via older electronic data interchange systems, Forrester says. EDI systems are small, private networks that predate the Web.

It's hard for a company to tweak its EDI to work with the Internet, says analyst Rubin. And since these companies rely so much on their EDI systems, they aren't as motivated to jump onto Internet e-marketplaces.

"It's going to be a while before this industry converts to more complete online systems," said Rubin. "The big question is how many of these exchanges will be able to hold out until enough retailers and manufacturers make the transition."

"B2B Recipe Eludes Grocers," *Investor's Business Daily*, December 4, 2001, p. A8. Reprinted by permission.

33

Silicon Valley techies suit up Army with sleeker gear
Engineers retool clunky gadgets quickly, cheaply

By Edward Iwata
USA TODAY

On a pitch-black night last fall, 40 Army Rangers parachuted into the forests at Fort Polk, La., simulating combat against an Eastern Bloc enemy.

They were outfitted with the "Land Warrior," a computer system full of high-tech firearms and communications gear.

On the ground, the troops used Land Warrior's satellite-mapping device and found each other in 30 minutes. It can take two or three hours using flashlights and paper maps.

One Ranger, peering through a heat-sensing thermal sight on his M-4 rifle, spotted "enemy" snipers in the dark 300 meters away and opened fire, "killing" them. The Rangers finished their mission twice as fast as a typical platoon.

"It's powerful technology," says Army Ranger Sgt. Chris Augustine. "We were apprehensive at first, but now we're begging for it."

That's a stunning turnaround from three years ago, when soldiers hated the clunky Land Warrior system and ripped it off their backs. The $2 billion project was on its deathbed after defense contractor Raytheon built a prototype called the "turtle shell" that was blasted by the General Accounting Office. Since then, the Land Warrior has been resurrected by a team of Silicon Valley engineers who retooled it in six months.

The firms—Pacific Consultants, Exponent, Pemstar and Computer Sciences—ignored rigid Army specifications and brainstormed ideas. They lightened the Land Warrior computer harness, wrote new software and worked closely with soldiers.

Today, the new Land Warrior is earning rave reviews from troops testing it. "A dramatic improvement," says Army Lt. Col. Scott Crizer. Military officials say

48,000 Land Warrior outfits may roll out by 2004 to be used by Army troops in training and combat. Even the Navy has tested the Land Warrior.

The tech firms hail the revised Land Warrior as a victory of their fast-track, entrepreneurial business model over the costlier defense industry model followed by the military for decades. They also tout their use of commercial products, such as Microsoft software and Intel computer chips, instead of pricier technology made by the government or large defense contractors. While corporate behemoths, such as Lockheed Martin

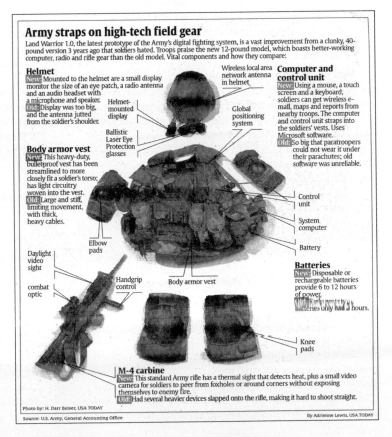

Army straps on high-tech field gear

Land Warrior 1.0, the latest prototype of the Army's digital fighting system, is a vast improvement from a clunky, 40-pound version 3 years ago that soldiers hated. Troops praise the new 12-pound model, which boasts better-working computer, radio and rifle gear than the old model. Vital components and how they compare:

Helmet
New: Mounted to the helmet are a small display monitor the size of an eye patch, a radio antenna and an audio headset with a microphone and speaker.
Old: Display was too big, and the antenna jutted from the soldier's shoulder.

Body armor vest
New: This heavy-duty, bulletproof vest has been streamlined to more closely fit a soldier's torso; has light circuitry woven into the vest.
Old: Large and stiff, limiting movement, with thick, heavy cables.

Computer and control unit
New: Using a mouse, a touch screen and a keyboard, soldiers can get wireless e-mail, maps and reports from nearby troops. The computer and control unit straps into the soldiers' vests. Uses Microsoft software.
Old: So big that paratroopers could not wear it under their parachutes; old software was unreliable.

Batteries
New: Disposable or rechargeable batteries provide 6 to 12 hours of power.
Old: Early rechargeable batteries only had 2 hours.

M-4 carbine
New: This standard Army rifle has a thermal sight that detects heat, plus a small video camera for soldiers to peer from foxholes or around corners without exposing themselves to enemy fire.
Old: Had several heavier devices slapped onto the rifle, making it hard to shoot straight.

Labels: Wireless local area network antenna in helmet; Helmet-mounted display; Global positioning system; Ballistic Laser Eye Protection glasses; Control unit; System computer; Battery; Elbow pads; Daylight video sight; combat optic; Handgrip control; Body armor vest; Knee pads

Photo by: H. Darr Beiser, USA TODAY

Source: U.S. Army, General Accounting Office

By Adrienne Lewis, USA TODAY

and General Dynamics, rule the defense world, the small tech firms say their Land Warrior success has caught the attention of military brass and defense companies.

"We made it the classic Silicon Valley way: quicker, cheaper and better," says Hugh Duffy, a former Pacific Consultants executive. "It's an uphill battle, but we think we can transform the old model."

Six years ago, the Army hoped the Land Warrior would revolutionize combat by creating the world's first digital soldier. Part of the Pentagon's sweeping $21 billion drive to create a digital battlefield, the Land Warrior would give the Army the same dominance on the ground that the Air Force enjoys in the skies.

In theory, the early Land Warrior would be an awesome fighting machine. Infantrymen would use a computer and radio harness, voice communication and wireless e-mail, a satellite-mapping system and other high-tech gear.

"The idea was to make our soldiers invincible," says Justus Decher, executive director of business development at Pemstar.

After intense bidding, the contract to develop Land Warrior was awarded to Raytheon, maker of the Tomahawk cruise missile and the world's No. 3 defense contractor, with $17 billion in revenue.

TROUBLED TIMES

But the first prototype by Raytheon was a 40-pound monstrosity, according to GAO reports, Army officials and defense industry experts. During testing, soldiers who rolled on the ground got stuck on their backs like tortoises. The helmet was so heavy, troops who were crawling couldn't lift their heads to fire rifles. A thick helmet cable got snagged in bushes so often that soldiers ripped it out.

The early Land Warrior software rarely worked, and batteries for computers and radios lasted far less than the desired 12 hours. The system failed water tests, leaking badly. During jump exercises, the bulky computer packs wouldn't fit under soldiers' parachutes.

"It was a classic example of guys sitting around a table, wishing they had this and that," says retired Army Lt. Col. Tim Eads, an analyst at the Center for Strategic & International Studies. "You ended up with a 50-pound piece of metal that soldiers hated dragging around."

Raytheon declined to talk about problems raised in the GAO report but said the company laid the foundation for the Land Warrior concept. "We believe our efforts were invaluable to (the success of) the Land Warrior," says Raytheon executive David Martin.

Meanwhile, the cost of developing the Land Warrior units had soared to $2.1 billion from $1.4 billion, according to the GAO. Congress was threatening to cut off funding, and Army officials were under pressure to kill the program.

An intense Army colonel named Bruce Jette revived the Land Warrior system, according to military and defense industry insiders. Jette, a no-nonsense engineer with a doctorate in physics from the Massachusetts Institute of Technology, has a personal stake in the project's success: His son is studying at West Point.

To troubleshoot, in early 1999 Jette brought in high-tech consultants Exponent, a Silicon Valley firm that studies engineering and structural failures and accidents.

The firm felt that Raytheon had followed Army specs for the project too closely. The old prototype had to be trashed and a new computer and radio system built.

Raytheon strongly objected, say military and defense industry sources. The company had spent four years and millions of dollars developing the Land Warrior. It needed more work, but not a complete overhaul, they felt.

"We fulfilled our contractual obligations and designed what the government requested," says Raytheon's Martin.

In tense meetings and phone calls, Army officials asked Raytheon several times to work with the Silicon Valley engineers to change the Land Warrior. Raytheon refused, according to military and defense industry experts.

"Raytheon had a lot of ego and technical talent invested in the project," says Dan Causey, the Army's chief of technical management for the Land Warrior program. "They felt they were at the top of their game, and we hadn't convinced them. It was a real impasse."

The Silicon Valley engineers felt Raytheon could build missile systems but couldn't make cheap, reliable computer setups the way they could. Over beers at nearby bars, the engineers clashed over everything from software standards to computer chip speeds.

The budding partnership crumbled when Exponent refused to sign a subcontractor agreement with lead contractor Raytheon. Frustrated Army officials told Exponent to charge ahead anyway and design a new Land Warrior.

GOING OFF THE SHELF

The Silicon Valley engineers slapped together a crude model in three months. They went to retailers Best Buy and Fry's Electronics and bought several

(Cont.)

cheap, off-the-shelf products, including Microsoft Windows CE software and a wireless card to allow Land Warrior computers to send data.

The most critical technical step: They wrote the software in common programming language used by most software engineers, rather than using old government programming language, as Raytheon had.

The Army sped up the months-long military procurement process by staging a Silicon Valley-style "bake-off" in late 1999 in Menlo Park, Calif. The bidders—Pacific Consultants, Raytheon and Motorola—demonstrated their proposed Land Warrior computer and software designs before a roomful of Army engineers.

"It was like the gunfight at the OK Corral," Duffy says.

Pacific Consultants said it could finish its prototype in six months for $2 million—more quickly and cheaply than the other bidders. The price tag for Pacific Consultant's prototype was $30,000 a unit, while Raytheon's version would have cost more than $60,000, say defense contractors and Army officials.

The Army decided in one day, choosing Pacific Consultants to design the Land Warrior's hardware, software and radio systems. The next year, Pacific Consultants led a consortium that won a $35 million contract to make the prototypes. In coming years, the military might dole out up to $18 billion to contractors to manufacture and repair Land Warrior units.

Soldiers say the newest Land Warrior is the best version yet. At 12 pounds, the vest and body armor fit snugly around a soldier's torso. Its Microsoft Windows 2000 software still has bugs but is nearing the project goal of 10 days of use without breaking down.

Soldiers who've grown up with computers love the Land Warriors, says Army Ranger Sgt. Don Boyle, who notes that a Delta Force Land Warrior video game is used during training at West Point.

Mindful that billions of dollars have been spent on ill-fated defense projects over the decades, the military hopes to buy more commercial technology. Even the Navy Seals have bought commercial speedboats and reinforced them to withstand gunfire.

"The Army may have led the world in solid-state electronics in the 1960s, but today, our technology expenditures aren't even one high-tech company's R&D budget," says Jette. "We have to use technologies in the commercial sector to our advantage."

Analysts say it's unclear, though, whether the Army's success with the Land Warrior will persuade the military and defense industry to change its ways. Too much is at stake, such as the $200 billion, 10-year contract won recently by Lockheed Martin to build the Joint Strike Fighter, a state-of-the-art jetfighter. Conservative military brass fear change. Politicians still want to funnel defense dollars into their districts.

"The forces arrayed against change are pretty formidable," says analyst Christopher Hellman at the Center for Defense Information.

Many of the large defense contractors have decades-old political ties to the Pentagon, Congress and the White House. Unless small tech firms own superior technology, they stand little chance of competing against the big guns.

Yet, the Silicon Valley model might be winning converts. Military experts say two new Army projects to modernize military vehicles and soldiers' communications systems will use commercial technology.

"That's a good sign," says Exponent executive John Geddes. "It means we've been successful."

"Silicon Valley Techies Suit Up Army with Sleeker Gear," *USA Today*, February 7, 2002, p. 1Bff. Reprinted with permission.

Getting Information for
Marketing Decisions

How To Lower Marketing Costs— And Eliminate The Guesswork

By Doug Tsuruoka
Investor's Business Daily

Marketing involves guesswork. It's hard to figure out why a housewife clips a coupon, or buys from one retailer and not another.

A technique called experimental design gets around those bumps. It gauges the impact of many marketing pitches by testing just a few.

It's like a poll or cross-section that uses the smallest sample possible. That makes it unnecessary to test all the marketing approaches.

The idea is to match up all possible combinations, such as pricing, perks and pitches. The process then filters out those that are the biggest hits with consumers.

"If you had 72 e-mails, we could predict which would have the most impact on customers by testing only 16," said Gordon Wyner, a vice president of Mercer Management in Boston. Wyner, with Mercer Vice President Eric Almquist, recently wrote of the approach in the Harvard Business Review.

The big plus is knowing beforehand what works. The technique applies to prices, ads, promos and other offers in various ways to get consumers to bite.

A Better Test

For instance, a test could determine if price sensitivity is higher on taco shells than on taco sauce.

"If there's less sensitivity on taco shells, you could raise prices on that product and improve overall revenues and profits," Wyner said.

You also might use it to test consumer reactions to tastes such as sweet, salty, crunchy and sour.

The technique is especially useful now. Computers make it easy to change prices, promotions and other marketing tools in the blink of an eye.

Many firms use this approach. They include retailer Staples, credit card firm Capital One and Pepsi Bottling Group.

In April, Staples.com slashed by more than half the number of shoppers who drop out of registration without buying anything.

To do this, the $10.9 billion-in-sales company started with a database of 10,000 sample shoppers. It included steady customers as well as those who never bought before.

All buyers register with Staples to have orders delivered. They give addresses and other data.

Fewer Dropouts

Staples found many customers dropped out because they didn't like being asked a lot of questions.

"People felt overwhelmed," said Colin Hynes, Staples' Web site usability director. Staples cut the number of questions from 35 to 30 by merging some queries and making others optional.

The upshot is Staples cut the dropout rate by 53%. "More than half the people who were leaving aren't leaving now, and a majority are buyers," Hynes said.

Capital One also uses the technique to craft credit pitches.

The firm might test six credit card teaser rates, six co-branded finance products with other firms and four annual percentage rates. It also might mix in four insurance packages and eight direct-mail offers. This could result in nearly 500,000 marketing sets to test.

But Capital One knows which work by testing 128 variables.

"Experimental design's really useful for companies like Capital One that have large numbers of customers and face rapid and constant change in their markets," Wyner said.

Pepsi Bottling used a form of experimental design to test its new Mountain Dew Code Red.

The high-caffeine offshoot of Mountain Dew is aimed at inner-city kids, computer geeks and other groups. The company tapped carefully chosen urban, ethnic and other focus groups to "design" the drink.

Each group had eight to 10 persons. They were drawn from a larger pool of 1,000 to 2,000. The group included regular Dew drinkers and those new to the product.

The tests were run by parent PepsiCo. Up to four groups met daily over several months.

That's how Pepsi calibrated the taste, color and packaging of Code Red, resulting in the drink's distinctive candy-red color and cherry taste.

"They wanted a bright, vivid red that we were able to home in on," said Tyler Ricks, a senior marketing manager for Pepsi-Cola Co.

Ricks says Pepsi even had some consumers use a meter-like device with a dial so they could give their answers on a scale of one to 10.

That was handy in choosing packaging. "We heard back loud and clear that the packaging needed to look and feel just like (regular) Mountain Dew," Ricks said.

Such testing saved Pepsi from doing a bigger, more costly survey before its launch in May.

It also saved Pepsi from missteps, like earlier plans for a blue-colored "Arctic Mountain Dew."

The company sold 17 million cases of Code Red in five weeks after the product came out in May. Pepsi thought it would take 34 weeks to sell that many cases.

A.C. Nielsen pegged Code Red as the No. 5 soft drink at convenience stores in June and July. The drink's launch helped Pepsi Bottling's third-quarter net jump 16%.

"It's the first time in a long time that a single product has helped drive growth," Ricks said.

WINGING INTO WIRELESS
It's cheaper and easier to install—and more companies are finding that it pays off big

Three years ago, U.S. Fleet Services considered building a wireless network for its drivers, but soon decided against it. Customizing mobile devices and developing software was too hard, and the company didn't have computer systems robust enough to make it worth the hassle. Then, last year, U.S. Fleet revisited the technology—and this time it put the pedal to the metal.

The reason? These days, wireless is cheaper and easier to deploy—and it's already paying off. In September, U.S. Fleet, which refuels vehicles for customers such as Coca-Cola and Nabisco, began equipping its 200 trucks with mobile devices and wireless connections to its corporate intranet. The price: $1.5 million, a quarter of what it would have cost three years earlier. Now, managers can check drivers' locations online, letting them rearrange routes on the fly—and increase the average number of daily deliveries per truck from six to seven. As soon as drivers fill a client's vehicle, the information is scanned into their handheld computers and zapped off to the network. That lets customers check deliveries immediately on U.S. Fleet's Web site, two days faster than before the system was installed.

Wireless "makes good business sense and doesn't cost an arm and a leg," says Saul Cohen, vice-president of information technology at U.S. Fleet.

Once written off as overhyped and underperforming, wireless is enjoying a resurgence in Corporate America. Thanks to plunging equipment prices, new standards for radio links, and increased cellular coverage, even small companies can afford wireless systems once available only to deep-pocketed giants such as United Parcel Service Inc. "During the past 18 months, companies staggered around, not quite sure whether to touch wireless," says Martin Dunsby, a partner at Deloitte Consulting. "Now the interest is accelerating."

What's fueling the growth? Device makers, ranging from well-known names such as Palm Inc. to industry stalwarts like Symbol Industries are churning out smarter and smaller handhelds. Symbol's standard machine, for example, has gotten a tenfold boost in performance since 1999, while its price and weight have fallen by a third. That makes it cheaper for companies to equip workers and has cut the price of wireless projects in half over the past two years, says researcher

IDC Corp. That, in turn, will help double the number of field reps with wireless devices, to 11 million, this year, says Yankee Group Research Inc. And in hospitals, offices, and factories, a standard called WiFi (a.k.a. 802.11b) that connects devices to wireless networks is simplifying installations. This year, employees using WiFi networks are expected to more than double, to 12 million, according to Gartner Inc. Another boost: Tiny radios can now track parts in warehouses or alert techies when machines are on the blink.

Still, lingering design and technical issues need to be ironed out. Some companies are waiting for the higher-speed wireless networks that phone companies such as Verizon Wireless and Sprint PCS Group are promising this year. Without those networks in place, companies fear their wireless initiatives won't have sufficient reach to make them pay. For instance, coffee distributor Millstone Coffee gave handheld computers to 400 field reps last fall but has delayed wirelessly linking them until connection speeds and coverage improve. And security holes uncovered last year in WiFi technology have sparked concerns about hackers intercepting corporate data.

Where the Wireless Web Works

Businesses flocked to wireless projects as their cost fell by more than 50% in the past two years. Here's what companies are doing:

PROBLEM		PROJECT	PAYOFF
Workers on the move: The roll-out of data networks helps companies improve customer service by getting info to reps more quickly.	**Pepsi Bottling Group's 700 technicians phoned in to get service-call data—and faxed back billing info.**	Now a wireless network sends details to the service rep's handheld. The device zips billing data to the office.	**Service response time cut by 20%. Errors from the old fax system gone. Correct parts ready for pickup.**
Wireless workplaces: Offices are setting up systems that transmit data from the Web or a company's intranet to employees moving about the workplace.	**Staff at St. Luke's Episcopal Hospital in Houston spent too much time on administrative tasks. Handwritten records had potential for errors.**	A wireless network for three of the hospital's floors lets staff check charts, lab results, and patient data, wiping out handwriting errors.	**Staff on the networked floor cut time spent on data entry 30%. The respiratory therapy group cut staff by 20%, saving $1.5 million a year.**
Smart machines: Wireless devices in plants and warehouses can automatically collect data from other computers around them, speeding up work flow and eliminating paperwork.	**Office Depot's 2,000 drivers sorted through info from 40-plus deliveries daily. This led to data-entry errors and slowed inventory tracking.**	Drivers' handheld devices automatically transfer customer data to the company's Web site when they return each evening.	**No more handwritten bills, which reduced customer complaints about missed deliveries by more than 10% last year.**

Data: Gartner Inc., International Planning & Research, Cahners In-Stat Group, Venture Development Corp.

The biggest action is in reaching out to field personnel. In years past, Pepsi Bottling Group Inc.'s 700 soda fountain technicians spent too much time on the phone instead of time fixing the company's 1.3 million vending and fountain machines. Customers called in problems, then a call-center employee paged a technician, who would ring for details about the job. At the end of the day, repair workers would fax in forms detailing their visits—with results not available on Pepsi's intranet until five days later.

That system is on its way to the trash heap. Pepsi's technicians now have off-the-shelf handheld devices from Armonk (N.Y.)-based Melard Technologies Inc. Dispatchers today retrieve from Pepsi's intranet everything the technicians need to know about a job and zap it off to the paperback-sized handheld. When the job's done, the technician sends an electronic bill to headquarters. At the same time, the handheld automatically tells the stockroom which parts were used, so when the technician stops in for supplies, replacements are waiting for pick-up.

The payoff? Pepsi answers calls 20% faster than it used to and has saved $7 million—meaning the project will pay for itself in just two years. And parts replenishment requests are now nearly 100% accurate, vs. 85% in the past, when legibility was a big issue. "We sell soda," says Gary K. Wandschneider, senior vice-president for operations of Pepsi Bottling Group. "When we tried to figure out why customers switched to our competitors, part of the answer was customer service and equipment failure."

Field workers aren't the only ones going wireless. In warehouses, offices, and hospitals, wireless technology gives mobile workers instant access to data. St. Luke's Episcopal Hospital in Houston spent $2.5 million on computers and a WiFi network for three of its 22 floors. Nurses and doctors bring laptops on their rounds, entering treatment info and zapping it to the hospital's intranet. Staff in the departments with wireless have cut data-entry time by 30%, says Gene Gretzer, the hospital's wireless project leader. The respiratory therapy group alone was able to shave staff by 20%, saving $1.5 million while handling 13% more patients.

Increasingly, companies are using wireless devices that talk to each other, cutting out humans entirely. Thermo King Corp., which makes cooling units for trucks and shipping containers, is selling self-monitoring equipment. When a truck returns from a delivery, a radio connected to the Net contacts sensors on the vehicle that track the performance of the cooling machinery. If there's a problem, an alert is sent to a Web site monitored by technicians. That can mean savings of up to $1,000 per truck annually by reducing spoilage and cutting maintenance staff.

Sure, the wireless Web hasn't lived up to expectations for consumers. For businesses though, the mobility of wireless combined with the wealth of data on the Internet are creating a one-two punch.

By Heather Green

"Winging into Wireless," pp. EB8–EB9. Reprinted from the February 18, 2002 issue of *Business Week E.Biz* by special permission, copyright © 2002 by The McGraw-Hill Companies, Inc.

36

Corporate Intelligence

I-Spy

Getting the lowdown on your competition is just a few clicks away

By Susan Warren
Staff reporter of The Wall Street Journal

Pssst! Wanna Get the skinny on a business rival?

The explosion of company Web sites, chat rooms and e-commerce has produced a gold mine of information just waiting to be unearthed by resourceful businesspeople eager for the scoop on a competitor. With time, patience and a few quick keystrokes, you can comb the Web for loads of facts and figures your competitors would rather you didn't know. While you're at it, you might want to check out what people are saying about you.

"The good news is your competition's kimono is more open than ever," says Larry Chase, publisher of Web Digest for Marketers, an online newsletter. "The bad news is, so is yours."

In corporate-speak, it's called gathering competitive intelligence. But let's not mince words. We're talking about good old-fashioned spying with a big plus: You never have to leave your desk.

Ethical Concerns

Sound shifty? Actually, business-ethics experts agree there's nothing wrong with learning what you can about your competitors from the wealth of public information available on the Web. Where you cross the line is if you anonymously coax proprietary information from an unsuspecting competitor, says W. Michael Hoffman, executive director of the Center for Business Ethics at Bentley College in Waltham, Mass.

Stephen Miller, a spokesman for the Society of Competitive Intelligence Professionals, says that his organization's ethical guidelines dictate that you should never misrepresent yourself when gathering information. But not misrepresenting yourself doesn't necessarily mean you have to identify yourself, he adds. Dropping anonymously into a competitors' Web site, Mr. Miller says, is akin to the time-honored business practice of wandering into a rival's store to look over his merchandise, how he's priced it, how he's advertised it and how he's displayed it.

"I'd be silly if I didn't try to find out—in an ethical way—about my competitor's

product," Mr. Hoffman says.

Within these parameters, there are lots of ways to gather tons of useful information using the Web. A multitude of companies have sprung up that will do your searching, sifting and sorting for a fee. But if you're more budget-conscious, or simply want to get a feel for the kind of stuff that's available, there's lots of basic information you can collect yourself. Get ready to spend some time at it, though.

One of Mr. Chase's favorite tricks is to use a standard search site to look up all of the Web pages a business has open on the Internet. For example, at Altavista.com, a list of such pages can be had by typing in the address of the company you're investigating in the following format: url://companyname.com.

Sometimes Mr. Chase has even come across pages that the company meant to keep confidential, but neglected to make secure. "I've uncovered new business presentations that way. People put them up and think nobody will find them," says Mr. Chase.

You can also judge your competitors by the company they keep. At Altavista, the search string link://www.companyname.com will reveal who has Web sites that are linked to those of your rivals. (Also check link://companyname.com—some companies are catalogued with the three w's, and some aren't.) That list will give you an idea of how well-connected your competitor is in the Internet community. It may give you the chance to figure out why some sites are linked to your competitor, and not to your own company's site.

Don't Neglect the Obvious

Before you get too fancy with your searches, though, start with the basics: Check out your competitor's corporate Web site. This seems obvious, but a keen eye and a little reading between the lines can reveal some less-than-obvious insights, spying aficionados say.

Start broadly. Evaluating the design and layout of the Web site can give you clues to the company's sophistication and the image the firm is trying to project. Company profiles can reveal partnerships and general business goals.

For a publicly traded company, comb through the investor-relations site, which lays out the company's financial details, including quarterly reports on profits, losses and unusual expenses. All this is required by law to be public, but it's nice to have it compiled in one place. There are often other useful features, such as management profiles that will tell you the background and experience of the people running the rival firm, and copies of business presentations and speeches laying out corporate strategies and outlooks.

Make sure to review any press releases posted, which can provide information about new products and ventures, or signal trouble with announcements of layoffs or restructuring plans.

Even a company's listing of employment

opportunities can provide fertile hunting grounds, says Curtis Cook, vice president of business intelligence for Global Trade Solutions, an Ottawa, Ontario, partnership that specializes in corporate intelligence gathering.

For example, does Brand X have a lot of openings for product engineers? "Then it would be a safe guess that they're ramping up to put a lot of research and development into a new product line," says Mr. Cook. Or maybe the company is seeking to beef up its sales force, signaling that it has finished the development part, and is getting ready to launch a new product that will need heavy marketing.

Realizing that they've been revealing more than is wise, many companies have begun scaling back the amount of detail they provide on their Web sites, including job postings and product prices. But with persistence, you can sometimes pick up the trail by searching through some of the Web sites that specialize in employment, such as Monster.com or Headhunter.net. There you might find listings that tell you not only what kind of jobs your rival is trying to fill, but how much the company is paying.

Working the Chat Rooms

While you're surfing, drop in on a few message boards and chat rooms dedicated to the company or business you're interested in. There's a lot of frivolous garbage to wade through, but with persistence, you can glean some valuable tidbits from exchanges between employees and between industry experts who also frequent the sites.

For instance, sniping and griping about a boss or policy can reveal chinks in a company's armor. More significantly, you might pick up talk of a new product or process that hasn't made it to the public eye yet.

"Oftentimes employees don't know that what they're talking about is confidential and proprietary," says Global Trade's Mr. Cook. "They're excited about what they're working on and the prospect of being on the cutting edge. So they share those types of things."

If you don't see anything interesting, toss out your own question, suggests Mr. Cook. You never know when you'll find someone eager to talk.

This is an area fraught with ethical concerns, however. Mr. Hoffman, the head of the Center for Business Ethics, views chat-room reconnaissance as ethically acceptable.

"A Toyota salesman can walk into a Honda dealership and ask questions [about nonproprietary information] like 'How do you make your gas tank? How do you sell your radio and CD combo?'" Mr. Hoffman says. This kind of information might be given to any inquisitive person who walked into a dealership. "I don't think I'm unethical in not saying, 'Oh, by the way, I'm with Toyota,'" Mr. Hoffman says.

If the person you're conversing with asks who you are, however, then without question you should reply truthfully. And if a rival should volunteer proprietary information to you during a chat-room conversation or anywhere else, Mr. Hoffman says, you have an obligation to immediately identify yourself.

Know Thyself, Too

Finally, sometimes the most useful information can be what you learn about yourself. It's a good idea to monitor those chat rooms and message boards for what's being said about your own company, too. Or check out the consumer reviews offered on sites like Epinion.com to find out how you stack up against your competitors in the customer's eye.

It all sounds relatively easy. But Internet spying has some big pitfalls, the experts warn. The biggest challenge is simply finding the time to wade through all the information you'll be bringing in. The more specific your intelligence goal (do you want to know more about your competitor's manufacturing processes? financial strength? marketing strategy?), the more focused your search can be. But even finely tailored research, when culling from the six billion pages indexed by the largest search engines, can bring in truckloads of information.

Sorting through your harvest can be a monumental task. And there's no guarantee that what you find is going to be current or accurate, so careful evaluation and analysis is important.

Otherwise, "before you know it, a day has gone by and you've found all kinds of interesting stuff, but none of it may actually be very valuable to you," cautions Mr. Cook.

Professional Help

Firms specializing in corporate intelligence combine their analysis and expertise with sophisticated technology to narrow searches and produce more useful information. One example is **Compete** Inc., Boston, which has developed software that can track Internet users around the Web, observing their shopping and buying habits.

"It's almost like watching shoppers move through Wal-Mart," says Man Jit Singh, Compete's chief executive, "watching which aisles they walk down, which products they pause to ponder, and what they finally buy."

For example, when Internet retailer BarnesandNoble.com put up three new product category tabs for shoppers on its home page, rival Amazon.com asked Compete to evaluate whether shoppers were using the tabs, and whether it was worth creating similar categories on its own site. By reviewing weeks of data from Internet provider firms, which showed what pages were visited and gave basic gender, age and income information, Compete was able to report back to Amazon that only one of the BarnesandNoble tabs was proving popular with shoppers. (BarnesandNoble declined to comment for this article.)

By reviewing user habits, Compete has also been able to guide banks on how to design their Web sites to attract the clientele they desire—young and malleable, or older and affluent, for example. Analyzing user data geographically allows the company to advise a car manufacturer to ship white cars to California and blue cars to Florida. By discovering which cars are proving most popular on a competitor's site, that same car manufacturer might find out that offering buying incentives on a similar car in its fleet could draw more buyers away from the rival.

Companies big and small benefit from corporate intelligence. **Cyveillance** Inc., based in Arlington Va., caters to larger companies with big brand names. Much of its business involves evaluating how a company's brands rank with customers and distributors, and how they're being used or abused. Information provided by Cyveillance has helped companies track down trademark and copyright violators, for instance, says Richard Moore, vice president of marketing.

Since the Sept. 11 terrorists attacks, Cyveillance's services have been sought by companies—and even some government agencies—concerned about security. The same kind of spying techniques used to cull intelligence on competitors can also pick up possibly threatening comments or behavior that might bear closer investigation in today's more security-conscious environment, says Mr. Moore.

Ms. Warren is a staff reporter in The Wall Street Journal's Dallas bureau.

McDonald's Asks Mystery Shoppers What Ails Sales

Undercover Customers to Rate Service and Food Quality; Our Own Give It a 81.9%

By SHIRLEY LEUNG
Staff Reporter of THE WALL STREET JOURNAL

CHICAGO—Sandra Bachmann says, "Two Quarter Pounders with cheese."

It's what hungry people poised at a McDonald's counter tend to say. But Ms. Bachmann actually is hungry for information: Does the employee smile? Is the kitchen clean? Will the order be accurate and hot?

Ms. Bachmann is a mystery shopper, and mystery shoppers represent the latest hope for a turnaround at **McDonald's** Corp. Since Jack Greenberg took over as chief executive in 1998, he has reorganized management, added new menu items and introduced a costly new made-to-order cooking system. But none of that has restored growth to the world's largest restaurant chain. Sales are sluggish at stores open more than a year, and profit has declined four quarters in a row. Just Friday, the company reported it expects to record a fifth straight quarter of profit decline, blaming a weak world economy and unusual charges of up to $245 million relating to severance and unrecoverable costs from its Monopoly-game fraud scandal, among others. U.S. same-store sales also remain slightly negative so far for the fourth quarter.

So Mr. Greenberg's latest strategy involves hiring experts such as Ms. Bachmann—more than 150,000 in all—to evaluate service, cleanliness and food quality using a single set of standards and measurements in more than 13,000 restaurants nationwide. The program is designed to enhance, perhaps even perfect, execution and is based on the premise that large improvements are needed.

The problem: The premise may be flawed.

To gain some sense as to how McDonald's restaurants would fare under such scrutiny, The Wall Street Journal hired one of the nation's largest mystery-shopping companies, Dallas's **Feedback Plus** Inc. Its mystery shoppers visited and prepared reports on 25 McDonald's restaurants in four markets: Dallas, Chicago, New York and Los Angeles.

McDonald's performed well.

The overall score of the 25 McDonald's was about 81.9%, compared with an 80% average for all restaurants—fast-food and sit-down—that are evaluated by Feedback Plus. To provide some comparisons with the 25 McDonald's, Feedback Plus also evaluated eight of **Diageo** PLC's Burger Kings (score: 80.1%) and four each of **Wendy's International** Inc. restaurants (score: 80.7%) and **Tricon Global Restaurants** Inc.'s Taco Bells (score: 77.1%).

A way-below-average score would have left McDonald's with enormous room for improvement. But this outcome raises the question of whether McDonald's could raise its performance to 90% or above. Of the 70 restaurant companies that hire Feedback Plus, very few boast average scores above 90%. And those that do are relatively small, especially compared with McDonald's.

Even if attainable for the giant chain, would a higher score boost its sales? Considering that the biggest challenge facing McDonald's is an overabundance of competitors and consumer choices, operational excellence could help the largest hamburger chain stand out. Not surprisingly, the mystery-shopping industry in particular argues that point. "If they raised their overall scores by a few percentage points, the sales impact could be huge," says Kelly Heatly, restaurant account executive at Feedback Plus and a board member of the Greater Dallas Restaurant Association.

But industry analysts and some restaurateurs aren't so sure. One McDonald's franchisee in Texas has hired her own mystery shoppers and used the evaluations to boost scores to 92% from just above 80%. As scores have risen, "we have not seen a swing in sales," says Karen Lopez McWilliams, a five-store owner who nonetheless supports mystery-shopping because "we ultimately want to make sure we deliver the best."

A spokesman for McDonald's, headquartered in Oak Brook, Ill., says Feedback Plus's scores are irrelevant because the chain is devising its own criteria for mystery shopping. "I don't think they would have the same level of expertise that McDonald's would have in our own restaurant operations and what the standards should be," says spokesman Bill Whitman.

He says mystery shopping can only help the company. "If we stay focused on the

---

We Love to See You Smile?

MCDONALD'S WEAKNESSES

Greeted customer with smile	64%
Repeated order for accuracy	52%
Mentioned food promotion or supersize	36%

MCDONALD'S STRENGTHS

Gave correct order	96%
Received order in less than 3 minutes	72%
Said 'Thank You'	72%

*Visit of 25 McDonald's in New York, Chicago, Dallas and Los Angeles regions Nov. 7 through 15
Source: Feedback Plus Inc.

---

needs of the customers, the sales will take care of themselves," he says.

So where can McDonald's improve? According to the Feedback Plus reports, the chain's weakest category is counter service, where it scored only 72.4%. The survey found that only 64% of employees greeted customers with a smile, even though that is the chain's motto. Only 36% of employees offered customers a food promotion or suggested a larger size, and only 52% of employees summarized the order for accuracy.

McDonald's drive-through service also could be better. Employees handed out proper utensils, such as napkins, only 70% of the time and thanked customers only 50% of the time. Employees mentioned food promotions or suggested a larger size only 20% of the time. Plugging promotions can be especially vital to boosting sales.

Only two out of the 25 restaurants surveyed received perfect scores. Larry Ingram, the owner of a McDonald's in Mesquite, Texas, that scored a 100%, says he doesn't use mystery shoppers. His secret to success? "I'm in my stores every day," says the 40-year McDonald's veteran.

HOW DO YOU FEEL ABOUT A $44 TOOTH-BLEACHING KIT?

Procter & Gamble discovers what the Web is really good for—test marketing.

By: John Gaffney

At Procter & Gamble (*PG*), the operative word these days is experimentation. Take heating pads. Simple enough concept. Millions of Americans get aches and pains and seek relief. So P&G developed ThermaCare Therapeutic HeatWraps, air-activated heat packs that last for eight hours. But one version just isn't enough for P&G. Stiff neck? How about neck-to-arm ThermaCare? Got cramps? Try ThermaCare menstrual. Sore back? Check out lower-back ThermaCare.

You won't find any of these products in a grocery store. But you will find them and many other surprises on P&G's corporate website, PG.com. Each month the $40 billion consumer-goods marketing powerhouse invites online consumers to sample and give feedback on new prototype products. If an item gets rave reviews, P&G might decide to bring it to retail stores. If not, it's history.

Since first dabbling in online research in 1998, the Cincinnati-based company has become the industry's most avid proponent of using the Internet as a fast, cost-effective means for gauging consumer demand for potential new products. It already conducts 40 percent of its 6,000 product tests and other studies online. Procter & Gamble spends about $140 million annually on research, and the company believes that it can cut that figure in half by shifting efforts to the Internet. "Let's say you're introducing a new iteration of a product we'll call Brand X," says Barbara Lindsey, director of the family care business unit at P&G. "It used to be that you would have to conduct traditional focus groups and surveys, and then wait more than two months for the results to be tabulated and interpreted. That's all changed. Now we can e-mail a concept test to our target audience on Thursday and have the results on Monday."

P&G brand manager Val Bogdan-Powers didn't work quite that fast, but aided by Web testing, she recently oversaw one of the most successful product launches in P&G history. In August 2000, when she was ready to launch Crest Whitestrips, a new home tooth-bleaching kit, P&G wasn't sure consumers would go for its steep $44 retail price. So Bogdan-Powers turned to the Web. She began an eight-month campaign offering the strips exclusively on P&G's Whitestrips.com. To promote the online sale, from August to May, Procter & Gamble ran TV spots and advertisements in lifestyle magazines such as *People* and *Good Housekeeping*. It also sent e-mails to customers who had signed up to receive product updates on its website.

"We wanted to pre-seed the marketplace so we could show retailers that there was a huge consumer demand for this product," Bogdan-Powers says. "Then when we introduced it at retail, we would be confident that the product and the price point worked. We were willing to sell a little and learn a lot." What P&G quickly learned was that it had a hit on its hands. In eight months it sold 144,000 whitening kits online. Twelve percent of visitors who registered for product information went on to make a purchase, an enviable conversion rate. With this sales data in hand, Bogdan-Powers was able to persuade retailers to stock the product, even at the high price. Introduced in stores in May and backed by print and TV ad campaigns, Crest Whitestrips had sold nearly $50 million worth of kits by late July—an unqualified success, even by P&G standards.

Despite P&G's conservative public image, the 164-year-old company has been at the forefront of Web innovation since the early days. In 1995 it launched a handful of product-specific sites. By 1999 it had 70-plus online destinations, most of which were little more than promotional vehicles for its more than 300 brands, including Folgers Coffee, Dawn, Pampers, and Tide. It still runs dozens of product-specific sites, but P&G is so sold on the Web that it gave over the staid corporate site, PG.com, to the product-sampling mavens. "P&G has tried absolutely everything on the Internet," says Forrester Research senior analyst Jim Nail. "But they haven't found that Internet advertising moved the needle on sales. Sampling is moving the needle, big time."

P&G is also finding the Internet exceptionally useful in refining existing products. Nowhere is this more in evidence than at Reflect.com, the San Francisco-based

(Cont.)

beauty-care dotcom spun out of P&G in 1999. The site, which lets consumers customize their own beauty products, uses customer feedback to fine-tune its offerings. In order to do so, Richard Gerstein, Reflect.com vice president for marketing and design and a 13-year P&G veteran, says he relies on a sophisticated customer relationship management system by E.piphany to provide his staff with detailed sales data. "Every day I have a report that tells me what's selling well, how much repeat business we had in a certain category, and even how quickly a customer who buys a moisturizer comes back for repeat business," Gerstein says. Gerstein shares this data with P&G and can also tap into any consumer research done at the parent company.

Based on such input, Reflect.com recently revamped its skin-care moisturizer line. "We heard our customers saying, 'I'd like to get even more specific benefits in a moisturizer,'" he says. They also wanted more upscale packaging. Reflect.com delivered both in early June, and skin-care product sales "exploded," Gerstein says, growing 500 percent in six weeks.

P&G's Internet success has not escaped its competitors' notice. During the past year, General Mills and Quaker have followed P&G's lead, embarking on several ambitious online test-marketing projects of their own. In addition, a handful of popular startup sites, including StartSampling.com, FreeSamples.com, and DealoftheDay.com, have sprung up to offer consumers samples of prototype products from big companies like P&G and mom-and-pop shops such as SweetSides, based in Mission Hills, Calif. According to a survey of national marketers by research firm MarketTools of Mill Valley, Calif., online spending by packaged-goods marketers went from $96 million in 1999 to $280 million last year. And if that speeds up the creation of more popular varieties of heat wraps or moisturizer, it has to be a good thing.

39

FACING UP TO CRM

*That pricey new technology promises to track your customers' every move.
But will it help your bottom line?*

By: Brian Caulfield

True story. One of the Big Three Detroit automakers put together a customer relationship management (CRM) system that helped it decide which cars to manufacture based on what was going out of dealers' lots. It worked great.

Well, except for one catch. According to Eric Almquist, VP at Mercer Management Consulting, the company's marketing team had just created sales incentives to get rid of a lot of lime-green cars, which no one wanted. As consumers snapped up the special deals on the cars, the CRM software noticed the surge of sales in lime-green cars and instructed the factory to produce more. The automaker lost millions of dollars before it caught the error.

No one doubts that CRM software is powerful stuff. It can slash call center costs, make a sales force dramatically more productive, and glue together offline and online sales efforts. Everyone knows stories like the one Stephen Pratt, global practice leader for Deloitte Consulting's CRM efforts, likes to tell about the telecommunications equipment manufacturer that used CRM software to coordinate its Web and offline technical-support teams. Tech support began running so smoothly that within six months, happy customers signed up for an additional $15 million in contracts.

But CRM can also go terribly wrong, causing interdepartmental chaos or never taking hold among key employees. The nightmare scenarios are all too common. Based on interviews with thousands of clients, Gartner Inc. projects that in the next five years, 55 percent of all CRM projects will fail to meet objectives. That failure rate represents a big financial risk, considering that CRM systems cost an average of $35,000 per call-center agent to deploy and that setup and maintenance of CRM sales software typically costs $28,000 to $40,000 per salesperson (over three years). How can you avoid ending up on

the CRM casualty list? Head off the most common mistakes before they happen.

EXTEND THE OLIVE BRANCH.

CRM projects usually involve different departments, which means skilled diplomacy is in order. "Traditionally sales, marketing, and service have been enemies," Pratt says. "Marketing would blame sales for not closing leads, sales would blame marketing for not generating enough leads, and service would blame them both for too-high expectations. Asking them to work together goes against their DNA."

The trick is to find leadership that can cajole or force various fiefdoms to do the right thing. Rob Schauble, director of technology for Hewlett-Packard's (*HWP*) customer support division, gathered managers from marketing, production, sales, and customer service in order to get the cooperation he needed to install CRM software from Motive Communications on all the computers HP sells. The package would let HP technical support more quickly diagnose and fix a customer's problem. Rather than going over anyone's head, Schauble invited everyone with a stake in the project to help map out a strategy from the start. His initiative paid off; more than a year after the project's completion, he estimates that the software saves HP millions of dollars by reducing the time it takes to identify problems.

EXPLAIN, EXPLAIN, EXPLAIN.

No amount of high-level cooperation will protect a CRM project from rank-and-file employees who hate it. Lisa Harris, CIO at HR-services firm Staff-Leasing, based in Bradenton, Fla., faced rebellion from the staff when she installed Oracle (*ORCL*) CRM software that helped solve some customers' problems online—without the help of a live operator. Call-center employees felt that the software

> **CUSTOMER RELATIONSHIP MANAGEMENT SYSTEM:**
>
> Enterprise software that helps a company track customers and their interactions with the company. Frequently used by customer-support, sales, and marketing staffs, CRM systems allow employees to quickly call up the past sales and service records of a customer, as well as outstanding orders or unresolved problems.

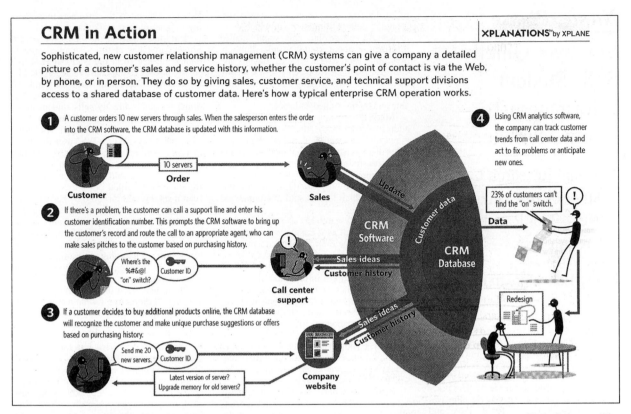

CRM in Action

XPLANATIONS™ by XPLANE

Sophisticated, new customer relationship management (CRM) systems can give a company a detailed picture of a customer's sales and service history, whether the customer's point of contact is via the Web, by phone, or in person. They do so by giving sales, customer service, and technical support divisions access to a shared database of customer data. Here's how a typical enterprise CRM operation works.

1 A customer orders 10 new servers through sales. When the salesperson enters the order into the CRM software, the CRM database is updated with this information.

10 servers
Order

Customer

Sales

2 If there's a problem, the customer can call a support line and enter his customer identification number. This prompts the CRM software to bring up the customer's record and route the call to an appropriate agent, who can make sales pitches to the customer based on purchasing history.

Where's the %#&@! "on" switch?

Customer ID

Sales ideas
Customer history

Call center support

3 If a customer decides to buy additional products online, the CRM database will recognize the customer and make unique purchase suggestions or offers based on purchasing history.

Send me 20 new servers.

Customer ID

Sales ideas
Customer history

Latest version of server?
Upgrade memory for old servers?

Company website

CRM Software

Customer data

Update

CRM Database

4 Using CRM analytics software, the company can track customer trends from call center data and act to fix problems or anticipate new ones.

23% of customers can't find the "on" switch.

Data

Redesign

---

threatened their jobs, so they quietly discouraged customers from using it. "Our operators would say, 'Wouldn't you rather call up? I'll take care of everything you need,'" Harris says. She stuck with the online CRM, but also began talking to employees about the software. She changed their work routines to include more customer hand-holding and less data entry, which was increasingly done online.

SHOP AND INSTALL WITH CARE.

CRM software is complex to install because it often touches many different legacy systems. Four years ago, Staff-Leasing's Harris says she spent millions of dollars integrating a CRM application for a previous employer. But when she was finished, it took operators too long to get data on screen. She had bogged down the performance of the new CRM implementation by trying to integrate too many complicated systems. The project ended up a total bust.

Harris says new products that link related applications into suites, like the one she's using from Oracle, typically work well together. But analysts say such

> **CALL CENTER:**
>
> A company department or a contractor that handles telephone duties such as sales or tech call support. There are 82,000 call centers in North America.

suites, a relatively new trend, are still immature. The technology is further complicated by the fact that CRM firms are making the leap from client-server forms of CRM to Web-enabled ones. For example, early versions of Oracle's Net-enabled CRM suite, introduced early last year, tried to do too much too soon, which resulted in client problems, according to Wendy Close, CRM research director for Gartner Inc. Close adds that the Net-based systems, such as PeopleSoft's (*PSFT*) latest offering, have fewer features than client-server versions.

Finally, make sure that the system your techies build is really what the company needs. Many problems arise from lack of planning and communication, says Larry Senn, of Senn-Delaney Leadership Consulting Group. "There is a blind spot here, and the more technical the organization, the bigger the blind spot," he says. "Engineers tend to think if something makes sense, people will do it—but that's not how people operate."

40

Name, Please

Surveyor Quietly Sells Student Information To Youth Marketer

National Research Center Stresses Its College Ties—Not Razors, Credit Cards

Many Educators in the Dark

BY DANIEL GOLDEN
Staff Reporter of THE WALL STREET JOURNAL

Each year, more than one million U.S. high-school students take time out of their school day to fill out a survey asking their names, addresses, grade-point averages, races, religions and social views. The organization that sponsors the survey, the National Research Center for College and University Admissions, tells the schools it will broaden students' higher-education options by distributing their names and profiles to hundreds of colleges and universities across the country.

But colleges aren't the only recipients of the survey results. Generally unknown to high schools, colleges, students and their parents, National Research for at least a decade has also sold the personal information it gathers to the country's leading supplier of young people's names to commercial marketers, American Student List LLC.

American Student List pays for the information by helping to fund the National Research survey. American Student List then sells student names and other information to companies that solicit students for a wide array of goods and services. Companies that buy student names from American Student List include shaving giant Gillette Co.; credit-card purveyors American Express Co. and Capital One Financial Corp.; Kaplan Inc., the Washington Post Co. unit that is the largest admissions test-coaching chain; Primedia Inc.'s Seventeen Magazine; and Columbia House Record Club, which is owned by AOL Time Warner Inc. and Sony Corp.

Huge Influence

From its base in Lee's Summit, Mo., National Research—a little-known company with just 30 employees—has become a hugely influential force in a burgeoning industry surrounding college admissions in which companies and colleges buy names and detailed information about young people. Publicly presenting itself as a service to students and colleges, National Research doesn't readily disclose its role in helping commercial marketers pitch their products to an impressionable and highly valued audience.

Marketers obtain teenagers' names and addresses from many other sources, such as magazine-subscription lists and Web sites. What distinguishes National Research is that it gathers student names in a classroom survey that many school officials believe will be made available only to educational institutions, but which then is sold to commercial marketers.

National Research has also made its presence widely felt as it competes with the influential College Board to sell student information to colleges and as it lobbies Congress to kill legislation that would restrict collection of some student information.

Many teachers and educational officials express anger and disbelief when told that National Research sells student names to commercial marketers. "It's so disgusting," says Barbara Henry, admissions director at Oglethorpe University in Atlanta, which buys student information from National Research. "Everybody's upset when their children are solicited" without parental approval.

Richard Bischoff, associate director of admissions at the University of Chicago, another National Research customer, says he also was in the dark. "To the best of my knowledge, any service we buy names from does not sell into commercial markets," he says. "That's certainly something we would care about."

Steven Danloe, who gave the survey to social-studies students for 15 years at Baboquivari High School in Topowa, Ariz., before leaving teaching this year, says if he had known about the commercial sales, he "would have thrown the surveys in the trash."

Few Ask

National Research's president, Don M. Munce, says it has never hidden its commercial ties from high schools or colleges who inquire about them. But few do.

Its survey includes a "privacy statement" explaining that responses are "used by colleges, universities and other organizations to assist students and their families." Mr. Munce says referring to "other organizations" is sufficient disclosure of National Research's commercial ties. He adds that the privacy statement was designed to be brief because "teachers are very busy."

Mr. Munce says he is confident that American Student List sells only to reputable marketers. American Student List's president, Donald Damore, confirms that his company aims to limit its sales to legitimate marketers.

He says it monitors its customers by reviewing samples of their marketing material.

But Mr. Damore acknowledges American Student List has at times supplied student names gleaned from the National Research survey to college-aid consultants targeted by the Federal Trade Commission for fraud.

The only other company to which National Research directly sells student information is the publisher of "Who's Who Among American High School Students," Mr. Munce says. Who's Who uses the information to cull entries for the book and then sells copies to students for $45 apiece.

As a 14-year-old sophomore in 1999, Rotem Ben-Ad filled out the National Research survey, administered by her guidance counselor during a school assembly at her Jewish day school in Irvine, Calif. Rotem hoped to showcase herself to East Coast colleges. She then received solicitations from test-preparation companies, financial-aid consultants, the high-school Who's Who and other marketers.

"I was like, 'How did they get my name?'" she says. "I didn't know what was legitimate and what wasn't."

As colleges step up their competition for promising students, National Research has become the leading private-sector rival of the College Board in offering colleges information on high schoolers. A nonprofit organization based in New York, the College Board sponsors the SAT college-admissions test. ACT Inc., a smaller nonprofit in Iowa City, Iowa, sponsors the competing ACT exam. Both the College Board and ACT Inc. gather information from students based on questionnaires filled out during registration for tests.

The two nonprofits sell the information and test scores to colleges but not to commercial marketers. They also tell students how information gathered from test-registration questionnaires will be used and give them the choice of not answering survey questions or not having their names sent to colleges.

'Participation Fee'

The College Board makes about 65 million name sales a year. It charges colleges a $185 "participation fee" each time they order a batch of names, plus a per-name fee of 24 cents. Mr. Munce declines to say how many name sales National Research makes a year. People in the student-marketing industry estimate the total may approach half of the College Board's.

College admissions officers say that National Research's competition has forced the College Board to try more-aggressive marketing tactics. National Research mailings prod high schools to survey freshmen and sophomores, for example, "so you can get a jump-start on reaching them." It also does its testing at the beginning of the year, meaning it can send its survey results to colleges as much as three months sooner than the College Board. Trying to catch up, the College

Board says it intends next year for the first time to sell names of freshman takers of the PSAT, a warm-up to the SAT. It also intends to introduce a "search on demand" feature enabling colleges to buy student names year-round.

National Research was started in 1972 by James Kunz, a former admissions director at now-defunct Tarkio College in Tarkio, Mo. Mr. Kunz, who has left the organization, wanted to help small Midwestern colleges with recruiting, Mr. Munce says.

National Research today charges colleges an annual membership fee of $250, plus a fee of 24 cents for the use of each student name for a year. Colleges typically order computer searches for one or more categories of students—the Massachusetts Institute of Technology, for example, buys names of minority and female high-school freshmen with A averages and an interest in engineering—at a total price of thousands of dollars per search.

American Student List pays National Research about $800,000 a year to help underwrite the survey's annual cost of more than $2 million, according to Mr. Damore of American Student List. Mr. Munce won't confirm the dollar figures. But he says that funds from his two commercial customers represent less than 10% of National Research's total revenue, the rest of which comes from educational institutions. Who's Who declines to comment on what it pays for the survey names.

National Research's solicitations to colleges state that "member dues cover the cost" of the survey. Asked about the statement, Mr. Munce says it is erroneous.

National Research distributes more than 100 million surveys each year to 18,000 participating high schools—three-fourths of the national total—expecting 1% or 2% of the surveys to be returned, Mr. Munce says. It has a database of four million students, including a majority of college-bound students, he adds.

National Research has a clever tactic to reach this coveted market: It ships surveys directly to teachers and guidance counselors, rather than to principals or superintendents. This approach makes some districts wary. Gwinnett County, Georgia's largest school district, bans the survey because National Research doesn't seek approval from the district's own research department.

Mr. Munce says National Research sometimes contacts school districts and has occasionally mailed forms to principals. But principals typically forward them to guidance counselors anyway, he says.

High-school teachers and guidance counselors administer the survey, without extra pay, during school hours. Most say they hope to improve students' higher-education prospects. "We're so rural that a great many colleges can't afford to send someone," says Kelly Palmer, a guidance counselor at Troy

High School in Troy, Mont. He has handed out the survey for the past six years. "It provides our kids good exposure," he says. Mr. Palmer didn't know about National Research's commercialization of student information but says it won't cause him to drop the survey.

Nearly a thousand colleges—including the University of Miami, Boston University, Tulane University and many lesser-known schools—are survey customers. "We feel like we need to get our name in front of students early to build recognition," says Ms. Henry, the admissions director at Atlanta's Oglethorpe University. Her school has bought the names of freshmen and sophomores from National Research but will reconsider the relationship now that she knows about the organization's commercial ties.

Battling in Congress

Relying partly on its loyal college and university customers, National Research has tried to block legislative restrictions on its activities. One target: an amendment to the main federal education bill, now pending before a congressional conference committee, which would require parental consent for collecting information from students for commercial purposes. The measure, backed by a bipartisan coalition opposed to commercialization in schools, wasn't specifically aimed at National Research but could sharply limit its commercial activities.

At Mr. Munce's request, Paula Tacke, admissions director at the University of South Dakota, wrote to Senate Majority Leader Thomas Daschle, a South Dakota Democrat, in June, expressing "serious opposition" to the bill. Mr. Daschle's office responded, acknowledging her concern.

Ms. Tacke says National Research assured her that survey information is used only for educational purposes and that National Research opposes the amendment because it might discourage college recruiting. Mr. Munce separately says National Research's opposition reflects only this interest in protecting recruiting as well as such activities as fund raising for high-school proms.

National Research's survey includes language describing the organization as a nonprofit, and it is registered as such with the secretary of state's office in Missouri. But the organization hasn't sought exemption from federal or state taxes because it doesn't collect charitable contributions, Mr. Munce says.

As for profits, he says, "some years we have a surplus, and some years we don't." He says there was a surplus in 2000, but he won't be more specific.

National Research's success has drawn new competition. In 1999, a second survey, distributed by Educational Research Center of America Inc., began arriving at high schools. Educational Research, established by a commercial-list company in Lynnbrook,

N.Y., sells colleges student names for 20 cents apiece, making it the low-price supplier.

National Research sued Educational Research in 1999 in U.S. District Court in Kansas City, Mo., for copyright and trademark infringement. In its defense, Educational Research contended in court papers that National Research had no right to accuse it of breaking laws, because the plaintiff itself had "intentionally deceived" students and educators. National Research "does not disclose to teachers that the information being collected from students will be made available to thousands of companies that want to sell those students everything from credit cards, cars, clothes and sporting equipment to formal wear and photographs," Educational Research alleged.

National Research, in its own court papers, called the allegations "irrelevant, mis-directed and totally unsupported." It dropped its suit in 2000, after a judge rejected its request for an injunction blocking Educational Research from using similar methods to survey students.

Federal law prohibits "unfair or deceptive acts or practices" that affect commerce. The FTC, which enforces this law, declined to comment on National Research.

During the court case, National Research identified 40 teachers who had contacted it because they were confused when they received the new rival survey. Through their involvement in the case, some of these teachers learned that National Research had been selling student names to American Student List, which sold them to marketers. The teachers were displeased.

Stanley Holliday, a social-studies teacher at North Central High School in Indianapolis, promptly stopped giving the survey in 1999. Susan Corbosiero, a math teacher at Westborough High School, outside Boston, dropped it the same year. She says she feared she could be held legally liable if student names weren't handled confidentially. Mark Beehler, a guidance counselor at Angola High School in Angola, Ind., also discontinued the survey in 1999.

The legal feuding and unease among some educators so far doesn't seem to have diminished the value of National Research's student-name list in the teen-marketing world. "The database is priceless," Mr. Damore of American Student List said in an affidavit filed in a separate 1999 lawsuit—since settled—was brought by American Student List against a former employee in U.S. District Court in Union, N.J.

American Student List, based in Mineola, N.Y., has one of the biggest names in teen marketing. It has its own list of 17 million high-school students, drawn from National Research and such sources as magazine-subscriber lists, youngsters who respond to commercial offers on the Internet, and—until federal law banned the practice last year—state automobile-registration records.

year, American Student List was acquired by Havas Advertising SA, a French advertising agency.

Dow Jones & Co., which publishes The Wall Street Journal, also buys student names from American Student List to market its publications to college students.

Most students included in the high-school Who's Who are nominated by teachers or civic organizations, as the company states in its promotional literature. But many aren't nominated at all. Instead, Who's Who takes their names from the National Research survey if they report a "B" average or higher. Paul Krouse, founder of the book's publisher, Educational Communications Inc., acknowledges it doesn't tell students it obtained their names from a marketing survey.

In "standards and guidelines" it distributes to high schools, Who's Who says that "under no circumstances" will it accept nominations from "standard commercial lists." Mr. Krouse, now a consultant to Commemorative Brands Inc., a manufacturer of class rings that in April purchased Educational Communications, says the statement is accurate because National Research ought to be considered an educational organization, despite its commercial ties.

The high-school Who's Who is unrelated to "Who's Who in America," published by a unit of Reed Elsevier PLC.

Wheaton Academy, a Christian high school in West Chicago, Ill., doesn't nominate students for Who's Who because guidance counselor Daniel Crabtree believes that colleges don't regard listing as a credential for admission. Nevertheless, because Mr. Crabtree administers the National Research survey to sophomores and juniors, about 10% of students there receive Who's Who solicitations annually. David Fiore, chief executive of Commemorative Brands, owner of Who's Who, says the nomination of one of these students, Paul Zeigler, came from the survey and from an "alternative source" he declined to identify.

"I thought I was nominated by a teacher who liked me," says Mr. Zeigler, a junior who took the survey last year. If it was just a survey, "that's crushing," he says.

Educated Guesses

Sampling Is Taboo, But the Census Does Plenty of 'Imputing'

It Fills In Missing Answers On Race, Sex, Age— Even Postulates Whole People

Whatever the Neighbors Say

BY GLENN R. SIMPSON

Staff Reporter of THE WALL STREET JOURNAL

WASHINGTON—In March, the federal government called the 2000 survey of the U.S. population "the most accurate census in history." It rejected the controversial idea of using statistical sampling to make up for people missed.

In fact, a significant adjustment had already been made: The 2000 total includes 5.77 million people the Census Bureau believes exist but didn't actually count.

When it received no answers from what it believed were occupied addresses, the bureau simply directed its computers to "impute" people, based on various clues, including how their neighbors responded. In some cases, officials acknowledge, they added such imputed residents to the count when they weren't even certain there was a home at a given address.

Imputed Americans made up more than 2% of the official 2000 census. In a few states, they made up more than 3%.

Besides inventing whole people, the Census Bureau used imputation to fill in lines left blank. When people filled out a form and were counted but didn't give their race, age, sex or marital status, the bureau attributed one to them anyway, basing it on data their neighbors gave.

The races of more than 11 million Americans in the count were determined this way. In California and New Mexico, the races of more than 8% of the population were imputed.

Imputation—also known as "hot decking"—is a technique the bureau has employed with little fanfare since the 1940s, when it was devised by the late management guru W. Edwards Deming. But its use increased dramatically in last year's census. The bureau imputed more than three times as many complete people in 2000 as in 1990. As for filling in a race line left blank, this occurred more than twice as often in the 2000 census as in 1990.

One State Sues

The extensive adjustments can be gleaned from reams of data the bureau has been releasing this summer. Meanwhile, Utah, which thought it should have gained a House seat after the 2000 census, blames imputation and is suing the bureau. A hearing in its case was held yesterday.

The surge in imputation comes against a background of intense legal and political battles over another practice—statistical sampling—that was long proposed as a cure for undercounting of minorities and immigrants. Republicans bitterly campaigned against sampling as scientifically dubious, while Democrats said it was the only way to keep people from being disenfranchised.

Both techniques fill gaps in survey data. In imputation, missing information for a particular person is drawn from a "donor," usually the nearest neighbor. In sampling, a broad swath of information believed to be missing is filled in using data from a large group.

After being heavily criticized in 1990 for undercounting minorities and immigrants, the Census Bureau wanted to use sampling to correct the shortfall. But the Supreme Court ruled in 1999 that sampling couldn't be used to meet the Constitutional mandate of an "actual enumeration" of the population to apportion congressional seats. The court did allow sampling in compiling the figures that states use when they redraw districts.

Bureau Turnabout

In February, the Bush administration stripped the bureau of the authority to do sampling for any purpose. Weeks later, the bureau reversed its own support of sampling and agreed with the White House that it was unnecessary. It would introduce more errors than relying on the "quality count" already done, said the newly appointed acting census director, William Barron, who added: "We can't give out adjusted data based on plausibilities."

Then what about imputation? Census officials defend this as essential for accurate results and stress the differences. The methods "are completely different techniques for different purposes," maintains Howard Hogan, chief of the Census bureau's decennial statistical studies division. One distinction he cites: Sampling is used in the initial data collection, while imputation is used at a later stage, data processing.

But Everett Ehrlich, a Democrat on an oversight panel called the Census Monitoring Board, says sampling and imputation serve the same function of making up for nonresponses. "One of the principal reasons for the success of the 2000 census is the large number of people that were made up at the end," Mr. Ehrlich says. "They were made up using statistical inference. And they are not qualitatively different from the people who would have been created using sampling."

The Census Bureau says congressional Republicans who opposed sampling knew about imputation and endorsed it. Chip Walker, staff director for the House subcommittee that oversees the Census, agrees. He thinks imputation is acceptable because "when the Census Bureau imputes data, they have an actual geographic location and an actual house or apartment in which they believe somebody resides." The Southeastern Legal Foundation, which brought the suit that led to the Supreme Court rejection of sampling, says it agrees that imputation is different and doesn't have a problem with it.

Statisticians have long considered imputation an imperfect but necessary tool in counting large populations. They say it's naive to suppose one could do a large count without some form of statistical adjustment. "The census is actually a fairly crude measurement instrument," says Kendall Prewitt, a Clinton appointee who led the 2000 census, resigning as census director soon after Mr. Bush took office. Without some such statistical conjecture, Mr. Prewitt says, the vast gaps in information that can be gathered "would really mess the data up."

After census forms have been sent and census takers have made their rounds, there remain many addresses from which there is no response. So bureau statisticians, using formulas they won't disclose, make educated

A Lot of Assumptions

PEOPLE FOR WHOM CENSUS BUREAU IMPUTED:	1990 CENSUS	2000 CENSUS	% CHANGE
Race	5,005,771	11,534,770	+130%
Sex	3,029,741	3,102,263	+2%
Age	6,079,408	10,522,996	+73%
Hispanic origin*	24,763,781	12,468,979	–50%
Marital status	3,966,805	5,960,599	+50%

*Can be of any race.   Source: Census Bureau data

Total U.S. population (in millions): 248.7 ... '90 '00

Number of 'whole' people imputed (in millions): 1.9 ... '90 '00

guesses as to how many people live there and their race, sex, age and marital status.

Sometimes the agency knows that at least one person lives at an address, and has to impute other residents. Other times it knows exactly how many people live in a residence, but nothing else about them. Sometimes it has to guess at everything.

Many people who do respond to the census withhold data they consider sensitive and personal, such as age or income. The race question is often left blank because some people are unsure whether it covers ethnic heritage—it doesn't—and some resist answering because they don't like the way the census categorizes races.

Mr. Deming, famous for the technique called Total Quality Management, devised a cure for missing data in the 1940s. At the time, recalls 85-year-old census veteran Joe Waksburg, many people were declining to give their age. He says that instead of inserting an average to replace the missing data, or worse yet a zero, Mr. Deming realized "you can do better by looking at other information"—namely, the neighbors.

In those days, cards were used to collect census data, and newly collected decks of the cards were dubbed hot. Hence the term "hot decking."

The bureau's computers still use data from neighbors to fill the gaps, though the process is now more refined. Instead of always picking the neighbor right next door, the program sometimes evaluates who in the neighborhood is the best match, then inserts the data. It also imputes data about Hispanic origin in part by checking surnames. Hispanic-origin imputation occurred far less often in 2000 than in 1990, apparently because the question was made easier to understand and wasn't left blank as often.

"When you first hear about [imputation] you think, 'My God, what a crazy thing to do,'" says Norman Bradburn, associate director of the National Science Foundation, a federal agency. But it has proved a highly accurate way of counting the uncountable, Mr. Bradburn says, because similar people do tend to live close to each other. "We are very, to put it politely, homogeneous," he says. "To put it negatively, we're very segregated."

That doesn't stop critics from decrying the practice. A census advisory committee of Asian and Pacific Islanders has expressed concern that "as increasing numbers live in non-Asian neighborhoods," imputation "may cause significant numbers to be reassigned to the white or other non-Asian race." George Washington University sociologist Amitai Etzioni charges that bureau computers "took people and put them into racial boxes" that they might not agree with.

Some economists object to income imputation, fearing it distorts important data. Economists from three universities objected on that ground in a 1999 letter to the bureau. States for which the bureau did the most

imputing in 2000 were those with large urban populations and some more sparsely populated ones in the West. They are Nevada, New York, Arizona and New Mexico. In the imputation of race, states bordering Mexico led: New Mexico, California, Arizona and Texas.

Even as race imputation rose, the 2000 census presented less of a problem with undercounting of minorities and immigrants. The bureau, pummeled by civil-rights groups after 1990, had grappled with how to address the undercount issue. When its answer—statistical sampling—ran afoul of the Supreme Court and some Republicans, the bureau said it would improve its counting methods.

When preliminary census results came out this spring, it appeared the bureau had done so. It told Congress that minority undercounts had fallen by 40% or more. The total undercount was estimated at 3.1 million, down from four million in 1990, even as the U.S. population grew by more than 30 million. "These numbers confirm what we have said all along, that you can dramatically improve the census without using a risky sampling scheme," said Republican Rep. Dan Miller of Florida, chairman of the census subcommittee.

But some experts say the bureau lowered the minority undercount by assigning a missing race answer more often. Data obtained from the bureau by Eugene Ericksen, a member of the Census Monitoring Board, show that of whites, 1.5% were imputed in the census totals, but imputations accounted for 3.3% of the black total and 3.8% of the Hispanic total. "It's quite possible the use of imputation . . . may very well have helped to reduce the differential undercount," says Mr. Ericksen, a professor of sociology and statistics at Temple University in Philadelphia.

Statistics professor Stephen Fienberg of Carnegie-Mellon University in Pittsburgh says that rather than trying to stay in the field longer to reach households for the 2000 count, the bureau actually pulled its census takers several months earlier—and increased imputation had to make up the difference. "When they closed up virtually all the census offices around the end of June, what that meant was inevitably they had to be doing a lot more imputation," Prof. Fienberg says.

The bureau's Mr. Hogan doesn't dispute that. "A lot of things went on, but that's at least part of the answer," he says. He says officials are seeking a more complete explanation for the surge in imputation.

Utah's challenge to the practice grows out of dogged research by a Brigham Young University statistics professor, Lara Wolfson. When the state learned it wasn't gaining a representative as it expected, it first claimed its residents had been undercounted because the bureau missed missionaries traveling abroad. About the time that claim was failing, Ms. Wolfson learned that a congressional census subcommittee had a document full of headings such as "Imputations," "Total Substitutions," "Substitutions of

3,4,5" and "Group Quarters." No one could explain the headings, but weeks later the bureau confirmed what she suspected: that the census totals had been statistically adjusted.

Utah filed a new suit challenging the bureau, this time saying the agency had illegally imputed tens of thousands of people in North Carolina, which gained a congressional seat. Utah argued that imputation was restricted by the same Supreme Court ruling that barred statistical sampling. "When it comes to counting the population for purposes of congressional apportionment, you've got to count people," says Thomas Lee, a lawyer for the state. "You can't use statistical methods to try to estimate them."

Utah says that in some cases, the Census Bureau isn't even sure houses exist for the people it imputes, and it has to impute those as well. Mr. Hogan, the bureau statistician, confirms that for some residences, "we do impute whether it exists or not." But in such cases, he adds, "someone at some time has told us they think there's a housing unit there."

The bureau, in addition to citing differences between imputation and sampling, argues that Utah was too late with its suit. The case was heard yesterday by a federal judge in Salt Lake City.

Mr. Prewitt, for one, takes Utah's claim seriously. "I think it's a very interesting argument," the former census director says. He says that while sampling and imputation aren't the same, they are both types of inferential statistics, and if the Supreme Court's ruling is interpreted as banning all such interpolations, "imputation could be disallowed."

Mr. Ericksen, the census monitor, adds that "this whole business of sampling became focused upon because it was thought that the people who got missed would be minority people who would help the Democrats. But there are other things that happen that also have political implications."

"If you really tried to put all this together and assess the rationality of it," he adds, "you wouldn't be happy."

Corrections & Amplifications

PROF. EUGENE ERICKSEN of Temple University is a consultant to the Census Monitoring Board. In a page-one article yesterday on the Census Bureau's method of supplementing its head count, he was misidentified as a member of the board. In addition, former Census Director Kenneth Prewitt's first name was given incorrectly as Kendall. In some editions, a lawsuit by Utah was described as an attempt to prevent losing a House seat; the case is an effort to gain a seat. (WSJ August 31, 2001)

Product

42

BUILDING 'EASY' INTO TECHNOLOGY
The user interface comes to the fore in product design

Ted Selker is ready to tear out some of his thinning hair. An associate professor at Massachusetts Institute of Technology's Media Lab, Selker is in a dither about MIT's new e-mail system that takes five times as many clicks to send a message as his old software did.

There's not much that bugs him more than clunky, baffling user interfaces—the screen or control panel that connects a human to a device. As the creator of the breakthrough red pointer that sits in the middle of the IBM notebook keyboard, Selker has built a career out of making computers easier to use. He wishes more equipment makers would do the same. But since no one is measuring the time consumers waste because of awkward design, "we put up with a lot of crap," Selker says.

OUT OF THE MIRE. Companies outside the computer realm are taking heed. For outfits such as Dassault, Whirlpool, and 3M, it hasn't taken complex statistical analysis to realize that users who must make life-and-death decisions, such as pilots and surgeons, want fewer buttons to run more functions on the equipment they use. The goal for all these manufacturers, of course, is to boost sales. But along the way, they're hoping to strengthen brands, save customers time, and even improve product safety by keeping users from bogging down in a mire of buttons and screen commands. "The design of a user interface can really make or break a product," says Robert J. Beaton, director of the Displays & Controls Laboratory at Virginia Polytechnic Institute.

Simplification is one of the best ways to improve usability. In the cockpit of its new Falcon Jet 7x, Dassault Corp. is taking just such a tack. Its new EASy cockpit scheme replaces a panel of knobs, switches, and levers with four flat screens arranged in a T pattern. All the information pilots need—from altitude to speed to where the plane sits relative to the horizon—is displayed on those screens, reducing a 450-page paper-based flight-management manual to 30 online pages. "We're trying to move to the paperless cockpit so the pilot doesn't have to carry 100 pounds of navigation books," says Jerry Tritt, Dassault Falcon Jet's chief pilot.

A pilot navigates through the data using a cursor control device mounted on the middle console, where his hand naturally falls. If the pilot wants to change the flight plan, he points, clicks, and follows the choices on the screen—all while looking ahead rather than down at the console. The controller has even been designed to hold steady during turbulence.

The intent behind this innovation is to increase what's called situational awareness—knowing where you are relative to the terrain and other planes. With the new system, changing a flight plan now takes seconds, down from as much as five minutes the old way. "Instead of flipping multiple switches and trying to remember how it's done, it's in front of him on screen," says John Uczekaj, a vice-president for business, regional, and general aviation avionics at Honeywell International Inc., whose Digital Engine Operating System is behind the high-tech panels. The new design still must pass muster with regulatory bodies before it can take wing. Dassault expects U.S. and European regula-

---

DASSAULT FALCON JET COCKPIT

OLD DESIGN Control panel is full of analog dials, switches, knobs, and levers. A change in a flight plan takes up to five minutes. In an emergency, the pilot runs through a paper checklist to troubleshoot. Flight-management system is described in a 450-page binder.

NEW DESIGN Four flat panels replace the dials and most of the switches and knobs. A mouse-like device selects pull-down menus to adjust settings. Flight plan changes take one minute. Pilot runs through an electronic checklist in an emergency. Flight-management system is 30 onscreen pages.

---

tors to certify the new cockpit by early 2003 and to have EASy in the air soon after.

Home appliances aren't so high-tech, but they can still leave consumers in a spin with a nonsensical array of dials and buttons. Whirlpool Corp. is trying to help its customers make sense of it all by creating control panels that are consistent across appliances within a price category. Charles Jones, vice-president for consumer design, calls it "leveraged learning." In other words, once you learn how to program your dishwasher, it's a cinch to drive the microwave because the systems are similar.

Whirlpool and its partner, Ziba Design Inc. in Portland, Ore., are trying to think like consumers. Within its appliances, Whirlpool has placed a layered interface resembling that of an automated teller machine, so the user isn't overwhelmed with cooking options when all she wants is some popcorn. The number of functions has jumped to 250, from 75, and they are grouped in three levels to accommodate all users—from children with basic skills to adults who may want to set up their own programs for the perfect tuna casserole. The appliances have a combination of so-called soft keys that control the liquid-crystal display, along with traditional buttons and dials, or hard keys. These are arranged in a hierarchy on the control panel to highlight major functions—the on-off switch is a large button—and downplay others.

Medical-equipment makers also are focusing on simplifying user interfaces—knowing that such changes can save lives. Take 3M Health Care's cardiovascular systems division, which is now owned by Japan's Terumo Corp. 3M wanted to double the number of functions of its blood monitors (gizmos used to track blood properties during open-heart surgery) while reducing the number of button pushes necessary to access them. The operator, faced with a range of displays that included pressure gauges, timers, and alarms—along with a spaghetti-like array of tubing carrying blood from the heart-lung machine—doesn't have the time to fiddle with a fancy user interface.

Lacking its own internal design experts, 3M hired IDEO, a San Mateo (Calif.) design-and-engineering outfit, to help. The result

(Cont.)

WHIRLPOOL APPLIANCES

OLD DESIGN Different control panels for every appliance. Shape and color of buttons or dials do not relate to function. One microwave offers 75 functions—many of them too complex to use.

NEW DESIGN Control panels now have a common look, feel, and function. Graphical user interface allows layering of functions so all buttons are not on the surface. A microwave user can now access 250 functions in less time, with 30% fewer errors.

---

potassium—a chemical used to stop the heart during the operation—users are more certain of when to start lowering the potassium to restart the heart. The advance takes 5 to 10 minutes off a 50-minute bypass procedure. Together, the improvements in form and function mean that "the new design helps the patient get off [the heart-lung machine] and recover quicker," says Gary Paul, who was the system's program manager for 3M.

The importance of the user interface is even becoming apparent with products that never had one. Companies such as Coleman Co. and First Alert Inc. have now made their smoke alarms interactive. The plastic boxes that used to hang, inert, from the ceiling can now be shushed without having to climb on a chair. The Coleman model has a button that chefs can push with a broomstick if cooking smoke sets it off. With First Alert's product, the touch of any button on a TV or other household remote control device will activate an infrared sensor to silence the alarm.

Now if only the VCR and DVD makers would be as sympathetic. Even after 20 years on the market, VCRs remain too complicated for many ordinary folks to program. So most people use them only to record shows in progress or play movies. The DVD is almost as troublesome to set up. That's probably because design engineers focus on adding the next cool function rather than simplifying its use. "They're paying more attention to the inner works than the outside," says Virginia Tech's Beaton. When they finally do think about how these gadgets

---

TERUMO BLOOD MONITOR

OLD DESIGN Systems often produce bad data, requiring a complex recalibration process. The monochrome display is tough to read at an angle. Users must pore through reference manuals to memorize the buttons to use.

NEW DESIGN Recalibration takes one push of a button. Fewer buttons are required to monitor 12 blood values vs. the old design's six. The readings are color-coded—red for blood coming from arteries, blue for veins. Training time is reduced.

---

was a modal approach, again like an ATM. The operator can choose among setup, calibration, or operation modes—and each level restricts the number of available functions, reducing errors and saving the user from having to memorize all the idiosyncrasies of the machine.

FASTER RECOVERY. And the results? A recalibration during an operation takes one touch of a button, getting rid of awkward paper printouts and reducing possible errors. And with more accurate readings of levels of

work, maybe we'll be able to relax in front of the TV without worrying about which button to push—or not.

By Faith Keenan in Boston, with Adam Aston in New York

"Building 'Easy' into Technology," pp. 92B–D. Reprinted from the December 3, 2001 issue of *Business Week* by special permission, copyright © 2001 by The McGraw-Hill Companies, Inc.

43

CRUISING FOR QUALITY
To catch up with Japan, Detroit redesigns how it designs

You'd think Ford Motor Co. would learn a lesson about keeping an eye on quality from the $3.5-billion Explorer tire debacle. And, indeed, the auto maker went to extraordinary lengths to ensure that its revised 2002 Explorer launched without a hiccup. It even took the unprecedented step of holding up vehicles in the factory for engineers to pore over them for defects. But that wasn't enough. Last May, the new Explorer had to be recalled. It turned out that while redesigning the car, engineers forgot to adjust a rail used to guide the vehicle along an assembly line. The oversight meant that some Explorers limped off the line with nine-inch-long gashes in their tires.

Try as it might, the U.S. auto industry can't shake its karma for shaky quality—even though its cars and trucks are better than ever. *Consumer Reports* recently found that the average number of problems per 100 new vehicles built by General Motors, Ford, and Chrysler dropped from 105 in 1980 to just 23 in 2000. But as the Explorer Redux episode highlights, U.S. cars still are not up to snuff. Despite the improvement, *Consumer Reports* pegs the quality of American vehicles at Japanese levels circa 1985. And the Big Three currently spend about $125 more per vehicle in warranty costs than their Japanese rivals.

Why the gap? It's not that American factory workers are sloppier than their Japanese counterparts. In fact, fewer than 15% of quality problems can be traced to shoddy workmanship or other factory errors, says Sandy Munro, president of Munro & Associates Inc., a Troy (Mich.)-based manufacturing consultant. The real problem, he says, is at the front end of the development process. "It has more to do with who designed it, how they designed it, and what processes and materials they used," Munro contends.

RAIDING TOYOTA. Now, in a drive to reduce costs and boost quality, U.S. carmakers are revamping their approach, trying to root out problems before assembly lines start rolling. They're borrowing strategies invented by the Japanese, or—in the case of Chrysler Corp.—raiding Toyota Motor Corp. for quality expertise. And they're bringing suppliers into the design process earlier and treating them like partners, in hopes of spotting problems with components as early as possible.

Detroit is finding, as it did back in the 1970s, that there is no better way to begin than with a close look at Japan. There, top car builders take an evolutionary approach to design, stressing continuous improvement. From year to year, if parts are working well, they are kept, not replaced. And by using common components across a range of vehicles, Japanese designs cut down on variability—the old, familiar foe of quality.

In stark contrast, U.S. auto makers tend to start with a clean sheet of paper whenever they redesign a vehicle. And this can lead to trouble. When Chrysler introduced the redesigned 1999 Jeep Grand Cherokee, former CEO Robert J. Eaton bragged that there were so few shared bits between the new and old models, they'd all fit in a bag in his hand. He should have kept mum: *Consumer Reports* says the Grand Cherokee's "reliability has been among the worst we've seen."

Another nagging problem at U.S. car shops is an overly narrow focus on component design without enough regard for the larger task of integrating parts on the factory floor. The trouble, points out Jay Baron, director of manufacturing systems group at the Center for Automotive Research in Ann Arbor, Mich., is that good components that don't fit together demand costly last-minute design changes. "This is one area where the Japanese are way ahead of us," says Baron. Instead of striving for perfection in the design of each component, the Japanese fast-forward to the manufacturing phase to make sure the parts fit, and then back up to make necessary adjustments, he says. Now, all three Detroit auto makers are beginning to follow suit.

TRICKY PROBLEMS. Ford, by any calculation, needs the most work. Last year alone, recalls and other quality gaffes cost the company at least $1 billion, says CEO Jacques A. Nasser. Now, Ford is pinning its quality hopes on Six Sigma, a data-driven method pioneered by industrial giants such as AlliedSignal Inc. and Motorola Inc.

It's an approach that depends on rigorous statistical analysis to unearth tough problems. And it's already helping crack some tricky ones at Ford. Ill-fitting doors on Ford's top-selling F-150 pickup truck, for example, were blamed for chronic wind noise and leaks. So, after studying the installation of hundreds of such doors, a Six Sigma team working at Ford's Norfolk (Va.) truck factory discovered that door-fit varied according to the order in which bolts attaching the door to the frame were driven in.

The problem implied its own solution. Experimenting with various sequences, the team reduced the defects rate by two-thirds—without changing a single part. The change immediately saved $35,000 on the plant floor by eliminating the refitting of bad doors. Larger savings in warranty haven't yet been tallied.

The truck team passed along its findings to other Ford truck plants and to teams developing future models. Ultimately, catching potential problems while the designs are still just sketches gives the biggest payoff. "In existing product, problems are easy to find, but hard to fix," says Louise Goeser, Ford's quality vice-president. "In future product, problems are harder to detect, but easier to fix."

Of the Big Three, GM has made the most progress on quality. This year, it climbed to No. 4 on J.D. Power & Associates' annual overall quality rankings, just a notch behind Nissan Motor Co. Now, GM is looking to close in on the leaders, Toyota and Honda, by working more closely with its suppliers, says GM manufacturing chief Gary Cowger. On some vehicles, GM is even handing over complete design responsibility for its interiors to large suppliers, such as Lear Corp. and Johnson Controls Inc. The subcontractors, GM figures, can better monitor quality by designing and building fully integrated systems—complete seats or dashboards as opposed to just seat frames or speedometers.

At Chrysler, the struggling U.S. unit of Germany's DaimlerChrysler, improving quality is an even more urgent mission. The company's new CEO, former Mercedes chief engineer Dieter Zetsche, has made it a cornerstone of his $3.9-billion turnaround plan. He's overhauling Chrysler's vehicle development processes by pulling together teams from all areas of the company—design, engineering, marketing, manufacturing, and purchasing—in a bid to drive out waste. By involving everyone up front, his goal is to avoid the kinds of last-minute design changes that lead to errors later on. Even before Zetsche arrived, Chrysler quality was improving: Its Dodge Intrepid beat out the Toyota Camry and the Honda Accord—long-time leaders in the midsize sedan segment—in J.D. Power's 2001 new car quality survey.

Chrysler also is adding more discipline to the development process by borrowing Mercedes' system of "quality gates." This refers to a series of a dozen or so checkpoints throughout the three-year vehicle development process. The concept is simple, says Don Dees, the quality guru Chrysler hired last year from Toyota. "You don't go through the gate if you're not ready. Otherwise, you'll have warranty problems for the customer."

Chrysler also expects to boost quality by sharing more parts among its vehicles and borrowing more components from Mercedes. Until now, some Mercedes execs were slow to release certain technologies and components to their counterparts at Chrysler.

But Zetsche, who joined Chrysler in November, has the influence to encourage sharing.

Some quality problems may still find their way into vehicles. But Chrysler is trying to identify them earlier—and fix them faster—at its new quality engineering center near its Auburn Hills (Mich.) headquarters. There, some 15,000 company-owned cars are serviced. The center also receives and scrutinizes every faulty part that is removed from a car at Chrysler's 4,600 dealers nationwide. That helps engineers quickly identify problems in the field and work with suppliers to find a solution. "As you fix things, you put that in your book of knowledge so you don't make the same mistake on the next vehicle," says Dees.

Sounds good. But Detroit has already shown that learning from its own mistakes is easier said than done. What's more, it remains to be seen whether the Big Three can turn the still harder trick of learning Japan's best practices too.

By Joann Muller, with Katie Kerwin, in Detroit.

44

BIG BRANDS (SMALL COMPANIES)
You don't need to be huge to become a household name. Here's how to do it

Ask people to name the big machine that lumbers around skating rinks resurfacing the ice, and chances are they'll say it's a Zamboni. In bike stores, customers looking for a super-strong lock usually ask for Kryptonite. And who can hear the name Archie without conjuring up that freckle-faced redhead from Riverdale?

Sure, you know these names. But you probably didn't know these brands are all owned by little companies, each with fewer than 100 employees and less than $50 million in sales. "Lots of people think we must be a $500 million company with two floors of a skyscraper in Midtown," says Michael Silberkleit, publisher of Archie Comic Publications Inc. Actually, it's a $15 million, 23-person outfit with modest digs in Mamaroneck, N.Y.

Standing alongside the Coca-Colas and P&Gs of the world, you'll find a good number of little companies whose brands loom large: Ovaltine, with $40 million in sales, is one of the famous old brands owned by the 30-person Himmel Group in New York. Tofutti frozen desserts come from a company with only 15 full-time employees and $13 million in revenues. Baby Jogger, a big wheel among the stroller set, is the product of The Baby Jogger Co. with a staff of 70 and $15 million in revenues.

How do you build a big brand without the ad budget or the marketing muscle of a giant corporation? The companies that have succeeded share certain traits:

■ They carve out a unique niche, often becoming the first and dominant brand in their category. Sixty-employee Kryptonite Corp., for example, owns 60% of the bike lock market.

■ They are masterful outsourcers, often farming out manufacturing and other functions that aren't central to building the brand. ID Software Inc., the 17-person creator of the computer games Doom and Quake, outsources everything but game development. Himmel, which manages other famous old brands like Bromo Seltzer and mouthwash Lavoris, farms out everything but advertising and marketing.

■ They often team up with bigger partners to boost distribution. The Republic of Tea, a 60-employee specialty company in Novato, Calif., got a big boost when Barnes & Noble bookstores agreed to sell its tea in their cafes.

■ They raise their profiles with astute public relations. Take Internet discount retailer Bluefly Inc., an $18 million company, which aggressively courted the business and fashion press to become an e-tailing success story.

Of course, establishing a big brand doesn't mean your work is over. Bigger fish, with much bigger budgets, may try to emulate your success. You may also spend a lot of time and money defending your patents and trademarks. And if you got big by standing on the shoulders of a giant, you could just as easily shrink back to the size of Tom Thumb if the relationship goes awry.

Here's what some small companies have learned.

BEWARE OF GIANTS. It sounds easy: Partner with a big corporation with a big distribution network to get your product out there. But as David Mintz, CEO of Tofutti Brands Inc., found, the strategy has its risks. In the 1980s, the onetime Kosher caterer in New York invented a soy-based frozen dessert called Tofutti, which he sold locally. Then, Mintz hooked up with ice cream maker Haagen-Dazs for exclusive distribution in major markets. "All of a sudden, I was the hottest thing," he recalls. "My products were in supermarkets nationwide. I was on TV all the time—Joan Lunden, Regis Philbin, *The MacNeil/Lehrer News Hour*."

As the buzz grew, so did sales—from $30,000 to $18 million over an 18-month period. His staff of 10 ballooned to more than 100. But in 1988, Tofutti and Haagen-Dazs began to quarrel over money and control. Haagen-Dazs executive Jack Lyons, vice-president of distribution for the eastern U.S., says the two company presidents had a "clash of egos." Mintz chose to dissolve the partnership—with disastrous results. Sales plummeted to less than $10 million, and Mintz had to lay off all but a handful of workers. Patiently, he rebuilt the brand until sales crept back to $13 million last year. To keep consumers interested, Mintz focuses on creating new products. His latest hit: Tofutti Cuties, little frozen dessert sandwiches.

Mintz says he doesn't regret dancing with a giant. "It did get me known. But it almost got me bankrupt, too." Today, the 15-person company has more than a dozen wholesale distributors—including, ironically, Haagen-Dazs, which is now a non-exclusive distributor of Tofutti products in New York.

VALUE YOUR DISTRIBUTORS. When customers come into Gregg's Greenlake Cycle in Seattle for a three-wheeled, all-terrain baby stroller, they're clear about what they want—a "Baby Jogger." They're not even aware it's a brand name with a legion of knock-offs, says store manager Marty Pluth.

How did Baby Jogger become a household name? In 1984, Mary Baechler and her then-husband, Phil, invented the big-wheeled carriage in their Yakima (Wash.) garage. At

---

HOW THEY DID IT
Words of Wisdom from CEOs with Big Brands

"Sixty years later, we are still squeaky-clean. It's who we are."
—**Michael Silberkleit,** publisher, Archie Comic Publications

"A good idea gets you started. When the tidal wave of competition comes, that's when brand matters."
—**Mary Baechler,** CEO, Baby Jogger

"We're never afraid to do what it takes to get our story out."
—**Gary Furst,** CEO, Kryptonite

"It's good to be well-known. It's not good to be generic. The machine is not a 'Zamboni.' It is a Zamboni ice-resurfacing machine."
—**Richard Zamboni,** president, Frank J. Zamboni

"Sometimes what's fast and easy is not the best route. Sometimes it's supposed to take time."
—**David Mintz,** CEO, Tofutti Brands

first, it was mostly runners who bought the Racing Stroller, as it was then called. But as more retailers picked up the product—and turned it into a mainstream lifestyle item for active Baby Boomers—Baechler realized those distributors were the key to building her brand. So she focused on training retailers to demonstrate its proper use to skeptical parents. The strategy worked: By 1994, sales of what by then was called the Baby Jogger reached $5 million, and by 2000, they had leapt to $15 million.

But like any great idea, this one bred numerous copycats around the world. Baechler, whose strollers sell for about $180 and up, was shocked on a recent business trip to Amsterdam to find about 30 different competing all-terrain strollers in a baby store. "I said: 'Yikes! How did this happen?'"

To goose her sales, Baechler started selling strollers online last year, but that strategy backfired. Some angry retailers called her up and screamed at her, she says. Others turned to her rivals.

The result: Baechler recently halted all Web sales, despite her hefty investment in an online shopping system. Ultimately, she realized, The Baby Jogger Co. needed its retailers far more than the Internet. "They're what built this company," she says.

INSPIRE AFFECTION. Few industrial products have the pop culture appeal of the ice resurfacer made by Frank J. Zamboni & Co. Hockey fans cheer the slow-moving Zamboni when it rolls out at National Hockey League games. "It's like a mascot," says Paula Jensen, who handles merchandising for the 50-employee, Paramount (Calif.) company.

That warm feeling translates into sales industry estimates peg at $16 million. Over five decades, Zamboni has kept its lead in the market despite growing competition from Canadian rivals such as Ontario-based Resurfice Corp. At about $80,000 a pop, these babies aren't cheap, and there's little to differentiate them—except for the Zamboni brand. Indeed, the Zamboni name is closely associated with skating culture, says a loyal customer, Ed Peduto, general manager of Burbank Ice Rink in Reading, Mass. "They have a commitment to rink operators.

They've been at every trade show I've ever been to, and they work hard to stay on top."

Not only do patrons applaud when the Zamboni rolls out, says Peduto, they eagerly consume Zamboni merchandise. His best-selling item: Zamboni die-cast miniatures featuring the logos of the NHL Stanley Cup winners.

The Zamboni's mystique isn't lost on Jensen. She's a former Walt Disney Co. merchandiser who joined Zamboni in 1997 and has expanded licensed goods from the usual caps and T-shirts to include everything from duffle bags to coaster sets. Such sales account for nearly 10% of revenues.

She let Wendy's International use a Zamboni in a 1997 Superbowl commercial, and in 1999 David Letterman was allowed to stage a mock Zamboni race outside his studio. But Jensen turned down the request of a beer maker that wanted to claim, "Our beer is colder than a Zamboni," because it clashed with the company's image. When it comes to protecting your brand, there are some brews that just don't mix.

STAY TRUE TO YOUR BRAND. Developed by Louis Silberkleit and his partners during World War II, Archie may well be the world's oldest teenager. But Archie's staying power isn't accidental. Silberkleit and later his son Michael, now the publisher and CEO of Archie Comic, have worked hard to keep Archie and his pals relevant while retaining their wholesome charms.

In the 1940s, Archie sold 6 million comic books a month. Then, TV supplanted comic books. Archie would surely have become a socio-cultural footnote if it weren't for Louis Silberkleit's move to put an Archie cartoon on TV in 1969. Today, the company sells about 800,000 comic books a month, but a growing share of its $15 million in revenues comes from licensing for television, movies, and merchandise.

Michael Silberkleit doesn't make decisions about the brand lightly. Residents of Archie's Riverdale now use cell phones and computers and grapple with contemporary issues such as race relations. But he resists pressure to modernize the illustration style. Just as vigorously, he defends Archie's apple-pie image and his trademarks. Sil-

berkleit has gone to court to shut smutty Web sites that used names of Archie characters in their domain names. He was no less forgiving when Melissa Joan Hart, star of the TV version of Sabrina the Teenage Witch, which is based on an Archie character, posed nearly topless for Maxim magazine in 1999. Silberkleit faxed Hart and Sumner Redstone, head of Sabrina licensee Viacom Inc., to express his outrage and exact a public apology from Hart. "Our brand has always been about entertainment that is clean and suitable for kids," says Silberkleit.

SEEK GOOD PRESS. Back in the 1970s, Kryptonite had the brand thing all locked up. Its unique, "U-shape" bicycle lock, protected by patents, was reputed by cyclists to be the toughest lock around. But by 1994, most of the patents were expiring. How did Kryptonite keep its brand out front? With publicity. Lots of it.

That year, to promote its line of locks in New York, then-CEO Michael Zane locked up his own bike on the city's mean streets. For 48 hours, he sat in a stakeout van with a *New York Post* reporter, watching several would-be thieves fail to snap the Kryptonite. The $30-million, Canton (Mass.) company, has been hyping itself shamelessly ever since. Its surveys, such as Top Ten Worst Cities for Bike Theft, regularly get ink. Last February, Kryptonite executives donned war paint and kilts to dole out bonuses to celebrate banner sales, and got themselves a writeup in the *Boston Business Journal*.

Tacky? Perhaps, but it seems to work: Sales have grown by an average of 12% a year, and the company continues to outpace huge rivals such as Master Lock Co. and Yale. "We're not bashful," says CEO Gary Furst. "We know how to make impressions." Great marketing, to be sure. But it doesn't hurt if the product behind the brand is pretty good, too.

By Ellen Neuborne

45

THE BEST GLOBAL BRANDS

Together with leading brand consultant INTERBRAND, we've ranked the leaders around the world

Not long after she started her new job as head of Boeing Co.'s marketing and public-relations department in 1999, Ford veteran Judith Muhlberg uttered the "B" word in a meeting of top executives. Immediately, a senior manager stopped her and said: "Judith, do you know what industry you're in and what company you've come to? We aren't a consumer-goods company, and we don't have a brand."

Boeing has come a long way since then. Today, branding matters in a big way at the aerospace giant. The company's first-ever brand strategy was formalized last year as part of an overall strategy to extend its reach beyond the commercial-airplane business. Now, everything from Boeing's logo to its plan to relocate its corporate headquarters from Seattle to Chicago has been devised with the Boeing brand in mind.

A belief in the power of brands and brand management has spread far beyond the traditional consumer-goods marketers who invented the discipline. For companies in almost every industry, brands are important in a way they never were before. Why? For one thing,

customers for everything from soda pop to software now have a staggering number of choices. And the Net can bring the full array to any computer screen with a click of the mouse. Without trusted brand names as touchstones, shopping for almost anything would be overwhelming. Meanwhile, in a global economy, corporations must reach customers in markets far from their home base. A strong brand acts as an ambassador when companies enter new markets or offer new products. It also shapes corporate strategy, helping to define which initiatives fit within the brand concept and which do not.

That's why companies that once measured their worth strictly in terms of tangibles such as factories, inventory, and cash have realized that a vibrant brand, with its implicit promise of quality, is an equally important asset. A brand has the power to command a premium price among customers and a premium stock price among investors. It can boost earnings and cushion cyclical downturns—and now, a brand's value can be measured.

That's exactly what we have done in our first annual report card of the world's most potent brands. To help assess which companies are managing their brands with skill and which ones aren't, *BusinessWeek* has teamed up with Interbrand Corp., a pioneering brand consultancy in New York, to offer a ranking of 100 global brands by dollar value. The ranking by Interbrand, a unit of Omnicom Group Inc., is based on a rigorous analysis of brand strength.

The basic theory is that strong brands have the power to increase sales and earnings. Interbrand tries to figure how much of a boost each brand delivers, how stable that boost is likely to be in the future, and how much those future earnings are worth today. Many of the brand names in our table are also the name of the parent company. The assigned value, however, is strictly for the brand. Coca-Cola's value is based on products carrying the Coke name, not on Sprite or Fanta.

Some big household brands won't turn

up in our ranking at all. Only global brands, generally defined as selling at least 20% outside of their home country or region, are included. That eliminates some familiar names such as Gatorade, whose sales are overwhelmingly in the U.S. In addition, each brand must have enough publicly available data for Interbrand to make a reliable assessment. That knocks out private companies such as Mars Inc. and even some publicly traded ones that don't break out enough data.

In other cases, it's too difficult to separate the strength of the brand from other factors. That's the case with airlines, where schedules and hubs often leave travelers with little

THE WORLD'S 10 MOST VALUABLE BRANDS

RANK	BRAND	2001 BRAND VALUE ($BILLIONS)
1	COCA-COLA	68.9
2	MICROSOFT	65.1
3	IBM	52.8
4	GE	42.4
5	NOKIA	35.0
6	INTEL	34.7
7	DISNEY	32.6
8	FORD	30.1
9	McDONALD'S	25.3
10	AT&T	22.8

Data: Interbrand, Citigroup

WIELDING A MEAN BRANDING IRON

Over the past two decades, factors ranging from the rise of the global economy to the rise of the Internet have helped make brands more powerful than at any time in history. Here are the milestones along the way:

JUNE 22, 1984 British record mogul Richard Branson launches an airline, extending the Virgin name from music to planes. Virgin goes on to encompass stores, movies, and financial services in one of the great brand-building stories of the '90s. Marketers take note that a strong, fertile brand can go in all sorts of new directions.

APR. 23, 1985 To stem defections to rival Pepsi, Coca-Cola introduces a new, sweeter formulation of its iconic soda pop, only to bring back Coke Classic 77 days later amid one of the biggest consumer backlashes in marketing history. The debacle offers one of the first glimpses at the latent power of brands.

NOV. 30, 1988 As the takeover era reaches a climax, buyout firm Kohlberg Kravis Roberts & Co. submits the winning bid for RJR Nabisco, walking away with a brand portfolio that includes Oreo cookies, Winston cigarettes, and Hawaiian Punch—all for a record-setting $25.4 billion. The vast premium paid over book value in this and other acquisitions brings home to corporate leaders just how valuable brands can be.

(Cont.)

APR. 2, 1993 Philip Morris takes decisive action against discount cigarettes that are stealing share from mighty Marlboro by slashing prices 20%. Other premium makers are forced to follow, and consumer-goods stocks tumble amid fears that brands are losing clout. Suddenly, "brand management" becomes part of every manager's vocabulary.

MAY 5, 1994 With companies in all industries starting to focus on building brands, IBM makes marketing history by consolidating its entire $400 million global advertising account at one agency, Ogilvy & Mather, citing the need to get maximum leverage from its marketing efforts.

MAY 15, 1997 With less than two years of operating history and no profits in sight, online bookseller Amazon.com goes public at $18 a share and the dot-com boom is born. Shares later reach a high of $106, forever changing our notion of what it takes to build a dominant brand.

choice when buying tickets, no matter what their feeling about a particular airline. Interbrand ranked some corporations, including Johnson & Johnson and Procter & Gamble Co., based on their portfolios of brands. The portfolio ranking follows the table of 100 brands.

DE RIGUEUR. This kind of rigorous assessment of brand value has been required for more than a decade in Interbrand's original market, Britain, where measures of brand value often must be included on corporate balance sheets. Some experts believe that the U.S. and other countries should also require companies to break out brand valuations for investors. While other rankings rely on surveys of fleeting consumer perceptions, we believe our analysis will provide a reliable benchmark for comparison in years to come.

The ranking reflects the important developments of the past year and shows just how much they cost in brand value. Fewer than half of the 74 brands for which Interbrand had a 2000 valuation showed a gain in value in 2001. Mighty Coca-Cola is still the world's most powerful brand, but the name lost 5% of its value last year, according to Interbrand's calculations, as it struggled against its longtime rival Pepsi, ranked at No. 44. If No. 2 Microsoft hadn't been mired in antitrust troubles and an overall technology slowdown—causing it to shed 7% of its brand value—it would have cruised into the top spot on the list.

The dot-com meltdown claimed a lot of casualties. Yahoo!, at No. 59, and Amazon.com, at No. 76, while still formidable brands, nevertheless lost 31% each of their brand value amid widespread uncertainty about their ability to deliver earnings in the future. Still, the news wasn't all bad. No. 88-ranked Starbucks was the biggest gainer in percentage terms, adding 32% in value to its fast-growing brand, which now encompasses 4,435 stores on three continents as well as branded coffee paraphernalia, music, and candy.

To see just how much—and how fast—a mismanaged brand can lose value, take a look at No. 8-ranked Ford. Everyone knows that Ford Motor Co. has had a tough year. Between the Firestone tire fiasco and a series of embarrassing quality gaffes, little has gone right for the Detroit carmaker. Investors certainly have been hurt: First-half earnings from continuing operations are down 91% from a year ago. But what does the blow to Ford's reputation really cost? When a brand is tarnished, its power to attract customers and command top prices diminishes—and so its value drops. That's what the numbers show for Ford. By Interbrand's calculations, the carmaker's name is worth $30.1 billion today—$6.3 billion less than last year.

SEA CHANGE. Numbers such as these make it clear why companies in all industries are suddenly becoming more vigilant brand stewards. Branding used to be practiced by companies that sold packaged goods to consumers—and almost no one else. Developing a brand included advertising, package design, and maybe a few promotions and was seen as far less central to the corporate mission than serious stuff such as floating debentures, quickening inventory turns, or boosting capacity utilization.

That was in a different millennium. As the new one unfolds, brands have been taking center stage in a sweeping shift that some compare to the wave of mass marketing that occurred in the years following World War II. Pharmaceutical companies, which have been liberated to promote their products directly to consumers, have been spending hundreds of millions to create entirely new brands such as Viagra and Claritin. Branding efforts in the financial services sector have taken off as that industry has consolidated and as federal legislation has knocked down the walls that used to separate banks from brokerage houses. Professional services companies such as Andersen Consulting, rebranded as Accenture, have realized that conveying a sense of trust and shared mission is as important as technical competence in winning multimillion-dollar contracts. Universities, government agencies, entertainment properties, and even individuals—Michael Jordan, Martha Stewart, Madonna—have come to be regarded as brands: Their names stand

WINNERS					LOSERS				
Whether it's Starbucks' iced lattes or the *Financial Times'* salmon-colored paper, ascendant brands all deliver a distinctive product to a growing legion of customers.					Amazon and Yahoo! lost brand clout when the dot-com bubble burst. Xerox did itself in with turbulence in the executive suite, while Ford got run over by the Firestone tire controversy.				
RANK	BRAND	2001 BRAND VALUE ($BILLIONS)	2000 BRAND VALUE ($BILLIONS)	% CHANGE	RANK	BRAND	2001 BRAND VALUE ($BILLIONS)	2000 BRAND VALUE ($BILLIONS)	% CHANGE
88	STARBUCKS	1.8	1.3	32	45	XEROX	6.0	9.7	−38
42	SAMSUNG	6.4	5.2	22	76	AMAZON.COM	3.1	4.5	−31
95	FINANCIAL TIMES	1.3	1.1	14	59	YAHOO!	4.4	6.3	−31
4	GE	42.4	38.1	11	62	DURACELL	4.1	5.9	−30
94	GUINNESS	1.4	1.2	11	8	FORD	30.1	36.4	−17

Data: Interbrand, Citigroup   Data: Interbrand, Citigroup

for an implicit promise of quality, innovation, or reliability.

ON A MISSION. That's why executives who earned their stripes at consumer-goods powerhouses such as Procter & Gamble and PepsiCo Inc. are suddenly turning up in the top ranks of companies that have nothing to do with detergent or snack foods. Back in 1994, General Motors Corp. was one of the first when it turned to Ronald L. Zarella, former president of Bausch & Lomb Inc., to teach it brand management. Citigroup, on the way to building Citibank into the 13th-ranked brand on our list, recruited a slew of marketing professionals from H.J. Heinz, Philip Morris, and other consumer-products companies.

Why do companies that sell to other businesses, rather than directly to consumers, need to manage their brands? For the same reason that Coke and P&G do: to give themselves a leg up in the marketplace. Just look what it did for No. 3-ranked IBM. Branding played a huge role in the computer maker's remarkable reinvention in the 1990s under Chairman Louis V. Gerstner Jr. One of Gerstner's first moves was to bring

the excesses of Web culture. And when the dot-coms imploded, IBM was well positioned as "a voice of reason—not about hype, but about steering a clear course," according to Maureen McGuire, IBM's vice-president for integrated marketing communications worldwide. Not surprisingly, in a year in which most technology brands took a bath in terms of their valuation, IBM held nearly steady, at $53 billion.

For technology marketers, IBM has become the model. Witness German software giant SAP, a brand that came in at No. 43 in our ranking. A massive but muddled advertising campaign in 1999 had left employees just as confused as customers about what the company's brand stood for. SAP hired a marketing veteran from Sony Corp., Martin Homlish, to orchestrate its next moves. "It became clear to us that technology marketing is not just talking about your technology," says Hasso Plattner, SAP's co-CEO. "You need a clear message."

When Homlish arrived at SAP as chief marketing officer, he and the seasoned marketing executives that he recruited first set

A strong brand not only helps customers understand an organization but it also imparts a sense of mission inside the company. Since employees embody the brand to consumers, it's vital that they understand and embrace brand values. "If they can't articulate to the outside world what the brand is all about, then who can?" says Shelly Lazarus, chairman of Ogilvy & Mather, whose clients, in addition to IBM and SAP, include American Express and Ford, both in the top 20 in our brand ranking. "Once an enterprise understands what the brand is all about, it gives direction to the whole enterprise. You know what products you're supposed to make and not make. You know how you're supposed to answer your telephone. You know how you're supposed to package things. It gives a set of principles to an entire enterprise."

UPWARDLY MOBILE? When managers have a clearly articulated sense of the brand, it can also help to guide basic strategy. When Boeing, No. 63 in our ranking, thought about expanding into areas beyond its core aircraft operations, top executives thought carefully about what, exactly, the Boeing brand stood for. Once the organization defined itself as a global aerospace-technology company instead of just an airplane builder, moving into satellites and aircraft services became easy decisions.

Likewise, a strong commitment to its brand strategy helped Samsung Electronics Co., whose Samsung brand ranked No. 42 on our list, make the tough decision to ditch Wal-Mart Stores Inc. as a major retailer of its products. Samsung, which gained 22% in brand value last year, is trying to move up the value chain. Selling Samsung products at Wal-Mart made sense back when the South Korean electronics company aspired to churning out low-end electronic gadgets. Now, however, the company is attempting to move into more innovative, higher-margin items, such as voice-activated mobile phones that double as digital music players and personal digital assistants. Those are products that many consumers may be trying for the first time, thus giving a new brand like Samsung a big opportunity. "That transition and our strategy to move upmarket very aggressively are the main reasons why our brand improved rapidly," says Eric Kim, Samsung's marketing chief. Having its products appear in a mass-market discounter such as Wal-Mart hampered Samsung's attempts to build a premium image.

Samsung has good reason to worry about protecting and enhancing its brand integrity. Companies that don't do so run the risk of seeing their brands degenerate into mere commodities that customers shop for strictly on the basis of price. That drift can lop off millions in brand value and market capitalization, sometimes with astonishing speed. Philip Morris Cos. found that out back in

BEST IN CLASS						
How some big brands stack up in two industries						
AUTOMOTIVE				**TECHNOLOGY**		
RANK	BRAND	PERCENT CHANGE IN BRAND VALUE		RANK	BRAND	PERCENT CHANGE IN BRAND VALUE
8	FORD	−17		3	IBM	−1
12	MERCEDES	3		6	INTEL	−11
14	TOYOTA	−1		15	HEWLETT-PACKARD	−13
21	HONDA	−4		16	CISCO	−14
22	BMW	7		24	COMPAQ	−15
35	VOLKSWAGEN	−6		32	DELL	−13
48	HARLEY-DAVIDSON	NA		49	APPLE	−17
	Data: Interbrand, Citigroup			64	TEXAS INSTRUMENTS	NA

in a marketing czar steeped in branding, Abby Kohnstamm, his longtime associate at American Express Co. Together, Gerstner and Kohnstamm reasserted the primacy of the brand in an organization that had degenerated into warring product groups. In a move that shocked Madison Avenue, Kohnstamm in 1994 consolidated all of Big Blue's advertising at a single agency, Ogilvy & Mather Worldwide Inc. Her goal was to give the far-flung company a unified and consistent message across all its products, services, and geographic markets.

After it took over, Ogilvy positioned IBM as a wise partner that could guide companies through their transformation into nimble, Net-savvy players. When Internet mania was in full swing, IBM's slice-of-life ads lampooned

about establishing a coherent message for the company. "The first mission was to have a mission," says Susan Popper, senior vice-president for global advertising and an ad-agency veteran. "We had to move from a product-driven to a brand-driven culture."

Homlish insisted that all the company's product names, logos, brochures, and Web pages have a consistent look: "speaking SAPanese," he calls it. To make that easier to accomplish, he borrowed a page directly out of the IBM playbook and consolidated all global advertising at Ogilvy & Mather. So far, the marketing pros seem to be succeeding: SAP was that rare phenomenon—a technology company with a brand that actually increased in value over the past year, posting a 3% gain.

(Cont.)

1993 when it slashed the price of its flagship Marlboro cigarette brand on what came to be known as Marlboro Friday.

That tacit acknowledgement that the rise of discount brands was burning into Marlboro's market share led investors to fear that the big brands were losing their pricing clout. The result: an immediate plunge in stock prices for consumer-goods companies across the board. The episode "really raised the bar on accountability," recalls Jan Lindemann, global director for brand valuation at Interbrand. "It was the point at which marketing directors and brand managers realized that what they did had a direct effect on shareholder value. Marketing departments had to recognize that brands and brand managers were going to be held more accountable."

Marlboro Friday turned out to be a wakeup call, not a death knell for big brands. At many companies, the soul-searching that followed ushered in a period of increased marketing budgets, stepped-up product innovation, and experiments with more compelling ways to reach consumers. Companies have learned the importance of the customer experience. They're scrutinizing every customer contact and every activity, from call centers to the way the company's trucks are painted to the selection of magazines in the lobby, to make sure they are in sync with the core values of the brand.

PERKING MERRILY. Perhaps no brand has done a better job of that than Starbucks. In 20 years, the Seattle company has grown from 18 coffee shops to 4,435. Over that entire period, it has spent maybe $20 million on traditional advertising, a pittance next to the $30 million that Pampers, ranked below it at No. 92, spent just last year. Instead, Starbucks plowed potential ad money into employee benefits. It was one of the first companies to offer part-timers stock options and health benefits. Why? Because for the Starbucks brand, the experience the consumer has in the store is crucial. A disgruntled employee or dirty restroom would break the pact Starbucks has with its customers. "If we want to exceed the trust of our customers, then we first have to build trust with our people," says Howard Schultz, Starbucks' chairman. "Brand has to start with the culture and naturally extend to our customers."

Employee benefits as a marketing tool? Why not, if that's what the brand requires. Besides, conventional advertising is no sure thing. As the dot-com bubble proved, massive advertising is not the same as brand-building. At the height of the boom, startups spent tens of millions of investor dollars familiarizing Web users with such new brands as outpost.com, eToys, and Pets.com. In the end, too many of the dot-com ads never got around to telling consumers what the brands stood for—or even what products or services the company offered. Now, many of those names are disappearing, along with the sock puppets and airborne gerbils that were their mascots.

Brand gurus predict that demands on brands will only increase in the coming decades. The 72 million members of Generation Y, who are now reaching their mid-20s, have exhibited the most social activism since the baby boomers in the 1960s. They are likely to base much of their consumption on the values they ascribe to the companies providing goods and services, predicts brand consultant Marc Gobe, author of *Emotional Branding: The New Paradigm for Connecting Brands to People.* This means that companies will have to make a far greater effort to ensure that the values communicated to consumers are consistent with its internal values. If it is not, they will be exposed. "You can fool some of the people some of the time—until they have a bad experience with your brand," warns David F. D'Alessandro, CEO of John Hancock Financial Services Inc. and author of *Brand Warfare: 10 Rules for Building the Killer Brand.* Those that make good on their promises, though, will be rewarded with a more loyal consumer base—and a brand that steadily grows in value. As managers are learning, a brand is not just an abstract concept. It's a treasured corporate asset.

By Gerry Khermouch in New York, with Stanley Holmes in Seattle and Moon Ihlwan in Seoul

"The Best Global Brands," pp. 50–57. Reprinted from the August 6, 2001 issue of *Business Week* by special permission, copyright © 2001 by the McGraw-Hill Companies, Inc.

46

SHOE FETISH

New Balance has no celebrity endorsers, does minimal advertising, and yet in the past five years has gained more customer loyalty than any other athletic shoe brand.

By: John Gaffney

Michael Jordan, Tiger Woods, and Mia Hamm hold court for Nike (*NKE*). NBA MVP Allen Iverson spins his hip-hop, straight-from-tha-playground style for Reebok (*RBK*). And Jordan's air-apparent, L.A. Lakers won-derkid Kobe Bryant, dunks for Adidas. All told, athletic footwear makers spent more than $5.9 billion on adver-tising and celebrity endorsements last year, and guess which company commands the most brand loyalty?

None of the above, yo.

The highest levels of customer devotion in one of the most volatile and hotly contested product categories on the planet belong to a small New England company that is proudly endorsed by . . . no one. According to market research firm Brand Keys, Boston-based New Balance Athletic Shoes hasn't simply replaced Nike as the footwear brand with the most loyal customers. It is also the only athletic shoe brand in the Brand Keys index's top 20, and during the past five years, its high-performance shoes have gained more loyalty than any other competi-tive brand.

More remarkable, New Balance has accomplished all of this in a period during which brand loyalty in gen-eral has been eroding faster than Ken Lay's credibility. Just ask Robert Passikoff, Brand Keys president and a professor at New York University. To create the Brand Keys brand loyalty index, he surveys 16,000 consumers twice a year about their level of satis-faction with nearly 150 U.S. compa-nies. Since the index began in 1997, Passikoff has seen significant erosion not just in athletic footwear but also in financial services, telecom-munications, and airlines, among

other categories. He attributes this to the sheer volume of products on the market. Today there are nearly 10,000 athletic shoe models, filling every niche from $15 Keds to $200 Nike Air Jordan XVII basketball shoes.

Measured by market share, New Balance is number four in this standing-room-only category, behind Nike, Adidas, and Reebok, but it has been gaining rapidly. Be-tween 1999 and 2001, its domestic share climbed from 3.7 to 11 percent, while revenues jumped from $550 mil-lion to $813 million. What's more, the growth came on just $13 million in national advertising last year. Nike, by comparison, spent $155 million and Reebok $49 million, according to Competitive Media Reporting.

How does New Balance do it? To start with the most basic reason, the company gives customers a truly unique product: athletic shoes in varying widths. No other athlet-ic footwear manufacturer makes shoes for wide or narrow feet, while New Balance covers all sizes from AA to extra-wide 6E. "I can't tell you how many people tell me that we make the only shoes they can wear," says Paul Heffernan, New Balance vice president for global marketing.

The company backs up its product with a marketing strategy that emphasizes consistency and subtlety and targets serious athletes between the ages of 25 and 45. These customers spend less on sports shoes than teens do—$2.3 billion compared with $3.5 billion—but ac-cording to Heffer-nan, they are far easier to hold on to. "Our customers are upwardly mobile, settled, very intense people," says New Balance marketing services manager John Donovan. "They're serious about fitness and their desire to achieve. Let me put

In Brand Loyalty, New Balance Dusts the Competition

By market research firm Brand Keys's measure, the average brand-loyalty rating is 100, and a swing of one or two points is considered dramatic. So New Balance's 11-point climb is exceptional.

(Cont.)

it this way: Our customers don't really think they can win the Boston Marathon. But they believe they can beat last year's time."

New Balance ads feature unknown athletes and run in niche magazines like *Outside, New England Runner,* and *Prevention* and on cable-TV channels favored by older viewers such as CNN, the Golf Channel, and A&E. New Balance's low-key slogan is "Achieve New Balance." It hasn't changed for five years. Even its ad tag lines go right after the Gen X and boomer mind-set: "Life sucks, go for a run." Or "Turn off your phone and fax . . . achieve New Balance."

The company's advertising didn't always play it so quiet. In fact, New Balance was the first athletic footwear company to offer a multimillion-dollar endorsement deal, to L.A. Lakers star James Worthy, in the mid-1980s. But after sales of its basketball shoes got no juice from Big Game James, New Balance pulled the plug on celebrity deals and has shied away from mass-market advertising ever since. "I don't have a poster of Michael Jordan in my bedroom anymore," Heffernan says, "and neither do our customers."

New Balance's low-key approach has worked well with brand extensions into kids' shoes and apparel, Donovan says, since both were designed to appeal to its core customers. Promotions for the kids' line, for example, aim at parents who wear New Balance sneakers themselves. Print ads tout shoe widths and urge parents to "nurture and care for kids" and their feet.

New Balance is also cautiously edging back into the youth market, from which it had retreated after the failure of the James Worthy basketball shoe. One strategy is built around PF Flyers, a casual-shoe label popular in the 1980s, which New Balance acquired in 2001 and plans to relaunch in 2003. The reasoning behind the sub-brand, Donovan says, is that PF Flyers will be positioned too far from the mother brand to fit under its wing. "PF Flyers is more about fashion and flash, and it will have some low price points," he says. "It's not a good brand extension for New Balance."

The brand's other bid for the youth market—to apply the New Balance "N" to a new line of basketball shoes—is far riskier. It will bring New Balance toe-to-toe with the likes of Nike, Adidas, and Reebok in a hyper-competitive category. Why not use another sub-brand? Donovan says the company decided that the shoes belonged under the New Balance umbrella because the focus will be on high performance, not high fashion, and the target audience will be serious athletes—albeit in the fickle 15-to-21 age range.

To promote the shoes, New Balance plans an uncharacteristically edgy campaign. A Hoop Troop featuring hotshot amateur ballplayers will visit street courts in 10 cities to talk up the basketball shoes and even give away a few pairs for free. Simultaneously, New Balance will roll out a $7 million TV and print ad campaign. Heffernan admits that the campaign is a stretch for the traditionally low-profile company but says it's what's needed to compete in the youth market. He does promise that one thing won't change: You won't see any NBA superstars. "We go about things our own way," he says. "We've become a celebrity brand by avoiding celebrities."

Shoes That Morph From Sneakers to Skates Are Flying Out of Stores

Maker Bets That Growing Fast But Staying Hip Will Allow Them to Avoid Scooter's Fate

By Leigh Muzslay

Staff Reporter of The Wall Street Journal

A company that never sold a shoe before last Christmas is marketing one of the summer's trendiest shoes for teens.

Heelys look like thick-soled sneakers, but they have a wheel embedded in each heel that allows wearers to switch from walking to skating simply by shifting their weight. The shoes, which sell for $89.95 to $109.95, make it easy to "heel" in places like malls and schools that frown on skating. They're also a logical successor to Soaps, which first appeared in 1997 and feature plates on the shoe-sole arch that allow wearers to "grind," or slide along rails, curbs and ledges.

Patrick Hamner first encountered Heelys one evening in March 2000, when he returned to his Dallas home. His sons ran to the door squealing about a video dropped off by a neighbor that showed young people skating through a parking garage. "Three boys, yelling, 'Daddy, Daddy, this is the coolest thing we've ever seen,'" recalls Mr. Hamner, vice president of the venture capital firm **Capital Southwest** Corp.

The Hamners' neighbor was in the same firm as a patent lawyer for Roger Adams, the shoe's inventor, and two months later, Capital Southwest fronted **Heeling Sports** Ltd. of Carrollton, Texas, $2.4 million to produce the shoes.

Armed with capital, Heeling Sports confronted its next challenge: figuring out how to become the next hot item for kids without flaming out, as the Razor Scooter did last year when knockoffs showed up everywhere.

To craft a strategy, Mr. Adams, who was Heeling's president, pulled together a shoe designer, a public-relations firm with youth marketing experience and a chief executive who had been a general manager of the RollerBlade unit of Benetton Group SpA.

The plan was to start small and stay hip. Heelys would first appear with little fanfare on the feet of cool kids, go into wide distribution in the spring of 2001 and grow in a swift but "noncorporate" way. The shoes made their debut at last September's Action Sports Retailer Trade Expo in San Diego, which features thousands of skate, surf and urban streetwear products. Trade-show director Court Overin says the shoes came off as "cool and kind of irreverent" because of their morphing ability.

From the start, Heelys avoided big-box stores, including toy retailers FAO Schwartz and Target, which were selling shoes with wheels in the front and back. Instead, Heeling Sports focused on skate and surf shops and the mall chains Journeys and Gadzooks, which target teens.

Heeling Sports put up an edgy Web site and hired many of the young people who had tested prototypes. The group of 40 hits malls, skate parks, college campuses and amusement parks in California, Texas and the Northeast on weekends, performing Heelys exhibitions.

By December, Heelys had buzz, and Mr. Adams was impatient. Rather than wait for spring, he paid $5 a pair to air-freight 7,500 pairs of Heelys from a manufacturer in South Korea to stores in 10 markets before Christmas. The company also sent free Heelys to top talk-show hosts and key TV stations and newspapers.

Stores that held demonstrations of the shoes quickly sold out. So many Journeys' salespeople began wearing Heelys to work, lapping the mall when sales were slow.

Shoe envy among kids was also key. In March, for example, Jake Jordan of Plano, Texas, saw a friend with Heelys and asked for a pair for his eighth birthday. Soon his three older brothers were clamoring for their own, washing windows and floors to earn the money.

John Mershaino, the sales manager at Shoe Palace in San Jose, says his three area stores have sold about 300 pairs a week since mid-March. Journeys President Jim Estepa says Heelys are the most important shoes of the year in his 460 stores, averaging sales of 50 to 100 a week in areas where Heelys are hot, including California, Texas, Arizona and Nevada.

As for Heeling, it says it expects to have shipped one million pairs by the end of 2001.

Cannibalize Your Own Products? If You Don't, Someone Else Will

Author: MIKE ANGELL
Investor's Business Daily

It's not an appetizing subject for many companies. But when should a new product cannibalize sales of an older product?

Cannibalization—when a company's new product takes sales from an older one—gets a bad rap. Marketing texts say it's bad, says Rajesh Chandy, assistant professor of marketing at the University of Minnesota's Carlton School of Management.

But he calls it "an important part of business. The whole reason is to create a larger revenue stream. The revenue impact of a new product should be greater than the loss of the older product."

Yet the downside is worrisome.

Home Depot successfully cannibalized older stores with new ones for years. Clustering stores built barriers to entry for rivals.

But Home Depot cut the number of new stores in 2001 because they steal sales from older ones. Analysts figure they stripped 6% to 8% from same-store sales.

Old For New

In 2001, Home Depot opened 204 stores vs. 225 planned. It now sees about 200 new stores a year over the next three years.

Retailers don't lend themselves to cannibalization, says Chris Conley, an assistant professor of product design at the Illinois Institute of Technology. "Stores tend to run into limited geographies."

But cannibalization is needed in technology, consumer products and autos. All of these products enjoy a period of strong growth followed by flat sales.

"It's very important to have a new product that can make the curve go back up," said Conley. "The best companies continuously manage product portfolios."

Before decline sets in, Conley says, a company at least should have a new product on the drawing board. Too many expect their products to have long shelf lives.

"I don't know if it's denial or just raw determination to keep selling a product," Conley said.

Question Is When

But how does a company know when sales of a product might decline before the fact? Answer: good market research.

Outside research firms or units within a company can do the job.

"That requires spending time with customers, or even the customers of your customers, since many products are sold to other businesses rather than consumers," Conley said.

EMC Corp. rode a decade-long wave of spending on large, very expensive storage computers. But that market cooled.

Clients needed smaller, less expensive storage computers that were coming from companies like Sun Microsystems, Dell Computer and Network Appliance. It wasn't until 2000 that EMC offered a less expensive system.

"Incumbent firms have a hard time cannibalizing because they have so much interest in existing investments," Conley said.

How a firm is organized can promote cannibalization, Chandy says. Internal units competing for resources are more likely to have instances where products cannibalize each other.

In the 1980s, Hewlett-Packard's printer unit mostly focused on laser-jet printers. They were faster and more durable than ink-jets.

But another HP unit sought to improve ink-jet technology, with the company's blessing.

Greg Wallace, marketing manager for HP's printer business, says the employees at the laser-jet unit weren't happy.

"There was a concern that ink jet would cannibalize sales from laser jet," Wallace said. "We had a lot of worries and a lot of angst over the decision. But we had the courage to attack ourselves."

At HP, product managers led the drive to improve ink jets. Conley says product managers are the best people to know when a product should be cannibalized. They're most familiar with what the current product does and what it should do in the future.

Salespeople should be involved in the process, but shouldn't lead it, Conley says. They're often too focused on short-term gains.

"Salespeople can't tolerate ambiguity and risk with a new product," Conley said. "In some cases, there's confusion in the marketplace because customers ask what product do we use."

At HP, the laser-jet people were up in arms about the ink-jet unit's plan to use the line "laser quality" in marketing. So the ink-jet crew eventually had to find other ways to tout quality in ads.

"There was some initial confusion about marketing," Wallace said. "But it resolved itself."

Other firms take a different tack. Gillette only advertises newer razors, not older ones, says spokeswoman Michele Szynal.

It expects the new razor, in this case the Mach3 Turbo, to take sales from the existing Mach3 line as well as older ones. The more expensive Mach3 Turbo is expected to more than make up for lost sales.

But there is a risk if the one product makes up too great a portion of a company's sales.

"If existing products are the primary source of revenue, it's very risky to move," Chandy said.

"Cannibalize Your Own Products? If You Don't, Someone Else Will," *Investor's Business Daily*, January 16, 2002, p. A1. Reprinted by permission.

Disc Jockeying

DVD Gains on Tape, But Economics Have Hollywood in a Tizzy

As Format's Sales Surge, How Do You Keep Wal-Mart, Blockbuster Both Happy?

Warner's Low-Price Crusade

BY BRUCE ORWALL, MARTIN PEERS AND ANN ZIMMERMAN

Staff Reporters of THE WALL STREET JOURNAL

The DVD movie format is on fire. In just four years, U.S. consumers have bought 31 million digital video disc players. They're snapping up DVD versions of big movies like "Shrek" and even buying second-tier titles faster than expected. In short, Hollywood—promoting the DVD format as a lucrative sequel to its videotape gold mine—looks to have another hit on its hands.

Yet even as DVD surges, it is on a different economic path than video, and one that is fraught with dangerous unknowns.

Where video enriched Hollywood through rental fees and sales, the hottest action in DVD right now is in sales. Chains like Wal-Mart Stores Inc., Target Corp. and Best Buy Co. have glommed onto DVDs to lure shoppers into their stores and are doing a booming business with them.

But DVDs are also a huge business for Blockbuster Inc. and other big rental chains, and that leaves the studios in a quandary over how best to balance the interests of their biggest customers.

While at odds about that, the studios are even more at loggerheads over pricing. One studio, Warner Bros., is crusading to drive down the prices of all DVDs, preferably so low they'll become an impulse purchase like magazines. Most of its rival studios are aghast. They had counted on years of charging premium prices for the small video discs, which offer viewers a better picture than videotape plus features such as the ability to skip around without rewinding or fast-forwarding. "It's like we're in a race to the bottom" in DVD pricing, complains the president of Universal Studios Home Video, Craig Kornblau.

How these struggles play out will go far to determine the ultimate shape of the evolving and fast-growing DVD business. The film studios could leave hundreds of millions of dollars on the table if they choose the wrong path. At stake is nothing less than the long-term value of the studios' principal asset: their huge libraries of movies.

Disc Breaks

DVDs are already selling for less than videotapes went for just a couple of years ago—as little as $14.99 for new Warner releases, and $10 for older ones like New Line Cinema's "Austin Powers: The Spy Who Shagged Me." Some studios fear that the trend is prematurely draining the life out of videotapes, a business they had hoped to milk for years to come.

The outcome of the DVD tug of war "will determine the future profitability of the film business," says Ann Daly, who oversees DreamWorks SKG's home-entertainment operation. The stakes are just as high for chains such as Blockbuster that get the bulk of their revenue from rentals.

For a variety of complicated reasons, most of the movie studios don't get a cut of DVD rentals at Blockbuster, as they do on rented videocassettes. That's hurting studio profits because Blockbuster is devoting an ever-bigger chunk of shelf space to DVDs. But to get a piece of the DVD rental business, the movie studios would probably have to make changes such as raising prices on DVD titles that they think consumers would prefer to rent. Another option would be giving those titles solely to rental stores for a few weeks before retailers could stock them.

Genie's Out

Those changes would upset the big retailers. Wal-Mart says it would resist any move to create exclusive rental periods for certain DVDs. Moreover, "Wal-Mart will not be happy if the prices start inching up," says the spokesman, Jay Allen, who says that "our customers want fresh DVD product for under $20." He adds: "You can't put the genie back in the bottle."

Wal-Mart's stake in DVD was clear at a Houston meeting last summer, where store managers were instructed on the importance of promoting the November release of DreamWorks' "Shrek." DreamWorks partner Jeffrey Katzenberg was on hand with a video in which the Shrek characters did the retailer's "Give me a W" cheer. It went over so well that Wal-Mart later used the promotional video in stores. Result: "Shrek" is the biggest selling DVD yet, nearly eight million so far.

"Wal-Mart or Target want to sell DVDs aggressively, not just to drive their own sales but to take a shopping trip away from a category-specific retailer like Best Buy," the electronics chain, says Brian Gildenberg of Management Ventures, a retail consultant in Cambridge, Mass.

But the Best Buys of the world are eager to sell DVDs, too, for a slightly different reason. DVDs bring in throngs of shoppers, whom the stores hope to "upsell" to expensive electronics gear. For electronics chains, DVD has become "what soda is to a grocer," Mr. Gildenberg says. Best Buy stocks more than 5,000 DVD titles.

Hollywood has to care what retailers think because their aggressive promotion is helping cement the DVD format in consumers' minds. Studios are expected to try raising the wholesale price of lesser DVD movies with limited ownership appeal, but they're fearful of being penalized by big retailers for doing so. Hollywood frets that if it doesn't listen to the retailers, the result could be a drop in their enthusiasm for the format, possibly followed by a drop in shelf space and orders.

Tale of the Tape

All this is in contrast to the economics that made videotapes a huge revenue source for studios, often the difference between profit and loss on a movie. Complex two-tier pricing maximized the studios' take. Some titles, such as Disney animated movies, carried relatively low wholesale prices because they were intended to be sold in large numbers to the public via mass-market retailers. Films that people might want to see just once—say, an Adam Sandler comedy—were aimed at the rental market and carried higher wholesale prices. To keep the rental business healthy, the studios made deals with Blockbuster and a number of other big chains to share the rental revenue.

In the DVD era, the delicate balance is wobbling. A big reason is the strategy of AOL Time Warner Inc.'s Warner Bros., in which every title is priced for the mass market, with no regard for the rental business Hollywood relied on so long. This is a crusade for Warren Lieberfarb, Warner Home Video's chief, who helped bring the DVD into existence a decade ago, at times against opposition from other studios. Warner has a greater financial interest in DVD than other studios because it holds several patents for parts of the technology.

The Warner executive takes glee in stirring the pot, describing the DVD situation as "another Lieberfarbian controversy." Indeed, the DVD endgame he envisions is a shocker: freeing Hollywood from Blockbuster, which controls close to 40% of the rental market and has long been a tough negotiating adversary. Blockbuster has "used that share to increase their margins at the expense of the studios," Mr. Lieberfarb complains. Blockbuster Chief Executive John Antioco says the chain uses its market power for the benefit of its customers.

Mr. Lieberfarb's bet is that people can be conditioned to buy just about any movie they want to see if it's priced low enough. If consumers insist on renting, he wants to cut Blockbuster out of the equation and steer the market toward "video on demand" services: movies delivered to the home by high-speed Internet connection. Warner is a partner with four other studios in such a service, called Movielink, which it hopes to launch later this year. Walt Disney Co. and News Corp.'s Twentieth Century Fox plan a rival service called Movies.com.

Blockbuster, which is majority-owned by Viacom Inc., doesn't think its core business of renting movies is in danger. Indeed, Blockbuster is currently feasting on DVDs itself, thanks to the low wholesale prices. The chain pays less for discs than for videotapes, in part because its long-term deals to share rental revenue with movie studios don't apply to DVDs.

As a result, the rental giant usually earns much more on the DVD version of a movie than on the videotape version, and is racing to redesign its stores to emphasize DVD. It's also forging a new business in selling used DVDs cheaply after they've been rented a few times. In a current promotion, it sells used copies of Universal's "The Fast and the Furious," released less than five weeks ago, for $9.99, or about half what new versions go for at Wal-Mart. Mr. Lieberfarb also sees used-disc sales damping the growth of the DVD sales market.

So far, owners of DVD players show a lusty appetite for buying movies. They buy an average of 16 discs a year, compared with the five or six videotapes that VCR owners have been purchasing, says Adams Media Research of Carmel Valley, Calif. Consumers spent $4.6 billion on DVD purchases last year, which was nearly 2 1/2 times the 2000 level and a windfall for the studios, whose videotape business is mature.

However Blockbuster's chief negotiator with the studios, Dean Wilson, argues that as DVD players are adopted by less-affluent consumers, a "higher percentage of households [will be] interested in rental versus purchase."

Blockbuster's relationship with Warner Bros. appears ready to come unglued, as their deal to share revenue from videotape rentals expires this month and they currently aren't talking about a new deal.

Generally, Blockbuster's Mr. Antioco says he is content with the DVD status quo,

in which he pays low wholesale prices without the complication of sharing the rental proceeds. If the studios keep dropping prices, "my margins would go through the roof, and customers would still rent," he says.

Still, he implicitly acknowledges the threat Warner's strategy poses to Blockbuster. The chain offers DVDs for sale but primarily rents them. Consumers are more likely to buy a movie when they're doing other shopping, Mr. Antioco says, while they "go to Blockbuster because [they] want to watch the movie that night and bring [it] back."

For an oligopolistic industry, Hollywood is unusually divided on the DVD issue. Currently helping Warner to push some prices lower is Metro-Goldwyn-Mayer Inc., which has cut prices mostly on older movies. Fighting to hold the line on prices are Disney, Dreamworks, Vivendi Universal SA's Universal Pictures and Viacom's Paramount Pictures.

Warner and MGM, as owners of vast film libraries, have an interest in low prices as a way to make those films, many obscure, throw off cash. But to studios with smaller libraries, cheap DVD pricing looks self-defeating, and they see rentals as still the best way to maximize revenue. "Will consumers change their behavior just because there's a format change?" asks Ms. Daly of Dreamworks. "My belief is that it's not going to happen."

The studios have all been dragged along with Warner's strategy to some degree, and they aren't happy about it. "One guy with a lot of movies can unfortunately seemingly dictate the way the market could go," complains Robert Chapek, president of Disney's Buena Vista Home Entertainment.

A few years ago, he says, an older title released on videotape might have initially carried a retail price of $19.99. At intervals of about nine months, the price would have dropped to $14.99, $12.99, and finally $9.99. With DVD, "there's pressure to get to the lower point much quicker."

Lost Empire

Disney and others have held their wholesale prices higher than Warner's, and sales have been so robust that it's been hard for any of them to complain so far. Retailers now sometimes drop prices below wholesale to draw shoppers. When Disney's animated "Atlantis: The Lost Empire" was released

last week, Best Buy sold the DVD for $16.99—a dollar below the price for the videotape. That makes studios nervous that consumers will increasingly get used to cheap discs.

Some studios are deeply concerned that declining DVD prices threaten what profits remain in the videotape business, which is still the main format used by the vast majority of U.S. households. Here, too, Warner has rocked the boat.

Whereas DVDs usually become available for sale and rental on the same day, in videotape the conventional approach is that consumers can't cheaply buy a title aimed at the rental market for several months after rental outlets get it. But last year, with the John Travolta thriller "Swordfish," Warner released a low-priced videotape simultaneously to retail stores and rental chains. The DVD came out the same day, for both rental and purchase. Warner priced both the DVD and the videotape for mass-market sales.

The DVD sold well, but the consensus in the industry was that Warner missed out on a lot of videotape rental profits. Mr. Lieberfarb says the DVD sales made up for "disappointing" tape sales, making it a wash. He is taking the same approach with titles such as "Training Day" and "Heist," even though Blockbuster's Mr. Antioco estimates that the result will be about 40% less revenue for the studio.

Mr. Lieberfarb wants to get the retail price of new releases down to about $10, not much more than the cost of a rental and a late fee. Some older titles from Warner like "Private Benjamin" can be found for $5.99.

Last year, Warner failed to clinch a deal to distribute DreamWorks' videos and DVDs, largely because of their very different views on pricing. Mr. Lieberfarb insists his low-price DVD policy is right: "Those people who are not doing this," he says, "are basically surrendering their business to Blockbuster."

Ready-to-Wear Watchdogs

'Smart' Garments Keep Track Of Vital Signs, Hide Odor; Skirt to Washer: 'Too Hot!'

By Susan Warren

Staff Reporter of The Wall Street Journal

Novelist John Jurek published a mystery, "KaeLF Skin," last fall featuring "smart fabric" underwear that can pleasure, addict, injure and even kill the wearer.

As it happens, the fiction isn't all that far from the truth.

The first generation of garments that couple nanotechnology—the science of making electronics on the tiniest of atomic scales—with high-tech fabrics to create "smart clothing" is beginning to roll out.

Motorola Inc. is working on developing clothing that can "talk" to washing machines, giving instructions on how the garments should be washed. Chemicals giant **DuPont** Co. and textiles concern **Burlington Industries** Inc. also see potential for a huge new market in clothing that looks like the same old thing but functions more like an appliance.

On the horizon: Expanding the waistline of your pants with a push of a button. Adjusting the color of a sweater from blue to green to match a favorite skirt. Tracking a wandering child through a global-positioning system woven into his jacket collar. Clothing a baby in sleepwear that sounds an alarm if breathing stops.

Last year, Burlington, of Greensboro, N.C., paid just under $10 million for a 51% stake in Nano-Tex Inc., a company using nanotechnology to engineer fabric that resists wrinkles and stays drier.

At Nano-Tex's laboratories outside San Francisco, researchers play basketball every day in the same socks, engineered with molecular-scaled sponges that absorb the rancid hydrocarbons responsible for body odor. The sponges are designed to release the smelly stuff only when they meet up with detergent in the washing machine. With this new fabric, "you could wear the same gym suit three or four times" without offending other players, says David Soane, chief scientific officer.

At DuPont, Wayne Marsh, a manager in the company's central research department, has been guiding efforts to engineer new fibers that can function as conductive "wires," as well as react to signals from electricity, heat or pressure. DuPont scientists have tinkered with the traditional circular shape of fibers to make them oval, square, or triangular. These shapes enable microscopic "wings" of different materials to be added to the core fiber, like blades of a propeller; the doctored material can then be made to contract or expand, loosening and tightening clothing, or making it warmer or cooler depending on what the wearer desires.

These fibers, already appearing in some new high-performance fabrics, will ultimately combine with electronic devices to enhance fashion as well as function. For instance, conductive, winged fibers could change the reflective quality of specially dyed fiber/cloth so that it changes color on command from an electric signal.

"The clothes that we wear might not look like the uniforms on the bridge of the Starship Enterprise, but they will be able to do the same things," DuPont product manager Stacey Burr says.

The Wilmington, Del., company hopes such research will renew its fibers businesses. DuPont's specialty-fibers business constituted $3.5 billion of the company's $28 billion of sales in 2000, while its slow-growing polyester and nylon businesses brought in another $7 billion. The now-tiny area of smart fabrics, or "textronics" as DuPont calls it, is considered an ideal opportunity for leveraging the company's knowledge in chemistry, textiles and electronics.

Scientists at the Massachusetts Institute of Technology are approaching smart clothing from the electronics side, trying to find ways to meld devices like phones and computers into garments. They have attracted several corporate sponsors to help fund their research, including **Philips** NV of the Netherlands, which last year collaborated with **Levi Strauss** & Co. to introduce a jacket with a built-in cellphone and MP3 player. Though briefly marketed, the system proved too cumbersome, observers say.

Last month, MIT researcher Steven Schwartz traveled to Russia to test a "smart" space suit outfitted with wearable computers. The suit, built in collaboration with **Boeing** Co., is designed to monitor the astronaut's condition while providing information and feedback during space walks outside the space station. Mr. Schwartz's pet project is the "smart vest"—an undergarment made with flexible conductive fibers that could be used as a kind of motherboard for plugging in wearable devices.

In New York, technology start-up **Sensatex** Inc. hopes to roll out an athletic T-shirt that will monitor heart rate, track body temperature and respiration and count how many calories the wearer is burning. It could even warn of a potential heart attack or heat prostration. Such a shirt might have prevented the recent death from heatstroke of football player Korey Stringer, the company says.

Sensatex moved into the "smart shirt" business after buying an exclusive license to technology developed at Georgia Institute of Technology for the military to monitor battlefield soldiers.

The company's first smart-shirt prototype is a T-shirt-like garment that looks and feels like a soft, ribbed-cotton knit. But the cotton and spandex cloth is interwoven with conductive fibers that can receive and transmit data from embedded sensors to a special receiver the size of a credit card. The "transceiver," worn at the waist, stores the information and can transmit it for playback to a cellphone, home personal computer or a wrist-mounted monitor.

Worn by an elderly person, the shirt could monitor vital signs or signal a dangerous fall. A GPS unit could locate a wandering Alzheimer's patient. Baby pajamas could be fashioned with a cellphone, so anxious parents could call home from the theater to listen to their infant's breathing, check his heart rate or even sing a lullaby.

For now, though, Sensatex says it is focusing on the fitness arena. The company's chief executive, Jeffrey Wolf, says he is working with sports organizations to test the athletic T-shirt on professional players by the end of the year. Also in the works: a version that could be used for weight-loss or fitness training. The company expects the T-shirt to sell initially for around $200.

Long Adept at Copying, Taiwan Takes to Patents

As the Country Becomes High-Tech Innovator, Its Copyrights Multiply

BY JASON DEAN AND TERHO UIMONEN
Staff Reporters of THE WALL STREET JOURNAL

TAIPEI, Taiwan—Not long ago, this island's high-tech industry was widely considered an outpost of copycats selling other people's designs. Now, the copycats have their own ideas to sell.

As Taiwan's tech companies blossom into major designers and manufacturers of everything from advanced semiconductors to notebook computers, they are embracing patents as a way to protect intangible assets that are the key to success in a hypercompetitive industry.

Taiwan's growing concern with intellectual-property rights is evident in the ranking for U.S. patents, which carry the most weight in the global tech industry. In 2000, Taiwan ranked fourth globally in the number of U.S. patent grants received, surpassed only by the U.S. itself, Japan and Germany—and up from 11th place a decade ago. Lawyers and executives familiar with the matter say Taiwan's patent-filing pace probably quickened last year.

The island's cutting-edge semiconductor manufacturers top the list of Taiwan patent holders, most for improved production technologies. But chip designers and makers of other electronic components are also receiving more patents for product innovations.

For tech companies, patents are at the core of doing business, enabling them to protect innovations and giving them leverage in dealing with competitors. "Intellectual property is the lifeblood of an organization," says Peter Blackmore, executive vice president at **Compaq Computer** Corp., which is seeking a merger with **Hewlett-Packard** Co. in part because the combined company would have one of the biggest patent portfolios in the tech industry.

Taiwan's patent explosion indicates that its companies are taking innovation more seriously—a crucial development in a country eager to focus more on creating techniques and products as its assembly-line jobs migrate to low-cost China. Some Taiwan companies have already begun using their patent portfolios to earn money through licensing deals, and they are growing adept at wielding their intellectual-property power in the frequent legal spats over perceived patent infringements.

"They're learning to play the game," says Lawrence Liu, an attorney at Lee & Li, one of Taiwan's biggest law firms. "Taiwan companies are beginning to realize that there is commercial value in patent protection."

Hon Hal Precision Industry Co. is just one Taiwan company flexing newfound muscles. The electronics maker's U.S. patents soared from zero in 1995 to nearly 400 five years later. It has also assembled an in-house legal army of about 300 intellectual-property specialists to help protect its inventions for products such as components that connect devices within computers, mobile phones or other gadgets. Company Chairman Terry Gou says Hon Hai has a war chest of $285 million with which to wage infringement suits. As a reflection of the company's strength in research and development, intellectual property "is a legal means to compete," says Y.P. Jou, Hon Hai's general counsel.

Taiwan's embrace of intellectual-property protection is far from universal. Illegally copied software, fake Rolex watches and imitation Louis Vuitton accessories are easy to find in the island's street markets. What's more, experts say, some Taiwan companies spruce up their portfolios with less-valuable patents just for bragging rights. "They use them as wallpaper," says Fred C.T. Yen, a patent attorney with a Taipei law firm.

Yet there is broad agreement that as Taiwan gets serious about intellectual property, the development is bringing real benefits to business. The island's legislature passed a patent-law amendment late last year extending protection of older patents, something foreign pharmaceutical companies have aggressively lobbied for. Among local companies, the island's biggest chip maker, **Taiwan Semiconductor Manufacturing** Co., now earns what it says are "substantial" fees by licensing its production technology to companies including **National Semiconductor** Corp. of the U.S., one of the world's oldest chip companies.

Until recently, Taiwan tech executives thought it frivolous to spend money protecting intellectual property. But that left them at the mercy of foreign competitors, who frequently took legal action against them, sometimes even when the Taiwan companies supposedly weren't infringing on their patents.

Hon Hai, for example, was on the receiving end of patent-infringement accusations by U.S. rival AMP Inc. for nearly a decade. But in October, Hon Hai sued the Taiwan subsidiary of U.S. conglomerate **Tyco International** Ltd., which bought AMP in 1999. The suit, filed in a Taiwan court, alleges infringement on a Hon Hai patent for a device that connects **Intel** Corp.'s Pentium 4 processors to computer motherboards. Tyco, which has countersued Hon Hai in a California district court, says its products "do not infringe any valid claims of certain patents purportedly owned by Hon Hai."

Still, Hon Hai's lawsuit is something of a landmark for Taiwan companies. Says Mr. Yen, the lawyer: "Now not only can they play defense, they can play offense, too."

Gel candies 'like rubber stoppers' linked to deaths

Consumer calls prompted action at one major chain

By Gary Strauss
USA TODAY

Michelle Enrile's life essentially ended April 10, 1999, when she fell into a coma after allegedly swallowing a popular gel-like candy made by Taiwan-based Sheng Hsiang Jen Foods.

Unable to breath for nearly 30 minutes after collapsing in her San Jose, Calif., home, the fourth-grader sustained brain damage from which there was virtually no chance of recovery, says her physician, Elaine Pico. Three weeks ago on July 30, Gil and Yvonne Enrile awoke to find that their daughter, 12 years old by then, had died.

"Even though everyone told us she would never recover, we still had high hopes that she'd come back to us as a normal kid," says Gil Enrile, a 48-year-old engineer at semiconductor equipment maker Applied Materials. "All this over a piece of candy. It's like bringing a gun into your house and not knowing when it will go off. We're still in shock."

Long popular in Asian countries, the gel candy has been removed in recent days from store shelves of three major U.S. retail chains—Safeway, Albertson's and Costco—in at least 31 states, Mexico and the United Kingdom.

The candies are marketed under a variety of brand names, including Fruit Poppers, Jelly Yum and Mini Fruity Gels. The candies also have been linked to last year's choking deaths of 3-year-old Deven Joncich of Morgan Hill, Calif., and Arturo Lopez, a Seattle 2-year-old. A Canadian girl, whose name has not been made public, also died last year.

The jellies, which until last year were sold primarily in small Asian and Hispanic markets in the USA, come in colorful foil-top plastic cups about the size of coffee creamer packs. Sheng Hsiang has said it has sold more than 3 billion of the snacks.

Attorneys representing Sheng Hsiang say Michelle couldn't have choked from a gel candy because physicians never found one lodged in her throat. Attorney Gary Soter has said that Michelle choked while being chased by her younger sister. "Any food product could cause a person to choke under those circumstances," he said.

TROUBLED HISTORY

The candies are made from konjac jelly, which comes from the fibrous Asian elephant yam plant. Billed in Pacific Rim countries as a health product, the candies are shaped and sized like the end of a hot dog. But health officials say the candy's rubberlike consistency doesn't easily dissolve, and can be almost impossible to dislodge if swallowed whole by small children.

The product is described on the Web site of U.S distributor New Choice Food as a healthy alternative to candy—fat free, cholesterol free and high in fiber. The 120-count tubs that were sold through Costco carry a 1-inch-by-1 inch label warning of a choking hazard. The warning reads: "Do not try to swallow whole! Take only in small bites and must be chewed carefully. Not suitable for children under 5."

The gel candies have had a troubled history, particularly in Japan, where they've been dubbed "the deadly mouthful" after being linked to 8 deaths and 80 choking incidents since 1995. But it wasn't until Michelle Enrile's death that much U.S. publicity surrounding the death surfaced—even in northern California. Attorneys for Sheng Hsiang maintain the product is safe. "Whether it was a mini-fruity gel, a piece of meat, a hot dog, or any hard candy, the result could have been the same," the company said in an earlier statement.

But Food and Drug Administration official Janice Oliver said Thursday that the agency has begun collecting samples from several manufacturers to decide whether the government should ask for a permanent ban from the nation's shelves. The Consumer Product Safety Commission says it has no jurisdiction to recall food.

Albertson's, Safeway and warehouse retailer Costco—who say they were unaware of choking incidents in Japan as well as at least two deaths in Taiwan—are taking no chances.

After ordering gel candy products to be removed from nearly 200 outlets in California—the biggest U.S. market for gel candies—Albertson's expanded its recall Thursday to 1,700 stores in 31 states, including

(Cont.)

Tennessee's Sessel's chain and Philadelphia-area Acme stores.

"Safety and health of our customers are our first concern," says spokeswoman Jenny Enochson. "We felt the right thing to do was to get it off the shelves."

Safeway began stocking the candies only within the past few months, says corporate spokesman Brian Dowling. "Everybody and their brother has been carrying it, so obviously our buyer saw some potential interest for consumer appeal," he says. News of Michelle's death generated enough calls from consumers to prompt Safeway to pull the product, something it rarely does without prompting from a manufacturer or government regulators, Dowling says.

Mom-and-pop store operators also are responding.

"We're trying not to sell them any more, because they're not good to sell," says John Truong, manager at Hai Thanh Supermarket in San Jose. "I didn't order any more. They were popular, really popular. Everybody buys them."

WARNINGS

Following Arturo Lopez's death in July 2000, Dr. Alonzo Plough, Seattle's director of public health, issued the nation's first health alert, warning parents of potential hazards. "We don't think they're a safe product, and there should be some serious thought to regulatory action," Plough said Thursday.

"You can pound on these products, and they keep their form. They don't dissolve easily, and they don't break up," Plough says. "They can lodge in the windpipe because of their shape."

Canada's version of the FDA, the Canadian Food Inspection Agency, issued a similar alert last August after consumer advocates in Hong Kong reported the two Taiwanese deaths. Besides the choking death of a 4-year-old Toronto girl, a 10-year-old boy almost died until he was revived by family members, says CFIA inspector Chris Tang. The candies are "like rubber stoppers," Tang says.

The Santa Clara County, Calif., Department of Public Health recommends that the candy be cut in pieces before it's given to small children.

"We decided to do something after the death of Michelle on July 30 and after learning of another death in Seattle," said Joy Alexiou of the county Health Department. "We want to make sure parents read those warning labels."

Terry O'Reilly, a San Mateo, Calif., attorney representing the Enriles, plans to file suit against Sheng Hsiang on behalf of the Joncich family next week.

"We've heard rumors of several other deaths in California," O'Reilly says.

O'Reilly, who has been handling product-liability cases for 32 years, says, "I'd like to get this product off the shelves. It's dangerous, and it's going to keep killing kids. There's no excuse for this."

Sheng Hsiang's U.S. distributor, New Choice Food of Irwindale, Calif., and Marina Foods, the San Jose grocery where the Enriles purchased the gel candies, have already agreed to pay the family a total of about $7 million. A trial date involving the Enrile's case against Sheng Hsiang is expected to be set within the next 2 weeks.

New Choice and Marina Foods declined to comment for this story.

Gil Enrile says no amount of money can assuage the pain of his daughter's death—nor his guilt.

"She was a perfect kid," says Enrile, barely keeping his composure. "She was very organized and a straight-A student. She liked to ride bikes. She liked to swim. Her wish was to go to Stanford University. Losing her is going to be with us for a long time."

He still blames himself for being unable to dislodge the candy from Michelle's throat. If there's one thing he hopes her death accomplishes, it's to see the candies permanently removed from store shelves. "Nobody should go through what we have gone through," Enrile says.

"Gel Candles 'Like Rubber Stoppers' Linked to Deaths," *USA Today*, August 17, 2001, p. 1Bff. Reprinted with permission.

Place

RETAIL RECKONING
There are just too many stores.
Warning: Big shakeout ahead

Lured by a Nordstrom store and nearly 70 other new retailers, Cheryl Campbell went straight to the Easton Town Center in Columbus, Ohio, on the morning after Thanksgiving. With shopping bags in each hand, the 52-year-old surety underwriter looked like many other shoppers who kicked off their Christmas shopping season by heading to this gleaming outdoor mall. But even by the free-spending measure of the 1990s, Campbell says the last thing this city needed was more new shopping space. "It's really a question of who is going to survive," says Campbell, juggling her shopping bags in front of the new Nordstrom.

Indeed, it doesn't take an expert to see that Columbus can't support all its new stores. The Easton center, built to look like a quaint town with a fake train station and streets like Worth Avenue named for luxe-shopping districts around the world, has doubled in size to 1.6 million square feet since the summer. In addition to Nordstrom, Easton added an Anthropologie store and an American Eagle Outfitters. Meanwhile, ten miles northwest, the Polaris Fashion Place, an enclosed 1.5-million-square-foot mall, opened in October, bringing the city's first Saks Fifth Avenue and 149 other new stores. That's on top of Tuttle Crossing, a 1-million-square-foot mall that opened in 1997, and six other big malls built previously. "They're all engaged in a big game of chicken," says local retail consultant Christopher Boring of Boulevard Strategies. "There's going to have to be a shakeout."

It's an outcome that's likely to be repeated across much of the nation. Rampant discounting may yet save this year's Christmas shopping season from utter disaster, but retailers are still expecting the slowest holiday sales since the 1990-91 recession. And with so many bargains and promotions, profits will take an even bigger hit. That's just for starters. With expansion-minded retailers and developers coming off a decade-long building binge, what comes after Christmas is likely to be even more frightening.

Like the bull market in dot-com stocks, retail is just starting to come to grips with its own bubble. The industry added 3 sq. ft. of new store space during the 1990s for every man, woman, and child in the U.S., according to research firm F.W. Dodge, like *Business-Week*, a unit of The McGraw-Hill Companies. That 20% growth rate was double the rate of population growth during the decade. Most of it occurred during the past five years, as low unemployment and soaring housing and equities markets left consumers feeling flush.

But even under those optimal conditions, many retailers did not perform well, as the total consumer-spending pie was sliced thinner. In fact, as space grew, the industry became less productive. Average operating profit margins for retailers, after rising

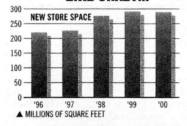

RETAILERS BUILT LIKE CRAZY...

NEW STORE SPACE

▲ MILLIONS OF SQUARE FEET

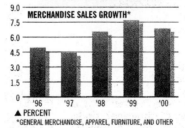

...TO KEEP PACE WITH GIDDY CONSUMERS...

MERCHANDISE SALES GROWTH*

▲ PERCENT
*GENERAL MERCHANDISE, APPAREL, FURNITURE, AND OTHER

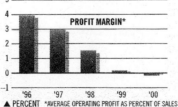

...BUT HAVE LITTLE TO SHOW FOR IT

PROFIT MARGIN*

▲ PERCENT *AVERAGE OPERATING PROFIT AS PERCENT OF SALES

Data: F.W. Dodge, Census Bureau, U.S. Bancorp Piper Jaffray

slightly to 3.97% in 1996, fell each year thereafter to a negative 0.17% in 2000, even as consumer spending accelerated, according to research by U.S. Bancorp Piper Jaffray (chart).

That was in the good times. Now, besides a shaky Christmas, store owners face a recession of uncertain depth and duration, one that could be magnified by another terrorist attack or other external shock. Adding more downside risk is that consumers are laden with record debt and worried about their jobs. There is also evidence that they are fundamentally realigning their priorities, suggesting that they may not return to their free-spending ways even when things improve. "Retailers who expanded, hoping that the consumption boom would continue, are in for a rude awakening," says Stephen S. Roach, chief economist at Morgan Stanley Dean Witter & Co.

This cycle is dealing out huge gains for a fortunate few. The dominant players are bigger and more aggressive than they were in the industry's last downturn. They will probably emerge holding a far greater share of the market, with two or three undisputed leaders in most sectors. In discounting, the likely winners are Wal-Mart Stores and Target; in consumer electronics, Best Buy; and in home improvement, Home Depot and Lowe's.

EMPTY SHELLS. The flipside? The next few months will be grueling for chains that are in the crosshairs, such as discounter Kmart, department-store giant Sears, Roebuck, and apparel specialist Gap. There is the potential for a much broader shakeout than last time, as weaker players are gobbled up, and survivors shutter underperforming stores and exit unprofitable product segments. While retailers have always "followed the rooftops," chasing new sources of population growth, this time the landscape could become even more littered with empty or underutilized retail shells, as a relative handful of megaretailers and regional malls consolidate their grip on the business. For shoppers like Campbell in Columbus, the wellspring of choice could narrow again.

No one is expecting the immediate succession of high-profile bankruptcy reorganizations seen in the early-1990s recession, when big department-store chains like Federated and Macy's sought Chapter 11 protection. True, 31 publicly traded retailers have already filed reorganization proceedings this

(Cont.)

year, more than the annual peak of 25 during the last recession, according to bankruptcy-data.com. But most of those were smaller or long-declining operators like Ames Department Stores Inc. or drug chain Phar-Mor Inc. By contrast, most big retailers carry less debt than a decade ago and will be able to hold on longer, even if many of the weakest players have trouble securing new debt lines.

The emerging key players are those that have clear and understandable positions in consumers' eyes. Just as important, they have developed logistical and financial systems to deliver the goods more efficiently. Wal-Mart has staked out the turf of price leader, while the slightly more upscale Target stands for cheap chic. Kohl's sells leading casual brands but is cheaper and more convenient than traditional department stores. "Customers want a place that is clearly defined so they don't waste their time," says Kohl's Corp. President Kevin Mansell.

"FIVE-YEAR PHENOMENON." This is leaving legions of retailers with identity crises. One thing that is remarkable about this turn of the retail cycle is the number and diversity of major players that were struggling to generate a decent financial return even before the economy headed into recession. That includes nearly the entire department-store sector, which has been hemorrhaging share to specialty stores and discounters. Whole categories that once seemed so promising, like sporting goods superstores, have been decimated. The resulting stresses could make the coming retail downturn last far longer than the one in the early 1990s. "This could be a five-year phenomenon," warns Edward Yardeni, Deutsche Banc Alex. Brown's chief economist.

The wild card, of course, is the impact of the September 11 terrorist attacks. Surveys of consumers have provided some evidence that the attacks, coming right after the popping of the stock market balloon, may have left shoppers ready to move away from 1990s-style conspicuous consumption binges in favor of more modest spending focused on the family and home. Already, that is taking a bite out of high-end retailers like Neiman Marcus, Saks Fifth Avenue, and Tiffany & Co. "Before September 11, I used to worry about what that new outfit was going to look like," said Faith Lipton, 30, as

she exited empty-handed from the Neiman Marcus store on Chicago's Magnificent Mile. "Now what matters is that my husband is going to come home from work to help raise our child. What used to be necessities are no longer necessities."

Plenty of other retailers are struggling to find a niche in the more crowded landscape, where retail concepts seem to grow stale faster than last night's eggnog. Remember the "softer side of Sears" campaign? Under former CEO Arthur C. Martinez, Sears spent nearly $4 billion in the mid-1990s to remodel its stores, spiff up its apparel offerings, and be more appealing to women shoppers. In October, new CEO Alan J. Lacy reversed course, saying he would remodel stores again, focus on a narrower but more potent range of apparel lines, and jettison its department-store heritage to find a new footing in an elusive niche between discounters and department stores. "We want to carve out a unique position," Lacy said.

Join the crowd. A similar strategy is in place at Toys 'R' Us Inc., which in recent years was leapfrogged by discounter Wal-Mart. Toys 'R' Us CEO John H. Eyler Jr. is repudiating past attempts to battle the discounters on their turf, narrowing product assortments and looking to add more exclusive items. Warren Kornblum, executive vice-president of worldwide marketing and brand management, recently told licensers that the retailer wishes to be viewed as a "large-scale, multiple-outlet specialty retailer. What we're not going to be is a discounter."

Will these stabs at reinvention work? Perhaps. But the strong don't plan to offer any quarter. Retail juggernauts like Wal-Mart, Target, Walgreen, and Kohl's are adding more new stores than ever. Even at the expense of a lower return on investment, they're determined to seize long-term market share.

Take Walgreen, which is poaching scarce pharmacists from rivals and opening a new store about every 18 hours, usually right next to a competitor. "It's almost like water dropping on a rock," Walgreen Vice-President Mark A. Wagner recently assured institutional investors gathered by UBS Warburg in New York. "It's a slow process, but eventually we're going to win the battle."

A steep downturn would accelerate an insidious cycle of weak finances that makes it even harder for the laggards to catch up. And even if they're not shouldering insupportable debt loads, some chains will be on the spot this coming year when unsecured debt lines come due, at a time when banks are retreating from lending, says bankruptcy attorney Conor D. Reilly, senior partner at the law firm Gibson, Dunn & Crutcher LLP. With new unsecured lines out of the question, those who are able will turn to the public-debt or commercial-paper markets, while others "may have to settle for a reduced facility of some kind with security involved," Reilly predicts. That will, in turn, reduce flexibility and constrain store upgrades and other improvements.

Suppliers, contending with their own sales declines, can ill afford to walk away from major retail customers. But they may be less inclined to extend payments and make other concessions to those, like Kmart and Saks, that were most aggressive in extracting concessions during the boom. Many retailers have "squeezed all the stuffing out of their suppliers over the last three to five years," says Burt Flickinger III, a consultant at Reach Marketing in Westport, Conn. "Now the suppliers have nothing to give, at a time that the appetite among retailers is the greatest." Capping the cycle, as sales and cash flow falter, retailers are forced to cut capital spending, including new stores and the information systems that are crucial to ordering the right merchandise mix and aiming marketing at the most loyal customers.

CASH SQUEEZE. Take the battle between Kmart and Wal-Mart. As Kmart's cash flow from operations sank this year, the company cut capital spending twice, to $1.2 billion from a planned $1.7 billion. It says it will hold investment at the lower level next year, and is spending all the money it needs. But after accounting for store closings and conversions of some stores to larger formats, it will open a net 10 new stores this year, and just seven next year. In some cases, rather than invest in expansive new sites for its grocery-and-general-merchandise Super K stores, the company is shoehorning food sections into existing discount stores. The cash squeeze could also make it harder to recoup ground it has lost in the important information-systems arena. Inventory control systems were so bottlenecked that at one point last year Kmart had to stash excess merchandise in 12,000 trailers parked at the stores.

Compare that with Wal-Mart. Its capital budget totals $9 billion, and that will climb by an additional $1 billion next year. Wal-Mart will open 199 net new stores this year and projects opening 248 the next, for 46 million sq. ft. of new space. Not only is Wal-Mart taking share from Kmart with new stores, but sales growth at existing Wal-Mart stores have far outstripped the rate of same-store sales growth at Kmart this year.

Similar stories are playing out in other sectors. Walgreen, the No. 1 drugstore chain, is planning a record 475 stores, up three from this year, while No. 2 CVS Corp. is scaling back openings as profits decline. Best Buy Co., the No. 1 big-box electronics store, will maintain its 60-stores-a-year expansion rate, while No. 2 Circuit City Stores Inc. continues to slow openings and gravitate upscale to avoid competing head-to-head on price against the leader.

Very few retailers thought of slowing expansion in the 1990s, even those already wrestling with operational headaches. Indeed, Wall Street was impatient with those who weren't willing to expand as fast as possible. That was particularly true in the second half of the 1990s, when retailers had to compete for investors' dollars against booming tech companies. But the avalanche of funding merely invited poor decision-making, particularly on the real estate front. "The first 50 locations are real good, the next 25 are O.K., the last ones are just deals: 'I'll take the crummy mall in Oshkosh to get a good location in San Diego,'" says Laura A. Weil, a former Lehman Brothers Inc. investment banker who joined American Eagle Outfitters Inc. as chief financial officer after helping to take the apparel chain public. Weil has had to fend off investor concerns that American Eagle's brisk 16% annual growth in square footage was insufficient.

But investors can't say there weren't signs of a looming retail glut. The feverish pace of new-store openings couldn't mask the fact that sales were hardly rising at existing stores. For most of the five years through 2000, total retail sales growth, excluding autos, grew at a faster rate than sales at stores open at least a year, according to Bain & Co. That's significant because when total sales grow faster, it suggests new stores are canni-

---

balizing sales at existing stores, lowering overall productivity. Indeed, total sales growth outstripped existing-store sales growth every month during 2000 and the first six months of this year.

Nowhere is this scenario more apparent than among narrowly focused "specialty" apparel stores. Those chains opened 64 million sq. ft. of new space, a 30% increase, between 1996 and 2000, according to securities firm Lazard Freres & Co. Gap accounted for much of that new building. Each year, CEO Millard S. Drexler increased the rate of growth, from 21% in 1997 to 30% in 2000. In that time, square footage more than doubled at its Old Navy, Gap, and Banana Republic units, to 31.3 million sq. ft. Drexler couldn't fund that kind of growth internally. So he turned to the debt markets, going from a net cash position of $17 million in the third quarter of 1997 to a net debt level of $1.75 billion for the same period this year. Gap's debt is now 36.5% of total capital. Drexler's gamble didn't pay off. Sales at existing stores have declined for 18 months in a row. Profits have fallen for six straight quarters, and the company expects a loss for the fourth quarter. Drexler now admits he grew too fast and has slammed on the brakes. "It's easy to get distracted and lose sight of the fundamentals," he said at an investor conference in September.

MORE MERGERS? The new specialty stores were also stealing sales from department stores, but they had only themselves to blame. Following a wave of mergers in the '80s and bankruptcy reorganizations in the early '90s, department stores became less willing to take the financial risk of creative merchandising. Except for a small portion of in-house brands, they mostly rely on selling the same national megabrands, from Tommy Hilfiger and Polo Ralph Lauren to Jones Apparel Group, in branded boutiques that make it hard to remember whether you are in a Macy's, a Dillard's, or a Lord & Taylor. "I don't know how Rich's and Macy's survive," says James Crutcher, a retired Atlanta physician who visits units of both in the area's Cumberland Mall. "They're so much alike, once you get inside the door you don't know the difference."

Now things are only going to get tougher for department stores. It's not hard to figure out who are the likeliest candidates for the

latest round of consolidation. Dillard's finances are deteriorating—sales have been declining, with the company posting a loss for the third quarter and analysts predicting it will post another for the fourth. The Dillard family, which controls 90% of the stock, could be forced to sell if business doesn't turn. The company won't comment on that possibility. Saks Inc., where cash flow from operations has dwindled as sales at existing stores have tanked, could face problems paying its debt, which is near the highest of any department-store chain. CEO R. Brad Martin denies Saks could run into liquidity troubles, but its junk-bond debt rating and low stock price say otherwise.

As the department stores and discounters have moved closer together in price, the importance of having a clear identity has grown. "The murky middle is where nobody should be right now," says Gwen Morrison, managing director of consulting firm Frankel Brand Environments. No retailer illustrates this better than Sears. While the chain is robust in home appliances, Sears has little credibility in clothing. Yet Sears needs apparel—it's far more profitable than appliances and electronics, where margins are thin and under mounting pressure from rivals like Best Buy and Lowe's.

DAUNTING TASK. That's why Lacy didn't exit the business when he announced the company's restructuring plan in October. But Lacy faces a daunting task moving Sears out of career wear to focus just on casual wear, in which Kohl's is the low-priced leader. Indeed, the two chains sell many overlapping brands, from Levi jeans to Nike shoes. To distinguish itself, Sears plans to create an overarching private apparel brand, much as it did on a smaller scale with its Canyon River Blues jeans brand. But it will be hard to stand out when there are already so many vibrant national and store brands, from Federated's Inc. line to Target's Mossimo. "When you think about Sears, you don't think about apparel. You think about screwdrivers and appliances," says Emanuel Weintraub, principal at retail consultants Emanuel Weintraub Associates Inc. of Fort Lee, N.J.

Although the strongest players are becoming increasingly dominant, that's not to say there won't be opportunity for newcomers— or for those willing to head in a radically new

(Cont.)

direction. Take once-sleepy Fred's Inc., a 374-store Memphis (Tenn.) discount chain that has more than doubled in size in five years with a concept that combines three of the fastest-growing formats—a dollar store, closeout store, and pharmacy. But for those chains that can't deliver on a crisp identity, there will be less and less room to maneuver amid the store glut. Once the holiday sales pass, the climate will only get chillier.

By Robert Berner in Columbus, Ohio, and Gerry Khermouch in New York, with Aixa Pascual in Atlanta and bureau reports.

54

Retailers discover leap to Web's a doozy

Transition trips even the top traditional stores

By Jon Swartz
USA TODAY

SAN FRANCISCO—When eToys.com, Pets.com and other high-profile e-tailers imploded a year ago, big retailers piled on the rhetoric: They would pick up the pieces of the eviscerated e-commerce market and clean up.

Mark Goldstein, then-CEO of Kmart's Bluelight.com, went so far as to highlight Pets.com's many gaffes on a whiteboard and vow not to repeat them.

But guess what? The world's best retailers aren't plundering the e-commerce market. Instead, they're licking their wounds and rejiggering online operations. Meanwhile, pure e-tailers like Amazon.com, which were hemorrhaging cash last year, are edging toward profits and—in the case of eBay and online travel sites—raking in cash and drawing a record number of visitors.

"Wal-Mart and Target are giants offline, but online they're shadows of themselves," Carrie Johnson, analyst at Forrester Research, says in a recent report. Instead of being overtaken: "Online, non-traditional retailers trounced offline goliaths," she says.

Amazon CEO Jeff Bezos says he expected as much. "There is wide recognition now that e-commerce is hard," he said in a recent interview. "For regular retailing, the key is location, location, location. The equivalent for online is technology, technology, technology. . . . These are just two completely different businesses."

ROUND ONE: INTERNET

So far, Internet companies are still on top when it comes to consumer retailing online. Online auction sites like eBay, pure Internet retailers like Amazon and Internet-based mom-and-pop shops captured two-thirds of e-commerce revenue this summer, Forrester says.

Meanwhile, Wal-Mart, the world's largest retailer, gleaned just 1% of retail sales online and Target even less.

What's more, some big real-world retailers appear to be struggling online. The number of visitors to Kmart's BlueLight.com in October, the latest data available, was off 25% from a year ago. Walmart.com

is revamping its strategy; CEO Jeanne Jackson resigned last month. In September, Target joined a long list of retailers who have sloughed off online sales to Amazon.com to oversee e-commerce operations.

"The same market forces that drove pure players out of business last year are hitting brick-and-mortar firms this year," says analyst Ken Cassar of Jupiter Media Metrix.

He says many simply need time to build their online business. They have to learn to compete with the more popular Amazon.com and eBay. They are scrambling to catch up with the efficient online businesses of catalogers L.L. Bean and Lands' End. And they overestimated online revenue because of overly optimistic research forecasts.

"The online channel is in its infancy, and it will just take time for the market to evolve," says Walmart.com COO John Fleming. In the meantime, some major offline retailers are:

▶ **Scaling back online.** Federated Department Stores said last month that it will stop selling products on its Bloomingdales.com Web site in February and dramatically reduce items on its Macy's site.

Meanwhile, Walmart.com and BlueLight.com have eliminated sales of apparel because they are low-margin items that come with comparatively steep shipping-and-handling costs.

▶ **Shifting plans.** Walmart.com expects loyal consumers to continue to buy lower-cost goods at its 3,500 stores nationwide. But it is starting to see the Web as a prime venue to hawk higher-priced goods such as laptops, DVD players and digital cameras. Those items aren't as visible in stores because of limited shelf space—which isn't a problem in cyberspace. Also gaining prominence on the company's Web site: movies, books, music, flowers and jewelry that can be ordered, gift-wrapped and shipped with a mouse click.

"We want to offer customers enhanced services online and sell them products they might not buy in our stores," says Fleming.

The huge retailer is also testing in-store kiosks.

(Cont.)

▶ **Cutting costs.** BlueLight.com has slashed operating expenses 75% from a year ago and could be profitable in early 2002, says CEO Richard Blunck.

But the cuts run deep. It slashed 120 jobs this summer, hired an outside firm to handle its technology operations and switched to a new customer-service partner. "I don't agree online divisions of major retailers should be non-profitable marketing arms," Blunck says. "This should be treated as a (profit-and-loss) business."

To get there, BlueLight.com requires a minimum $10 margin on products sold online. That means an emphasis on pharmacy orders, photo reprints, jewelry and high-priced toys.

▶ **Farming out operations.** Rather than build expensive infrastructures themselves, a growing number of big retailers are letting Amazon.com do it for them.

While retailers such as Target had to start their online presence from scratch, the transition was easier for catalog companies, such as L.L. Bean and Lands' End.

"The only difference between e-commerce and the catalog business is the front end," says Rich Donaldson of the L. L. Bean Web site. "We just added an Internet site. The warehouses and delivery systems are already in place."

L.L. Bean's site has been profitable since its fall 1996 debut. Landsend.com has been profitable since its mid-1995 launch. Its online revenue represented 16% of the company's total merchandise sales in 2000.

ONLINE SUCCESS

Ultimately, major retailers say, there are numerous ways to reach success.

Major retailer Best Buy's Web site is already profitable. One reason: Its core audience is technically adept, and they're looking for high-cost goods.

What's more, some online retailers have cashed in on narrowly focused markets that big-name players don't specialize in. Online jeweler Blue Nile and movie-ticket broker Fandango, for example, have built $50 million to $100 million businesses.

Another formula companies are pushing is the concept of "three- tailing," in which retailers such as J.C. Penney use multiple channels—stores, Web site and catalogs—to reach consumers.

Yahoo's Rob Solomon, vice president and general manager of Yahoo Shopping, says all retailers have to have some online presence, because the sector is "too big, and growing, to ignore." The mistake is expecting profits too soon, he adds.

"If 1999 was the holiday season of pure Internet plays, and 2000 was the year of big-name retailers, then 2001 is the year when retailers realize they need a Web site," agrees eBay spokesman Kevin Purs-glove.

Contributing: Michelle Kessler

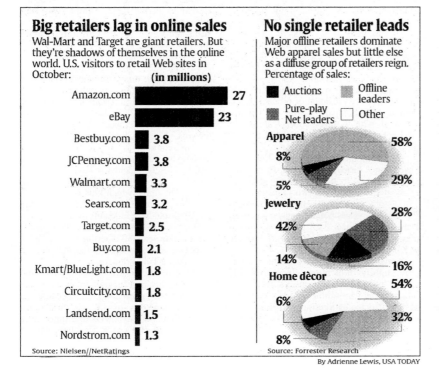

Big retailers lag in online sales

Wal-Mart and Target are giant retailers. But they're shadows of themselves in the online world. U.S. visitors to retail Web sites in October:

(in millions)

Amazon.com — 27
eBay — 23
Bestbuy.com — 3.8
JCPenney.com — 3.8
Walmart.com — 3.3
Sears.com — 3.2
Target.com — 2.5
Buy.com — 2.1
Kmart/BlueLight.com — 1.8
Circuitcity.com — 1.8
Landsend.com — 1.5
Nordstrom.com — 1.3

Source: Nielsen//NetRatings

No single retailer leads

Major offline retailers dominate Web apparel sales but little else as a diffuse group of retailers reign. Percentage of sales:

■ Auctions
■ Pure-play Net leaders
▨ Offline leaders
☐ Other

Apparel
58%
8%
29%
5%

Jewelry
28%
42%
14%
16%

Home dècor
54%
6%
32%
8%

Source: Forrester Research

By Adrienne Lewis, USA TODAY

Most recently, Target, Toys R Us and Circuit City arranged for Amazon.com to sell their products on Amazon's popular site. In exchange, Amazon gets a percentage of sales. That accounts for about 7.2% of Amazon's third-quarter revenue, or $46.2 million. Amazon expects that figure to grow, Bezos says.

"Retailers Discover Leap to Web's a Doozy," *USA Today*, December 18, 2001, p. 38. Reprinted with permission.

119

Retailers Won't Share Their Toys

Rather Than Cutting Prices, Stores Sell Exclusive Wares; Who's Got 'Monsters' Dolls?

By JOSEPH PEREIRA

Staff Reporter of THE WALL STREET JOURNAL

NORTH READING, MASS.—Clutching an advertising flier, Marie Deschene was hunting for bargains at a **Wal-Mart Stores** Inc. outlet here recently. High on her list was a $9.99 package featuring two stuffed animals based on characters from the new movie "Monsters, Inc."

"My kids just love those guys," says the 31-year-old mother of three, referring to Mike Wazowski and Sulley, the two heroes featured in the **Walt Disney** Co. animation. But a few minutes later Ms. Deschene stops dead in her tracks. "I'm so embarrassed," she exclaims, "I'm in the wrong store."

Tucked away in the corner of the Monsters ad were three words that had escaped her notice: "Only at Kmart."

Products carried at only a single chain have long been a part of the toy business. But this holiday season, the practice is bigger than ever. Does your child crave one of the new G.I. Joe "Urban Military" action figures, dressed like soldiers in many National Guard units? They're only at Toys "R" Us outlets. **Target Stores** Inc. is pushing Parents' Play and Learn, an educational toy line of musical instruments, games and puzzles sold only at its stores. And **Sears, Roebuck** & Co. is trumpeting a proprietary line of Blue's Clues toys, based on a popular children's TV program.

The trend is being propelled, in part, by toy retailers tired of cutthroat pricing. In recent years, many discount chains have been slashing prices on nationally advertised toys to draw customers into their stores, hoping to generate sales of more-profitable items such as clothing or candy. Rivals usually match the cuts, prompting price wars. The result has been a general decline in profit margins among toy retailers.

Exclusive products, by definition, can't be undercut on price, because no other chain has them. John Taylor, a toy industry analyst at Arcadia Investment Inc., figures that retailers typically earn between 40% and 50% gross profit margins on exclusive toys, compared with 20% to 35% margins on the more widely distributed variety.

"With exclusives, there are no profit margin pressures," says Neil Friedman, president of **Mattel** Inc.'s Fisher-Price division, which has been supplying many more proprietary products lately.

Which is particularly good news in this lackluster selling season. In the first ten days of the holiday shopping season, beginning with the Friday after Thanksgiving, same-store sales rose 2.1% compared with 3.2% in the same period a year ago, according to TeleCheck Services Inc., a check-acceptance company.

The Toy Manufacturers of America was already predicting flat sales for the year. But Mr. Taylor of Arcadia says that so far this holiday season toy sales are flat to down 5% behind last year, excluding videogame sales, which are up briskly. A few toys, including "Harry Potter" and "Monsters, Inc." products, are selling well. But they haven't been able to make up for the falloff in sales of Pokemon, scooters and electronic pets that were hot last season, Mr. Taylor says.

To stimulate sales, **Toys "R" Us** Inc., Paramus, N.J., estimates exclusive products will make up 20% of all sales this year, up from 12% last year and 5% the year before. It plans to boost that mix to 30% over the next two years, says Andy Gatto, the company's senior vice president of product development. The company's Web site (jointly operated with Amazon.com) features an "R-Exclusives" page that lists more than 30 proprietary brands and categories.

KB Toys Inc., a chain of 1,400 mall-based stores based in Pittsfield, Mass., this year has upped its only-at-KB toy selection to about 28% from 10% two years ago. The 1,400-store chain's best-selling item for both this and last year's holiday season has been Dance Diva, a musical toy that allows kids to play karaoke at home. It is sold exclusively at KB outlets.

Sometimes the exclusive products differ only slightly from more widely available goods. In the case of "Monsters, Inc." toys, other retailers are selling a wide assortment of items , including figurines and plush products. But only Kmart, Troy, Mich., has the rights to sell plush versions of Mike and Sully in a single pack.

The toy industry isn't unique in turning to exclusives to help offset the thiner profit margins of its mass-marketed products. Retailers in general have been increasing their reliance on private label brands. Among the best known proprietary brands are Kmart's Martha Stewart Everyday, and Target's line of household products designed by famed architect Michael Graves.

Exclusives, however, can be risky for toy retailers. Many of the toys aren't advertised on television, leaving a retailer to generate demand on its own. There is a danger of being left with a shelf full of duds that are difficult to shift through other channels. And with more widely advertised toys, manufacturers sometimes take back unsold inventory or provide future credits. That's almost never done with exclusives.

The trend also promises to frustrate a lot of parental Santas this year. Instead of buying their Christmas gifts all from one place, many shoppers have to visit multiple stores. Ms. Deschene is a case in point. After purchasing a couple of Barbie dolls and a Lord Faraquuad action figure tied to the movie "Shrek," from Wal-Mart, she grumbles as she leaves the cash register: "Now I got to go to Kmart for 'Monsters.'"

Manufacturers are of mixed mind about exclusives, in part because they're worried about ceding marketing power to retailers. Adrienne Fontanella, president of Mattel's Girls Division, which makes Barbie and other lines, says her unit has recently been pushing exclusive deals for sales outside the Christmas period. One example was Halloween Kelly, featuring Barbie's younger sister and sold exclusively by Target Stores this past October.

Ms. Fontanella adds that Mattel turns down many exclusive propositions from retailers. For one thing, the retailer has to be able to generate a big enough sales volume to provide Mattel a certain level of profit, which she wouldn't disclose. "There's a cost on our part and the benefit has to outweight the cost," Ms. Fontanella says.

But retailers say they're determined to keep up the push toward exclusives. One that will be closely watched is Toys "R" Us' attempt to revive the faded Cabbage Patch brand. The dolls, which kids could "adopt" with hospital papers, were the rage during the 1980s but have fallen off the toy charts in recent years. Toys "R" Us bought rights to the line this year and is setting aside a lavish display at its newly opened flagship store in New York's Times Square.

To give the dolls a one-of-a-kind look, factory molds are changed almost weekly—an expensive undertaking. But because the doll is exclusive to Toys "R" Us, the chain is selling them for $80 apiece, four times more than its previous price tag. The chain plans to roll out Cabbage Patch nationally beginning early next year.

Erin White contributed to this article

Tres Chèap

Taking Aim at Costco, Sam's Club Marshals Diamonds and Pearls

Wal-Mart's Warehouse Club, Long the No. 2, Invades Its Rival's Upscale Turf

In This Aisle, Bronze Sculpture

By Ann Zimmerman
Staff Reporter of The Wall Street Journal

Greg Kline, a Dallas real-estate lawyer, has a regular shopping list for his monthly trips to the Sam's Club warehouse store: a 44-pound bag of dog food, a box of oversize blueberry muffins and a 3 1/2-pound bag of frozen stuffed pasta shells.

On a recent Saturday, he added another item: a two-carat diamond.

Mr. Kline and his wife, Lisa, didn't think of Sam's for diamonds when they first decided to upgrade her engagement ring. Then, when a new Sam's store opened in nearby Plano, an affluent Dallas suburb, it sent them a flier promoting "a diamond extravaganza." This traveling gem show—Sam's Club's first—featured diamonds priced as high as $1 million, still just half what the chain said the stones could fetch at retail.

The Klines and shoppers like them have become the prize in a battle between Sam's Club and archrival Costco Wholesale Corp. for pre-eminence in the wholesale-club business. Long known for selling huge quantities of diapers, detergent and diskettes at discounted prices, Sam's Club is now using diamonds, along with luxury watches, fine wines and even sculpture, to woo the well-to-do customers who for years have helped Costco consistently best Sam's.

Bigger Spenders

In the U.S., Costco's approximately 229 stores had average annual revenue of $114.3 million in the fiscal year ended last September, while Sam's 439 stores open a year averaged only $61.1 million in the fiscal year ended last January. Costco's profits have slipped some this year because of energy and technology woes in California, its biggest state, and the cost of expansion in new markets such as Texas. But Costco shoppers still spend an average of $110 at each visit. Sam's won't provide its comparable number but acknowledges that Costco's is higher.

Costco, based in Issaquah, Wash., lures its more affluent clientele with warehouse prices for gourmet foods and upscale brands such as Waterford crystal, Raymond Weil watches and Ralph Lauren clothing. Costco also is one of the largest purveyors in the world of Dom Perignon champagne, which it sells for about $94 a bottle.

Warehouse clubs traditionally have served small business and consumers who like to buy in bulk. But Costco devotes 25% of its merchandise to what it calls treasure-hunt items: the deeply discounted TaylorMade golf clubs, the Prada and Coach handbags and the Ashworth golf shirts shoppers stumble upon on their way to the paper towels. The largest buyer of Bordeaux in the country, Costco says its wine buyer prides himself on finding up-and-coming premium wines before they hit Wine Spectator magazine. And Costco has sold diamonds for years; the company promises to give members a refund plus $100 if one of its diamonds is appraised for less than double the Costco price.

Designer Bedding

Now, taking its cue from Costco, Sam's is making its stores brighter and adding colorful signs to brighten its grungy girders-and-cardboard-boxes image. The Wal-Mart Stores Inc. unit is adding brand names such as Maytag appliances and Ralph Lauren bedding and clothes, and beefing up its fresh-foods department with steamed shrimp and bagels. Last winter, Sam's unveiled a revamped jewelry division that offers a wider assortment and higher grade of diamonds, pearls and other gems, plus watches by Ebel, Concord and TechnoMarine that sell for little more than half of department-store prices.

"I highly respect that company in the Northwest," says Tom Grimm, Sam's chief executive. "But now they have to contend with a Sam's organization that knows where it wants to go. We're better at a lot of the pieces." And, he insists, "we're taking [the stores] to a new level."

With Labels by Erte

A Sam's Club in Scottsdale, Ariz., recently sold a case of Courvoisier cognac with labels designed by Deco artist Erte for $10,000. "We still don't know yet how high is up," Mr. Grimm says.

In the slower-growth economy, wholesale clubs generally are doing better than retailers overall as consumers become more price-conscious. And Sam's in particular is seeing results from adding higher-end products to its mix. The average sales ticket has increased about 7% this year. In June, a tough month for many retailers, Sam's sales at stores open at least a year jumped 7.1% from a year earlier, when sales increased 4.5%. By contrast, Costco's same-store sales rose 5%, compared with a 9% gain a year earlier. And in each company's most recent quarter, Sam's operating earnings increased 15%, while Costco's net income slid 13%.

"There's no question Sam's is getting better, and I wouldn't be a retailer if I wasn't paranoid," says Jim Sinegal, chief executive of Costco. "They're zeroing in on an aspect of our business, so we have to get a new target. We have no illusions."

Intense competition has been a defining characteristic of the warehouse-club business since it was born in 1977, when Sol Price opened his first Price Club in San Diego. The concept of charging membership fees to small businesses and individuals for the privilege of buying bulk goods just a sliver above wholesale prices was a huge hit in the 1980s. But by 1993, the industry was in trouble, with way too many stores packed too closely together.

A series of consolidations and store closings ensued. Costco acquired Price Club. Sam's bought Kmart's Pace Club chain. The two emerged with 85% of the wholesale-club market. But they took different tacks to reinvigorate the business.

Costco, considered the innovator, created a fresh-food department modeled not on supermarkets, but on upscale gourmet food shops. The move helped drive repeat business, increasing average visits to every 10 days now from once every three weeks in the mid-1990s.

With only 3,600 different products, compared with about 40,000 at an average supermarket, Costco wanted to break up the potential monotony for its more upscale customers. Enter the high-grade jewelry, crystal and other posh products that justified a basic membership fee of $45, $10 more than the Sam's fee.

"No matter what community you're in, business owners are on the top end of the demographic scale," Mr. Sinegal says. "So we figured if our customer is not going to buy Waterford, who is?"

Demographic Differences

With its roots in the more rural, lower-end Wal-Mart chain, Sam's focused on its members' business needs, offering bulk packages of the kinds of items sold in Wal-Mart's discount stores and supercenters. "Costco's membership base is a little more affluent, so it allowed them to get to a better merchandise mix faster than Sam's," says Lee Scott, Wal-Mart's chief executive. "We also took our operational standards down as we continued to expand."

In the last fiscal year, Sam's sales accounted for 14% of Wal-Mart's total revenue of $191 billion, when Wal-Mart's earnings increased 17% to $6.3 billion. Shares of the Bentonville, Ark., parent have hovered in the mid-50s recently, off their 52-week low of $41.44 last October.

(Cont.)

After Costco first encroached on Sam's territory, opening several locations in Atlanta, Sam's in 1998 launched a promotional campaign called "The Secret to Living Well," heralding its move to "more high-end merchandise and services," according to material it sent suppliers. In 1999, it unveiled a new prototype called the Millennium Club, which was supposed to incorporate 300 new ideas, such as track lighting for product displays and letting customers weigh their own produce, instead of buying it already bagged.

The Millennium Club fizzled. "We oversold and underdelivered," says Sam's spokeswoman Melissa Berryhill.

Plagued with revolving-door management, Sam's in early 1999 brought in Mr. Grimm, who was retired and living in Salt Lake City when Wal-Mart called. A veteran of the wholesale-club business, Mr. Grimm had founded Pricesavers, a Utah-based chain that he eventually sold to Kmart.

After investigating what members wanted, Sam's unveiled its vision of the future in Plano this summer. The new store opened just a mile up the road from Costco's first Texas store, which opened last fall.

With its new blue-and-orange logo proclaiming "It's a Big Deal," the new Sam's Club is bigger than most, and with its steel casings pushed to one side, it has a more open, orderly feel than a typical Sam's Club. Each department is designated by a brightly colored blimp-size sign with a picture of the category offerings underneath. Costco still eschews signs in its stores, hoping to encourage shoppers to walk through the whole store.

The new Sam's Club has a cafe, where the menu includes root-beer floats, baked pretzels and gourmet pizza, and is outfitted with computer kiosks along the wall for accessing the Sam's Club Web site. In the fresh-food section, a large copper kettle churns out caramel popcorn and nut clusters.

On a recent Saturday, staffers handed out Oreo cookie chocolate mousse cake, Old Bay-seasoned shrimp and other treats. The store's added space allows it to hold more road shows, like the three-week diamond extravaganza and a show of bronze castings of Remington sculptures.

"When you have an income demographic like east Plano, you can bring in very interesting merchandise," Mr. Grimm says. In its first month, he says, the store sold a $10,500, 10-foot-tall Remington sculpture of a cowboy on a bucking bronco and a pair of $40,000 diamond-stud earrings. Sam's accepts only its own credit card, so the buyer of the earrings bought $40,000 of Wal-Mart gift cards at a Wal-Mart (redeemable at Sam's) to get the air miles on his credit card, a Sam's spokesman says. The buyer declined to be interviewed.

Mr. Grimm hopes soon to roll out many of the features in the Plano prototype chainwide, including a new 8-by-23-foot display case of premium wines, some so expensive that they are kept under lock. Just days after the Plano store opened, it sold out of the tightly allocated Opus One, a California red wine that went for $114 a bottle, about 30% less than retail.

"Costco over the years had a better wine program in quality and selection. But Sam's realized that they had to upgrade and be tops in selection and quality as well," says Michael Mondavi, chairman of Robert Mondavi Corp., an international wine producer that supplies both Sam's and Costco.

Sam's still has a way to go to catch up to Costco, which did $123 million in wine sales last year, a 26% increase over the prior year. But Costco has definitely taken notice. Shortly after Sam's upgraded its jewelry department, Costco's jewelry buyers checked out the competition. They bought and inspected several rings, concluding the clarity level of the stones was lower than what Costco would carry, says Megghan Harruff, Costco's assistant merchandise manager for jewelry. Sam's confirms that it allows a lower level of clarity in some of its diamonds.

"They are doing better and they look better, but we're convinced we can stay ahead of the game," says Ms. Harruff, adding that Costco sold 50,000 carats of diamonds last year. Jim Sweet, manager of Costco's Plano store, says his store's volume hasn't slipped since Sam's opened.

"You don't bring in a pallet of fancy merchandise and think you can cultivate a certain customer," says a Costco executive. "They might bring in a pallet of Ralph Lauren shirts for $37. But while our customers will buy five of them, their customers won't spend $37 on a shirt."

Glass Walls

Still, Costco isn't sitting still. For the last year, the chain has been testing a food factory in a Seattle store that produces smoked meats and tortilla chips, bottles a private-label sports drink and makes fresh-squeezed orange juice behind glass walls so customers can watch. But there are no immediate plans to try the factory in any of its other stores. Costco is also testing special-order kiosks for items ranging from top-brand faucets to expensive area rugs.

Mr. Sinegal, Costco's CEO, says he believes there is plenty of market share for both companies. In the end, he says, "it is the customer who will decide."

A few weeks after Greg Kline visited Sam's, his wife spent an afternoon checking out the diamond offerings at both Sam's and Costco. Neither had precisely what she wanted, but she was impressed with a new feature at Costco—an 800 number she could call to order a specific solitaire that would be shipped to her Costco within 48 hours.

"My husband thought I would be offended when he suggested I go to Sam's," Mrs. Kline says. She still hasn't decided where they will buy the new stone, she says, but "I'm not someone who has to get their jewelry at Tiffany's."

"Tres Chèap: Taking Aim at Costco, Sam's Club Marshals Diamonds and Pearls," *The Wall Street Journal*, August 9, 2001, p. A1ff. Copyright 2001 by Dow Jones & Co Inc. Reproduced with permission of Dow Jones & Co Inc. in the format Textbook via Copyright Clearance Center.

57

WHEN MACHINES CHAT
XML is about to spark an efficiency revolution

Life for manufacturers is about to get a lot easier, thanks to an emerging Internet technology dubbed XML. That moniker is short for extensible markup language, but don't confuse XML with cryptic programming languages like C and Pascal. Rather, think of XML as a combination Rosetta stone and *Oxford Unabridged Dictionary of the Web*—a tool that will smash the language barriers now segregating different breeds of computer, different business-process software, and different database formats. For manufacturing, XML will transform Web sites from online parts catalogs into doorways for collaborating on everything from product design and prototyping to optimized production and intricately coordinated supply chains.

XML's sweeping implications have Bill Gates, Steve Jobs, and many other CEOs hopping with excitement—along with manufacturing engineers and project managers like Maytag Corp.'s Bryan Patty. In the past, shipping the specs of a new dishwasher or other appliance to retailers such as Sears, Roebuck & Co. was a "Herculean process," Patty recalls. A team of programmers would download all the information from a mainframe, then retype the information into an Excel spreadsheet. The manual-translation process was both tedious and ripe for error. "That's not where you want to be in terms of efficiency," Patty says.

DATA DISTINCTIONS. With XML, Maytag now simply labels, or "tags," each chunk of data. Model number, price, and all the other numbers and words are marked to identify what they are. Then Maytag's mainframe zips out the specs to retailers and trading partners. Their XML-savvy computers automatically pick out each spec and insert it in the proper column. The price information, for instance, will wind up in the price column—no matter whether the price column is named B or E, or whether the document is an Excel spreadsheet or an entry form for a database from Oracle Corp. Maytag figures it can squeeze out as much as 80% of its catalog-production costs.

How can a mere coding protocol produce such startling gains? It's all in the eye of the beholder—in this case, a computer. To PCs and mainframes alike, everything is black or white, a one or a zero. Strings of digital bits are recognized as numbers, but a computer has no way of telling whether "10049" is a price, a part number, or a Zip Code. Today, spreadsheets and database forms provide the context needed to, say, sort part numbers. But when the raw data is transferred from engineering to marketing, which uses a different database system, the data will probably have to be reentered manually.

One obvious solution to this incompatible babble of bits would be special translation programs for converting from one format to another. Sounds simple. But despite the untold millions spent on such software, the manufacturing world is still divided into fenced-off camps running different design, engineering, and logistics systems. Electronic data interchange (EDI) networks are perhaps the most successful tool for relaying digital data across supply chains, but EDI is too limited for big producers and too costly for most smaller manufacturers.

"MARKETING DISASTER." So XML looks like the best bet yet for enabling different computers and programs to understand each other. The concept has been around since the mid-1990s. But only in the last three years have companies begun to define the required tagging standards. Manufacturers are at the forefront because, by some estimates, automating business practices and supply-chain systems with XML will save industry a mind-blowing $90 billion a year worldwide.

Cisco Systems Inc. is one leading proponent of XML. And nearly all software companies are scurrying to add the language to their applications. If you don't, says Robert Austrian, an analyst at Banc of America Securities in San Francisco, "it's a marketing disaster waiting to happen." He believes XML will quickly become essential for any program used in manufacturing and business-to-business relationships.

Indeed, some say XML ranks in importance just below the creation of the Net itself. It started five years ago when a group of programmers began working with the World Wide Web Consortium, which coordinates Web standardization projects. Building on earlier efforts by IBM Corp. and others, they sought to enable networked machines to not only read the information on each other's Web pages but also to understand the associations and relationships among the pieces of data.

That could pave the way for business between Web sites—computers dealing with computers automatically, in a fraction of the

---

DIFFERING DIGITAL DIALECTS

XML will eventually replace HTML as the lingua franca of the Net. But first, industries that use the language must agree on the different dialects. Here are the organizations trying to set standards:

W3C The World Wide Web Consortium first developed XML and wants to be the arbiter of XML standards across all industries

OASIS The Organization for the Advancement of Structured Information Standards is creating XML standards for e-business

ROSETTANET Wants to define how consumer-electronics companies and the electronic industry's other high-tech players use XML

BIZTALK.ORG A Microsoft-led effort to standardize XML in the software and e-business arena

ISO The U.N's International Standards Organization seeks a unified, global approach to using XML in manufacturing and design systems

VOICEXML FORUM IBM, Motorola, Lucent Technologies, AT&T Labs, and others are hashing out XML standards for wireless communication

time humans need, yet exercising far greater rigor. XML by itself may not be a panacea, admits Timothy Bray, one of XML's authors and now CEO of Antarcti.ca Systems Inc. in Vancouver, British Columbia, "but it provides a framework to solve critical business issues."

For example, if a company uses Oracle's financial software to track production costs, the program might be able to uncover new insights to improve efficiency. With XML, it will understand all the Byzantine manufacturing commands spit out by the plant's mainframe as well as the PCs controlling shop-floor operations, work cells, and individual machines. Running routine financial analyses on production data at that level of detail is now just a dream.

Still, reaping XML's benefits in manufacturing may have to wait a bit. While companies like Maytag have done plenty of XML work on the customer-facing side of their business, bringing XML to supply chains has lagged—and that's where the biggest payoffs will probably come. So Richard L. Hunter Jr., Dell Computer Corp.'s vice-president of supply-chain management in Austin, Tex., figures he'll have to twiddle his thumbs for "three to five years before we see any meaningful impact to the business from XML."

The devil holding things up is, as usual, in the details—agreement on precise definitions for I.D. tags. The trouble is, XML has been floating around for so long that some companies have already developed their own variants, and more XML "dialects" continue to spring up.

LACK OF TRUST. In addition, many competitors remain leery of the basic XML concept. They fret that customers may no longer be as motivated to buy the same brand of system to maintain easy data portability. But solutions must be found, says Jan Harris, vice-president of global sales for Motorola Inc.'s semiconductor business, because "standard tags are a must."

As a bare minimum, all the players within a given industry need to use identical tags. Otherwise, "you'll never get the payoff," says Jennifer Hamilton, chief executive at RosettaNet, an industry group that is defining XML standards for the electronics sector. Several more groups, including BizTalk.org, have sprung up to address the dialect problem. So far, their success has been mixed. One problem: Like feuding suppliers of computer-aided design systems, the groups don't quite trust each other.

RosettaNet is perhaps the main success story to date. It has 105 members and at least 87 of them have some sort of XML project up and running. It hasn't been easy "to get an entire industry to sit down and agree on things," says Hamilton. "That can take several years even within the walls of one company." But if XML is to live up to expectations, every other industry is going to have to follow RosettaNet's lead.

By Jim Kerstetter in San Mateo, Calif.

58

INSIDE CISCO'S $2 BILLION BLUNDER

How the world's most admired supply chain screwed up, and how CEO John Chambers plans to fix it.

By: Paul Kaihla

As corporate humiliations go, it had to be one of the worst. In May 2001, Cisco Systems (*CSCO*) announced the largest inventory write-down in history: $2.2 billion erased from its balance sheet for components it ordered but couldn't use. The gaffe was made all the more embarrassing by waves of prior publicity about Cisco's brilliant integration of its vast information systems. The network was so responsive, gushed Cisco CEO John Chambers, that the company could close its books in 24 hours, any day of the year. Yet the system wasn't responsive enough to stop building billions of dollars' worth of stuff nobody wanted.

Cisco blamed the fiasco on a plunge in technology spending that Chambers called as unforeseeable as "a 100-year flood." If company forecasters had only been able to see this coming, Cisco implied, the supply-chain system would have worked perfectly. But *Business 2.0* has learned that, in fact, flaws in the system contributed significantly to the breakdown. Cisco recognized many of these problems even before last year's inventory bubble, and ever since, an elite group of execs and engineers has been working on a top-secret remediation program called eHub. Here's the first inside look at how this ambitious, multimillion-dollar project could help avoid a repeat of last year's disaster . . . if it works as planned.

INFLATING THE BUBBLE

During the late 1990s, Cisco became famous for being the hardware maker that doesn't make hardware. Instead, Cisco farms out most of its routers and switches to electronics contract manufacturers. This arrangement has several advantages. For one, it allows Cisco to concentrate on marketing and product innovation. It also liberates Cisco from much of the hassle and expense of maintaining inventory, as Cisco's information systems make it possible to ship fully assembled machines directly from the factory to buyers, more or less on demand.

But the Great Inventory Wreck of 2001 highlighted some ugly bugs in the system. Cisco's supply chain is basically structured like a pyramid, with Cisco at the point. On the second tier reside a handful of contract

manufacturers—including Celestica (*CLS*), Flextronics (*FLEX*), and Solectron (*SLR*)—responsible for final assembly. These manufacturers are fed by a larger sub-tier supplying components such as processor chips (Intel and Xilinx) and optical gear (JDS Uniphase and Corning). Those companies, in turn, draw on an even larger base of commodity suppliers scattered all over the globe.

Communication gaps between the tiers eventually got Cisco into trouble. To lock in supplies of scarce components during the boom, Cisco ordered large quantities well in advance, based on demand projections from the company's sales force. What the forecasters didn't notice, however, was that many of their projections were inflated artificially. With network gear hard to come by, many Cisco customers also ordered similar equipment from Cisco's competitors, knowing that they'd ultimately make just one purchase—from whoever could deliver the goods first.

The result was double and triple ordering, which bloated demand forecasts and put the squeeze on component supplies. A missing link in Cisco's supply-chain management system magnified this problem. Suppose Cisco projected sales of 10,000 units of a particular router. Each of the company's contract manufacturers would compete to fill the entire order, and to gain an edge, they often tried to lock up supplies of scarce components. Suppliers would be swamped with orders, but Cisco's supply-chain system couldn't show that the spike in demand represented overlapping orders. If, say, three manufacturers were competing to build those 10,000 routers, to chipmakers it looked like a sudden demand for 30,000 machines. Cisco became enmeshed in a vicious cycle of artificially inflated sales forecasts, artificially inflated demand for key components, higher costs, and bad communication throughout the supply chain. Eventually, the bubble burst.

BETTER LIVING THROUGH AUTOMATION

Cisco's inventory woes highlighted the shortcomings of a communication system that stopped only partway down the pyramid. That's where eHub comes in.

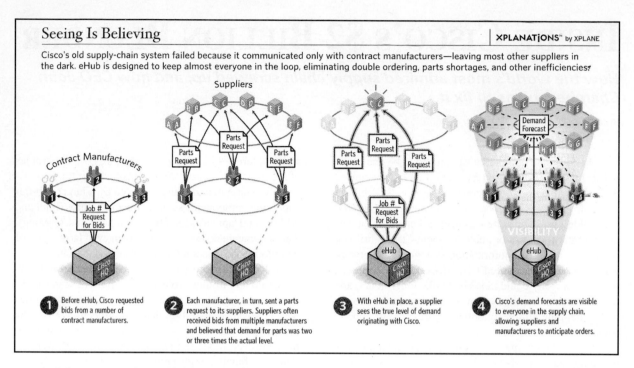

Seeing Is Believing

XPLANATIONS™ by XPLANE

Cisco's old supply-chain system failed because it communicated only with contract manufacturers—leaving most other suppliers in the dark. eHub is designed to keep almost everyone in the loop, eliminating double ordering, parts shortages, and other inefficiencies.

① Before eHub, Cisco requested bids from a number of contract manufacturers.

② Each manufacturer, in turn, sent a parts request to its suppliers. Suppliers often received bids from multiple manufacturers and believed that demand for parts was two or three times the actual level.

③ With eHub in place, a supplier sees the true level of demand originating with Cisco.

④ Cisco's demand forecasts are visible to everyone in the supply chain, allowing suppliers and manufacturers to anticipate orders.

As it happens, work on eHub began in 2000, when the last thing on anyone's mind was a slump in demand. Instead, the project was intended to help eliminate bidding wars for then-scarce components. "It was created for scaling *upward*," says Carl Redfield, Cisco's head of worldwide manufacturing and logistics. "It was put in to ensure that enough material would always be on hand."

By the summer of 2000, Cisco had produced a 3-inch-thick specification binder that served as a blueprint for eHub. Its central nervous system would be run by Irvine, Calif., supply-chain integration firm Viacore, which would take Cisco's already advanced supply-chain engine to a new level.

Private exchanges that link members of a supply chain are nothing new. In the past, companies like Dell (*DELL*) and GM (*GM*) have created electronic hubs that feed supply-chain data to outsource manufacturers and suppliers, and vice versa. These exchanges typically provide a Web interface where vendors manually type in things like sales forecasts, purchase orders, and shipping schedules. The systems are not real-time, and they're plagued by data-entry errors.

eHub practically eliminates the need for human intervention. Instead, the system automates the flow of information between Cisco, its contract manufacturers, and its component suppliers. The key ingredient is an XML technology called Partner Interface Process, or PIP.

eHub's dozen or so PIPs indicate whether a document requires a response—and if so, how quickly. For example, a PIP purchase order might stipulate that the recipient's system must send a confirmation two hours after receipt and a confirmed acceptance within 24 hours. If the recipient's system fails to meet these deadlines, the purchase order is considered null and void.

Under eHub, Cisco's production cycle begins when a demand forecast PIP is sent out, showing cumulative orders. That forecast goes not only to contract manufacturers but also to chipmakers like Philips Semiconductors and Altera Corp. (*ALTR*) "Before, if Celestica, Flextronics, and Solectron all came to Philips at the same time, and each said they wanted 10,000 of a certain chip, that was a total of 30,000 chips," says one senior engineer who worked on the eHub project. "Now, Philips can say, 'Hold on, I'm on eHub. I know that total aggregated demand is only 10,000.'" By requiring all the systems in the supply network to talk to each other, eHub ferrets out inventory shortfalls, production blackouts, and other screwups almost as fast as they occur.

Complexity and cost have put eHub a bit behind schedule. Cisco originally planned to connect 250 contractors and suppliers by the end of 2001. Instead it linked roughly 60, including Agilent Technologies (*A*), Hitachi, IBM (*IBM*), Intel (*INTC*), LSI Logic (*LSI*), Motorola (*MOT*), and Xilinx (*XLNX*). This year the number

(Cont.)

should rise to 150 or more, and Cisco's ultimate goal is to integrate as many as 650 supply-chain participants.

eHub is just the first stage of Cisco's plans for the future. Ultimately, Cisco hopes to automate the whole enchilada: A customer purchases a product online, and that order goes into both Cisco's financial database and supply-chain system simultaneously. For now, however, eHub will be plagued by a timeless software limitation—it's only as good as the data it receives. Garbage in, garbage out.

"If the inputs are wrong, the world's best supply chain can't save you," says Steve Kammen, an analyst who covers Cisco for CIBC World Markets. Nevertheless, when the next tech boom comes, Cisco expects eHub to provide the parts it needs; the next bust, eHub might keep it from getting stuck with so much unwanted stuff. Cisco isn't ready to boast about all of this—yet—but the buzz is building. "I walk into our customers today," marvels Viacore CEO Fadi Chehade. "They say, 'Oh, we heard that you are operating the Cisco eHub. Can you copy it for us?'"

59

The Friction Economy

American business just got the bill for the terrorist attacks: $151 billion—a year.
■ *by Anna Bernasek*

It's a frigid early morning in January, and Michael DePasquale, or Rusty, as he prefers to be called, has finished loading his van with containers of milk, sugar, cups, and coffee-brewing equipment. Barreling into the front seat, the heavyset 33-year-old, a driver for national coffee distributor Filterfresh, begins his haul to downtown Boston, looking more like a bouncer than a deliveryman. Everything about Rusty, with the possible exception of his wild Fu Manchu mustache, calls out "no nonsense." He wants to cover his route, get the job done, then pick up his two kids from school. That's it. No messing around. But just 45 minutes after he leaves the company warehouse in Woburn, Mass., a mess is exactly what he gets. He used to be able to unload his freight and walk right in the building at 53 State Street, a 40-floor office tower that's home to many financial services firms. Not anymore.

Now there's a guard on duty at the loading dock who carefully inspects Rusty's paperwork and the brand-new ID badge he has to carry. The guard knows him—but still has to call upstairs and double-check. No one answers. The guard waits a few minutes and tries again. This time the receptionist is there to give the okay. "I hate this building," Rusty spits out. "A few weeks ago I came in the front door as I always do to clean the coffee machines—it's much faster than waiting for the freight elevator, which can take 15 minutes—and they wouldn't let me in because I wasn't on the list. Nothing worked, and I couldn't do my job."

Since Sept. 11, Rusty and his fellow Filterfresh drivers have at times felt as if they're fighting a new war, battling their way into office buildings. Vans are often searched inside and out at some buildings—and those are the few that still permit on-site parking. Such nuisances are minor, it would seem, but they add up. Indeed, they add up in a surprisingly large way. For Filterfresh's 250 drivers across the country, delays have tacked on an estimated full hour per day to each route.

Back at Filterfresh's head office in Westwood, Mass., CEO Daniel Cousineau is explaining what that extra hour means to the $300-million-a-year business. A sophisticated, clean-cut French Canadian, Cousineau speaks with soft precision as he leans forward in his chair. Five additional hours a week per delivery person, he says, equals an extra 1,250 hours a week. By that measure, Filterfresh needs 24 more delivery people to do the same work it did prior to Sept. 11. "That's a 10% increase in our labor costs just so we can hold our ground," Cousineau says.

Four months after the savage terrorist attacks, American business is back to normal in many ways. The headlines have shifted from the Afghan front to the homegrown blight of Enron. Fear and uncertainty, once pervasive, now mingle with resignation. Leading economic indicators, as measured by the Conference Board, have risen for the past three months, and even Fed Chairman Alan Greenspan seems to believe the recession has turned toward the exits. Yes, things are back to normal. What's remarkable, however, is how much "normal" has changed.

It wasn't so long ago that corporate chiefs and management gurus were boasting that godlike efficiency was within the reach of their businesses. The unrestrained flow of goods and capital—thrust forward by free trade, the borderless Internet, and deregulation—made the productivity marvel possible. Companies like Dell were fast shrinking the inventory they kept on their shelves, shipping off products as quickly as their virtual supply chains could package them. American companies connected with suppliers and customers halfway around the world, it seemed, almost as easily as with those in neighboring states. The effect was massive. Allen Sinai, chief economist at Decision Economics in New York City, estimates that the free flow of money and merchandise alone contributed at least three-quarters of a percentage point to annual U.S. growth from 1995 to 2000.

One can't help but feel nostalgic. Today, post-Sept. 11, the economy faces a subtle new reality: Call it friction. It's as if fine sand has been sprinkled into the gears of American business—the intricate productivity machine that had been so well oiled during the 1990s. From higher security costs to airport delays, from planning for supply-chain breaks that might arise to dealing with personnel problems that have already occurred, companies are staring at substantial new costs in their operating budgets. The bill this year may top $150 billion, a full 1.5% of U.S. domestic output. (More on that later, we promise.) And worse still, Wall Street's economic models—you know, the ones pointing to a full, if sluggish, recovery by midyear—don't appear to have factored these costs into their scenarios. The surprise could be nasty for CEOs and shareholders alike.

The already weak economy doesn't help. In an environment where price discounting is rampant and excess capacity abounds, even the smallest bump in expenses can do big damage to a company's bottom line. Indeed, if the trends continue, the U.S. could well see the reverse of what happened during the past decade.

Whether the squeeze will be proportional to the dramatic expansion of the '90s has yet to be seen. But consider where just some of that sandy friction is falling, and you realize that it's landing all around us: in the higher premiums companies are forced to shell out for property insurance, in the jacked-up rent on office buildings as new security measures are passed on to tenants, in increased IT spending to beef up Internet security, and in extensive new spending on backup computer operations. Longer waits at the border (to say nothing of office lobbies), higher shipping and air-freight costs, and less predictable mass transit are also grinding the gears. So are heavier inventories, mail delays, rising premiums on workers' compensation, and a raft of new government regulations.

How painful is the final bill? To come up with a fair estimate, we've added and subtracted, rounded off, eliminated double counting, and vetted the findings against a consortium's worth of economists. That left us with the staggering figure of $151 billion, not including the tip. What it does include is $18 billion of new costs related to workplace security, $15 billion for IT security and contingency operations, $65 billion for logistical changes to supply chains, $12 billion for employee travel, $35 billion for insurance and liability, and $6 billion for employee absenteeism. (See table for specifics.) Yes, there's plenty of guesswork here, but we've deliberately erred on the side of conservatism. Nor have we included the squishy costs—things

(Cont.)

like morale, psychology, fear, distraction from strategic goals—all of which exist but prove even more difficult to quantify.

There's another rub, besides. Many of these friction costs are ongoing and must be figured into future company expenditures. A firm that hires ten new security guards, for instance, has to pay those ten salaries each year. That means the $151 billion tab facing corporate America could well be an annual one. As most of that cash is diverted to protective uses from productive ones (such as spending on research, product development, and more efficient technology), that $151 billion—while still a small part of GDP—can have a wallop on growth. Richard Berner, Morgan Stanley's chief U.S. economist, figures the cost over time to be a half-percentage-point reduction in annual growth in domestic output.

If all these projections seem too high in the ether of theoretical science, consider your monthly insurance bill. Business after Sept. 11 is simply a riskier proposition, and companies have little choice but to swallow the additional risk in the bitter form of surging premiums. It's happening right now. "We're seeing broad-based hikes," says Bill Yankus, a managing director at investment firm Fox-Pitt Kelton, which studies the insurance industry. "And it's of a magnitude we've never really seen before." Not only are property and life insurance premiums jumping by large percentages and even multiples of what they were a year ago, workers' compensation costs are rising between 30% and 50%, Yankus says. Wall Street analysts estimate a $35 billion rise in corporate insurance costs this year—which alone is likely to cause rumbles on the bottom line. Alice Cornish, an analyst at Prudential Securities in Boston, calculates that pretax profits for the companies in the S&P stock index could drop by an average of 2.5% in 2002 because of higher insurance premiums.

Airport delays are an equally obvious if potentially more costly friction point for businesses. If you thought your preflight wait was bad during the high-alert weeks just after the terrorist attacks, well, get ready to visit that airport bar. New baggage security rules imposed by the federal government on Jan. 18—mandating that every bag be screened or matched with a passenger—are likely to compound the wait. Some airlines are recommending that domestic passengers check their luggage not just two hours prior to departure, but three.

To be conservative, however, consider what only a single extra hour at the airport costs the economy. Economy.com, a West Chester, Pa., economic consulting group, has actually done the math. With 17 million business travelers

STICKER SHOCK

Did someone say profit recovery? Last year FORTUNE 100 companies earned a total of $277 billion. Start subtracting . . .

Logistics $65 billion

David Closs, a professor of logistics at Michigan State University, has calculated a best-case and worst-case scenario for the increase in costs associated with supply chains, transportation, and inventory storage. The best-case scenario, he says, is a $50 billion rise. The worst case: $80 billion. After conferring with other logistics experts, we took the midpoint.

Insurance and liability $35 billion

Forecasts on Wall Street range from a $25 billion increase in insurance costs to a $50 billion hike. A credible if perhaps low-end figure may be $35 billion.

Workplace security $18 billion

Security consultants believe that business spending on security will increase 20%, or $24 billion, in 2002. Zurich Financial chief economist David Hale estimates a slightly lower increase in security costs of 10% to 15% in 2002. Spending would cover 300,000 new security guards, screening equipment, new ID systems, video surveillance, and other gear, he says. We went with Hale's conservative estimate of 15%, or $18 billion.

Information tech $15 billion

Experts say that as many as 10,000 companies will need disaster-recovery backup systems, and figure the average cost of such a system to be $1 million. That represents a total of $10 billion for backup IT systems alone. Including other security-enhancing IT, contingency sites, and backup operations, technology analysts say firms could easily spend $15 billion.

Travel and transportation $12 billion

Economy.com calculated the cost of an extra hour's wait at airports to be an annual $8 billion. We added an extra half-hour to that, for the latest baggage security procedures, to reach $12 billion. That still doesn't take into account extra costs associated with overnight hotel stays to ensure timely arrival at meetings, or delays in other areas, like customs and immigration at the 301 ports of entry into the U.S. Taking those delays into account, the cost could be much higher.

Employee costs $6 billion

In the year ending June 2001, the direct cost to business from unscheduled absenteeism was $755 per employee, according to the Society for Human Resource Management. The Bureau of National Affairs has reported a 20% rise in absenteeism due to the terrorist attacks, though several workplace consultants FORTUNE queried put the figure lower. With 100 million people in the work force, and assuming a modest 8% upswing in absenteeism, we figured a $6 billion tab. Estimate does not include tardiness and lost productivity.

TOTAL $151 billion

flying each month, the loss in productivity neatly adds up to 17 million hours a month. At last year's output per worker of $40, Economy.com figures a loss in output of $680 million a month, or $8 billion a year.

The effect, unfortunately, has been magnified at the Long Island headquarters of Audiovox, a major supplier of wireless products like cell phones. For CEO Phillip Christopher and his 50-member sales and engineering team, travel is a way of life. If they're not on the road showing off new products to telecom outfits like Qwest and Sprint, they're not doing their job. But more than four months after the initial shock of Sept. 11, flying remains something of a dirty word at the firm. "Most of our people are fearful and really reluctant to travel," says Christopher. "It has presented quite a challenge to us."

So the boss found a solution. His staff, he discovered, was more willing to fly if each person had a buddy so they could travel in pairs. While that has coaxed his sales and engineering team back into the air, it has meant a loss of productivity to the firm—a meeting that would normally involve one person now takes two.

Aggravating the situation, Audiovox's salespeople and engineers carry loads of electronic equipment, making the routine of airport security that much more arduous and time-consuming. The compounded delays have meant that Christopher now has to send his staff the night before to ensure that they're on time for morning meetings in distant cities. Thus, the one-day visits Christopher and his team used to make to a company like Sprint in Kansas City have turned into two-day affairs, requiring an overnight hotel stay. So far, Christopher calculates that all this has raised the firm's total operating costs by 1%. "Not huge," he says, "but in this economic environment, every dollar counts."

No kidding. And the fact is, higher airport security costs have already raised costs elsewhere in the economy. The annual $29 billion cost of air freight has risen 3% since Jan. 1, according to Jim Valentine, a transportation analyst at Morgan Stanley. UPS and FedEx have likewise increased their general shipping charges by 3% to 4% since the start of the year instead of the more typical 2.5% annual increase. Both firms say the higher costs reflect new inefficiencies caused by heightened security. On top of general charges, both FedEx and UPS have jacked up some other prices by 20%, including those for pickups and, naturally, the transport of hazardous materials.

Remember just-in-time inventory? Well just-in-time has morphed into "just in case." The change is having a significant impact on costs. It's not merely delays at American airports that are causing problems. Certain

European hubs now require a 24- to 96-hour hold on cargo. At the same time, all border crossings into the U.S. are taking longer, though nowhere near the chaotic delays seen immediately after the September attacks. Many industrial companies have had to "buffer" their operations by stockpiling more parts, components, and materials at plants, says Joseph Martha, vice president of global supply-chain management at Mercer Management Consulting in Cleveland. But some firms, particularly those in the electronics, automotive, and high-tech industries, will have to go further, he says, by "looking carefully at their suppliers and deciding what should now be sourced domestically."

It's an issue Jim Commiskey doesn't need to be reminded of. Vice president of global services at Vector SCM in Michigan, he helps manage GM's $5.5-billion-a-year global logistics operations. Commiskey used to assume a one-hour lag for U.S. customs in his planning estimates when it came to GM parts arriving from Canadian plants. Now it's more like four. "Are we going to return to the days when going to Canada was like crossing from Michigan to Ohio?" he asks. "No. Those days are gone, and you have to build it into your supply chain."

The new frictions, in some capacity, affect virtually every company that moves its products around the country—but that's especially true if what's being moved could be turned into a weapon. Witness the recent experiences of Du Pont, the country's largest chemical company, where Jerry Donnelly, director of its $1.6-billion-a-year logistics operations, has had a trying couple of months. "I don't anticipate it's going to settle down much in the next year either," he says. "I'd like to get back to the business of shipping safely and saving money, but there are all these other things to deal with."

Like what happened on Oct. 7, 2001. That was the day the U.S. went to war in Afghanistan, but for Donnelly it marked the start of a focused period of contingency planning. That Sunday evening he got a frantic call from a colleague, informing him that Washington had stopped the shipment of hazardous materials by rail. Some 20% of the group's sales are from substances classified as hazardous, and he feared the worst. Du Pont normally keeps two to three days of feedstocks at its plants, and without those supplies they'd be forced to shut down.

On Monday morning Donnelly mobilized his team of 150 people at Du Pont's Wilmington headquarters, and they went to work—first figuring out inventory levels at 15 plants across the country, then coming up with alternative ways to move the chemicals. Donnelly

felt they could probably ride out the crisis in all but one case—Du Pont's shipments of chlorine, a chemical used extensively to purify drinking water. The main obstacle: Chlorine, which is toxic if breathed into the lungs, can be transported only by rail. Checking inventories, Donnelly knew that after 72 hours several of its plants needing chlorine would sit idle. The problem "tied up our whole group for three days," says Donnelly. "We were running around with our heads off."

Luckily for Du Pont, the government called off the red alert by Wednesday afternoon. Yet for Donnelly the lesson was so clear that he's been planning for threats to the company's supply chain ever since. "Things that we thought would never happen have, and we need to adjust," he says. And that means considering shipping chemicals by trucks or barges—and in the case of chlorine, deciding whether to relocate the entire supply chain, a far more costly enterprise.

Uncertainty in and of itself is a frictional cost. And Donnelly is facing it from all sides, even from the government. For example, the Chemical Security Act, now being debated in Congress, would require companies to do everything from conducting more thorough inspections of chemical shipments, to providing detailed documentation of their production and delivery systems, to beefing up security at plants. The effect of new regulations for Du Pont will mean one thing, says Donnelly—adding operational cost. "We'll either have to use more equipment and have higher carrying costs, or we'll keep more inventory and that will increase our costs too," he says.

Smart logistics are the cornerstone of an efficient economy— indeed, many economists credit the relentless drive to lessen the costs of moving and storing goods as a key factor in the supercharged 1990s economy. Michigan State University logistics expert David Closs measures the progress this way: By 2001 the average large American business held 1.36 months of inventory, compared with an average of 1.57 months a decade earlier. Closs, unfortunately, thinks that progress is over—at least for a while. He expects the figure to rise to 1.43 this year as higher transportation costs and security measures lead companies to hold more just-in-case inventory. New logistics costs alone could add $50 billion to $80 billion to corporate America's bill in 2002, he estimates.

Security, you wonder? David Hale, chief economist at Zurich Financial Services in Chicago, estimates that the nation's businesses will cough up big money to hire 300,000 new security guards. John Santora, an executive vice president at real estate giant Cushman & Wakefield in New York City, believes that security costs at corporate headquarters

(Cont.)

will rise by an average $250,000 per year. The majority of firms don't have complete disaster-recovery or backup computer systems yet, according to several experts. They may have to add them—at a cost of $1 million for a typical software system. Throw in a few thousand background checks for new employees—at an average cost of $2,500 to $5,000 per person—and the security bill grows bigger still.

Few of those expenses are likely to be productive in terms of generating sales or improving operating margins. The new security measures divert scarce funds from R&D and technology that might improve a firm's operating efficiency—at a time when industry titans like Intel, General Motors, and Calpine have said they will slash their 2002 capital-spending budgets even further than previously announced. In a December survey of 3,200 CFOs by Financial Executives International and Duke University, a surprising 47% of companies said they will reduce cap-ex spending this year. Duke professor John Graham, who ran the survey, says that it's the largest number of firms making such cuts since the poll began in July 1996. "Before Sept. 11, cap-ex spending was flat," he says. "That really pushed it over the edge."

But the biggest costs may not be the nuts-and-bolts expenses associated with airport delays, insurance premiums, and Internet firewalls. They may instead be what we've called the squishy costs— the kind that are hardest to isolate, to quantify, and perhaps to avoid. Squishiest of all is the stuff of hundreds of management books and how-to seminars: thinking big. Whether you call them strategic initiatives or Big Hairy Aggressive Goals, the seeds of growth come from the mindset and often the sheer will of a management team—a commitment to invest in an uncertain future, to take risks.

That mindset seems to be a short-term casualty of the war on terror. Just ask Joe Forehand, managing director of global consulting group Accenture. Forehand has found that his biggest challenge since the terrorist attacks is boosting the morale of his 75,000 worldwide employees. "The loss of economic and personal security removed the anchor a lot of people had," he says.

The expense—in terms of the boss' time, at least—has been real. Forehand estimates he's budgeted an extra 20% of his hours to focus on employee issues. Rainmaking, to a minor extent, has given way to regular town meetings, which he conducts in Accenture offices around the world. "There's been a shift in my emphasis," he explains, "inwards—to our business and people—and away from business strategy." The candor is telling in itself. What modern-day CEO (a management consultant, no less!) admits to not being consumed with growth 24 hours a day?

The country's work force appears to be adjusting its priorities as well. Some people are focusing on family rather than career; others are suddenly shunning urban commutes and high-rise office towers. Morale, of course, is a messy thing to measure. But at least one recent survey, conducted by the Bureau of National Affairs in Washington, D.C., has tried. Out of 146 employers queried, a stunning 74% reported "fear and anxiety among employees" more than two months after the attacks. Some 27% said they'd seen a greater need among workers for counseling services, a quarter saw a decline in productivity, and a fifth claimed a drop in morale.

Some of that anxiety clearly comes from the nation's response to the terrorist attacks rather than the terror itself—for example, not being able to get into downtown office buildings. Which brings us back to Filterfresh and its 60-person sales team. The harder it is to get inside, the harder it is to generate new sales, a fact that plainly bothers CEO Cousineau. Before Sept. 11, the company's sales force would generate new accounts by walking from floor to floor in every office building, knocking on doors. Until recently the big worry for Cousineau's salespeople was whether they could get a meeting with an office manager to pitch their products.

Now they have a bigger concern—how to get in the door to set up the meeting in the first place. It's simply impossible now for the salespeople to enter most buildings without permission. And if you think Filterfresh is alone in this challenge, take a walk over to the photocopy machine. Companies like Xerox, snack-food groups like Hostess, and linen and bottled-water companies all generate sales by knocking on office doors.

Morgan Stanley's Berner calls these new economic drags a "terrorism tax" and adds pointedly that they're here to stay: "Even if we catch bin Laden, part of the way we'll continue to feel safe is by being prudent and cautious," What's more, the terrorism threat could have lasting global impact, retarding the advances made in the 1990s on macro issues like free trade and deregulation. "I'm worried

we'll back away from our commitment to keep markets open and competitive," Berner says. Many executives in the trenches agree. "The ability to trust people has been a great strength of this economy," says Don Schneider, who presides over one of the world's biggest trucking companies. "When all of a sudden you have to check and double-check everything, it becomes embedded in our costs and makes us less efficient."

So the question becomes, Is there any way to shelter the already fragile American economy from all this falling sand? Some would answer with a resounding yes. A lesson that can be taken from the events of Sept. 11 is how economies adapt—and American business has proven in the past to be particularly resilient. The new frictions, say some economists, will offer a fresh incentive to improve efficiencies in other ways.

Paul Strassmann, a former head of IT at Xerox, General Foods, and Kraft, and now a productivity consultant, is one of those who predict a robust efficiency rebound. He contends that the new frictions will ultimately lead to savings as companies become smarter in dealing with them. Unnecessary business travel will be cut out, he says. Costly office space in metro areas will be shunned in favor of highly distributed office locations in less expensive areas. And firms will realize that the best defense is to be strategic about long-term security, not simply to throw money into lobby guards in the rush of panic. "It's an environment of using your head," says Strassmann, "not your muscle."

Optimists also point to the example of Israel. In the two years following the onset of the intifada in December 1987, productivity and business investment dived. But then both began to tick up as firms adjusted to the new environment. Richard Kasmin, head of research for Hotspot FX, a foreign-exchange trading firm in New Jersey, says Israel eventually built an economy that could function under the threat of terrorism. For the U.S., he says, the shock of domestic terror is going to diminish productivity, but firms will readily adjust.

In the meantime, however, anyone counting on a swift and strong recovery should think twice. And don't worry—you'll have plenty of time to think at the airport.

60

THE NEW TEAMWORK

This generation of collaboration technologies is making it easier for companies to work with partners and deliver products in record time

Mark the time and place: Oct. 26, 2001, Lockheed Martin Aeronautics Co. in Fort Worth. On that day, the defense contractor won the first piece of the biggest manufacturing contract ever—$200 billion to build a new family of supersonic stealth fighter planes for the Defense Dept. That Friday also marks the kickoff of a new technology era, one that could transform the basic workings of every major corporation.

Lockheed's mega-win will require some intricate teamwork. More than 80 suppliers will be working at 187 locations to design and build components of the Joint Strike Fighter. It's up to the 75-member tech group at Lockheed's Aeronautics division to link them all together, as well as let the U.S. Air Force, Navy, and Marines, Britain's Defense Ministry, and eight other U.S. allies track progress and make changes midstream if necessary. All told, people sitting at more than 40,000 computers will be collaborating with each other to get the first plane in the air in just four years—the same amount of time it took to get the much simpler F-16 from contract to delivery in the 1970s.

A project this enormous requires a feat of computing to keep all its moving parts in sync. Lockheed and its partners will be using a system of 90 Web software tools to share designs, track the exchange of documents, and keep an eye on progress against goals. Major partners such as Northrop Grumman Corp. already are hooked up. In about six months, the rest will be on board. "We're getting the best people, applying the best designs, from wherever we need them," says Mark Peden, vice-president for information systems at Lockheed Martin Aeronautics. "It's the true virtual connection."

Management experts have long talked about the so-called virtual corporation: a company that focuses on what it does best and farms out the rest to specialists who can do it better. Now, a new generation of Net-collaboration technologies is making it easier for companies to work hand-in-hand with their partners to bring new products to the market in record time—and on penny-pinching budgets.

These jazzy new technologies could take the Web a step closer to delivering on its potential. Companies can reinvent entire business processes, such as product design, supply-chain management, and sales and distribution relationships. The Net allows people from different companies with incompatible computing systems to meet in the middle on Web sites that speak a common language. And, instead of simply sending data from PC to PC, these Web tools let people separated by oceans interact with one another as if there were not even a wall between them. They can talk via their computers while looking at shared documents, carry on e-mail chats, and use electronic white boards—where two or more people can draw pictures or charts, in real time, as the others watch and respond.

If this stuff takes off, the corporation as we know it could be turned inside out. Picture it: Companies that have done everything in the past from ordering parts to bolting them together to selling them could instead use the Web as a giant electronic Yellow Pages—to find experts to do many of these jobs and then to collaborate with them over the Net on a minute-by-minute basis. The same company could offer its expertise to other firms, assembling and disbanding teams as projects begin and end. Tighter relationships between companies also could spur innovation as they tap the best talent from anywhere in the world. Workers might end up identifying less with their company than with their cross-company team—and get bonuses based on the team's performance. Potentially more radical than reengineering, Web collaboration could reshape the traditional corporation, says George Colony, CEO of tech market researcher Forrester Research.

For now, most companies would be content with technologies that make them far more flexible and efficient. Previously, they mostly relied on a pricey older technology called electronic data interchange, or EDI, to trade basic information like purchase orders. Because of the limits of the technology and resistance to changing business processes, only about 10% of large

---

Expediting the Xbox

Working with manufacturing partner Flextronics, Microsoft Corp. used a Web collaboration system to bring its new Xbox video game console to market last Nov. 15. The system helped slice about two months off the original production schedule. In one case, Microsoft decided that a metal bracket for holding the disk drive in place was too heavy, so it replaced it with a plastic one that was several ounces lighter and stronger.

Step 1 Microsoft creates a 3-D design for the new part and, tapping into the system, tells Flextronics to make the change. The system automatically sends an e-mail alert to Flextronics' manufacturing and design teams.

Step 2 Flextronics engineers log on to the system, see the change order, and discuss it among themselves. They determine that the change doesn't cause any problems with manufacturing.

Step 3 Microsoft makes a prototype of the part and discovers the bracket isn't a perfect fit. It e-mails Flextronics with some proposed changes to the design.

Step 4 Flextronics logs on and approves the changes. An e-mail alert is sent to the Flextronics unit that makes the plastic part.

Step 5 The parts people see the e-mail, log on to the system, and approve the change. The manufacturer modifies its tooling machines and builds a new version in two weeks.

Step 6 Microsoft makes another prototype, tests it, and approves the part to go into full production.

companies are collaborating with partners, according to Raymond E. Miles, professor at the Haas School of Business at the University of California at Berkeley. "People don't know yet how to do this, but they have to do it," says Miles. "You're not going to create wealth in the 21st century the way you did in the 20th."

The new tools are barely out of the box, but some early experiments are showing solid results. By using the Web to coordinate auto design by internal engineers and external suppliers, General Motors Corp. can get a car into production in 18 months, down from the 42 months it took in the mid-1990s. Land O'Lakes Inc. has saved $40,000 a month since September by using the Web to stuff butter and cheese into trucks it shares with companies such as Georgia-Pacific Corp. And Deloitte Consulting says it can bring a new team member up to speed on a project in a day or two, down from three weeks, by keeping everything they need to know on a Web site.

If this stuff delivers on its promise, it could help drive productivity growth for years. Yankee Group Research Inc. says that over the next five years, collaborating over the Net can save companies $223 billion by cutting transaction, production, and inventory costs. "There's an opportunity for a whole new level of business-performance improvements in the collaborative redesign of processes, using the Internet as the great enabler," says James A. Champy, chairman of consulting at Perot Systems Corp. and author of *X-Engineering the Corporation: Reinventing Your Business in the Digital Age.*

Still, Net collaboration is only in its toddler phase. Network connections aren't always reliable, so real-time collaboration sessions sometimes cut off suddenly in midstream. Technology novices tend to be flummoxed by logging on to Web sites and uploading documents. And even when the software works as advertised, it isn't always quickly adopted. Culture is the main hangup. Like squirrels burying nuts for winter, companies and their divisions have traditionally hoarded information—even from each other—as a competitive advantage. The challenge is to come up with ways to reward employees for working in new ways.

Tight technology budgets also have slowed adoption of new software. Many companies delayed collaboration projects in the second half of 2001. "They weren't going full-bore because they got burned before" by earlier Internet technologies that didn't deliver, says analyst Heather Bellini of Salomon Smith Barney. "Next year is when we'll move beyond initial deployments, We're still very much in the early adopter phase."

Being a collaboration pioneer has paid off big-time for Juniper Networks Inc. It farms out operations like manufacturing, logistics, and customer support so it can concentrate on

---

New Ways to Get Work Done

Web sites where workers can collaborate change the game for corporations by saving time and money on everything from product design to mergers

BUSINESS PROCESS	PAYOFF
Product Development: Companies are making products more cheaply and quickly by using the Web to synchronize the design process with suppliers.	Using a collaborative system at 11 General Motors Corp. factories, the company has cut the time it takes to finish a vehicle mock-up from 12 weeks to two weeks.
Supply Chain: Companies can use shared Web sites to work closely with contract manufacturers and suppliers—reducing inventories.	By purchasing food ingredients and other goods via an online service that allows it to interact with suppliers, H.J. Heinz Co. has cut its supplier costs by 10%.
Sales Channels: On Web sites, companies and their resellers share technical information, conduct employee training, and track sales leads.	Toshiba Canada Office Products Group has reduced by half the time it takes to process orders handled by its resellers and has cut printing and mailing costs.
Transportation: Logistics exchanges take the hassle out of delivering goods by offering quick price quotes, truck availability, and shared trucks.	Georgia-Pacific Corp. has saved $600,000, or 19%, since June on a single cross-country route that it shares with General Mills Inc.
Project Management: Law firms, consulting firms, and banks can use electronic bulletin boards to manage complex deals and projects.	Deloitte Consulting can bring a new team member up to speed on a project within a day or two rather than the three weeks it used to take.

---

what it does best: designing and selling networking equipment. Because the company is so efficient, even when revenue growth slowed to 32% in 2001 from a fivefold jump in 2000, it was able to increase research and development spending by 80%. "We were able to manage costs to protect strategic investment," says CEO Scott G. Kriens. "This has a lot to do with the outsourcing."

Juniper's network links its own operations with those of partners—setting off a digital chain reaction. Customers place an order via the Web, which relays the order to Juniper's core planning software, which spits out the details to every internal department that needs the info—from finance to supply chain and to outsiders like contract manufacturers. Juniper's production planning system automatically vets the manufacturer's inventory, raw materials, and production lead time—then coughs up a date when the product will be shipped directly to the customer. If a customer changes her order on short notice, a team of material planners and process engineers from Juniper and its contractor manufacturers are alerted by e-mail. They get together in a Web conference to figure out what needs to be done to deliver on time.

One of the most effective uses of the new collaboration technologies is in the area of product development—everything from designing cars to developing new prescription

drugs. This kind of teamwork not only increases efficiency but boosts innovation—the holy grail of companies hoping to produce the Next Big Thing in their industry. General Motors, for one, has chalked up big wins since setting up a collaborative engineering system in 1999 that allows GM employees and external auto parts suppliers to share product design information. Previously, GM had no way of coordinating its complex designs across its 14 engineering sites scattered across the world, plus the dozens of partners who design subsystems.

Now, GM's collaboration system serves as a centralized clearinghouse for all the design data. More than 16,000 designers and other workers use the new Web system from Electronic Data Systems Corp. to share 3-D designs and keep track of parts and subassemblies. The system automatically updates the master design when changes are finalized so everyone is on the same page. The result: GM has slashed the time it takes to complete a full mock-up of a car from 12 weeks to two. The time saved by online collaboration frees up workers to think more creatively—mocking up three or four more alternative designs per car.

After products roll off the assembly line, Web collaboration software can help sell them. Companies with complex sales channels are turning to the Net to help sign up

(Cont.)

resellers and coordinate marketing. PTC, in Needham, Mass., which makes product-design software, is using Web-collaboration software to reach out to resellers it needs to expand to new markets not already served by its sales force. The software from Channel-Wave Inc. automates the recruiting and certification process. It now takes a day to sign up a partner—down from a week. In a year, PTC has signed up about 170 partners. PTC expects to recoup the $22,000 a month it pays for ChannelWave with an improved rate of converting leads for resellers to sales—35%, vs. 20% in the old days. It will be able to use the Web site to hand off leads to specific resellers and track their attempts to land customers. If a reseller is having trouble, PTC can step in to help cement the deal.

Once a sale is made, the next step is delivering products. Collaboration technologies are saving money in warehouses and on 18-wheelers. A dozen companies including Land O'Lakes and Georgia-Pacific use a collaboration system devised by Nistevo Corp., a software company in Eden Prairie, Minn., to use the fewest trucks possible and keep them full by matching loads and routes. The companies submit all the details about their routes and contracts with truckers to the Nistevo Web site. The company matches up the participants' schedules and notifies potential partners by e-mail. Once the companies agree to terms, they log on to a Web site to place an order for a truck and track the shipments.

The rewards are starting to roll in. In just six months, Georgia-Pacific says it has saved $600,000 on one, six-legged route from Chicago to Maine and back again. And Fernando Palacios, vice-president for operations and supply chain at Land O'Lakes, says, based on initial results, the company expects to save a half-million dollars this year. Payoffs like that more than cover the average $250,000 annual cost for Nistevo and the $75,000 installation fee.

There's no matching Net collaboration when a crisis breaks out. Web sites can be set up in minutes. People are able to share data, schedule meetings, conduct forum discussions, and view up-to-date drafts of documents they're working on. Using a Web site

provided by New York-based IntraLinks Inc., 80 people from seven consulting firms produced a report for the New York City Partnership on the economic impact of the September 11 attacks. It took just six weeks—rather than the normal six months or more. The timing was crucial since the city needed facts to back up its pleas for relief funds. The Web site made sharing information a snap. Every morning, Jenny Abramson, an associate with Boston Consulting Group, posted links to newspaper articles on the Web site—alerting her colleagues with e-mails. "We were able to spend more time on the content issues, and less on logistics," says Abramson.

Those are some of the best-case scenarios. In other cases, collaborative projects have yet to deliver the goods. Last spring, Baker & McKenzie, a Chicago law firm with 3,000 attorneys and 62 offices worldwide, was enthused about a new multimillion-dollar collaboration system from Lehi (Utah)-based Nextpage Inc. that would allow its lawyers to manage cases and corporate mergers with other parties over the Web. The company had an ambitious plan to roll out the service to 10 of its offices in the second quarter and get the other offices online by the end of the year.

It didn't happen. The firm underestimated the training costs and the difficulties of changing peoples' behavior, especially among workers who weren't computer-savvy. During an early training session, one older lawyer actually confused a Microsoft PowerPoint presentation they were using to train people for the collaboration service itself. "Getting people to practice in a different way is a very ambitious exercise," says Mark Swords, a partner heading the initiative. Now, Swords says, Baker & McKenzie plans to roll out the service in the second quarter, a year later than expected, and in only two offices instead of 10 or more. The firm remains committed to it because he believes it could help land new clients.

Changing old habits is only one of the roadblocks to smoother collaboration. Technology bugs and a competitive wariness are making people move gingerly. One tech

manager at Boeing Co. complains that Microsoft Corp.'s NetMeeting software for online meetings "is terrible. . . . Everything freezes so people have to reconnect." Engineers fret about the time it takes to transfer bulky design files. And early users of a collaboration system made by Groove Networks Inc. in Cambridge, Mass., complain that they have to reformat Microsoft Word documents before they can share them in cyberspace. Software companies are scurrying to work out the bugs so their tools catch on faster.

One of the key early lessons is that for collaboration to work well, it has to be between people, not just machines. Management experts say digital workspaces can't completely replace more traditional interactions, especially in the creative process. In-person communication is important for training, building relationships, and riding herd on a difficult project. Nistevo addresses that by mixing tech wizardry with old-fashioned meetings. Palacios of Land O'Lakes says companies participating in Nistevo's trucking project build trust and sort out their problems by meeting face-to-face every quarter.

Lockheed won't have the luxury of waiting for in-person confabs to get over hurdles. Its suppliers span 26 states and three countries. But it's willing to put up with the glitches that are inherent in electronic collaboration. The Lockheed team is heading into the digital wilderness with no thought of turning tail. "This wasn't an accounting decision," says Lockheed's Peden. "It was a what-do-you-want-to-be-when-you-grow-up decision."

Other companies will face similar choices as these teamwork tools improve. For many outfits, finding a way to make collaboration work across corporate boundaries may be the surest path to reaching a ripe old age.

By Faith Keenan and Spencer E. Ante
Contributing: Ben Elgin and Steve Hamm

"The New Teamwork," pp. EB12–EB16. Reprinted from the February 18, 2002 issue of *Business Week E.Biz* by special permission, copyright © 2002 by The McGraw-Hill Companies, Inc.

Promotion

Another Advertising Star Is Born as Viewers Embrace Dell's Pitchman

'Dude, You're Gettin' a Dell' Is in Gen X's Vernacular, Echoing 'Where's the Beef?'

By SUZANNE VRANICA

"You're the Dell guy," shouts French restaurateur Alain Denneulin across a crowded room in his trendy Manhattan eatery, Felix. Heads turn and people point at Benjamin Curtis, a 21-year-old college student—and star of a popular ad campaign for Dell computers—who smiles and moves hastily to a table.

Dell Computer Corp., of Austin, Texas, has made a celebrity out of Mr. Curtis in commercials admired for their clever blend of humor and salesmanship. Mr. Curtis plays "Steven," a blonde surfer dude, who gives expert advice to people shopping for a home computer.

Steven is the first fictional Generation X pitchman to rise up from Madison Avenue and win wider acclaim since "Stuart." Stuart, some TV viewers will recall, was the redheaded know-it-all who turned his geezer boss onto online stock trading with **Ameritrade Holding Corp.**—a glamorous and exciting thing to do back in March 1999, when that campaign hit the airwaves.

Now, it's Steven's turn to generate buzz. The "Dell Guy" boasts one of the largest advertising fan club message boards on Yahoo, with 535 members. Louie, **Anheuser-Busch Cos.'** popular Budweiser lizard, claims only 15. A New York radio station, WHTZ-FM's Z100, recently yammered on about him for days. The station eventually tracked him down through his agent and got a call from him.

Steven first appeared in late 2000, in a spot created by **Interpublic Group's** Lowe Worldwide in which he makes a video for his parents to explain why they should buy him a Dell. Dell switched agencies, hiring the Chicago office of **Omnicom Group** Inc.'s DDB, but Steve and the campaign survived.

In July, DDB added the quip: "Dude, you're gettin' a Dell." The line hasn't quite achieved the status of Anheuser-Busch's "Whassup?" or **Wendy's International**

Inc.'s "Where's the beef?" But it is slowly seeping into the pop-culture vernacular, a kind of all-purpose "Good Job!" for slackers.

For the 2001 holidays, "Steven" wore a green elf suit and hawked Dell's $899 desktop computer. Now, Mr. Curtis is getting ready to shoot new ads in Los Angeles.

The new campaign comes at a dark hour for the home PC industry. Domestic sales of consumer PCs declined 31% for the first three quarters of 2001, according to the Gartner Group, a technology research firm. But thanks in large measure to the Steven ads, during that period Dell has managed to increase its share of the market to 16.5%, more than double the 7% share Dell had for the same period last year.

Hewlett-Packard Co. remains the leader in consumer PCs, with a market share of 21.9%. But Dell is a major advertiser, spending $196 million on ads for its brand in 2000. For the first nine months of 2001, Dell's advertising outlays totaled $137 million, up 18.1% from the same period earlier, according to CMR, an ad tracking unit of London-based Taylor Nelson Sofres PLC.

A large portion of the spending has gone to support the ubiquitous Steven ads, although Dell won't specify exactly how much. "Dell was previously known as a company that dealt with large enterprise customers and not necessarily a company consumers would relate to," says Erin Nelson, Dell's marketing director.

Dell rival **Gateway Inc.,** whose market share declined for the first nine months of 2001 to 15.4%, has run ads that also emphasize the personal side of PC shopping, with the tagline, "You've got a friend in the business." And **International Business Machines** Corp., though not a major player in consumer PCs, has been using its own Generation X pitchman, "Leon," in commercials for IBM.com.

"I would choose a Dell over a Gateway because Steven is cuter than Gateway's cow," says Libby Marie LeForce, a 17-year-old student from Chandler, Ariz. Chas McAvoy, a 35-year-old Web site designer, has created a site dedicated to Steven. Mr. McAvoy, owner of a Sony Vaio computer, has recommended Dell to clients. "I am much more aware of the company because of

Benjamin Curtis, the **'Dell Guy'** in an ad campaign, is bringing Generation X appeal to the computer maker.

the commercials," he says.

Gartner Group analyst Charles Smulder credits Dell's tactic of targeting second-time computer buyers with direct marketing methods, leaving first-time buyers to continue seeking guidance in retail stores. The Steven campaign is "icing on the cake of a business model that they carefully crafted and used successfully to take market share away from the competition," Mr. Smulder says.

The ads are appearing on shows such as "Who Wants to Be a Millionaire," which airs on Walt Disney Co.'s ABC, and "Friends," on General Electric Co.'s NBC. Mr. Curtis hasn't appeared in radio or print ads but has made appearances at Dell events to rally employees and at Comdex, the giant computer industry show.

All the attention has taken Mr. Curtis a bit by surprise. "I wasn't ready," he says. "People look at me and stare." He got the role at an audition and declines to say how much money he earns as Dell's pitchman but notes it is paying for half of his tuition at New York University, where he is studying acting. He got the role in an audition, after having appeared in a local TV commercial for a Long Island, N.Y., crisis center.

Already, some Hollywood doors have opened. Two weeks ago, he read for a role in "Terminator III." But he worries about being typecast. "I have been training in theater for years not to be typecast as a surfer dude," he says.

Spotlight falls on drug ads

Does song and dance drive sales, or give public vital information?

By Rita Rubin
USA TODAY

Turn on your television, and you could just as well see a commercial for Nexium, a heartburn remedy, as for Nikes. Flip open a magazine, and you'll find ads for Claritin—by now, just about everyone knows that's an allergy medication—next to ones for Clairol.

More than ever, drugmakers are pitching their prescription products directly to consumers instead of relying on doctors to spread the word. Five years ago, few non-medical types had ever heard of erectile dysfunction, generalized anxiety disorder or gastroesophageal reflux disease. Thanks to Bob Dole, the Heartburn Hotel's talking stomach and other pitchmen, though, such ailments are nearly as well-known as, well, Dole and Elvis.

No wonder. Spending on direct-to-consumer, or DTC, advertising of prescription drugs rose roughly 39% in 2000 from the previous year.

And spending on prescription drugs has kept pace. In the mid-1990s, as DTC marketing started to take off, total spending on drugs began rising faster than doctor and hospital costs, notes Larry Levitt, a Kaiser Family Foundation vice president. Today, prescription drugs represent 10% of the nation's annual personal health care bill.

Coincidence? Some consumer advocates and managed-care plans think not. They claim that DTC ads spur patients to demand prescriptions for expensive, newer drugs when cheaper, older medications would do. On the other hand, the pharmaceutical industry argues that DTC ads play a vital role in educating patients, sometimes motivating them to seek needed medical attention.

The ads "are intended to provide enough information to patients so that they are able to have an informed conversation with their doctor about new treatments that may be available to them," says Alan Holmer, president of the Pharmaceutical Research and Manufacturers of America, a trade group.

Clearly, the drugs most heavily promoted to consumers, such as the painkiller Vioxx and its competitor, Celebrex, also rank among the top sellers.

In the USA last year, according to a new report by the National Institute for Health Care Management, a non-profit group in Washington, D.C., Merck spent more promoting Vioxx to consumers—$160.8 million—than PepsiCo spent advertising Pepsi.

That concerns pharmacologist Raymond Woosley, dean of the University of Arizona College of Medicine.

"The thing that's missing is the bigger-picture warning, the fact that, hey, these are new drugs," says Woosley, who has long studied drug safety.

DTC ads should alert consumers that drugs are tested in only a few thousand patients before coming on the market, he says. "I think they should move more

Consumer direct

Dollars spent by drug companies on advertising prescription drugs directly to the consumer:

$1.8 billion — 1999
$2.5 billion — 2000

Source: National Institute for Health Care Management

By Julie Snider, USA TODAY

"There's only indirect information right now on whether patients are asking for things that are inappropriate."

— Richard Kravitz, University of California

How drugs rank in ad spending

The 2000 consumer advertising budgets, in millions of dollars, of the top 10 most heavily advertised drugs, with sales rankings for that year.

Drug	Ad budget	Sales rank
Vioxx	$160.8	10
Prilosec	107.5	1
Claritin	99.7	6
Paxil	91.8	8
Zocor	91.2	5
Viagra	89.5	17
Celebrex	78.3	7
Flonase	73.5	22
Allegra	67.0	13
Meridia	65.0	41

Source: National Institute for Health Care Management

toward a PSA (public service announcement) approach and get away from the hype," Woosley says.

Expensive as they are, DTC ads represent a relatively small chunk of drugmakers' marketing budgets. Last year, only about 16% of the $15.7 billion spent promoting prescription drugs went toward DTC ads, according to the National Institute for Health Care Management. Half of that total covered free samples distributed to doctors, a quarter went toward sending sales reps to doctors, while the rest went to medical journal ads and sales calls to hospitals.

Although DTC ads unquestionably are a windfall for television networks, magazines and newspapers, surprisingly little is known about their impact.

For example, it's not clear how much—if any—DTC ads actually contribute to sales, says Scott Neslin, a marketing professor at Dartmouth College. Apparently, Neslin says, drug companies believe that marketing products to consumers raises brand awareness. But that doesn't necessarily translate to increased sales, he says.

And, while some observers worry that ads may drive consumers to seek drugs they don't need, "there's only indirect information right now on whether patients are asking for things that are inappropriate," says Richard Kravitz, director of the Center for Health Services Research in Primary Care at the University of California-Davis.

Geriatrician Jeffrey Berger says his elderly patients frequently come in asking for drugs similar to those they're already taking.

One patient excitedly asked about a drug he'd learned about from a direct-mail advertisement, recalls Berger, director of clinical ethics in the department of medicine at Winthrop University Hospital in Mineola, N.Y.

While the man did indeed suffer from the ailment treated by the drug, "he had a heart condition that made it impossible for me to prescribe the medication," Berger says. "He was so disappointed."

Critics of the ads say they tend to hype the benefits and downplay the risks. "It's just hard to do justice to some of these issues in a 30-second television spot," says Martin Lipsky, chair of family medicine at Northwestern University Medical School in Chicago.

In 1997, the FDA decided that drug companies did not have to include detailed information about side effects in commercials as long as they directed viewers to call toll-free numbers, buy a magazine or go online for more information. "To rely on the observer to go pursue more information, I think, is unrealistic, for the most part," Berger says.

Even if consumers do go out and buy a magazine to see a drug's print ad, they might not get much out of it, says Rep. Pete Stark, D- Calif., who is pushing for more balanced ads.

"There's a page of mouse tracks that I swear to God, with my eyes, I can't read," says Stark, referring to the fine print accompanying such ads that often is simply lifted from prescribing information for doctors in the drug's package insert.

Since the FDA relaxed rules about television commercials in 1997, they've come to represent nearly two-thirds of the DTC advertising budget, according to the National Institute for Health Care Management.

A new Kaiser Family Foundation study provides an intriguing glimpse at what consumers take away from prescription drug commercials.

The study involved a nationally representative random sample of 1,872 volunteers. About 30% of them had at some time talked to a doctor about a drug they'd seen advertised, the study found. Of those, 44% said their doctor prescribed the drug they'd asked about.

As part of the Kaiser study, three-fourths of the volunteers were shown ads for Nexium for acid reflux, Lipitor for high cholesterol or Singulair for asthma. Immediately afterward, they were asked what they remembered from the drug ad. Overall, those who had just been shown a commercial were more likely to know about the drug's benefits and side effects than those who had not watched a commercial.

Still, only about 40% of the commercial viewers said they knew "a lot more" or "somewhat more" about the medication.

About 30% said they knew a lot more or somewhat more about the condition for which the drug is prescribed.

Says Linda Golodner, president of the National Consumers League: "Unfortunately, it looks like a lot of the messages aren't getting across to consumers."

"Spotlight Falls on Drug Ads," USA Today, December 11, 2001, p. 9D. Reprinted with permission.

Pass It On

Advertisers discover they have a friend in 'viral' marketing

By William M. Bulkeley

Staff reporter of The Wall Street Journal

Because of anthrax, people aren't opening strange paper mail. Because of computer viruses, they aren't opening strange e-mail.

What's a direct marketer to do?

Persuade people to pass along corporate pitches to personal friends.

It's called "viral marketing." And some direct marketers, who have seen growing use of the technique in recent years, think it's going to become an increasingly important part of marketing campaigns.

"You'll see more of it because the open rate"—how many of the e-mail pitches are actually opened—"is so much better," says David Kenney, chief executive of **Digitas** Inc., a Boston marketing firm that has run viral-marketing campaigns for such blue-chip advertisers as **General Motors** Corp., **Johnson & Johnson** and **Gillette** Co.

Infectious Idea

When Boston-based Gillette was introducing the three-bladed Venus razor for women last spring, one target group was college students, and Digitas designed a truck that traveled the spring-break circuit in Florida, parking daily near a beach. The truck crew invited women to come in and get some aromatherapy, learn about Venus, enter a sweepstakes and make a digital greeting card with a picture of themselves enjoying the beach.

The viral part came when they e-mailed the cards to friends. The messages automatically included a chance to enter the sweepstakes, "Celebrate the Goddess in You," and if e-mail recipients entered the contest, they saw a pitch for the Venus razor. Mr. Lynch says some 20% of the entries came from the viral-marketing cards, significantly expanding the audience for the product beyond the beach-site promotions.

Viral marketing is designed to mimic that most-valued of all advertisements—a word-of-mouth recommendation. Ad veterans say one of the all-time best viral marketing campaigns was MCI Corp.'s "Friends and Family" calling plan. It gave people reduced rates for calling a circle of people, who were encouraged to buy MCI long distance in turn.

Viral marketing works because friends "are better at target marketing than any database," says Steven Lynch, creative director at Digitas. "The idea is to get your constituency to do your marketing for you." Mr. Lynch

says that "the Web has transformed viral marketing" because it's easier to pass on e-mail than messages in any other medium.

But most people don't want to pitch products to their friends, even for a small payment from the advertiser. So viral campaigns are designed to woo their cooperation. Mr. Lynch says people will forward pictures, such as those used in the Gillette campaign, or they will pass along entertainment or compelling offers—the trick is to make sure the marketing message is in the e-mail along with the goodies.

Uncertain Count

Viral e-marketing hasn't exploded yet, in part because it isn't clear how well it works. Advertisers can tell if an item is forwarded from their client's site, but they have no easy way of knowing how often that message is subsequently passed along. It's also tricky to craft campaigns that aren't so heavy-handed that people will be turned off and refuse to send them along. And sometimes campaign techniques, such as sweepstakes entries, don't get forwarded because people fear they'll reduce their own chances of winning.

Still, advertisers are warming to the idea. Annette Lloyd, director of advertising at GM's Pontiac division, says viral marketing on the Internet works well with the young crowd Pontiac wants to reach. Pontiac has been running a television campaign around the theme of taking road trips with friends and urging viewers to check out its Web site. She says that from there "somewhere between 20% to 30% actually e-mail a friend" about Pontiac's contest to win weeklong car trips and record them, with a chance that the footage will be used in new TV commercials.

Another success story is told by London-based **MiniClip** Ltd., which last July built a 600,000-name mailing list of registered users after it created DancingBush—an animation of the president boogeying to music from the movie "Saturday Night Fever." Tihan Presbie, a London futures trader who started MiniClip, estimates that at least 10 million people must have viewed the animation to get such a large number of registered users. Nearly all of them came to the Web site because friends and acquaintances sent them the animation or the address.

Mr. Presbie says MiniClip is currently working with a U.S. rap singer on a viral campaign slated for later this year. "The future is targeted marketing," he says. "If we wanted to reach women under 25 that play soccer, we could make a MiniClip of young women playing soccer, and it would be forwarded to that target group."

At its most basic, when Digitas creates a direct e-mail campaign promoting, say, a handbag sale at client Neiman-Marcus, it routinely includes a "forward to a friend" button. Presumably, women who have given their e-mail addresses to Neiman-Marcus, or who are on lists that Digitas buys for the campaign, will know other women who like

Kate Spade purses.

Johnson & Johnson, based in New Brunswick, N.J., came to Digitas seeking ways to get teenage girls to check out its Clean and Clear skin-care products. Mr. Lynch says Digitas created a "microsite" from which teens could "send a talking postcard to your friend." The pop-up advertisement appeared at teen site www.bolt.com.

Easy Audio

Digitas was taking advantage of a new technology that lets users send sound without first downloading online software—a "plug-in" program—to make it work. The challenge of downloading and retrieving plug-ins turns off many users, Mr. Lynch says.

When users clicked onto the pop-up, they were linked to a Web site where they could design an e-greeting card, choosing decorations such as animated flowers or messages such as "Best Friends 4ever." They were offered a phone number to dictate a short voice message. When the e-mail was sent, the recipient would open the message and hear the recording through the computer's speakers. As soon as they played the message, they were invited to click on a button called "Skin analyzer." Then they would see Clean and Clear's main Web site, "where the marketing work gets done," says Mr. Lynch.

Digitas has also helped GM develop its online marketing, and as part of Pontiac's current road-trip contest, has a Web-site survey labeled "the Destinator."

Sample question: "Which sign would you get off the highway for?"

Sample answers: "Homemade pecan pie"; "Warning, hitchhikers may be prison escapees"; and "Wooden chain-saw bears $19.95."

After taking the quiz, viewers are urged to pass along their results to friends to "see if they travel well together," says Mr. Lynch.

In an effort to augment TV advertising with the Web, Digitas created an unusual addition to **AT&T** Corp.'s sponsorship of the Discovery Channel's "When Dinosaurs Roamed America." During the show people were urged to check out an associated Web site. When they did, they got the opportunity to send a virtual, animated dinosaur egg to a friend. Recipients could answer paleontological questions and then see the dinosaur hatch. Then they were invited to click through to a master site, where AT&T branding was heightened.

More than 100,000 people hatched dinosaur eggs and clicked to go to AT&T's Dino site, says Mr. Lynch.

Networks of Hasidic Women, Other Tightly Knit Groups Help Shaklee Sell Products

BY HEIDI J. SHRAGER

Staff Reporter of THE WALL STREET JOURNAL

A group of women are gathered around a dining room table in Brooklyn, talking about nutrition. Shaklee Corp.'s "new soy protein is very exciting," says hostess Sarah Stauber. She asks her guests to share what they love about Shaklee. "I just live on it, that's all," says one woman. Adds another, "I love the protein. I use it in my gefilte fish. . . . We are hooked on it."

This group knows its gefilte fish. They are Hasidic Jews, and 33-year-old Mrs. Stauber is part of a contingent of Hasidic salespeople among Shaklee's 500,000 representatives. Like other multilevel marketing companies, 45-year-old Shaklee relies on individual distributors to sell its wares—in Shaklee's case, food supplements, water filters, and personal-care and cleaning products. And many of these companies have found sales momentum builds quickest among tightly knit groups.

The largest such company, **Alticor** Inc.'s Amway Co., has historically had success in small, blue-collar towns; Salt Lake City-based **Nu Skin Enterprises** Inc. sells products through countless Mormons.

Shaklee has excelled at recruiting salespeople from groups most companies would consider unrecruitable, including the Amish, Mennonites and Hasidim, a movement within ultra-Orthodox Judaism that began in Eastern Europe in the 18th century. Shaklee has done so partly by accommodating the special needs of such highly insular communities. For the Amish and Mennonite sales force, Shaklee awards "bonus buggies" instead of cars. For the Hasidim, company representatives hold separate meetings before the Sabbath and find synagogues for husbands to pray in on convention trips. When women complained the products' kosher certification wasn't strict enough, Shaklee switched to one of the strictest kosher-certification companies.

The payoff is an army of enthusiastic salespeople. Just before Yom Kippur last year, when Hasidim fast for 25 hours, 27-year-old Chaya Suri Friedman distributed to customers and prospective clients a homemade flier that read, "Fasting is no pleasure; Now you can fast without the common challenges like . . . Weakness, Headaches, Dehydration . . . Shaklee Performance drink mix

is the answer!" Saleswomen spend hours on the phone counseling their patrons—mostly friends and family—on which ailment invokes which Shaklee salve. Last year, before Passover, when the kitchen must be painstakingly cleaned, Pessie Herzl, 33, hawked a "Sha-clean Pre-Pesach package" that included laundry detergent, hand lotion, vitamin B tablets and industrial-strength cleaner.

With lives of strict religious observance, Hasidic women seem unlikely candidates for entrepreneurship. Procreation is a chief commandment, so the typical family has at least five children. Mothers have little time for work between weddings, births, frequent holidays and religious observances. "What we look forward to is the building of generations, not of careers," says one Hasidic Shaklee consumer.

But laws and customs cost money. Expenses like elaborate weddings, private school, handmade wigs for the women and fur hats for the men—worn to cover their heads in keeping with Hasidic tradition— can strain family budgets. "Our lifestyle is more expensive," says Mrs. Herzl, one of Mrs. Stauber's recruits who has six children.

With a home-based business, "I'm making the money and I'm there for the children," says Mrs. Herzl. She says she has 300 to 400 customers, and of those, about 70% are ultra-Orthodox. "It's easier to build trust in your own community, where you're accepted." And selling primarily to other women allows them to avoid contact with men who are not their husbands or close relatives, in accordance with Hasidic custom.

Then there is the promise of high earnings, achieved as distributors deepen their network of recruits, or "downlines." Mrs. Stauber, a petite woman who wears a short brown wig, is a "coordinator." In 2000, Shaklee estimated average annual income for coordinators was $42,000. "Master coordinators"—Shaklee's highest-ranked salespeople, of whom there are 124 nationwide—earn an average of $300,000 a year, says the company. The climb, scaled by only a determined few as recruits beneath them sell more products, begins with a membership and discounts on products.

Since his wife first started selling Shaklee seven years ago, Jacob Stauber, 36, a social worker who practices private psychotherapy in Brooklyn, has grown to depend on her income. With six children under the age of 15, the couple says Shaklee earnings have enabled them to move out of an apartment in Mrs. Stauber's grandparents' house early last year, travel to Shaklee conventions in places like Portugal and Hawaii, and drive a Chevrolet Venture van with a built-in car seat.

Multilevel marketing has its critics, some of whom say an insular community like the Hasidim is especially vulnerable to

corporate promises of riches. Robert L. Fitzpatrick, co-author of the 1997 book "False Profits, Seeking Financial and Spiritual Deliverance in Multi-Level Marketing and Pyramid Schemes," says the chance to make as much as $300,000 a year without having to leave the community is "electrifying." But he also says such profit is illusory, and that over 90% of the people who get involved in such businesses will ultimately lose money. Most quit the business within the first year, having spent thousands of dollars on promotional and training material and other business-related necessities, and never moving beyond breaking even, he says.

Critics say part of the problem is simple math. Shaklee writes in a recent brochure, "Discover the Shaklee opportunity: find three who find three." The fallacy in this, detractors say, is that if everyone were successful at finding three who found three, a mere 11 levels deep into the pyramid would yield 177,147 Shaklee salespeople—more than all the ultra-Orthodox Jews living in Brooklyn.

Shaklee, a subsidiary of **Yamanouchi Pharmaceutical** Co. in Tokyo, asserts its business plan works for people who recruit successful downlines. "Our model has worked well because we have legitimate, wonderful products, and a viable, productive business opportunity," says Karin Topping, director of public relations at Shaklee, which is based in Pleasanton, Calif. "People know the difference between illegal pyramid schemes and legitimate multilevel marketing companies."

At least one Orthodox rabbi who is not Hasidic, Eli Teitelbaum, is speaking out against multilevel marketing. Since his wife was almost recruited into an unrelated illegal pyramid scheme in 1997 that ensnared large numbers of Brooklyn Jews, he has urged other rabbis to forbid participation in multilevel marketing companies. He also warns of "false promises" made by distributors and notes that making them is forbidden in Jewish custom.

Mrs. Stauber says Rabbi Teitelbaum "didn't do his research," and is reacting to the notorious 1997 sting. She knew "it was a scam," and so rejected recruiters who approached her, she recalls. As for false promises, if they are made it's the distributor's fault, not Shaklee's; disclaimers appear all over product labels and promotional literature, she adds.

Popular as Shaklee is among the Hasidic women who sell it, the constant focus and determination needed to generate an income drive many of them out of the business. "Even when you're home, you're not totally home," says 31-year-old Mindy Stauber, Sarah Stauber's sister-in-law, who has five children and left the business after about five years. But like most former Shaklee saleswomen, she is loath to criticize friends and

(Cont.)

family still in the business, and she remains a loyal Shaklee customer.

Sarah Stauber, meanwhile, has the burgeoning population growth of Hasidim on her side. "There's always new potential," she says. "Youngsters are getting married all the time and they have their own children, and then you have a fresh wave of clientele."

"Closed-Circle Commerce: Networks of Hasidic Women, Other Tightly Knit Groups Help Shaklee Sell Products," *The Wall*

How Newspaper Overcame Loss Of Big Advertisers

BY PATRICIA CALLAHAN

MODESTO, Calif.—The anticipated shuttering of many **Kmart** Corp. stores across the country means that hundreds of newspapers are poised to lose one of their largest advertisers.

But a look at one progressive newspaper suggests that, through hard work and unconventional sales methods, such a critical advertiser can be replaced.

McClatchy Co.'s Modesto Bee, an 85,000-circulation paper in California's Central Valley, lost one of its biggest advertisers a year ago when Montgomery Ward & Co. closed. This is exactly what could happen to other newspapers when Kmart, which filed for bankruptcy reorganization this week, begins a downsizing effort that analysts believe could close 250 to 500 of its stores.

At the Bee, Publisher Lynn Dickerson faced not just the loss of Montgomery Ward but also a local grocery chain that closed around the same time. She was determined to replace those lost dollars—and did, by offering discounted rates to dozens of far smaller businesses. It was a daring tactic in an industry that years ago priced small businesses out of its ad pages.

Although it takes at least 50 small ad accounts to make up for one Montgomery Ward, Mrs. Dickerson focused her staff on mom-and-pop businesses. "We didn't want to be at the mercy of a corporate office in Chicago or New York making decisions," she says.

For 2001, the Bee—located in a blue-collar area with 10% unemployment—posted a 6% rise in ad revenue. The overall U.S. newspaper industry, meanwhile, saw a decline of about 8.6%—the worst in more than 50 years, according to Peter Appert, an analyst with Deutsche Banc Alex. Brown.

The Bee's staff had to rethink the paper's rate schedule. Newspapers typically price ads according to categories: Grocers pay a food rate; car dealers, an auto rate. What about a hearing aid shop or a small shoe store? They usually have to pay retail rates that are designed for much larger businesses. So the Bee created cut-rate packages that made advertising affordable for even the smallest businesses, while preserving its large-advertiser rates.

To make sure it didn't anger its biggest advertisers, the Bee placed restrictions on the small-business ads, much like airlines restrict cheaper fares. The cheaper ads were smaller, couldn't include prices and had to run on certain days of the week or on pages that wouldn't appeal to larger advertisers.

To kick off the program, the paper held a seminar for small businesses explaining the importance of frequent advertising. The crowd of 300 was filled with people like Julia Dutton Haidlen, an interior designer who had been in business for 20 years but rarely placed ads in the Bee because of the cost. Mrs. Haidlen committed to running ads the size of a big business card every other day for about $1,000 a month. Last year, her revenue jumped 20%, and she added three employees to bring her staff to 12.

In another promotion last summer, advertisers who agreed to go above their normal spending could buy a full-page ad for as little as $1,299—a savings of nearly $4,000. Hy Step Corner, a small strip-mall shoe store, bought four full-page ads. "Normally, I couldn't afford it," says owner Allen Goldberg. The promotion earned the Bee $821,000 in revenue.

The paper even expanded beyond its distribution area to appeal to real-estate agents who said they would buy ads if the paper reached readers in the east San Francisco Bay Area. The Bee bought 52 news racks in that area and filled them with free copies of a revamped, stand-alone real-estate section. The result: 2001 real-estate ad revenue jumped 33%, requiring the Bee to add a full-time sales assistant just to handle such ads.

Mrs. Dickerson finished the year with ad revenue of $46.3 million compared with $43.6 million in 2000, and her paper's profit margin edged upward. While she is hopeful that Kmart will continue to be a big advertiser as it emerges from bankruptcy, her paper is pushing ahead with plans to diversify its ad base even more. She budgeted a 2% increase in ad revenue this year. "It's the same song, second verse," she says.

Selling Iced Tea in February: Inside One Campaign

BY BETSY MCKAY AND SUZANNE VRANICA
Staff Reporters of THE WALL STREET JOURNAL

Al Roker and Pat O'Brien were invited to "cover" the big event. Creative agencies in England, New York and Los Angeles were busy in production. And **PepsiCo** Inc., which usually reserves the pricey Super Bowl time for its biggest, splashiest brands, had already committed to a 60-second spot to showcase a new campaign for its top-selling Lipton Brisk iced tea. The plot: the foot-tall latex puppets that have been the drink's spokesthings for five years would be "fired" during the Super Bowl, since the reformulated Lipton Brisk "tastes so good it sells itself."

But then came the Sept. 11 terrorist attacks. Suddenly, pitching products during the Super Bowl, and the humor and expense that entails, seemed frivolous. The zeitgeist of the country changed, prompting marketers and agencies to question the tone and flavor of their creative product. Most were petrified to act for fear of offending consumers, and many started questioning the steep ad prices that have long been associated with the Super Bowl.

PepsiCo stopped running its TV commercials for two weeks as the nation mourned but didn't waver on its Super Bowl strategy. Company officials concluded that neither campaign it planned to run—two new Britney Spears ads for Pepsi-Cola and the Lipton Brisk spot—had the bald kind of humor that might turn viewers off. The Britney ads, says Dawn Hudson, Pepsi's senior vice president of strategy and marketing, were "exactly the right thing for the tenor of country," while the Lipton Brisk ad was simply light and fun.

Besides, the beverage company had already learned a lesson from hesitating when it comes to the big game. After 14 years of heavy spending on Super Bowl ads, it had pulled back in 1999 and ran only one spot for its new diet drink, Pepsi One. As a result, Pepsi lost the coveted "1A" top ad slot—the first ad to run during the first break in the game—to Anheuser-Busch Cos.

What's more, the Super Bowl has always delivered the kind of vast, general audience Pepsi seeks. "With the proliferation of cable stations and the Internet, there are fewer places out there where you can hit a large audience in one fell swoop." Ms. Hudson says.

Still, making a Super Bowl ad isn't easy—especially one involving celebrities, special effects, a mix of live action and animation. And the New York office of J. Walter Thompson, a unit of London's **WPP Group** PLC and the agency for Lipton Brisk, hadn't done a Super Bowl ad in about 25 years.

Larry King and Geraldo Rivera were originally asked to do the spot, but they declined. So J. Walter Thompson approached Mr. Roker, the NBC weatherman, and Mr. O'Brien, host of "Access Hollywood" instead. Their role: to "cover" the revolt of the Lipton Brisk puppets when they learn they are no longer wanted. Messrs. Roker and O'Brien interview a dejected and livid puppet with the voice of Danny DeVito, who leads his fellow puppets in a picket outside a Hollywood studio.

Worried about the time such a project would entail, Lipton had given J. Walter Thompson the go-ahead to begin sculpting the puppets last summer, even before Mr. DeVito signed on. Lipton had used puppet likenesses of other celebrities—including Frank Sinatra and Bruce Willis—before, but this was Mr. DeVito's first time. Each puppet takes about three months to make, at a cost of as much as $15,000, and the ad called for several. And each two seconds of "stop motion animation," as the technique for recording the puppets' movements is called, took an entire day to shoot.

Mr. DeVito's approval of his puppet didn't come easily. The star, who got about $650,000 for his voiceover work, at first thought his puppet head "looked like a bullet," according to Mickey Paxton, J. Walter Thompson's group creative director. Six versions were cast out of a claylike material, and J. Walter executives flew to England to make the final choice. Mr. DeVito's publicist wouldn't comment on Mr. DeVito's fee but said Mr. Devito was "extremely pleased" with his puppet and that he couldn't wait to watch the ad with his kids.

As the puppets were cast across the Atlantic, Messrs. Roker and O'Brien filmed their parts in Los Angeles. Mr. O'Brien asked questions to an empty chair, where footage of a puppet would later be superimposed. To simulate an attack by the puppets, Mr. Roker rolled around on the ground outside a studio after film crew members threw guacamole on him.

All told, PepsiCo and its joint-venture partner **Unilever** PLC, the consumer-products company that owns Lipton, spent more than $5.3 million on creating, producing and airing the 60-second Lipton Brisk spot.

As the game approached, Pepsi marketers grew concerned that the ad's tone wasn't light enough. With puppets protesting in the streets and jumping on Mr. Roker, they wanted to make sure it would be perceived as more mischievous than violent. The Danny DeVito puppet looked "too mean," Gary Rodkin, Pepsi's North American beverage chief, said at an editing session earlier this month. Other Pepsi officials agreed. With Mr. Paxton looking on, a graphic artist spent four hours easing wrinkles out of the puppet's face and softening his burrowing eyebrows.

Keeping it light was important also to allay concerns that firing puppets would be an unpleasant reminder to viewers of the layoffs sweeping corporate America. Dan Trott, who heads sales of noncarbonated beverages for Pepsi, says he considered how viewers would react. But the puppets don't actually leave, he points out: In two more ads to be aired later this year, they strike back. Plus, he adds, "They're puppets."

MTV'S WORLD
Mando-Pop. Mexican Hip Hop. Russian Rap.
It's all fueling the biggest global channel

It's the Suit vs. the Tattoo Set. Foggy Bottom and the Hip Hop Crowd. The General and the Veejay. It's, it's . . . well, it's another weird but fascinating cultural moment on MTV, the Viacom-owned music network that supplements its core mission of delivering 150-decibel music to the world's teens with straight-talking programs on issues such as AIDS, drugs, and racism. On Feb. 14, U.S. Secretary of State Colin L. Powell will lead *Be Heard,* a no-holds-barred talk show on MTV Networks, where he will field questions on the crisis in Afghanistan from teens from Boston to Berlin to Bombay. The program will air on MTV's 33 channels worldwide and reach almost 375 million households. MTV's video jockeys—the ones who usually deliver wall-to-wall Hindi film music, German hard rock, Mando-pop, and Mexican hip hop to local viewers—will moderate the meeting, and translators will be on hand to turn questions into English. It will be, in other words, an Event.

Powell's appearance is a media moment that only MTV could pull off. Media moguls can babble on about the global village, about how CNN or BBC can reach out and touch the world. But those news shows are bush league operations compared with MTV's clout. Thanks to the roaring success of its subsidiary, MTV Networks International, the music channel and its sister operations, VH1 and Nickelodeon, reach 1 billion people in 18 different languages in 164 countries. Eight out of ten MTV viewers live outside the U.S. CNN reaches an international audience less than half the size of MTV's. Its impressive global reach has earned MTV membership in that elite of such globally transcendent brands as Coke and Levi's.

MTV seems not to have missed a beat as turmoil roils the executive ranks at parent Viacom, whose board in late January called upon CEO Sumner Redstone and Chief Operating Officer Mel Karmazin to cease feuding. The stock is down almost 20% since early January, but analysts say the strife should have no impact on operating units like MTV. MTV Networks International makes buckets of money year after year from a potent combination of cable subscriber fees, advertising, and increasingly, new media. Few other transnational media operations can claim to make profits at all. But revenues at MTV Networks International increased 19% in 2001, to $600 million, while operating profits grew a hefty 50%, to $135 million. They are expected to more than double by 2004, according to Merrill Lynch & Co. media analyst Jessica Reif Cohen. In the past three years, the growth of MTV Networks International has outpaced the domestic network, accounting for 16% of MTV Networks' revenues, says co-founder and Chairman Tom Freston. He aims to increase that to 40% within five years, as MTV in the U.S. starts to plateau. MTV's international success is attracting a host of imitators, one of them spawned by the relentless Rupert Murdoch. But for now, MTV's version of globalization rocks.

MTV Networks International owes its success to a lot of factors. First, demographics: There were 2.7 billion people between the ages of 10 and 34 in 2000. By 2010, there will be 2.8 billion. Increasingly, this age group is acquiring the bucks to buys CDs, jeans, acne cream—whatever brands are hot in each country. That means advertisers increasingly love MTV International. Second, music: All that stuff about music being a universal language is true, and rock is the universal language for Planet Teen. What MTV does is customize the offering in a brilliant way. Third, television: The number of sets in the world's living rooms—especially in such places as China, Brazil, Russia, and India—is exploding. So are the globe's cable networks. "Everyone who has a TV knows there's something called MTV," says Chantara Kapahi, a 17-year-old student at Jai Hind College in Bombay. The fourth reason: Bill Roedy.

Roedy, a 53-year-old West Point grad, is president of MTV Networks International and, theoretically, is based in London. Theoretically, since his real office is more of a semi-perpetual airborne state involving him, his trademark army green pen and paper, and a business-class round-trip ticket to wherever. To give kids their dose of rock, he has breakfasted with former Israeli Prime Minister Shimon Peres, dined with Singapore founder Lee Kuan Yew, and chewed the fat with Chinese leader Jiang Zemin. Roedy even met with El Caudillo himself—Cuban leader Fidel Castro, who wondered if MTV could teach Cuban kids English. Says Roedy: "We've had very little resistance once we explain that we're not in the business of exporting American culture."

Roedy & Co. are shrewd enough to realize that while the world's teens want American music, they really want the local stuff, too. So, MTV's producers and veejays scour their local markets for the top talent.

On the Move

NORTH AMERICA	
HOUSEHOLDS REACHED	84.6 million
CHANNELS	6
WEB SITES	2
LANGUAGES	2
HOTTEST MARKET/ REVENUE GROWTH	United States/ 5%
ARTIST TO WATCH	Jennifer Lopez

LATIN AMERICA	
HOUSEHOLDS REACHED	28.1 million
CHANNELS	4
WEB SITES	2
LANGUAGES	2
HOTTEST MARKET/ REVENUE GROWTH	Mexico/ 27%
ARTIST TO WATCH	Alejandro Sanz

EUROPE	
HOUSEHOLDS REACHED	124.1 million
CHANNELS	15
WEB SITES	9
LANGUAGES	7
HOTTEST MARKET/ REVENUE GROWTH	Russia/ 80%
ARTIST TO WATCH	Alsou

ASIA/PACIFIC	
HOUSEHOLDS REACHED	137.9 million
CHANNELS	8
WEB SITES	6
LANGUAGES	8
HOTTEST MARKET/ REVENUE GROWTH	China/ 80%
ARTIST TO WATCH	Na Ying

Data: Viacom Inc.

(Cont.)

The result is an endless stream of overnight sensations that keep MTV's global offerings fresh. Just over a year ago, for example, Lena Katina and Yulia Volkova were no different than most Moscow schoolgirls. Today, Katina, 16, and Volkova, 15, make up Tatu, one of the hottest bands ever to come out of Russia. Tatu has won a cult following among local teens since their debut single, *Ya Soshla s Uma* (*I've Gone Crazy*), first aired on MTV Russia 15 months ago. Universal even plans to promote Tatu's next recordings in the U.S. "Our producers could have signed a contract with Sony or Warner, too. We had offers from all of them," says Katina.

Tatu is just one of a slew of emerging local music groups gaining international exposure through MTV and a wider audience in the U.S., too. Colombian rock singer Shakira, unknown outside Latin America until she recorded an MTV Unplugged CD—the acoustic live concerts recorded by MTV—in 1999, is now the winner of one U.S. Grammy and two Latin Grammy awards. Her CD has gone platinum, selling more than 2 million copies worldwide. After releasing four CDs in just three years, Taiwanese pop star Jolin Tsai, 21, is gaining popularity in mainland China thanks to heavy airplay on MTV.

Viacom is now counting on MTV to be one of its biggest growth drivers in the next decade. There's plenty of room to launch new channels on cable and satellite outside the U.S., where penetration, at 38%, is about where the American market was in 1983. As digital television takes off in Europe, MTV plans to introduce more music channels, such as the seven it has in Britain that focus on such genres as rhythm-and-blues and dance. Another part of the strategy: make MTV "a vehicle to develop business [for other Viacom brands]," says Viacom COO Karmazin. "Let's face it, the way people know Viacom is through MTV." Viacom can parlay growth abroad for its lesser-known VH1, Nickelodeon, and TV Land brands "off MTV's reputation."

MTV also is betting heavily on emerging technologies. In Scandinavia, it recently premiered MTV Live, which goes to homes with broadband cable. Viewers can play virtual games, such as *Trash Your Hotel Room*, where users get the chance to be a rock star and wreak virtual havoc. Meanwhile, in July, 2000, MTV Asia launched LiLi, a virtual animated veejay who interacts with viewers on air and online in five Asian languages. An actor behind the image controls LiLi's responses, letting her interview artists and offer viewers tips on pop culture in real time.

RECORD SALES ABROAD
MTV INTERNATIONAL REVENUES
IN MILLIONS OF DOLLARS
$231
$722
'96 '97 '98 '99 '00 '01 '02 '03
EST.
Data: Viacom, Merrill Lynch & Co.

LiLi is now so popular with Asian teens that Ericsson has launched a line of LiLi mobile phones. In Japan, an MTV wireless Internet service lets users download entertainment news, vote for their favorite veejays, or choose music. MTV "tries to make a lot of noise off the channel," says Nigel Robbins, CEO of MTV Group Japan.

MTV's early international expansion—it got into Moscow in 1993, for example—puts it ahead of the competition in nearly every market. Hong Kong-based Channel V's 24-hour music channel, owned by Rupert Murdoch's Star TV, reaches nearly 47 million homes but has yet to make a profit. VIVA—owned 45.9% by AOL Time Warner, EMI, and Vivendi Universal—is MTV's biggest rival in Europe. It reported a net loss of $9.4 million on sales of $40 million in the first nine months of 2001 but expects to be in the black in 2002. "The market is big enough for both of us," says VIVA CEO Dieter Gorny.

MTV faces some risks in a handful of countries, such as Italy and Brazil, where it operates with a local partner. "It's really a question of whether they can maintain distribution on outlets they don't own," says Sanford C. Bernstein & Co. media analyst Tom Wolzien. Wolzien says News Corp. and Vivendi have much stronger relations with local regulators, giving them an edge in launching music channels they can control.

MTV's best response to these threats is to make its programming as strong as possible. Its policy of 70% local content has resulted in some of the network's most creative shows, such as MTV Brasil's monthlong *Rockgol*, a soccer championship that pits Brazilian musicians against record industry executives. In Russia, the locally produced *Twelve Angry Viewers* was voted one of Russia's top three talk programs. In a colorful

studio amid bright blue steps and large green cushions, a dozen teens watch and discuss the latest videos. Periodically, they break into spontaneous dance or pop one another over the head with inflatable lollipops. O.K., it's not Chekhov. But Russian groups beg to be featured on it. Says producer Piotr Sheksheyev: "MTV trusts that we Russians know best what works."

Ceding so much control to local channels does result in the occasional misstep. While watching MTV in Taiwan, Roedy was aghast to see nude wrestling. That was one time he had to intervene. When MTV first entered the Indian market in 1996, Hindi film music—the romantic soundtracks of Bollywood movies—was wildly popular, but the channel's locally hired programmers disdained it as uncool. Viewers abandoned the channel, forcing it to air Bollywood music. Since then its ratings have soared by some 700%.

India is one of the giant markets that MTV is determined to dominate. The other big-country play is China. Analysts believe it is likely to be some time before the government grants 24-hour broadcasting licenses to foreigners on a nationwide basis. Still, in 2001, MTV's advertising revenue in China almost doubled—even though the network airs only a maximum of six hours daily through Chinese cable systems.

Roedy has spent the past decade cultivating relationships in China. At one long dinner with Chinese cable operators, he desperately attempted to hold his own through countless toasts and karaoke songs. After his Chinese counterparts sang Chinese opera arias, Roedy sang a few songs from *Madame Butterfly*, while MTV Chairman Freston belted out *House of the Rising Sun*, the bluesy ballad about a New Orleans whorehouse. They must have been in tune: MTV Mandarin is seen in 60 million homes in China via 40 Chinese cable systems. Last year, more than 10,000 teens came from all over China to audition to become the next veejay on MTV Mandarin. One finalist, who had traveled 18 hours to Beijing, was so distraught at losing that MTV offered to let her veejay for a day. Anything to keep a viewer.

By Kerry Capell in London, with Catherine Belton in Moscow, Tom Lowry in New York, Manjeet Kripalani in Bombay, Brian Bremner in Tokyo, Dexter Roberts in Beijing, and bureau reports

68

Ads Click

According to a major new survey, some types of online advertising may deliver the goods, after all

BY PETER GUMBEL

Internet advertising has been subjected to such a barrage of bad publicity over the past 18 months that it's a wonder anybody still believes in it. The online ad market, once frothy, has crashed. Hundreds of Web companies that depended on advertising for their revenue have gone out of business. And some so-called usability experts—Web scholars who carefully track how ordinary people actually use the Internet—have declared that the very nature of the Web may be incompatible with effective advertising. Users simply have too much ability to ignore or click off what they don't want to see.

But now comes a glimmer of good news for the beleaguered sector: Internet advertising, it seems, may not be quite as ineffective as its rock-bottom reputation would suggest.

A major new study of companies that use the Internet for at least some of their advertising suggests that many are relatively satisfied with the results they have been getting. Theirs is not just an abstract, touchy-feely sort of satisfaction, but an actual hard number based on return on investment and other criteria. At the same time, the survey shows that some types of online marketing—particularly those that deliver highly targeted and relevant messages to consumers—are substantially more effective than other, more general approaches, such as banner ads.

More than 2,000 companies were polled for the Internet advertising effectiveness survey, which was conducted in June and July by Harris Interactive Inc. and Jupiter Media Metrix Inc., both based in New York, and is believed to be the first broad study of its kind. Jupiter Media Metrix says that the findings are particularly relevant for small businesses, but that medium-size and big companies also responded.

"It's good news for the advertising industry that companies are reporting good returns from online advertising," says Marsha Loewenstein, a Jupiter analyst who worked on the survey.

What Scored Highest

When it comes to the different types of advertising, there is no single winner that stands head and shoulders above the rest. But two methods score consistently well: using e-mail to deliver targeted marketing messages to consumers who have agreed to receive them, or "opted in," and what's known as "pay for placement." With pay for placement, sites bid to show up high on the list of search results at a search engine. The highest bidder gets the top slot. **Overture Services** Inc. (formerly known as GoTo.com Inc.) is the market leader in offering this kind of search engine.

According to the Jupiter/Harris study, pay for placement won the most points for overall satisfaction and produced the highest return on investment. But e-mail scored better when it came to "converting" browsers into customers who actually make purchases.

In the middle of the rankings is what's known as "paid inclusion." This involves paying search engines such as AltaVista and LookSmart to have your site included in the directory. Then, when somebody puts in a query, your site will show up according to some relevancy criteria the search engines use.

At the bottom of the list are banner ads sold on what's known as a cost per mil, or CPM, basis. This means that an advertiser pays a Web site a fixed amount for every one thousand "impressions," or Web pages that contain the ad. Just 20% of the companies polled in the survey expressed satisfaction with the results from banners—half the per-

centage that said they were satisfied with the pay-for-placement model. Even so, given the banner ad's fall from grace over the past two years, a 20% score appears to be a respectable consolation prize.

The survey does have some important weaknesses. It's inevitably biased toward companies that continue to use the Internet for their marketing, rather than ones that tried and gave up. It also doesn't take into account two of the biggest and most important sites used for searching—**Yahoo** Inc. and **Google.** Yahoo charges an express processing fee to companies that want to be considered for listing in its directory, but doesn't guarantee inclusion, so it doesn't feature in the "paid inclusion" category. Neither does Google, which uses strict relevance criteria in its search results, although it does sell advertising space that can be geared to a search query. For example, a user searching Google for "wireless phone" will see a paid advertisement for a vendor at the top of the search-results page.

A Change at Sears

Despite such shortcomings, the survey confirms what some companies that use the Internet for their marketing have been finding in practice. Just ask Joe Charno. Mr. Charno is vice president of online management and marketing for Sears.com, the online operation of **Sears, Roebuck** & Co. in Chicago. He recalls how the company two years ago spent a good part of its marketing budget on banner ads and sweepstakes promotions on other sites. The aim was to raise the general awareness of Sears.com as a

Spreading the Message

How effective are online ads? A recent survey went to advertisers to find out what results they'd seen from a variety of types of ads. "Overall satisfaction" measures the percentage of respondents who ranked the ad types 1 or 2 on a scale of 1 to 5, with 1 as the highest rating. "Return on investment" is the average actual return on investment that respondents gave for each of the ad types.

TYPE OF ADVERTISING	OVERALL SATISFACTION	RETURN ON INVESTMENT
PAY FOR PLACEMENT Companies list themselves on an ad search engine and pay an agreed fee every time a user clicks on their listing	41%	29%
OPT-IN E-MAIL Companies send promotional e-mail to customers who request it	33	24
PAID INCLUSION Companies pay a flat fee to be included in sites such as AltaVista	31	23
CPC BANNERS Companies place banner ads on a site and pay per surfer who clicks on the banner (cost per click)	21	16
CPM BANNERS Companies place banner ads on a site and pay per thousand times the page containing the banner is viewed (cost per mil, or thousand, impressions)	19	12

Source: Jupiter Media Metrix Inc.; Harris Interactive

(Cont.)

brand, collect e-mail addresses and entice surfers to click through to the Sears site.

But these days, Sears.com marketing efforts could hardly be more different. The company now runs sweepstakes only on its own site and "has pulled back rather significantly from banner ads," Mr. Charno says. Instead, the company's focus is on developing the sophistication of its e-mail marketing program to tailor specific promotions to individual consumers. It's also using a variety of techniques to prime search engines. The aim is to ensure that consumers looking anywhere online for product information for, say, appliances or lawn and garden equipment are directed to the relevant parts of the Sears site.

"Our biggest win is to be where the consumer is looking," Mr. Charno says. Part of the challenge involves constantly testing all the various forms of online marketing now available, and being ruthless with discarding or retuning the ones that aren't working cost-effectively. The maxim, Mr. Charno adds, "is optimize, optimize, optimize."

The results are quite striking. One out of every 10 major appliance purchases in a Sears full-line store—that's upwards of $500 million in sales a year—are now influenced by Sears.com, the company says, with customers first checking out the Web site before buying. How does Sears know? Among other things, by surveying in-store customers on a regular, systematic basis.

Such experiences and the survey results point to two important shifts in online marketing. The first is the crucial importance of relevance. Give users an ad for something they're interested in or actively searching for, the argument goes, and they'll be far more inclined to click on it, and perhaps even buy the item online. The second is a change in the most-watched Internet advertising metric. These days, it's not the one tabulating the number of page views, or even the number of surfers who click on an ad—it's the return on investment.

The relatively high score given to e-mail in the survey won't come as a surprise to many big companies, which have been increasingly using it as a cheaper alternative to traditional direct mailings for sending promotional materials to consumers. But it has only been in the past 18 months that the pay-for-placement model has emerged as a potent online advertising medium. That rise is best reflected by the ascendancy of Overture.

At a time when even industry titans such as Yahoo and AOL have been hurt by the ad slump, Overture's fortunes have risen. The Pasadena, Calif., company now says it has 45,000 advertisers, and its revenue tripled in a year, to an albeit still modest $62.5 million in the second quarter of this year from $21 million in the year-earlier period. Before last month's terrorist attacks, Overture forecast that it would swing into the black for the first time later in the year—and is sticking to that forecast.

Overture runs a huge ad network of listings that are featured on the search-results pages of many major sites, including AOL, Lycos and AltaVista, where they are sometimes labeled "featured listings" or "partner search results." Businesses bid to have their Web sites show up as a link when a user searches a particular keyword or phrase, with the highest bidder winning the top slot. The companies then pay Overture the agreed fee every time a user actually clicks on the link and is taken to their site.

This auction model makes for big differences in prices between categories. For example, a company that wanted the top spot for "computer laptop" recently would have had to bid 66 cents for every user who clicks, more than 10 times as much as for the top listing for "apple juice." But even that is a far cry from the stratospheric costs—sometimes in the hundreds of dollars—that it took to acquire customers online at the height of Internet mania using other marketing methods such as sponsorships or costly portal deals.

Nader's Complaint

There are some gripes about Overture. One big issue is the quality of the listings themselves; traditionally, search engines rank results by relevance, rather than by how much an advertiser is prepared to pay to be at the top of the list. Consumer activist Ralph Nader has complained to the Federal Trade Commission that consumers allegedly are being misled because Overture's results that show up on other sites aren't labeled as paid advertisements. (On Overture's own site, by contrast, the amount each advertiser is paying per click is listed.) And some companies that use the service to advertise several products say that its bidding-for-keywords arrangement can be quite complex, sometimes requiring daily adjustments.

Ted Meisel, Overture's chief executive officer and president, concedes, "We are probably taking up too much of [advertisers'] time, and not enough of their money." The company has been working to address the issue of complexity for advertisers, and he says it plans to introduce new listings-management tools in the next couple of quarters. As for relevance, he says, "It'll always be our challenge to convince [critics] that quality actually matters to us."

Josh Needle is one Overture customer who isn't too bothered about such controversies. Mr. Needle spent 23 years as a criminal defense lawyer before setting up a small business in 1999 selling original cartoons. His idea of marketing is to spend $100 to $150 a month buying keywords on Overture, including "cartoons" and "cartoon art."

Mr. Needle says his Santa Monica, Calif., company, Impolitic, derives a lot of initial interest from the Overture listings. But he says that most people who see one of his cartoons online will call to discuss it, rather than just immediately click on the online purchase button. And he cautions, "I've yet to see a direct correlation between eyeballs and sales. That's just the nature of e-commerce."

69

THE MEDIUM IS THE INSTANT MESSAGE

A New York software company is the first to deliver custom ads via IM, the last great untapped mass-market channel.

By: Marc Weingarten

By some estimates, about 75 million people—not all of them teenage girls—already have access to instant messaging, that addictive hybrid of e-mail and old-fashioned telephone party line. So it comes as no surprise that somebody has finally found a way to turn the technology into a tool of marketing.

The somebody in question is a New York software company called ActiveBuddy. On behalf of corporate clients, ActiveBuddy creates custom bots, or intelligent agents—software applications that connect IM users to data they want, all the while mimicking, in a crude way, the banter of a fellow IM user at the other end of the data link. The databases can convey a client's marketing messages, or the client's ads can appear in the bot's IM dialogue box. It doesn't matter to ActiveBuddy CEO Peter Levitan, as long as major clients like Keebler's, Capitol Records, and Warner Bros. Records keep signing up. "People have got that IM screen up on their desktop seven hours a day," he says. "We think we're just scratching the surface of its potential."

ActiveBuddy bots are elegantly simple applications to use. After you add the name of one to your IM buddy list, type "Hi" or ask it a question to get things rolling. The bot is programmed to respond to natural-language questions in something approaching age-appropriate prose. For example, if you type "Hi" to LindsayBuddy,

an ActiveBuddy bot launched in August to promote Warner Bros. Records's new teen artist Lindsay Pagano, it responds, "Wassup yournamehere0434! Glad to see u again. What can i help u with?" The bot, essentially a front for a Pagano website, goes on to field questions about the singer ("Click this link to read Lindsay's bio!"), her tour dates, and, of course, where to buy her new CD. To keep fans amused, it also plays hangman and trivia games and provides Web links to streaming audio and video clips of Pagano. LindsayBuddy won't initiate a conversation, but that's not because it's trying to mimic a sullen teen; like all ActiveBuddy bots, it "speaks" only when spoken to. You can find all of the bots on ActiveBuddy.com, but most people hear about them from other IM users.

For Warner Bros. (which is owned by AOL Time Warner (*AOL*), *Business 2.0's* corporate parent), LindsayBuddy is an experiment. Looking to generate publicity for Pagano before her debut CD's December release, the music label decided a bot might be an effective way to reach the 13 million teens who use IM. So far, so good. By late November, 600,000 people had added LindsayBuddy to their buddy lists, and the bot had received more than 38 million messages. "It's been amazing for us," says Betty Lin, Warner Bros.'s senior manager of new media. "We've generated a ton of traffic for an unknown artist."

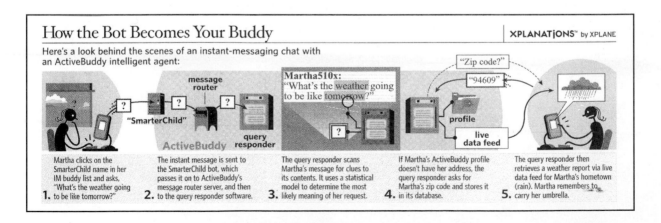

How the Bot Becomes Your Buddy — XPLANATIONS™ by XPLANE

Here's a look behind the scenes of an instant-messaging chat with an ActiveBuddy intelligent agent:

Martha510x: "What's the weather going to be like tomorrow?"

"Zip code?" — "94609"

1. Martha clicks on the SmarterChild name in her IM buddy list and asks, "What's the weather going to be like tomorrow?"
2. The instant message is sent to the SmarterChild bot, which passes it on to ActiveBuddy's message router server, and then to the query responder software.
3. The query responder scans Martha's message for clues to its contents. It uses a statistical model to determine the most likely meaning of her request.
4. If Martha's ActiveBuddy profile doesn't have her address, the query responder asks for Martha's zip code and stores it in its database.
5. The query responder then retrieves a weather report via live data feed for Martha's hometown (rain). Martha remembers to carry her umbrella.

(Cont.)

Equally impressive to Lin is the fact that LindsayBuddy—like most bots ActiveBuddy creates—is a word-of-mouth phenomenon. Traditional advertising contributed somewhat to the bot's popularity: LindsayBuddy was advertised on ActiveBuddy's other bots, and Pagano appeared in a commercial on network television last fall. But the lion's share of LindsayBuddy signups come from fans who, having discovered the bot, pass word of it along to their friends.

There's even more buzz around SmarterChild, Active-Buddy's newest creation. The general-interest bot can answer questions about anything from news and stock quotes to sports scores, movie showtimes, and biblical trivia. Unlike other bots, it's sponsored by multiple advertisers and runs ads on its message screens. Last June, when Active-Buddy posted a beta version of SmarterChild on its site, 3 million people added it to their buddy lists. Within months it was the company's most popular program.

Advertisers are pleased with it too. Snack-food giant Keebler's recently placed a two-line advertisement and Web link on SmarterChild to promote a sweepstakes for its Cheez-Its brand. Some 6.5 percent of IMers followed the link to the Cheez-Its website—a very good response rate, considering that the average clickthrough for e-mail newsletters is just 2.5 percent.

Granted, there are still some bugs to be worked out. As conversationalists, the best that can be said about ActiveBuddy bots is that they get to the point. There's certainly no mistaking their canned responses for human conversation. And their comprehension skills leave a lot to be desired. For example, a query about the New York Yankees on the Sporting News bot referred me to a fantasy football website. Sometimes you have to repeat or rephrase your question several times to get a relevant answer.

Still, ActiveBuddy is clearly on to a rapidly growing medium. And with as many as 150 million potential IM users projected by 2004, others are likely to catch on too. In fact, a competitor called FaceTime has recently popped up, offering customer-service bots for high-profile clients such as Alaska Airlines (*ALK*), Dell (*DELL*), and FAO Schwartz. Active-Buddy, meanwhile, has plans to create an IM bot for Reuters news agency later this year. "For some reason," Levitan says, "we've discovered that people really like to talk to computers."

"The Medium Is the Instant Message," *Business 2.0*, February 2002, pp. 98–99. © 2002 Time Inc. All rights reserved. Reprinted by permission.

Grown-Ups With Buddy Lists (Adult IM Users)	
GENDER	
Men	50%
Women	50%
AGE*	
18-29	30%
30-49	50%
50+	19%
EDUCATION	
No college	36%
Some college	34%
College graduate	30%
ANNUAL HOUSEHOLD INCOME*	
Less than $50,000	45%
$50,000-$75,000	19%
More than $75,000	24%
Source: Pew Internet & American Life Project, March 2001	

*Some respondents didn't know or declined to answer.

70

Dialing for Dollars

Marketers see mobile phones as the dream advertising platform. But will consumers?

By Jeanette Borzo

It's a marketing fantasy—preferred customers who are never out of reach, ready to react immediately to the latest promotion. But a growing number of companies, especially in Europe, are trying to turn dream into reality using the latest advertising platform—mobile phones.

"The ultimate value [of mobile advertising] is it's targeted to an individual person and that person can interact to participate in a promotion or a competition or whatever," says Allison Webb, a mobile telecommunications analyst in the London office of Frost & Sullivan, a global marketing-research firm based in San Jose, Calif. "You establish a relationship. It gives an advertiser the ability to read the market in real time."

Mobile marketing has begun modestly, focused mainly on a youth audience, but according to Ovum Ltd., a London-based research firm, the sector's revenue could grow to an estimated $12 billion globally by 2006, up from less than $48 million this year.

At first glance, a mobile-phone screen, half the size of a credit card, hardly looks like an auspicious advertising vehicle. But unlike television, newspapers or billboards, mobile phones generally belong to just one person, they're on most of the time, and they go just about everywhere. And marketers are taking advantage of that to beam their promotional offers to the select groups they most wish to reach.

Already, this type of mobile advertisement is generating response rates as high as 40%, compared with 3% generally expected for direct mail and less than 1% for Internet banner ads, says Frost & Sullivan's Ms. Webb.

Mobile Spasm

As it grows, mobile advertising's biggest challenge may well be to navigate the tightrope stretched between attracting and aggravating consumers. If you want to see a mobile advertiser jump, just whisper the phrase "mobile spam" into his or her ear.

"It's more intrusive to receive ads on the mobile phone than through e-mail, and people are already annoyed with that," says Katrina Bond, a senior analyst with Analysys Research Ltd. in Cambridge, England.

Avoiding that sense of intrusion is key to today's mobile-advertising market, and the industry hopes to achieve this by following an unbreakable rule: Get permission first. Radiolinja Oy customers, for example, either agree to receive marketing messages when signing contracts with the Finnish mobile-phone operator, or later on the Web. Such caution appears to pay dividends. In a summer promotional campaign the company conducted on mobile phones, television, radio, direct mail and in print, Radiolinja got a 30%

response rate on ads sent over the mobile phone. The next best—direct mail—garnered a 10% response rate.

Such feedback is partly due to the newfangled flavor of mobile ads. "I'm the first to admit that there is something of a novelty factor," says Chris Havemann, joint managing director at the **Mobile Channel**, a U.K. start-up that launched its mobile-ad service last month, and which has worked on test campaigns with Danish brewer **Carlsberg** AS and the Mars Confectionery unit of **Mars UK** Ltd. "But we're not trying to change consumer behavior. We're trying to tap into it."

Eventually, mobile advertisers will integrate more images, sound effects, melodies, animation and video into their communications, but for now marketers more often tap into consumer familiarity with short text messages that cellphone users send and receive in real time, known as SMSs. Mobile users in Germany sent an average of 38 messages a month at the beginning of 2001, according to Yankee Group, the Boston-based research and consulting firm. In the U.K., more than a billion SMSs are sent each month, says Enpocket, a media sales partner of British Telecom PLC, and the world as a whole will have sent a billion SMSs daily by the end of 2001, according to the GSM Association, a global body of telecom operators and equipment makers.

Ads in Concert

Asia is also SMS crazy, but Europe has a "wonderful proliferation of companies" that know how to use mobile marketing in concert with other advertising media, says Rosalie Nelson, digital-media research director at Ovum. "You haven't seen that integrated approach in the Asia-Pacific."

Mobile-Marketing Pioneers Share Seven Ad Axioms

GET PERMISSION
"This is opening a one-to-one dialogue with the customer," says Vesku Paananen, co-founder and chief technology officer of Add2Phone, a Finnish wireless-marketing and software firm. "Whatever we do, it should be permission-based."

S STANDS FOR SHORT—KEEP IT THAT WAY
"If the message is too detailed, the response rate is horrible," says Paul Smith, U.K. media manager for Mars Confectionery, a division of Mars UK Ltd. "We have to learn to be creative, short and sweet."

TARGET ADS BASED ON PROFILES
"People will not take kindly to random messages to buy washing detergent or toothpaste," cautions John Fletcher, senior consultant in Analysys Consulting Ltd.'s mobile-telecom sector in London. "These

advertisements can't be as random as with television."

PROVIDE INCENTIVES
By forwarding to other cellphone users an SMS ad for Warner Bros.'MovieWorld amusement park, located in Bottrop, Germany, the 25,000 participants in the ad campaign earned a 25% discount on the park admission price. "The response rate was near 15%," says Ingo Lippert, chief executive officer at MindMatics AG, a wireless advertising agency in Munich that managed the campaign.

ADD A CREATIVE SPARKLE
"It has to be cool or it's no fun," says Peter von Schlossberg, vice president and director of marketing and business development at Simon & Schuster New Media in New York. Mr. Von Schlossberg's latest campaign, "Let

Freedom Ring," encourages enthusiasts for the "Real War" game to sign up to download a ring tone of the U.S. national anthem.

INTEGRATE WITH OTHER MEDIA
"We don't look at wireless advertising as a stand-alone," says Lars Becker, chief executive officer at Flytxt Ltd., a mobile-marketing firm. Recently, the London start-up signed a partnership with the French outdoor advertising contractor JCDecaux for a new service called PosterTxt, which melds mobile marketing with billboard advertising.

DON'T HANG UP
Consumers who get an SMS promotion don't want to go to the Internet or elsewhere to reply. "The highest response rates are always to ads that remain within the mobile confines," says Chris Havemann, joint managing director at the U.K.'s Mobile Channel.

—Jeanette Borzo

(Cont.)

Mobile advertising can offer high returns, but with the increased costs of developing a new style of advertising and of placing individual calls, some consider the price high as well. Ranging generally from two cents to six cents per SMS, cellphone ads can run to $20 to $60 a thousand. Internet advertising, however, has stabilized at $4 to $30 a thousand, says Ms. Webb, though some premium sites can command up to $50.

"You have to be very smart because the cost per thousand is much higher," says Paul Smith, U.K. media manager for Mars Confectionery.

In the U.S., meanwhile, where the SMS market is stymied by numerous noncommunicating mobile standards and charges for incoming SMSs, mobile advertising is rare but not unknown.

Some U.S. advertisers have found inspiration in Europe. After a 10-day trip to Finland, Peter von Schlossberg, vice president and director of marketing and business development at **Viacom** Inc.'s Simon & Schuster New Media unit in New York, decided to use the mobile phone to promote a new game title. With help from a mobile-marketing firm in Finland, **Add2Phone** Ltd., Simon & Schuster New Media launched its "Turn Your Cellphone Into a Communicator" campaign and some 8,000 enthusiasts signed up to receive SMS game tips and tricks for the "Dominion Wars" Star Trek game.

Such campaigns often do target the youth audience, which is already known for its SMS enthusiasm. Consider the promotion **Flytxt** Ltd., a London-based wireless-marketing firm, ran for Momentum Pictures, the U.K. distribution unit of Toronto-based **Alliance Atlantis Communications** Inc. This summer, Alliance released "Get Over It," a U.S. film about a guy whose girlfriend leaves him. Six weeks before the film opened, Flytxt recruited a "GOI" fan club, offering film-ticket prizes along with a bikini like the one actress Kirsten Dunst wore in the film.

There was also a contest to come up with the best SMS to dump your boyfriend. More than two-thirds of the teenagers in the fan club submitted entries, including, "U r my alphabet. A letter between W & Y" and "Our relationship is like this text, short and sweet. Itz ova."

"Nothing in the movie is about SMS," says Lars Becker, chief executive officer at Flytxt, which has also run campaigns for London-based **Cadbury Schweppes** PLC. But 60% of the youngsters who signed up for the fan club went to see the movie the weekend it opened.

Many industry analysts expect mobile-advertising campaigns eventually will appeal to the older set as well. SMS itself began as a teen craze but worked its way into the adult population.

"Once this form of advertisement ties into [airline] mileage programs, then the older age range will join," says Ingo Lippert, chief executive officer at **MindMatics** AG, an interactive advertising firm in Munich, which has run campaigns for brands such as Coca-Cola and Ben & Jerry's.

Frost & Sullivan expects that by 2006 wireless banner-ad revenue in Western Europe will increase to $464.7 million from $51.5 million in 2001, and the number of wireless advertisements delivered by SMS will grow to 18.6 billion by 2006 from 676 million this year.

To prevent unwanted intrusion and take advantage of viral marketing's strengths, consumers generally complete a profile that is used to match ads to interests. Services often promise a limit to messages, send only targeted ads and let users modify their profile in case of a mismatch.

Frost & Sullivan's Ms. Webb, for example, signed up for information about London nightlife at www.nightfly.com and got far too many SMSs on Fridays and Saturdays. So she adjusted her profile about when and how often she could be contacted. The result "was very encouraging," Ms. Webb says, as the service thereafter "matched my profile."

Some 3% of Western Europe's mobile-phone users have agreed to receive some type of mobile-phone-based marketing alerts and promotions, Ms. Webb estimates. She boldly predicts that by 2006 that figure will balloon to 65%, as long as mobile-phone technology continues to improve and advertisers continue to restrict their campaigns to interested consumers.

'Emotionalize People'

In addition to permission-based and targeted ads, mobile-marketing executives emphasize that promotions need to stand out—and ideally strike an emotional chord with consumers. The use of voice is a "key element to emotionalize people," says Cyriac Roeding, co-founder and chief marketing officer of **12snap** AG, which has run campaigns for **McDonald's** Corp. and **News** Corp.'s 20th Century Fox studio.

Mr. Roeding, who is also chairman of the Wireless Advertising Association, points to 12snap's summer promotion for cosmetics and hair-care company **Wella** AG of Darmstadt, Germany.

From its 10 million-person database, 12snap sent SMSs to 200,000 Germans asking if they wanted to send a mobile kiss to someone. Those who said "yes" got a phone call with a long kissing sound and a voice announcing "your first mobile kiss . . . brought to you by Wella." To pass it on, participants entered someone's name and mobile number, and the routine repeated. Those who sent the most kisses were eligible for prizes.

"The response rates were so high I don't want to disclose them because it will inflate expectations," says Mr. Roeding. "Wella had to stop the campaign because all the prizes were gone."

"We were very satisfied with the effect of the campaign, which generated more than 750,000 contacts," says a Wella spokeswoman.

Customers were happy, too. "It was very funny," says Monica Trestian, a 27-year-old who says she bought Wella products a few weeks after getting a mobile kiss from her boyfriend. "It was new and innovative—it was not a normal SMS. When I get a boring SMS, I delete it."

That response underlines an important element in mobile marketing. In addition to being permission-based, mobile ads have got to be clever. Traditional, plain-vanilla advertising concepts simply won't fly.

"Good creativity is key," says Mr. Roeding. "If you can get that close to the consumer, than you must do it right."

Ms. Borzo writes about technology from Paris.

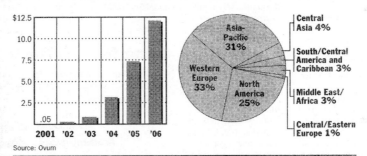

Pennies From Heaven

Global wireless marketing revenue is projected to see huge growth over the next few years (see chart at left; figures are in billions). At right, an estimate of how that wireless marketing revenue will be distributed around the world in 2006.

$12.5 10.0 7.5 5.0 2.5 .05
2001 '02 '03 '04 '05 '06
Source: Ovum

Central Asia 4%
South/Central America and Caribbean 3%
Middle East/Africa 3%
Central/Eastern Europe 1%
Asia-Pacific 31%
Western Europe 33%
North America 25%

71

Super Bowl Gets Competition

Some Longtime Advertisers Opt for Alternatives Instead; Expensive One-Night Stand

By Vanessa O'Connell
Staff Reporter of The Wall Street Journal

Cingular Wireless, then a new and little-known telecom venture, won nationwide recognition when it broadcast four offbeat commercials before an estimated 84 million people during last year's Super Bowl. But several months ago, Cingular decided against spending millions advertising on this year's event. "We are looking to have a longer-term impact this year," says Daryl Evans, the company's vice president of advertising and communications.

Other Super Bowl big spenders are making the same calculation. Amid the worst advertising recession in recent memory, marketing executives are running the numbers and concluding that there are more cost-effective alternatives to television's highest-rated but also highest-price event.

Some of the nation's best-known marketers are opting instead for the Academy Awards, the Grammies, the Golden Globes and other venues that offer younger, more sophisticated viewers for less cost. Some are choosing to spread their marketing dollars over long-term commitments instead of an expensive one-night stand.

Cingular, for example, is opting for pop-culture events such as Nascar racing, whose season begins in February, and tie-ins with movies like "Spider-Man," due in May. "We are trying to invest our money in those things that give us several weeks—if not months—of mileage," Mr. Evans says. Cingular is a partnership between **BellSouth** Corp. and **SBC Communications** Inc.

News Corp.'s Fox, the network that will broadcast the Super Bowl on Feb. 3, is still likely to sell out its total inventory of almost 30 minutes of commercial time. But demand is definitely weaker this year. Some advertisers say they have paid as little as $1.5 million for 30 seconds of ad time, though Fox disputes the rates have fallen that low. How Fox ultimately fares will be determined largely by the prices it can get this week for the handful of remaining commercial slots. Thirty-second commercials during last year's game general-

ly sold for about $2 million, down from an average of $2.2 million in 2000.

Another big obstacle for this year's Super Bowl is the 2002 Winter Olympic Games, which offers advertisers more broadcast opportunities and more sophisticated viewers.

Electronic Data Systems Corp. launched the first of a trilogy ad campaign, "Cat Herders," in the 2000 Super Bowl, followed by "Squirrels" last year. But this year, EDS directed its agency, Fallon Worldwide, a unit of **Publicis Groupe** SA, to create a series of commercials to debut during the opening ceremony of the Olympics, on Feb. 8. "The Olympic Games provide 17 days to sell the EDS story, and that gives us a better chance to make an impact," says Don Uzzi, the company's senior vice president, advertising, marketing and communications.

EDS has purchased roughly 29 minutes of Olympic advertising time, and will broadcast four new ads for a total of 58 times over those 17 days. It won't disclose its total outlay but 30 seconds of prime-time advertising during the Olympics runs about $600,000 on average.

There's also growing sentiment that the Super Bowl has turned into an expensive beauty pageant for big agencies such as **Omnicom Group** Inc.'s BBDO Worldwide, which handles **PepsiCo** Inc.'s Pepsi brand and Visa USA, rather than a bona fide launch pad for new brands and products. "The Super Bowl has been the altar of branding, and everybody prayed to the Super Bowl god. This year is different," says Simon Williams, chairman of Sterling Group Inc., an independent branding firm in New York.

In addition, some companies that had long been Super Bowl advertisers are today run by new chief executives or marketing heads, and others have cut back on the number of products they intend to launch.

"Media events don't drive our marketing strategy," says Larry Flanagan, the chief marketing officer at MasterCard International, which

advertised on the Super Bowl in 1998, 1999, and 2001 but will buy time during the Academy Awards this year. "When we were in the Bowl, it was because we were launching things, such as our travel and entertainment program," he says. "We don't have anything on tap for January or February that would coincide with the game."

MasterCard will look to tweak its "Price-less" campaign with new ads this year, but Mr. Flanagan says it will reserve its advertising splash for the Grammy awards, which are scheduled to air on Feb. 27.

The National Football League still has some defensive moves of its own. To broaden the game's appeal with young viewers, the game's half-time show will feature the rock group U2, whose music has been included in a lot of the NFL's own promotional ads.

NFL marketing executives also are trying to extend the Super Bowl with new opportunities for advertisers that choose not to pay television's highest commercial prices. This year for the first time, the NFL is organizing a Friday-night pregame concert. The league

Bang for the Buck?

Estimated price, in millions, for 30 seconds of ad time on each broadcast, followed by a rating measuring the percentage of U.S. households tuning in.

Broadcast	Price (Rating)
Super Bowl*	$1.90 (40)
Academy Awards	$1.60 (26)
NCAA Final Four	$0.90 (16)
Prime-time Winter Olympics	$0.60 (15)
Grammy Awards	$0.57 (17)
Barbara Walters Pre-Oscar	$0.55 (12)
'Survivor' finale	$0.53 (15)
Golden Globe Awards	$0.45 (15)
'E.R.'	$0.37 (17)
'Friends'	$0.35 (17)

Advertisers paid an average of $2 million for 30 seconds of television commercial time on last year's game. How some of the advertised products fared during 2001:

BRAND	AGENCY	% MARKET SHARE	SHARE POINTS GAINED OR LOST
MasterCard	McCann-Erickson	27.0%	+ 1.4
Dentyne Ice	Bates Worldwide	14.9	+ 0.6
Doritos	BBDO Worldwide	37.6	− 0.1
Visa	BBDO Worldwide	50.5	− 0.2
Pepsi-Cola	BBDO Worldwide	14.4	− 0.4
Budweiser	Various	12.1	− 0.5
Cingular	BBDO Worldwide	17.0	− 3.0

(Cont.)

presold the show to advertisers including **AOL Time Warner** Inc., **Philip Morris** Cos.' Miller Brewing Co., and **Motorola** Inc. Miller can't advertise on Fox's official Super Bowl programs this Sunday because rival Budweiser is set to be the exclusive beer marketer on the telecast.

John Collins, the NFL's senior vice president-marketing and entertainment programming, says Fox opted not to air the NFL-produced concert, which will feature rock artists Sting and No Doubt. So he sold it to a rival, **Viacom** Inc.'s CBS, which plans to broadcast the concert after its own advertising pageant—a special look back at the best recalled Super Bowl ads of past years.

Joe Flint contributed to this article.

72

NBC Olympic Campaign Sports Plugs Inside Plugs

Network's Ads Show Athletes Zooming Past Movie Posters That Were Put in Digitally

BY VANESSA O'CONNELL

In the theater, there's sometimes a play within a play. Now Madison Avenue has the plug within a plug.

To lower its costs amid the crippling advertising recession, **General Electric** Co.'s NBC is bringing commercial marketing to a new level by inserting other companies' products into its own promotions for the Winter Olympics. In a new ad campaign to promote the games, for example, NBC has inserted several prominent mentions of the rerelease of the 1982 movie "E.T. The Extra-Terrestrial" from **Vivendi Universal SA's** Universal Studios. For viewers, the result is in effect two ads in one, and they see billboards that don't really exist.

The ad campaign, which is aimed at drawing young viewers, was created by the network's internal agency. It revolves around a chase scene involving two Olympians, the snowboarder Chris Klug and Cammi Granato, a hockey player who helped the U.S. team win the gold medal at the 1998 games.

In the spots, Mr. Klug zooms through a mountain of fresh powder as police and state troopers chase him for speeding. After a pretty girl shows up on the slopes, Mr. Klug crashes through a window into a hockey arena, disrupting a game being played by Ms. Granato, then boards away down the mountain and runs into the pretty girl again. As the police zero in on him, a helicopter appears. "Meet me in February in Salt Lake City," Mr. Klug tells the girl as he grabs a rope thrown to him by his helicopter rescue team and is whisked away.

Careful viewers are likely to notice a billboard on the mountain plastered with an enormous ad for "E.T. The Extra-Terrestrial."

Halfway through the chase, Mr. Klug slides by another sign for the movie on the side of the ice rink. The technique, called "virtual video advertising," is commonly used to project stadium billboards during baseball games, but hasn't been widely used in commercials. It allows advertisers to reach viewers who avoid commercial breaks.

"I have never seen this done in ads," says David Sitt, chief executive of **Princeton Video Image** Inc., which creates virtual signs for sporting events. Madison Avenue has previously shied away from adding signs to commercials, he says, partly because advertisers feared that the networks might charge them extra for promoting two companies at the same time.

Barbara Blangiardi, vice president of marketing, NBC, says the network invited outside companies to pitch their brands in the Olympic promotion—and pick up part of the tab—to offset its costs to make the ads and air them in movie theaters and on a home video. NBC paid $545 million for the rights to broadcast the XIX Winter Games in the U.S., and it has been hurt by the ad slowdown and the enormous costs of covering the war on terrorism. Beginning Feb. 8, NBC intends to broadcast 375.5 hours of figure skating, ice hockey, snow boarding and other events.

Ms. Blangiardi says NBC is considering using virtual signage and other product-placement deals more broadly to offset the cost of advertising. She says the network may even consider inserting other products into ads for its fall lineup of TV shows or for other big sports events.

A similar ad for the Olympics appears on home rentals of the movie "A Knight's Tale" from **Sony** Corp.'s Columbia TriStar unit, but viewers see plugs for the home-video release of "The Animal" instead of "E.T." In exchange, NBC gave Sony some commercial time on the network to promote its home video division.

In baseball—and some international broadcasts of soccer, football and bullfights—inserting virtual ads has become quite common. Princeton Video Image created virtual signs for Radio Shack, Claritin, Century 21 and other brands during **Walt Disney** Co.'s ESPN Sunday night baseball package last year. The signs changed every half inning to reflect a new commercial message from different advertisers.

But NBC won't be able to line up advertisers for any kind of billboards at the Olympics because the International Olympic Committee prohibits such ads.

"All Olympic venues are clean venues,

and there will be no advertising allowed, even for our Olympic sponsors," says Caroline Shaw, chief communications officer for the Salt Lake Organizing Committee. The rules are intended to keep the focus on the athletes and not on advertisers, she notes. The only signs people will see in the background will be pictures of the athletes, signs to promote the Salt Lake Organizing Committee, which uses a snowflake logo, and the five Olympic rings.

"E.T." and "The Animal" aren't the only products that get some time during the NBC Olympic promotions. In the ads, NBC arranged for the snowboarder to have this sign added to the bottom of his board: "How's my boarding? Hot Snow." Hot Snow is a Web site that was created by MSNBC.com to help young viewers follow the game.

NBC's Olympics marketing scheme is one of the network's most expensive in recent years. It spent close to $800,000 just to make the stunt-packed snowboarder-chase ad. That's far more than the $150,000 to $300,000 NBC typically spends to make its promotions.

Part of the reason for the high cost is the fact that NBC chose to run the spot in movie theaters, beginning Jan. 4, at an additional cost of several hundred thousand dollars. Some shorter versions of the movie commercials were broadcast on the network late at night starting last month.

John Miller, president of NBC's internal agency, says the network was able to create the virtual sign in the ads using a so-called "green screen" on the shoot locale that could carry any message the network wanted to add. Initially, he says, NBC wasn't sure whether it would enlist a movie theater, consumer-products company, or job-placement firm as a partner.

"We only had so much money to promote the Olympics and we had a bunch of big ideas," he says. "One of the reasons we were able to pull this off is that we have some currency: our own air time, the inventory we sometimes use for our own promotional purposes."

Mr. Miller notes that while many middle-aged viewers aren't conditioned to notice virtual signs, the young people NBC is chasing spot them easily.

Price

Ways To Boost Sales Right Now: Price Wisely, Do What You Know

By DOUG TSURUOKA
Investor's Business Daily

Don't get trapped in old thinking when it comes to boosting sales. Consumers often do the opposite of what you expect.

Take flea powder. Cats and dogs have the same fleas and use the same powder.

But cat owners happily pay double for the same product. Why? Studies show feline fans can and do spend more on their animals.

Less-savvy firms might miss the point and charge everyone the lower price. But the best companies stick to simple rules that boost sales. They don't work in a vacuum. They work best when rivals stumble.

"Take advantage of companies that are building giant holes in the ground. While they're digging, find chances to win customers, build profits and dominate new markets," said Peter Meyer, a marketing and sales consultant who runs the Meyer Group in Scotts Valley, Calif.

They price to market, not costs.

As with cat owners, they raise the price of a product if the market wants it, rather than cut prices just because they can.

Johnson & Johnson, with $30.7 billion in sales, isn't afraid to keep prices high on certain lines. Some shoppers are comfortable paying a higher price for certain products.

An example is Band-Aids. Other brands cost less, but J&J knows shoppers will pay more for the sense of trust they impart.

"There's room for an additional price increase because of the comfort you get from buying the Band-Aid brand," Meyer said.

Prices vary by locale. But at a Duane Reade drugstore in New York, a box of 30 fabric Band-Aid strips costs $3.19, over two and a half times more than a box of 30 Duane Reade fabric strips.

That adds up, when you consider J&J has sold over 100 billion Band-Aids since they came out in 1921.

They create and lead new markets.

Human tests on J&J's new polymer-coated stent—a tiny tubular device that clears clogged arteries—shows it stops scarring and reblocking in heart surgery patients.

Reblocking is a problem with ordinary metal stents. Johnson's breakthrough should help boost sales in 2002 and 2003. Analysts say J&J sees new sales of up to $3.75 billion by charging into the new market.

They focus on marketing approaches and products where they already do well.

Discounter Family Dollar, with $3.7 billion in annual sales, sticks to sites and products where it's already successful.

Rather than build stores all over the U.S., Family Dollar, which has over 4,153 outlets in 39 states, focuses on areas where it knows it can do well.

"There's lots of efficiencies in clustering stores," said Executive Vice President George Mahoney.

The company keeps margins high and costs low by running stores of just 6,000 to 8,000 square feet.

"We don't need a large customer base to support a store," says Mahoney. The average outlet takes in slightly less than $1 million a year.

Family Dollar also boosts sales by sticking to goods that appeal strictly to its core low- and middle-income groups.

Ninety percent of Family Dollar's goods are priced at $10 and under. Nothing's over $20—yet its pretax profit margin, at 8.6% last year easily top Wal-Mart's.

Despite the down economy, its September sales grew 17%, with same-store sales up 6.7%.

They throw extra effort into meeting customer needs.

Compuware gets more sensitive to customers when times get tough. "We don't wait for customers to complain. We're already in there with them," said Paul Johnson, Southeast sales vice president for the software maker.

Case in point: Compuware set up automated software testing several months ago for a North Carolina bank. It tests software used to process depositor accounts, transfer funds and access account data.

Compuware let bank staffers sit down with its technicians to help design each facet of the system.

Most clients buying such a system normally would deal with many vendors. Compuware made sure they didn't have to go anywhere else.

They forge new products from old.

PepsiCo ramps up sales by spinning new products from old.

Take its Tropicana juice line. PepsiCo has spun off dozens of new juices from its main Tropicana orange juice product in the last few years. Its latest successes include health-type Pure Premium and Twister-brand juice drinks.

These products helped PepsiCo raise its share of the refrigerated juice market 1.3 percentage points to 26.4% in the second quarter.

The spinoffs helped sales at Tropicana surge 6% in the second quarter to $584 million from a year earlier. After a rough patch in the mid-1990s, Pepsi has stolen momentum from rival Coca-Cola.

Tropicana now is the No. 1 maker of not-from-concentrate juice, with a U.S. market share almost double that of its nearest rival.

"Tropicana's gained two full share points this year, despite increased competition," PepsiCo's Chairman and CEO Steve Reinemund said recently.

"Ways to Boost Sales Right Now: Price Wisely, Do What You Know," *Investor's Business Daily*, October 15, 2001, p. A1. Reprinted by permission.

Decisions, Decisions

Where are the high-priced traps— and how can I avoid them?

BY REBECCA BLUMENSTEIN

NEW YORK—So, you're on the road and think you're being savvy by using the calling card your phone company sent when you signed up for their plan.

Think again.

Exorbitant calling-card fees are just one of the reasons customers often end up with sticker shock when they open their monthly phone bills. An increasing array of charges are turning simple phone calls into a minefield of potential fees—and outraging consumers who are surprised by them.

Some charges are unavoidable, such as a universal service fee, usually 9.9% of long-distance bills, to cover the costs of providing Internet access to schools and libraries. But other fees can be circumvented if consumers read the fine print and make their calls in smart ways that avoid the biggest traps.

Still, a tour through phone bills reveals that calling the right way is easier said than done and often rewards high-volume users over consumers who don't make many calls.

AT&T Corp., for example, charges customers who use its calling card with the company's flagship 800 number a $1.25 service charge for each call, plus a per-minute rate of 89 cents. If customers using the card also require an AT&T operator's help to place a call, the service charge jumps to $5.50 plus the 89-cent per-minute charge. But if those same customers asked to be on the company's special calling-card plan for $1 a month, they would fare significantly better on the same kinds of calls—incurring a per-minute rate of 25 cents and no per-call service charges. The plan is mentioned on AT&T's Web site but isn't widely known. **Sprint** Corp. and WorldCom Inc.'s **MCI Group** offer similar bifurcated plans that reward those who know enough to call in and request the right plan. All you have to do is ask.

"Calling cards can be an enormous ripoff," says Gene Kimmelman, co-director of the Consumers Union Washington, D.C., office. He says recent proposals to lower phone bills seem to have accomplished little. "We are seeing more and more fees loaded onto bills."

An AT&T spokesman responds by saying the company tries to encourage customers to sign up for the cheapest plan. "If you make any volume of calling-card calls, even one a month, you want to be on a [discounted] calling-card plan," says the spokesman. He points out that with the growth in wireless calling and prepaid cards, fewer people are using calling cards.

But phone companies aren't just going to give their lowest rates to everyone, though some could argue that they should. Instead, discounted plans are tailored for those callers who shop around for the best rates, which allows the companies to continue to profit from the inertia that prevents many consumers from switching out of more expensive plans. AT&T, for its part, has learned that it is best to give customers choices, rather than, for example, sticking them on a cheap plan with a monthly fee they may not want to pay. "It is a tricky proposition to assume that you know what people want," says the spokesman. "That is fairly presumptuous."

Collect calling is another area where consumers need to tread very carefully—or better yet, avoid altogether by using cellphones. If you're at the receiving end of an AT&T collect call made through the company's flagship 800 number, you'll be billed 59 cents a minute plus a $2.99 service charge. If your caller gets help from the operator through the 800 number, the charge goes up to $5.50. If a caller simply dials 0 plus the number, the service charge is $4.99, but the per-minute charge goes up to 89 cents a minute.

These levies for credit-card and collect calls come on top of a bunch of recent price increases that can be difficult to avoid, such as pay-phone rates rising to 50 cents in states where **Qwest Communications International** Inc. and **SBC Communiations** Inc. offer local services. Basic charges for directory assistance and digital-subscriber lines for Internet service are going up as well, as are charges for standard subscriber lines—the basic copper phone lines that go into homes and businesses. In July, the regional Bell companies, in accordance with federal regulations, raised their monthly charge for standard subscriber lines to $5 from $3.50 a year earlier. And by 2003, the charge is scheduled to increase to $6.50. Second lines increased to $7 a month.

The Bell companies say some of these increases are the result of fees being shifted from long-distance companies to the local-service providers. The fee that long-distance companies formerly charged for standard subscriber lines, for example, has been removed from customers' long-distance bills and added to the amount being charged for the lines on the local bill.

For other fees, however, the justification seems less clear, such as Sprint's Carrier Property Tax. The tax, which amounts to 1.08% of the charges for a customer's interstate and international calls, allows Sprint to recover a portion of the property tax the company pays on its properties.

"It's ridiculous. Pretty soon we are going to see an electricity fee because they need the lights on at corporate headquarters," says Edgar Dworsky, a former Massachusetts assistant attorney general who is a founder of a public-service consumer Web site called Consumerworld.org, based in Somerville, Mass.

Call Tolls

Here's a sampling of some of the fees phone companies add to your bill. (Rates are examples chosen from a number of phone companies; costs vary from market to market.)

National directory assistance	95 cents to $1.99 for two listings. Some carriers charge to complete the call.
Local directory assistance	Once free, it now carries a fee in most areas. Verizon, for example, gives about three free listings a month and charges 35 cents thereafter.
Home voice mail	$5 to $8 a month plus set-up fee of about $10
*66 busy-signal redial service	50 to 95 cents, with a monthly cap of $9
Caller ID	About $7.95 a month
Call Waiting	About $3.75 a month
Collect calls	At least 45 cents a minute with $2.99 service charge
Calling-card calls	Without special plan, at least 89 cents a minute plus $1.25 service charge
Call trace *57	$7 per use
Airfone	$2.99 connection fee plus $3.28 per minute
Subscriber line charge	$5 a month, $7 for second line
Universal Service Fee	usually 9.9% of long-distance calls
Basic long-distance rates	30 cents a minute, Monday through Friday, (no calling plan) 7 a.m. to 7p.m, 25 cents a minute, 7 p.m. to 7 a.m. 16 cents a minute Saturday and Sunday.

Source: phone companies

Mr. Dworsky finds other fees unreasonable as well, such as a fee of as much as $1.98 a month that Sprint charges in five states, including Massachusetts, New York and Michigan, for Sprint calls made to local Bell customers in those states. These so-called termination fees, Sprint says, are the result of charges it's required to pay to the Baby Bells for putting the call through at the receiving end. Sprint officials say that by charging such fees, the company is trying to simply break out its costs of doing business. "We made a business decision to pass that along to customers rather than raise rates," says a Sprint spokeswoman. So far, other companies have not followed Sprint's lead in breaking out a property-tax fee for consumers.

Mr. Dworsky says the notion of loading up customers' bills with so many fees is troubling, particularly fees that must be paid in order to receive a more favorable rate. In one example typical of many long-distance service plans, Sprint offers long-distance rates as low as seven cents per minute for customers who pay a monthly fee of $5.95. "Why should a consumer pay a monthly fee for the privilege of having a reasonable per-minute rate?" Mr. Dworsky asks.

Indeed, it is those customers that don't pay monthly service-plan fees that are hit with the highest basic rates, which range as high as 30 cents a minute during the day for MCI customers.

Of course, it may seem insane to pay the higher rates, but millions do. A whopping 28 million consumers are still on AT&T's basic rate plan, despite the company's best efforts to alert them about other plans. Still, AT&T says that the percentage of its customers on optional plans has increased to about 80% of its total minutes. For some—mainly consumers who don't make many calls—it doesn't make sense to switch to a monthly-fee plan. Such customers are those who make so few calls that the higher rates they pay still amount to less each month than most service-plan fees.

However, lots of other consumers end up paying the basic rates by mistake. Take, for example, the thousands of people who move every month. When they receive a new telephone number, they are required to pick a long-distance company, but they stay on that company's basic rate unless and until they call to subscribe to a special calling plan.

And many consumers, such as Mary Harada of West Newberry, Mass., report unexpected charges after making adjustments in their phone service. Ms. Harada says she was cut from her AT&T international calling plan when she switched to an AT&T long-distance deal. When she got her bill, she says, it was a stunning $229, with $7-a-minute calls to Brazil and 26-cent-a-minute calls to Japan. On her previous international plan, she says, the same calls would have cost her a few cents a minute, plus the usual monthly fee.

"It set off a day of making telephone calls to try to figure out why this happened," says Ms. Harada, who eventually got virtually all of it rebated.

Some consumers complain that their phone company keeps no written records of what service they have requested. "I am beginning to deal with phone companies the way I deal with health insurance," says Ms. Harada. "I have a file and I keep everything. I date it and keep the name of the person I talked to."

Adding to customers' confusion and frustration, the number of services local phone companies offer has exploded in recent years, making bills more complex—and expensive. **Verizon Communications** Inc., for example, charges $7.99 a month in New York for Caller ID and an average of $3.75 for Call Waiting. Home voice mail, another popular option, costs an average of $5 to $8 a month, plus a one-time set-up fee of $10. Such services have been hugely profitable for the Bells since they cost virtually nothing

to deliver; they simply involve rewriting software in the companies' computer and phone networks.

But while consumers have taken to the services, they aren't exactly happy with the state of their bills. So, local companies, too, have begun offering plans that can lower customers' monthly payments. In Michigan, for example, SBC's Ameritech unit now has a plan that offers unlimited local calling, 300 minutes of toll calls, Caller ID, Call Forwarding, Call Waiting and three-way calling for $49.95 a month—a savings of more than $34 if customers were to purchase those services separately. Ameritech this month plans to begin aggressively advertising its unlimited-local-service plan in Michigan and to launch a similar plan in Illinois.

One thing almost everyone can agree on is that the most outrageous fees out there are for the calls you make on airplanes. The service never really took off, and now the companies that still offer it are not exactly trying to entice customers with low rates. Take Verizon's Airfone rates: a $2.99 connection fee plus $3.28 per minute. Verizon officials say the rates are comparable to those of other carriers and reflect the cost of deploying the technology and the volume of use.

No wonder flight attendants are yelling at passengers for refusing to turn off their cellphones.

Ms. Blumenstein, a staff reporter in The Wall Street Journal's New York bureau, served as contributing editor for this Report.

75

Dell Does Domination

It's a terrible time to be selling computers—unless you're Michael Dell, who is slashing prices and stealing share from less efficient rivals. Is it "game over" in PCs?
■ *by Andy Serwer*

Over the years I've spent a fair amount of time hanging out with Michael Dell, and what I noticed during my latest visit with him in Austin is how things have changed. Yes, he is still unflappable. And yes, he greets me in his new glossy offices with the same Stepford Wife-like grin he has always had. But he appears thinner now, as if he's lost baby fat. While he's still slow-moving, as if he's conserving energy, he now cuts to the quick in conversation. And when he zeroes in on the point he wants to make, when he reiterates why Dell Computer is in a better position than any other PC maker in the world, you realize that the 36-year-old has lost what was once one of his greatest advantages: No one underestimates him anymore.

Instead, Michael Dell looms over the PC landscape like a giant, casting a shadow over all his unfortunate competitors. This is a terrible time in a difficult business. PC sales were down for the first time last year. Dell's sales will be down, too, also for the first time. Yet even with that, even with recession, even with the threat of a Hewlett-Packard/Compaq Goliath, this is the only PC maker you can count on to grow and grow and grow. Almost single-handedly, Dell is forcing this industry to consolidate. Could this mean "game over" in the PC biz? Not even the ambitious CEO buys that. "Game over?" he looks back at me incredulously. "No way. We only have 14% global market share."

The Dellites may not admit to "game over" aspirations, but clearly they are thinking of a kind of domination never seen before among PC makers. "We think 40% market share is possible," says Dell's No. 2, Kevin Rollins. That's a remarkable goal; what's more remarkable is that it really is attainable. Don't look for Dell to hit that kind of number anytime soon. Rather, the company's growth will come from grinding out gains on several existing fronts, while shrewdly expanding into new target markets. But the growth *will* come—just ask Oracle CEO Larry Ellison, who has watched Dell take great chunks out of the market for Windows servers, which are

essentially high-powered PCs that can help manage Websites or data on corporate networks. "If you want to be in the PC business, you have to compete against Dell," says Ellison, "and that is very, very difficult."

The reason is simple: There's no better way to make, sell, and deliver PCs than the way Dell does it, and nobody executes that model better than Dell. By now most business people can recite the basic tenets of Dell's direct-sales model. Dell machines are made to order and delivered directly to the customer. There is no middleman. The customer gets the exact machine he wants cheaper than he can get it from the competition. The company gets paid by the customer weeks before it pays suppliers. Given all that, the company that famously started in Austin out of a University of Texas dorm room now dominates the northern side of this city the way giant steelworks

once lorded over old mill towns. Dell has some 24 facilities in and near Austin and employs more than 18,000 local workers. Dell did over $30 billion in sales in 2000, ranking 48th on the FORTUNE 500, ahead of names like Walt Disney, Johnson & Johnson, and Du Pont. Michael is the richest man under 40 in the world, worth $16 billion.

Two facts show how well the Dell model is working, even in tough times: Dell is on track to *earn* over $1.7 billion in 2001, taking almost every single dollar of profit among makers of Windows-based PCs. (Intel and Microsoft, of course, earn good money too—but they extract profits *from* the PC makers.) And Dell is gaining market share. That's not true for any other major PC maker.

Quite the contrary. The others are going *splat* for the same reason that Dell is succeeding: commoditization. The desktop PC

Profits? Higher market share? Nobody but Dell.
On the lower end of the worldwide computer market, only Dell is both gaining points of market share and garnering profits.

has become a commodity. That's great for consumers, who get standardized, easy-to-use, cheap PCs. But it's horrible for all but one manufacturer. As prices plummet, CEOs of most PC makers find it so hard to make a dime that they must justify to shareholders staying in the business at all. Commoditization relentlessly drives consolidation. And so it is no surprise when former highflying PC makers like AST crash. Or when IBM stops selling PCs in stores. Or when Gateway pulls back from selling overseas. Or when Micron shunts its PC business off to LBO artist Alec Gores. And the latest chapter of the consolidation story, of course, is the proposed HP/Compaq deal.

Commoditization has been going on in the industry for years. Dell, as master of the direct model, spent most of the 1990s operating in techno-Nirvana. The PC market was growing by 15%-plus per year, and the decade ended on a frenzied upswing as companies loaded up on new Y2K-ready machines. For its quarter ended January 2000, Dell did a record $6.8 billion in sales, up 31% from the previous year's quarter. In a sign of things to come, sales growth slowed later in 2000. Then the growth disappeared in 2001.

The economic slowdown was bad news for everyone, but Michael Dell and Kevin Rollins, who is increasingly his equal partner in running this business, made sure it was terrible news for Dell's competitors. In late 2000 they decided to slash prices. "It was advantageous for us, actually, because in periods of slow demand component prices drop, and, unlike our competition, we can pass those savings on immediately to customers," explains Rollins, a fine violinist who grew up in a hard-charging Utah family—his father was an engineering professor at Brigham Young—and came to Dell from the Bain consulting firm. Dell could make more money selling more computers at lower prices than it could selling fewer computers at higher prices. The low prices wreaked havoc on competitors. Compaq, HP, and Gateway all lost market share for the 12 months ended Sept. 30, 2001, while Dell's share of the U.S. market climbed 31%.

Of course Dell's price war made customers very happy. Sometimes you bump into one of them on an airplane. On a recent flight to Atlanta my neighbor was working on a Dell laptop. "Excuse me," I asked, "how do you like your Dell?" "Funny you should ask," he replied. Turns out he was Bob Perrett, the CEO of a company called Miltex, a dental- and surgical-supply firm in Bethpage, N.Y. Perrett came over to run Miltex two years ago as a dedicated IBM ThinkPad man. And he said as much to Frank Velardo, Miltex's head of IT. But Velardo was a Dell guy with an installed base of several dozen desktops and servers, and he persuaded his new boss to leaf through a Dell brochure. "We picked out a Dell Latitude," says Velardo. "The price was right. It's small, light, and fast. Then we got a large LCD monitor, a wireless keyboard and mouse, and docking stations—one for work and one for home—and he has been in love with it. And now that Miltex does more than $50,000 of business a year with Dell, we get our own dedicated rep." Back on the airplane, Perrett wants to me to hold his new baby. "Pick it up," he says. "It's great."

Success stories like Miltex were the exception for Dell in 2001. Sales to businesses were sluggish, and other markets propped up the company. "The government and education market had really good years," says Joe Marengi, co-head of Dell's Americas business, which produces about 70% of the company's sales. "To a large extent these businesses are driven by taxes, and 2001 was a tremendous year for tax collection." But government spending is almost certain to slow in 2002, which means that Dell is counting on business sales to pick up again. Michael Dell says the case for a second-half recovery is simple: "You've got 150 million computers that are over three years old, 45 million of which are in the large corporate-account sector in the United States of America, where Dell has about 40% market share. If we capture our 40% share of those 45 million, that alone would be 18 million units—which is what people expect us to do for the entire year."

Dell may be right, but some PC industry analysts think he's wrong. They argue that today's machines are so high-powered that companies are likely to put off their upgrades. In fact, as you look across the areas in which Dell has traditionally looked for growth, every single one poses a significant challenge. Some analysts, for instance, want to see great gains from Dell in overseas markets. "In the future, instead of 70% of revenue coming out of North America, you'll see that dip into the 50s or 60s because the U.S. market is not growing as fast as the foreign markets," says Lehman Brothers' Dan Niles. But Europe, the company's second-biggest market, has been problematic. Dell has made several missteps there over the years, so success is hardly a given.

T hen there's the consumer PC business. For years, business and home PCs were essentially the same machines. That's changing now. "The consumer wants the PC to be a home entertainment/multimedia experience," Michael Dell wrote to me in a recent e-mail. "The product lines are totally different." He believes his company will win here too, especially given the weakness of Gateway, the leading direct seller of consumer PCs. This Christmas season, Dell saturated 86 television channels with its "Steven" commercials, which touted all the cool things consumers can do with Dell PCs. The CEO wants consumer PCs to account for 20% of sales—up from 15% now—but Dell's home PCs aren't yet known as superior consumer machines. When it comes to the home, Sony's Vaio and Apple's iMac are the *crème de la crème*, the machines with all the buzz.

Other companies, most notably IBM, have turned to services for growth. IBM sells a wide range of hardware, but its meat and potatoes now is business services—the company's army of consultants who advise customers on how to use and implement its technology. (Credit CEO Lou Gerstner for realizing that selling hardware wouldn't get him the margins he wanted, and for building up IBM's strengths in services.)

Competitors think services are Dell's great weakness. They say that Dell, which often partners with companies like EDS, doesn't have what it takes to truly serve large corporations. As an example, they point to the fact that Dell lost a big global account with Shell. Indeed, one of the key reasons supporters of the proposed HP/Compaq deal are pushing hard for the merger is that they think the combination would create a services business that could successfully compete with IBM and steal sales from Dell. Michael Dell dismisses the criticism. "Services is now a $3-billion-a-year business at Dell," he says. "In the large-account space it's becoming a critical factor in many bids. We don't, however, need to copy IBM. We can keep doing it our way and win." Dell Computer will have enough of a consulting business to satisfy large customers—and no more.

That's because Michael Dell believes he can get higher margins from any number of hardware businesses. He is actively pushing the company into a wide range of peripheral products. How does he decide which products fit the bill? A few criteria must be met: The product must be (1) PC-related, (2) sizable, (3) profitable, and (4) increasingly a commodity.

Two product lines that make the list are storage and switches, and Dell is pushing like mad into those businesses. (Hey, EMC and Cisco! Guess who's coming to dinner?) The company has talked a lot about those efforts over the past year or so, but only now are the products being rolled out to any significant degree. Kim Crawford, who has an engineering degree from Stanford and an MBA from Harvard and who also did a stint at Bain, is the head of Dell's switches business. Crawford pulls out a chart diagramming the product life-cycle of switches, those black boxes that connect computer networks. "Here," she says. "Here's where we want to be. The sweet spot." She's pointing at so-called Layer 2 switches, which are used by customers looking to link computers in small to medium-sized networks, and are selling like crazy. And with operating margins reaching up to 50%, switches are a perfect Dell target: more profitable than PCs, and yet sufficiently overpriced that Dell can come in on the low end and steal market share from the likes of 3Com and Cisco. "It won't be a cakewalk," Crawford admits, "but this is a $17 billion market, and we aim to get our fair share."

Dell has entrusted its storage business to Russ Holt, a 40-year-old Georgia Tech computer science grad by way of NCR. Holt has targeted the boxes that hold data for low-end and medium-powered servers. Five years ago Dell ranked sixth among makers of these non-Unix-based servers, and the conventional wisdom was that corporate IT folks would never put their networks at risk by running Dell's cheap machines. The conventional wisdom was wrong. In 2001, Dell soared past Compaq into the No. 1 spot in the U.S. "It's breathtaking what they are doing," marvels Oracle's Ellison. "Dell gained six points of market share in one year. I've never heard of that before." (Actually, Larry, it was seven.)

Holt's charge is simple: Reenact the success Dell has had with servers in the $30-billion-a-year storage market by persuading customers to change brands. In a sense that becomes easier every quarter, since the IT manager who was a tough sell for his first Dell server is an easier sell for his first piece of Dell storage. Endeavors like Holt's also entail going to war with former allies. Some competitors scoff at the idea that Dell will ever get a firm hold in storage, where it ranks just seventh now. But the company already has a $1.4 billion run rate in storage, its revenues are growing at 27%, and the business is ripe for a low-price alternative. Sure sounds like Windows servers a few years back. . . .

While switches and storage make sense to the CEO, other hardware markets don't fit the plan. PDAs, for instance, are a nonstarter. (Interestingly, Dell and Steve Jobs see eye to eye on this one.) According to one Dell employee, Michael goes around dissing PDAs with a simple query: "Question: What is the biggest button on a PDA? Answer: The button that syncs it to your PC." Simply put, they aren't big enough or profitable enough for Dell. To wit: Palm just reported second-quarter revenues of $290 million, down from $522 million the previous year. As for the bottom line: It lost $36 million.

Those kinds of numbers just aren't interesting to Dell, especially when you consider his greatest worry: the stock. Yes, it was up some 50% in 2001, but over the past three years it's languished. Making matters worse, Dell shares are not cheap. On calendar 2001 earnings, it has a P/E of 42. On 2002 estimates, the P/E is still 37. For the stock to get back to its all-time high of $58, which it hit in March 2000, it would have to more than double, giving the company a market cap of $150 billion—a lofty perch occupied by the likes of Merck and SBC Communications. That's not implausible, but it sure is challenging, given that the company may not do $8.7 billion of sales in a quarter (as it did at the end of 2000) for years. Look long term, says the CEO: "Our stock went on the same wild ride as Nasdaq, but now we are faring very well. If we execute, the stock goes up bigtime over several years. I remain focused on where we want to be five to ten years from now, and beyond." Dell himself went out on the open market last September to buy tens of millions of shares. Of course, the stock then sold for under $20, not its current $28.

The CEO's confidence about Dell's long-term prospects hasn't done much to sway his Wall Street critics. Some naysayers whisper that the company is too aggressive with its accounting and makes suppliers hold back inventory at the end of a quarter to goose its numbers. Michael Dell doesn't completely disavow this: "I'm not going to suggest that there couldn't be incidents where we did things that could appear like that," he says, "but on a broad scale, no, that does not reflect our activities at all." The problem is that analysts question the big picture as much as the details. "We've been negative on Dell even though we think the business model is the best in the industry," says Lehman's Niles. "But that model doesn't matter at the end of the day, if the market you're serving is shrinking [for now]." If you buy into that kind of skepticism, you've got to question the value of Dell's ambitious long-term goals. "I believe 40% [market share] is a completely feasible number," says Morgan Stanley's Gillian Munson, and Niles concurs. But what does that really mean, assuming that the PC business is likely to be a slow-growth business with increasingly tight margins? Slow growth with low margins sounds a lot like a supermarket! Nonsense, counters Dell. "We have a multitude of opportunities," he says. "Market-share consolidation in PCs, servers, storage, services, software and peripherals, networking, financing, etc., and an advantaged business model. Net it all out [and] we should be able to grow much faster than most companies. Who of the large techs is better positioned to grow?"

No one, of course. And so Dell is hell-bent on growth, skeptics be damned. He won't say how much growth how fast, exactly, but here's how he expressed his ambition in a recent e-mail to me: "There are many different ways to look at it but we will grow. It's hard to beat our own 42% CAGR [compound annual growth rate] over the past six years. Comparing it to others Wal-Mart grew 29% CAGR in the six years up to $30 billion in revenues. In the six years after $30 billion, Wal-Mart grew 26%. Hope that helps."

Oh, it helped me, sure. If Dell can pull off something this audacious, he'll put a big hurt on competitors, of course, not to mention ratcheting up the pressure on Dell suppliers. Dell seems to be well on its way to becoming the Wal-Mart of the PC industry. With its huge and growing volume, it demands—and gets—more and more and more from companies that supply it with PC components. If Dell gets big enough, it could even put heat on Intel and Microsoft, which have never had to deal with a customer with this kind of potential clout. Executives at Microsoft deferred to CEO Steve Ballmer on this question, but he was unavailable for comment. Intel's Paul Otellini dismisses the notion that Dell could ever become as dominant as, say, Microsoft.

Otellini's probably right that Dell will never gain the kind of 90% market share in PCs that Microsoft enjoys in operating systems. That's a good thing for us, the PC consumers. The last thing we need is a company with anything approaching monopoly power in hardware. The very thought strikes Dell as odd. "But we keep lowering prices," he tells me, with a quizzical look, when I raise the subject. Can't argue with that. Once again, think of Wal-Mart. Dell could well keep growing to what we once thought was an impossible size, squeezing out competitors—some of which we will be sad to see go. But when was the last time you heard about Wal-Mart raising prices?

So sure, don't look for Dell to grow its revenues 40% a year anymore. This company is simply too big to guarantee that kind of growth. But there's no reason Dell can't begin to look like some sort of superbad blue chip. Which brings me to a final Wal-Mart analogy. For years and years Wal-Mart was a stock market superstar. Then, in 1992, WMT, which was then trading in the (split-adjusted) mid-teens, stalled. The company had various problems relating to operations and management, and some critics said its long run was over. For years these critics appeared to be correct. WMT never broke $20, even as the rest of the market was on the move. In the meantime though, after straightening out its problems, Wal-Mart just kept on doing what it always done: growing and cutting costs. Finally, in 1997, the stock took off on another run. Today, WMT trades in the high 50s.

As with Wal-Mart, with Dell you get the feeling that it's not *if* this stock will take off again, but *when*.

Reporter associate Julia Boorstin

DRUG PRICES WHAT'S FAIR?
How can we encourage research and still keep prices within reach . . . For Cipro and beyond?

For drugmakers, this fall's Cipro saga contains the germ of a potential nightmare. No, not because of worries that the antibiotic is scarce or that anthrax will bring America to its knees. The scary part for the industry was watching tough-talking Health & Human Services Secretary Tommy G. Thompson bully Cipro manufacturer Bayer into slashing its price by threatening to take away its patent-protected monopoly.

In one fell swoop, Thompson highlighted the fact that Cipro costs about 10 times as much as equally effective drugs, he emboldened Brazil and other countries to break patents to lower drug costs, and he set a worrisome precedent for future government meddling in the cost of medicines. If a free-market Republican Administration can force Bayer to cut its price, how will the government be able to resist stepping in when the soaring cost of a future Medicare drug benefit threatens to break the bank?

Make no mistake: In a few years, America's bill for drugs could well bust the health-care budget because of a triple whammy of expensive new medicines, a tremendous jump in the use of drugs, and the aging of the population. Already, there are drugs such as Pharmacia Corp.'s colon-cancer treatment, Camptosar, that can cost more than $60,000 per patient per year. And as today's gene wizardry becomes tomorrow's amazing new drugs, some of the price tags will be equally amazing.

The nation's drug bill has been rising at 14% to 18% a year, and for 2001 it will be between $160 billion and $170 billion, according to private sector estimates. The bill will climb even faster as seniors' ranks swell with aging baby boomers. The upshot: a clash between soaring costs and payers' ability to foot the bill. "The countdown has already started on the collision course," says Alan L. Hillman, director of the Center for Health Policy at the University of Pennsylvania's Wharton School. "We simply don't have enough money to pay for these future technologies."

The prospect of this collision is already prompting insurers, governments, and other payers to take direct aim at the pharmaceutical industry. To keep costs from soaring even higher, health maintenance organizations (HMOs) and pharmacy benefits managers (PBMs) are trying everything from pushing patients to use generics to demanding that drugmakers prove that their new medicines are cost-effective. States from Florida to Michigan are legislating discounts for residents, and companies like Chrysler are teaming up with others to negotiate lower prices. Meanwhile, a new World Trade Organization agreement gives other countries more leeway to make cheap knockoff drugs in times of medical need. All this comes at a bad time for Big Pharma, which is facing the imminent expiration of patents on many of its blockbusters and fewer-than-expected new drugs in the pipeline. "We are under enormous pressure," says Novartis Chairman and Chief Executive Daniel Vasella.

The industry is fighting back. In an advertising campaign, it is arguing that spending more on drugs actually saves money by reducing costly hospitalizations and other health-care expenses. Companies are also rushing to assure patients who cannot pay that they won't be left out. GlaxoSmithKline PLC announced in October that it would give discounts of 30% to 40% to needy elderly Americans, for instance. Novartis is providing its $28,000-per-year leukemia drug, Gleevec, free to those who can't afford it, as well as discounting other drugs for poor people. And the bioterrorism attack "gave the industry the opportunity to put its white hat back on," says Lehman Brothers Inc. analyst Nancy Myers. Glaxo, Bristol-Myers Squibb, and others rushed to donate antibiotics and expertise to the government. "If industry doesn't make such an effort, we will face a backlash," says Vasella.

Big Pharma's do-gooders, however, can't paper over the underlying issue: Just how will the nation cope with the rising cost of drugs? It's a far from simple question. A close examination shows that this is not a black-and-white case of medical breakthroughs that bust the bank or of lifesaving drugs priced out of reach of ordinary citizens. Instead, the tale is replete with paradoxes and puzzlements. Take one classic example: Some expensive new drugs, such as Gleevec or cholesterol-lowering medicines, do save money by reducing the need for expensive bone-marrow transplants or bypass operations. Yet in terms of overall health-care costs, a quick death is cheap. By living longer, patients will get other diseases that require more costly care. On the other hand, premature deaths rob the economy of productive citizens and workers.

These complexities make it extremely difficult to figure out whether any given drug increases or decreases health-care costs. Add in the larger picture, including productivity and quality-of-life measures, and the economics gets even murkier.

The whole debate is further muddied by the country's schizophrenic attitude toward drugs and drugmakers. Americans want powerful new medicines, along with smashing returns for stockholders. At the same time, people demand that drugmakers deliver their remedies at prices ordinary folks deem reasonable. If drug prices soar, Americans worry that medicines will have to be rationed by the patient's ability to pay, which wounds our sense of social equity.

So how is it possible to understand this complex situation? And more important, what can be done to soften the impact of the collision between soaring costs and ability to pay?

What follows is a step-by-step tour through some of the key questions and answers. The bottom line: The U.S. does spend more than it needs to on drugs, although in certain cases it should be spending more. Drugmakers need big profits to provide the innovative new medicines that the public demands—even though companies also need to boost research and development productivity. Market forces are already beginning to rein in the drug-cost monster, but there are steps the health-care system should take to speed the trend. BusinessWeek estimates that these steps could cut the nation's annual drug bill by as much as $15 billion and reduce other health-care costs as well.

WHY WE SPEND TOO MUCH ON DRUGS. One fact is crystal clear: The U.S. drug bill is higher than need be. Americans take more drugs than necessary, often popping expensive pills such as Cipro when cheaper ones will do. And because of overuse and misuse, studies estimate, the U.S. wastes an extra dollar for every dollar spent on drugs—fixing the ills medicines cause. Some patients don't get, or don't take, the right prescription, for instance, leading to lost work or unnecessary hospitalizations. Others suffer because of dangerous side effects or drug

(Cont.)

interactions. One famous 1998 study in the *Journal of the American Medical Association* estimates that adverse reactions to drugs in U.S. hospitals may cause more than 100,000 deaths a year. "When you see someone taking 14 drugs, the last seven are typically to treat the side effects of the first seven," observes Albert I. Wertheimer, director of Temple University's Center for Pharmaceutical Health Services Research.

Reduce these problems, and the savings are huge. If the estimated $150 billion spent each year to fix drug havoc could be cut to $50 billion, "we'd save enough to afford a Medicare drug benefit," says J. Lyle Bootman, dean of the University of Arizona's College of Pharmacy.

For each of these problems, there's plenty of blame to go around. Employers, doctors, and health insurers often fail to steer patients toward the drugs that offer the best value or to teach them to take the medicines properly, experts say. Meanwhile, Americans too readily seek pharmaceutical solutions to ailments that are better tackled through prevention. Public-health officials warn that we are on the cusp of a budget-busting diabetes epidemic, triggered by Americans' couch-potato habits. The incidence of the disease has jumped more than 33% since 1990, mirroring

a similar rise in obesity.

Drugmakers are culpable, too—although not necessarily because of the prices they charge. Selling drugs is, after all, a business, and companies have a duty to shareholders to maximize profits, observes Dr. Alan M. Garber, professor of medicine and health policy at Stanford University. "It would be unfair to portray the industry as greedy or irresponsible if they charge what they can get," he says. But companies may cross an ethical line when they market expensive drugs to those who don't need them or manipulate the patent system to extend their patent-protected monopolies.

Today, the rise in drug spending is not being fueled by headline-grabbing, $15,000-a-year AIDS or cancer drugs, which are used by too few people to add up to meaningful. Instead, Merck-Medco, a large PBM, figures that more than half of the projected doubling in its spending over the next five years will come from just two main types of drugs: cholesterol-lowering and other heart-related medications, and neurological medications, such as psychiatric drugs or painkillers, that are used by tens of millions of people.

When they develop new classes of drugs, companies typically price them far higher than the older medicines used for the same

conditions—even if the extra benefits are small. Expensive drugs called calcium channel blockers, for example, are routinely prescribed for patients with high blood pressure, even though studies show that cheaper beta-blocker and diuretic drugs can work as well or better.

What's more, drugmakers market many medicines directly to consumers, spending billions on ads that critics say are often misleading. "Pharmaceutical companies are coming out with these very expensive new drugs to replace existing drugs, sometimes in the absence of good evidence that their value is worth the extra costs," charges Dr. Sharon Levine, associate director of Kaiser Permanente's physician unit. For instance, the heavily advertised painkillers Celebrex and Vioxx, with combined worldwide sales of $5.6 billion, "are not more effective than Motrin, but they cost up to 60 times as much," Levine says. The new drugs do offer an important benefit for some patients: less stomach bleeding. But most people have no problem taking the older drugs. The Food & Drug Administration has cracked down on Pharmacia for painting too-rosy pictures of its drug's merits in consumer-focused ads.

Meanwhile, one study found that as many as two-thirds of people taking Schering-

Plough Corp.'s heavily advertised Claritin and other allergy medicines don't even have allergies. Schering responds that patients wouldn't take Claritin if it didn't work. But "there's no doubt that the direct-to-consumer advertising increases drug consumption," says Barrett A. Toan, chairman and CEO of Express Scripts Inc., a PBM. Claritin sales? About $2.2 billion per year.

WHY DRUGS COST SO MUCH. Investors won't fault companies for persuading consumers to buy more products than they actually need. And the more money drug companies make, the more they can spend developing tomorrow's lifesaving medicines. Indeed, industry execs argue that if prices were squeezed, the world can forget about new and better drugs.

Many economists agree—up to a point. Consider today's protease-inhibitor drugs for AIDS, which have dramatically cut deaths and hospital costs for those with HIV. If Congress had put price controls in place back in the early 1990s when lawmakers were screaming about high prices, "there would be no protease inhibitors now," says Eugene M. Kolassa, professor of pharmacy at the University of Mississippi. While drugmakers would have tried to develop AIDS drugs anyway, they would not have moved as quickly as they did without the promise of blockbuster revenues.

On the other hand, drugmakers wouldn't need to charge such high prices if they could boost R&D productivity. Overall, the average tab for developing a new drug is $500 million to $880 million, the industry says. But the amount actually spent on any one marketable product is roughly one-quarter of that.

To understand why, just look at the drug-development process. In the past, scientists made many variations of existing chemicals and tested them to see which ones had the ability to fight a particular disease. Now, with the explosion of information about genes and biology, the process has gotten more complicated—and oddly enough, more difficult. Researchers try to identify the best target in a particular disease—for instance, a

damaged gene that causes cancer—then they make a drug to hit the target and cure the disease.

That process can take 10 years or more. Such a long period means that about half of the calculated $500 million to $880 million total isn't actually spent at all. Instead, it's the opportunity cost—the measure of what the money tied up in the drug for so many years could have earned with alternative investments.

Moreover, there are pitfalls every step of the way. Making drugs from previously unexplored types of chemicals increases the chances of problematic side effects, explains John F. Niblack, R&D chief at Pfizer Inc. And new targets that look great in the test tube or in animals often don't pan out in humans. "If you develop a drug that hits one of those unvalidated targets, you are likely to spend a lot of money and find out that it doesn't work," says Niblack.

That's why, of the thousands of potential drugs that start development, only a tiny percentage make it into animal tests. Only a few of those will be given to people in so-called Phase I trials to test for safety. Then come Phase II trials for safety and the first hints that a drug works. And then Phase III: wide-scale tests to gather proof of safety and efficacy. Only about 1 in 10 of the drugs that enter human trials makes it through Phase III.

The high attrition rate means that about half of drugmakers' actual R&D spending represents the price of all the failed projects. The corollary, therefore, is that reducing the failure rate and the overall development time can dramatically cut total R&D costs. Pfizer's Niblack, for one, believes that new technologies for screening drugs, smarter clinical trials, and other measures will soon slash the attrition rate. But for now, industry productivity is going down and R&D costs are going up. With all the advances in biology, "we had expected a lot more [new drugs] by this time," admits Fred Hassan, chairman and CEO of Pharmacia. "The reason is that the new stuff is difficult to find."

That's why drugmakers are increasingly letting others take the big risks. More and

more, they're filling their pipelines by picking up drugs from biotech corporations and startups—after the medicines have already shown promise in clinical trials. Case in point: Bristol-Myers Squibb's $1 billion investment in ImClone Systems' promising cancer drug, C225.

Although drugmakers spend billions on R&D, they also rake in huge profits. Too big, some analysts believe. Since 1988, the return on equity of the five biggest U.S.-based drugmakers—Merck, Eli Lilly, Pfizer, Pharmacia, and Schering-Plough—has averaged 30% a year. Last year, it was 36%, compared with 27% for Microsoft Corp. and 21% for companies in the Standard & Poor's 500-stock index.

Industry execs say that the high returns are justified on the basis of the high risks they take to develop drugs. But economists point out that such risks ought to translate into variable returns—and drugmakers show a consistent high return on equity compared with companies in other sectors. Merck's return, for example, has not fallen below 28% since 1988. "If you went to Vegas with $1,000 and routinely came back with $1,400, could your family accuse you of gambling?" asks Alan Sager, co-director of the Health Reform Program at Boston University.

By this analysis, Big Pharma's prices are higher than needed to cover R&D costs and risks. But that's not surprising, because the price set for a drug typically has little to do with its development cost. Instead, pharmaceuticals are just like any other product: The producers charge what the market will bear. The usual price calculation includes an assessment of the medical benefits the drug brings and how much competition it faces.

If a new drug offers a lifesaving treatment where none existed before, or if it helps avoid costly hospital procedures, the price can be astronomical. An example is Genzyme's drug Cerezyme for the rare Gaucher disease, which has an average price tag of $170,000 a year. The alternative, after all, is severe disability or death. "In reality, if a drug is going to save a life, we will find a

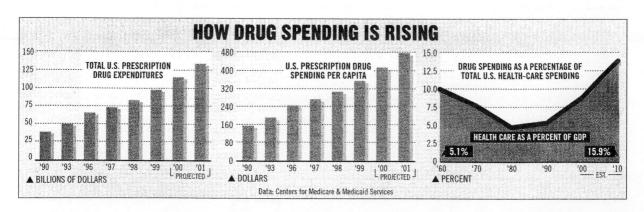

HOW DRUG SPENDING IS RISING

TOTAL U.S. PRESCRIPTION DRUG EXPENDITURES
▲ BILLIONS OF DOLLARS

U.S. PRESCRIPTION DRUG SPENDING PER CAPITA
▲ DOLLARS

DRUG SPENDING AS A PERCENTAGE OF TOTAL U.S. HEALTH-CARE SPENDING
HEALTH CARE AS A PERCENT OF GDP 5.1% 15.9%
▲ PERCENT

Data: Centers for Medicare & Medicaid Services

(Cont.)

way to afford it," says C. Daniel Mullins, associate director of the Center on Drugs & Public Policy at the University of Maryland School of Pharmacy.

And when it comes to new painkillers or other drugs, Big Pharma has been able to get away with charging high prices because most consumers, shielded by their insurance coverage, have little or no incentive to pick cheaper options, explains Kenneth L. Sperling, head of health-care analysis at Hewitt Associates LLC. That, however, is beginning to change, as the health-care system takes a harder look at the value of drugs.

SO WHAT IS THE VALUE OF DRUGS? AND CAN WE AFFORD THEM? Despite the concern over drug costs, pharmaceuticals represent only about 9.5% of the nation's $1.4 trillion health-care bill. In the U.S., drug spending is less, per person, than it is in many European countries, which have lower per capita medical bills. To economist H.E. Frech III of the University of California at Santa Barbara, the conclusion is clear: If the U.S. spent more on drugs, health-care costs would be lower. Argues the University of Mississippi's Kolassa: "We should be happy that pharmaceuticals are the fastest-growing component of the health-care budget, because it means that other components aren't growing as fast."

There's some merit to the argument. Health experts can point to case after case in which a new drug or a boost in drug use replaces hospital outlays. The advent of stomach-acid blockers, for instance, dramatically slashed the number of ulcer surgeries. Even at $28,000 per year, the leukemia drug Gleevec is cheaper than a bone marrow transplant. And a newly updated study by Columbia University economist Frank R. Lichtenberg finds that for every extra dollar spent replacing many older drugs with new, costlier ones, four dollars are saved in medical costs.

Even WellPoint Health Networks Inc. in California, which has been particularly ag-gressive at trying to curtail drug spending, has learned that additional drug use sometimes can save money. In 1998, WellPoint became concerned about rising emergency-room and hospitalization costs for its asthma patients. For help, the company turned to Kathleen A. Johnson, a pharmaceutical economist at the University of Southern California. She helped set up a program to identify patients at risk and train them to monitor their symptoms and use drug inhalers when needed. "We found that even though drug costs went up [about 20%], hospital admissions and emergency-room visits went down by 80%—and overall costs by 48%," says Johnson.

But as usual, the story is more complex than it seems. Many drugs don't replace costly procedures. Glaxo's new flu drug, Relenza, simply shortens flu symptoms by a day or so. Other drugs may cut some costs but raise others. Do AIDS drugs save money, for instance? "The jury is still out," answers Maryland's Mullins. Yes, AIDS-related hospitalizations and deaths are down. But the drugs also have serious side effects. HIV-infected patients are now getting cancer, heart disease, and other diseases that are costly to treat.

Even drugs that help prevent hospitalizations or surgeries may increase health-care costs—because so many people take them. Cholesterol-lowering "statin" drugs reduce the need for bypass and other heart operations. But they are now used by millions of Americans, and scientists estimate that only a minority would have needed operations without the drugs. The total statin bill: $15.5 billion this year, rising to $24.0 billion by 2005, predicts SG Cowen Securities Corp. Economists say it's not clear whether the health-care savings would be greater than that.

The problem of paying will grow even more complicated. Companies are experimenting with genes that help build new blood vessels to the heart, for instance, or cancer treatments where patients' own tumor cells are used to boost the immune system's ability to fight the disease. These approaches, some customized for each individual, will be hugely expensive. Yet if they work, Americans will demand them. "The limiting factor will be affordability," says Dr. August M. Watanabe, executive vice-president for science and technology at Eli Lilly & Co. "Can society afford them for its citizens?"

The nation can easily pay the tab, economists generally agree. "We're a long ways from reaching any limit," says Harvard University economist David Cutler. After all, he points out, GDP is rising faster than total health-care costs. That leaves a bigger and bigger piece of the pie to pay for drugs.

But while a rich nation like the U.S. can foot the bill, many Americans will be left out. In fact, de facto rationing is already common. Look at two of the latest drugs for rheumatoid arthritis, Immunex Corp.'s Enbrel and Johnson & Johnson's Remicade, both of which cost $10,000 to $12,000 a year. The companies do offer some assistance to poor patients. But, says Dr. John H. Klippel, medical director of the Arthritis Foundation, "just because of the expense, they are largely limited to people who have insurance plans that pay for them."

Overall, when it comes to health care, "we're moving to a three-tier system: the haves, the have-littles, and the have-nots," says Wharton's Hillman. "The more technology we have and the more that it costs, the more we have to ration it."

WHAT WE SHOULD DO. For Americans worried that they will be among the have-nots, the good news is that the market has begun to rein in drug costs. Insurers and payers will also get a break because blockbuster drug after blockbuster drug, from Claritin to stomach drug Prilosec, is coming off patent or other monopoly protection. Overall, drugs that are now worth $35 billion per year in U.S. sales could face competition from generics by 2005.

Large employers such as General Motors Corp. stand to reap windfalls. "If you take a look at three of the drugs that will lose exclusivity—Prilosec, Claritin, and Glucophage—we are talking about $75 million in potential savings for GM over a three-year period," says Cynthia Kirman, GM's director of pharmacy. That's why insurers and PBMs are already pushing generic drugs hard. When Prozac went off patent recently, Merck-Medco was able to convert 80% of mail-order customers within a week—an amazingly quick substitution. The savings from the coming flood of generics? Up to $3 billion per year.

Drugmakers are responding as many other companies would—by protecting their profits. For example, they're doing everything in their power to delay competition from generics, sometimes using tactics that even some drug company execs call "brazen" and "embarrassing". Generic competition is not the only threat, however. In

TOMORROW'S BLOCKBUSTERS

New medicines with mass appeal will keep drug costs soaring

PRODUCT AND APPLICATION	COMPANY	2005 PROJECTED SALES MILLIONS
CIALIS Erectile dysfunction	Eli Lilly/ICOS	$2,000
ARCOXIA Arthritis and pain	Merck	2,000
VANLEV Hypertension	Bristol-Myers Squibb	2,000
BEXTRA Arthritis and pain	Pharmacia/Pfizer	2,000
CLARINEX Allergy	Schering-Plough	2,000
CRESTOR Cholesterol reduction	AstraZeneca	3,500

Data: SG Cowen Securities Corp.

(Cont.)

the past couple of years, the market has also begun to generate another set of checks and balances on drug prices, called pharmaco-economics. In essence, experts scrutinize the value of individual drugs, aiming to get more bang for the buck.

Pharmaco-economics is already slowing the rise in drug costs for insurers and other payers. In Britain, for instance, a government panel made the controversial recommendation that Glaxo's Relenza not be made available to the public through the National Health Service. The benefits didn't justify the cost, the panel said. Similarly, U.S. military pharmacists have decided that all new patients with allergies will be put on only one allergy drug, Allegra. The government has negotiated a price of 60 cents per daily dose for Allegra, less than half the cost of competing Claritin. The savings: $7 million in fiscal 2001.

Kaiser Permanente is another believer in pharmaco-economics. Under its plans, only 6% of arthritis patients—those at higher risk for gastric bleeding—get expensive Cox-2 inhibitor painkillers like Vioxx. The rest take cheap ibuprofen. Nationwide, the ratio is 50-50. "If people can be switched from drugs of very little marginal benefit to drugs that are as good and a lot cheaper, there is an opportunity to save many millions of dollars," says Stanford emeritus professor Alain C. Enthoven. With seed money from BlueCross BlueShield, Enthoven is helping to set up an institute, RxIntelligence, to provide drug-effectiveness data that insurers can use to save money.

Meanwhile, insurers are giving patients incentives to choose cheaper drugs. According to a spring, 2001, survey by market researcher Scott-Levin, 50% of people enrolled in HMOs tracked by the firm were in three-tiered prescription drug plans, up from 5% just three years previously. In such plans, patients typically pay little or nothing for a generic drug. They have a bigger co-pay for the brand-name product, and a still higher co-pay for the most expensive drug.

Some cost-cutting tactics can be risky, leaving some patients with substandard treatments. Economists have shown that simpleminded measures, such as capping drug benefits, can actually raise overall costs since patients may not get the medicines that work best. But done correctly, with the emphasis on effective treatments instead of drug costs alone, this type of scrutiny can lead to better care.

One model, pharmacists say, is the approach used by Active Health Management for companies such as Merrill Lynch and Sears, Roebuck & Co. The idea: Give people more medical attention, not less. When doctors find and treat diabetes, heart disease, or other illnesses early, hospitalizations decline, yielding savings of more than $100 per person per year, calculates Dr. Lonny Reisman, CEO of Active Health Management.

Inevitably, the nation's drug bill will continue to rise, fueled by the introduction of new drugs and by aging baby boomers, now reaching their prime prescription years. "I think we will pay more for drugs and we will have less available for other things," says Express Scripts' Toan. But it is within America's power to use those drugs more effectively.

Health-care experts say there are some simple remedies. The nation's doctors and hospitals should be able to trim scores of billions per year by avoiding health-care costs that occur when drugs are used incorrectly. Steps include computer systems to spot dangerous drug interactions and better patient education about the need to take medicines as prescribed. Health care must also harness market forces more effectively. Back in the 1960s, when Americans paid out of their own pockets for drugs, consumers had a strong incentive to pick the medications that offered the best value. That incentive vanished when insurers began to pick up the tab. But it could be restored and boosted by expanding use of tiered co-pay plans, saving about $1 billion annually. Or for more savings, insurers could require patients to shoulder a specified percentage of each drug's cost; the percentage would increase for more expensive drugs. The nation could also educate consumers, doctors, and payers about which drugs deliver the most for the money, by setting up an independent pharmaco-economic institute. The information it provides could shave $10 billion or more off the annual drug bill, economists estimate. In addition, Congress could close loopholes that drugmakers use to delay introduction of generics. Tightening rules for advertising drugs directly to consumers could reduce overuse of expensive drugs. And Big Pharma must learn to cope with the flood of new knowledge about biology to boost its productivity.

The future could get ugly—not just for have-nots. Maryland's Mullins, for instance, fears that the health-care system may decide not to pay as much for treatment for those who helped bring on their own illnesses, such as smokers. Medical progress, though, will clearly continue on its current fast track. "America is in love with innovation—and it wants new drugs," says Jean Paul Gagnon, director of public policy at Aventis Pharmaceuticals. Now, we need to figure out how to pay for those drugs without breaking the bank.

By John Carey and Amy Barrett
With Arlene Weintraub in Los Angeles, Catherine Arnst in New York, Kerry Capell in London, and Michael Arndt in Chicago

Pfizer Offers Seniors a Flat-Fee Drug Plan

By Scott Hensley

Staff Reporter of The Wall Street Journal

Pfizer Inc., responding to pressure from consumers and politicians over drug prices, announced a plan to provide its prescription medication to financially strapped senior citizens at a flat fee of $15 a month.

Called the Share Card, Pfizer's deep-discount program will be available to single Medicare beneficiaries who don't have prescription-drug coverage and who earn less than $18,000 a year or couples with less than $24,000 in annual income. Patients can begin enrolling Feb 1. Participating retail pharmacies, including chain-store giant **CVS** Corp. and **Wal-Mart** Stores Inc., will start accepting the cards March 1.

By offering such deep discounts to lower-income seniors on some of the most widely prescribed medicines in the country, Pfizer could defuse mounting pressure on prices for all customers and spur rivals to make similar moves. But at least one analyst worries that Pfizer's plan could inspire the government to force similar costly discounts from other pharmaceutical companies.

With little prospect for a federal prescription-drug benefit in the near future, Pfizer said it decided to act on its own. "We're challenging others in the health and healthcare industries to join us with the appropriate reform of Medicare," said Henry McKinnell, chairman and chief executive of Pfizer.

Several other drug companies, including Britain's **GlaxoSmithKline** PLC and **Novartis** AG of Switzerland, introduced drug-discount cards for the elderly last year that could shave retail prices of their medication by as much as 40%. But critics say those discount programs, and others like them, still leave brand-name medicines beyond the means of many patients and also are difficult programs to administer.

But Pfizer, the world's biggest pharmaceutical company, is making its drugs available at a flat fee, on par with the co-payments charged by commercial insurers. An analysis by Sanford C. Bernstein & Co. estimates the flat fee represents a 69% discount off the average retail price for a month's supply of Pfizer medication of $48.22.

All Pfizer medicines, including cholesterol reducer Lipitor, blood pressure remedy Norvasc, and antidepressant Zoloft, would be covered by the plan. Celebrex, a popular arthritis drug that Pfizer co-markets with **Pharmacia** Corp., isn't included. Pharmacia says it already offers free Celebrex to indigent patients.

As many as seven million people might be eligible for Pfizer's discount plan. The company estimates that about 17 million of 40 million Medicare beneficiaries don't have any insurance coverage for prescription medication.

"This is a terrific boon for seniors," said Albert Wertheimer, a professor of pharmacy at Temple University, Philadelphia. Dr. Wertheimer said some other discount cards, by contrast, were "cruel hoaxes" that delivered minimal discounts on expensive medicines.

Wall Street was less enthusiastic. "From a humanitarian point of view, I think this is fantastic," says Richard Evans, drug analyst at Sanford C. Bernstein. "But they didn't have to go this far to defuse the political pressure on the affordability of medicine for the elderly. What Pfizer is putting in place here is more generous than the most onerous proposal I saw on Capitol Hill."

Mr. Evans fretted that Pfizer's action might lead to legislation requiring such deep discounts. A decade ago, Mr. Evans said, **Merck** & Co. offered unilateral discounts for the poor that emboldened Congress to pass a law requiring all drug makers to slash the prices they charged state Medicaid programs for medication. In the past year, these Medicaid drug programs have become a flashpoint for the debate on pharmaceutical pricing.

In the worst case, Mr. Evans estimates Pfizer could lose $450 million a year in retail sales because of the discount plan, though the actual loss is likely to be less because not all eligible patients may sign up. The New York company declined to estimate the cost.

Shares of Pfizer slipped 11 cents to $40.41 as of 4 p.m. in New York Stock Exchange composite trading.

German Shoppers May Get 'Sale Freedom'

Pressure Mounts to Soften a Strict Law of Competition

By Neal E. Boudette

Staff Reporter of The Wall Street Journal

BAD HOMBURG, Germany—Despite the best efforts of Hans-Frieder Schoenheit, Germans may soon get to test the theory that they can't tell when a bargain really is a bargain.

Mr. Schoenheit is deputy director at the Competition Center, an organization dedicated to protecting shoppers from the ordeal of discounts. Buy One, Get One Free? Today Only: 20% Off? Those, he says, are gimmicks that dupe consumers and destroy small shops. "If every store had a sale any time it wanted, there would be no price transparency," he says. "It would be totally confusing."

Many Germans used to agree with him, but not anymore—especially after the center pounced when clothing retailer **C&A Mode** announced it would give 20% off credit-card purchases in the first four shopping days after the Jan. 1 debut of the euro.

C&A figured it could ease currency confusion at cash registers that way, but hours after the appearance of advertisements plugging the offer, the center's lawyers took C&A to court and got a restraining order. A judge in Dusseldorf said the lure of a discount for only four days would put consumers under such pressure that they wouldn't be able to make sound buying decisions. Under the 93-year-old Law Against Unfair Competition, C&A was fined 250,000 euros ($221,100).

Many consumers find it silly. "They should just allow the stores to do what they want. It's idiotic," says Kirsten Koob, a mother of a two-year-old in Frankfurt. "If C&A wants to cut prices, let them."

Outraged by the C&A case, state secretaries in both the economics and consumer ministries are now calling for changes to the law, which, among other things, strictly limits when stores can mark down prices.

Big retailers condemn the law as obsolete, although mom-and-pop stores say they could be crushed by mammoth corporations without some amount of protection. Other European countries still have laws limiting sales, but Germany makes claims to maintaining the strictest on the books as well as the tightest

enforcement.

Mr. Schoenheit says the center hears "some voices that consumers don't necessarily want this protection," but vows to fight any changes to the competition law. For now, the law remains on his side. It allows price reductions on small lots of merchandise anytime but bans storewide sales unless they occur during one two-week period in the winter and another in the summer. Anniversaries are an exception, but only big ones divisible by 25, such as the 50th or 75th.

Founded in 1912, when Germany still had a kaiser, the center represented family-owned shops and small companies. Mr. Schoenheit acknowledges he is looking out for his members, although the center usually justifies its actions as taken in the interest of consumer protection. For decades, lawmakers and voters agreed with the center, buying the argument that people aren't smart enough to decide for themselves.

The center's objections have prevented bakeries from selling half-price bread at closing time and a pet store from putting goldfish on sale in slow afternoon hours. Suing under another German consumer law, the center fought to stop **Lufthansa** from linking frequent-flier miles to credit cards. The center also went after U.S. retailer **Wal-Mart** Stores Inc. when it advertised it would beat any competitor's price if a shopper showed up with the ad—tantamount to selling one product for two different prices, a court said. Under German law at the time, consumers had to pay the same price.

In a celebrated battle fought all the way to Germany's supreme court, the center and **Land's End** Inc. tussled over the Dodgeville, Wis., mail-order retailer's lifetime guarantee on its outdoorsy shirts and shoes. The center argued that the guarantee was bad for consumers, because it would benefit the company only if customers didn't take advantage of it, making it a ruse that hoodwinked unwitting buyers. The high court ruled that Land's End couldn't advertise the guarantee in Germany because the promise to replace any product any time for any reason amounted to selling two products for one price, a violation of a Nazi-era law against giving shoppers free gifts.

The political winds began to shift when the Competition Center's victories started fueling resentment among Germans who couldn't help but notice that the discounts and deals denied them are widely available outside of Germany.

Last summer, the law against free gifts and another against rebates were repealed. Land's End's guarantee and Lufthansa's frequent-flier-mile credit card are now legal. (Mr. Schoenheit says he is disappointed.)

In its eagerness to protect consumers, the center's actions have ended up ticking them off, instead. In 2000, it sent a letter to Kurt Krummenacher, the head of **Boa Lingua,** a

Swiss company that arranges language-instruction vacations across Europe. Boa Lingua's Web site—www.sprachen.ch—uses the German word for languages. The letter said using a general term like that gave Boa Lingua an unfair advantage over other language companies that could have used the word Sprachen.

Threatening a 5,000-mark ($2,261)) fine under German competition law because the Web site can be seen in Germany, the letter said the site had to be changed. Also enclosed was a bank transfer slip—so Boa Lingua could cough up 315 marks to cover the center's legal cost to that point.

"It was ridiculous. I threw it away," Mr. Krummenacher recalls. Weeks later another letter arrived, and soon Swiss lawyers and the media were defending the use of general terms, and ridiculing the notion that Swiss firms should comply with an odd German law. Mr. Krummenacher hasn't heard from the center again.

"Their whole idea about using general terms doesn't make sense," he says. "It's first come, first served. If we don't use Sprachen, then who should? No one?"

Last year, the center picked another target, sending a letter this time to Herbert Huber, a computer administrator in southern Germany whose personal Web site includes a page displaying articles criticizing the center. The letter demanded he stop using its name and threatened to sue if he didn't. The letter contended Web surfers might mistake it for the center's own official site, although Mr. Huber's site was mainly about his family and the town where they live. In the letter, the center demanded 350 marks for legal fees, which Mr. Huber paid.

Now his site refers to "the center who's name I cannot use" and adds, "For details, call me up!"

The clearest sign of how the tide has turned against the center is the aftermath of its fight against C&A, the clothing retailer. The court ruling sparked a torrent of media coverage: TV cameras showed up in C&A stores, and morning and evening news programs covered the sale—the kind of positive publicity even the most lavish ad budget couldn't have achieved.

C&A, which went ahead with the sale while filing an appeal, was mobbed by shoppers. Asked how the fourth and final sale day went, a C&A sales clerk in downtown Frankfurt smacks her palm on her forehead. "Women were buying 10, 15 pairs of pants each," she says. "Sometimes 20."

Revealing Price Disparities, the Euro Aids Bargain-Hunters

BY SARAH ELLISON

Staff Reporter of THE WALL STREET JOURNAL

RONCQ, France—For Marie-Claude Lang, a 72-year-old retired Belgian postal worker, the euro is the best thing since bottled water—or French country sausage.

Always on the prowl for bargains, Ms. Lang is now stalking the wide aisles of an Auchan hypermarket in Roncq, France, a 15-minute drive from her Wervick home. She isn't buying anything just yet. Instead, she's scribbling down the prices of products she passes on the shelves, pushing a large shopping cart that holds only her mammoth handbag.

Ms. Lang has been coming to France every other week for years to stock up on bottled water, milk and yogurt. But the launch of the euro on Jan. 1 has opened her eyes to many more products that she now sees cost less across the border. Today she sees that "saucisse de campagne," is cheaper "by about five euro cents," a savings she didn't notice when she had to calculate the difference between Belgian and French francs.

At Europe's borders, the euro is turning into the coupon clipper's delight. Sure, price-conscious Europeans have long crossed into foreign territory to find everything from cheaper television sets to bargain bottles of Coca-Cola. But the new transparency is making comparisons a whole lot easier.

For the moment, the euro may have brought something else: an uptick in inflation. Based on January figures from Italy, it looks like many stores rounded up their prices to switch to euros. Over the long run, a measure of the new currency's success will be whether it levels prices around Europe or sparks inflation.

David Ceri, store manager of a Carrefour SA supermarket in Mouscron, Belgium, a five-minute drive from the French border, bets price transparency will win out. He says a quarter of his customers are French. They come for cheaper tobacco and fuel, which are taxed less heavily in Belgium than in France, as well as generally lower prices on electronics and televisions. Mr. Ceri plans to send a new euro-priced catalog to nearby northern France. "It'll be the first time we've actively sought out customers abroad," he says.

Alain Picquet and his wife, Carole, used to come to Spain from their home in France looking for bargain-basement prices on fuel, beer and cigarettes, products that are cheaper in Spain because they carry lower taxes. Now, the Picquets travel to Irun, just across the Spanish border, every week to stock up on other stuff. "Much of what we buy here is cheaper than back in France," Mr. Picquet says. "And we're starting to notice that a bit more now that the prices are easier to compare."

Alcampo SA, the Spanish division of **Auchan** SA, says Spanish hams and spirits are the most sought-after purchases of French shoppers crossing the border. Cathy Collart, head cashier at an Auchan store in northern France, says lower taxes on bottled water draw a lot of Belgians to the store. "You can see who is Belgian based on who has the most water in their baskets," she says.

To figure out how much to charge, most big retailers use "zone pricing," which evaluates different factors in a region, like the average wealth of a customer and how much competition there is. Zones don't usually straddle borders, but they are sensitive to prices in surrounding zones, so that French prices near the border are closer to those in Belgium than to those in Paris.

"Prices are converging anyway because the retail business is more international," says Cees van der Hoeven, chief executive of Dutch retailing giant **Ahold** NV. But "regardless of the euro, prices in Paris will never be the same as in Appingedam," a small town in the Netherlands.

To be sure, the euro hasn't made everyone a bargain-hunter. Says Daniella Galan, a Spanish computer technician shopping in a Carrefour store just outside Biarritz in France: "I just like the feeling of shopping in France."

But the new currency is giving new leverage to budget-watchers like Ms. Lang, who lives on a fixed income with her divorced daughter and granddaughter. At the electronics section of the Auchan store in Roncq, she also priced TV sets. "I want to replace my black-and-white," she says, "but I hear they're cheaper in Germany."

Bargain Hunters' Paradise

The same goods, but different prices in euros

Country	Supermarket (City)	6 bottles of Evian 1.5 liter	4 pack vanilla Dannon yogurt	1.5 liter of Martini Rossi	1 baguette
France	Auchan (Roncq)	2.95	1.67	11.24	0.38
Belgium	Carrefour (Mouscron)	4.26	1.64	6.99	0.59
France	Carrefour (Anglet)	3.18	1.28	13.62	0.40
Spain	Alcampo (Irun)	3.78	N.A.	4.56 (1 liter)	0.56

Survival Tactics

The Dollar's Strength Tests the Ingenuity Of U.S. Manufacturers

Some Firms Pay More Heed To Sales; Others Diversify Or Cultivate Allies Abroad

How Many Parts in a Leg?

BY TIMOTHY AEPPEL

Staff Reporter of THE WALL STREET JOURNAL

For years, American manufacturers have watched with dismay as the dollar surges to new heights, making it harder for them to wring profits out of exports. Now the dollar is setting off a small revolution in factories across the country, one that could leave them stronger than ever when the economy bounces back.

Take Automatic Feed Co., a Napoleon, Ohio, company that makes machinery used in auto plants. Today, the company is in the midst of the most extensive product redesign in its 52-year history. The effort is aimed squarely at neutralizing the cost advantages its foreign competitors enjoy because of their weaker home currencies.

Then, there's Dormont Manufacturing Co., which is honing a skill that once took a back seat to production: salesmanship. The Export, Pa., company, which makes flexible metal hoses, is aggressively courting customers. It keeps track, for example, of how each client prefers to have its orders shipped and invoiced.

German Joint Venture

Angell Manufacturing Co., a Dayton, Ohio, car-parts maker, has adopted yet another strategy. Last year, it opened a joint-venture factory in Germany—its first production plant outside the U.S.—to supply German clients with aluminum wheel covers and other parts. That's less expensive than shipping the parts to Germany from an Angell plant in Lebanon, Ky. "We felt that the exchange rates were going to stay relatively high, so this was something we had to do," says Richard Anglin, the company's chief executive.

While manufacturers always are under pressure to increase their efficiency, the dollar's relentless ascent since the mid-1990s has sorely tested their ingenuity. The strong dollar, now at a 16-year high against a basket of foreign currencies, is forcing some manufacturers to find more creative ways to tap overseas markets and defend their home turf. They also are recognizing, some for the first time, that sales and marketing are almost as important as knowing how to make things.

Some manufacturers probably won't survive the double whammy of the dollar's strength and the global downturn. But those that do are likely to be more efficient and poised to thrive when the economy recovers. "There is a good side to a strong dollar in that it inspires greater productivity," says Neal Soss, chief economist at Credit Suisse First Boston.

Although a strong dollar hits all manufacturers hard, it hits small and midsize manufacturers harder. While many big companies can shift production to foreign factories, small and midsize companies seldom have that option. Those small and midsize companies account for a huge chunk of the nation's manufacturing sector. The only way most of them can gain a foothold in foreign markets is to export their products. But the strong dollar has all but dried up that option.

Indeed, an annual survey by the National Association of Manufacturers of its small and midsize members found that the proportion that export at least 25% of their output peaked at 8.8% in 1998 and has since plunged to 3.8%—less than in 1993. The trade group finds the export decline especially worrisome because exports helped drive the record-long U.S. expansion that followed the recession of 1990-1991.

Sipco Molding Technologies, a Meadville, Pa., tool-and-die maker, hopes for a respite from the dollar's rise, but the company has made sweeping changes to survive it. For years, Sipco has had a partnership with an Austrian company, which designs a special line of extrusion tools that Sipco once built in the U.S. Now, because of the strong dollar, the Austrian company both designs and builds the tools and Sipco simply resells them. Meanwhile, Sipco is exploring production opportunities in China and Mexico.

Over the past year, Sipco has laid off 30% of its work force of more than 100 people. But over the same period, the company added three salespeople, bringing its sales staff to four. The company, which says it didn't have any salespeople at all until four years ago, is relying on its new staff to search out domestic customers that need jobs done quickly. The idea is that the need for speed will give Sipco an edge over foreign rivals.

"We're trying to find markets more sensitive to time, so [the customers] don't have time to go around the world shopping," says Sipco President Larry Sippy. "We're either going to change the way we do business or we're not going to survive."

On the Rise

Inflation-adjusted index of the value of the dollar against a basket of other major currencies

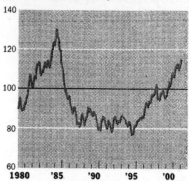

Source: Federal Reserve

It is an issue confronting companies across the country. At American Machine & Gear Inc. in Portland, Ore., the strong dollar has meant fewer orders from the steel mills and paper plants that buy replacement parts for industrial machinery from the 36-employee operation. The company bought a competing machine shop last March to help make up for the slackening business. And the strong dollar is a major reason the Paper Converting Machine Co., Green Bay, Wis., has had to cut jobs at its main U.S. plant. The company makes a variety of machines used for processes such as making tissues and color printing on plastic bags. But the company's Italian factory, acquired in 1998, has more than doubled its work force from 45 to 90 people in recent years. "That's where we're securing business and where our cost of manufacturing is more competitive," says Frederick Baer, president and CEO of the company.

Supervised Economists

In the past, Automatic Feed might have waited for the dollar to weaken. But now it's tough to predict when that might happen. Many economists are suprised that the dollar's value hasn't declined as U.S. interest rates have fallen and the economy has entered a recession.

Typically, falling interest rates would have prompted foreigners to pull money out of the U.S. and seek better returns elsewhere. But other economies don't look much better at the moment. So, the U.S. remains a haven.

Kim Beck, Automatic Feed's president and chief executive, says he has gone through plenty of downturns since he took the company's helm in 1983. He says the business, which was founded by his grandfather, Alvin Groll, is prone to booms and busts. He runs it according to a philosophy that has served it well through wars and recessions: Stash away money in good times to help pay for what it takes to get through the bad.

But this downturn seems different, Mr. Beck says. The strong dollar has exacerbated what was already a lousy global business climate. Never before, he says, have his foreign competitors attacked him so directly, not just in Europe, but in the U.S. as well. Automatic Feed's annual sales have fallen to less than $30 million, from $55 million in 1998, and the company has laid off half of its 180 workers.

"Normally, we're the kind of company that would pull in and wait for the market to come back, but you can't afford to do that anymore," Mr. Beck says.

So last year, Automatic Feed reached a deal with a similar manufacturing company in Reus, Spain, 4,000 miles away. Both companies make machines that car factories use to unroll giant coils of steel and feed them through presses to make parts. When projects come in, the two companies huddle to figure out which plant should make which parts, in essence divvying up the work to keep both factories operating. Mr. Beck can share in the benefits of having a European production base without having to take on the risks of building his own factory there.

Meanwhile, the company is overhauling its system for making its bus-size machines. It is also redesigning the machines themselves to make them easier and less expensive to build.

Leading the way out onto the factory floor—past a "hall of history" that includes a painting of stern-looking company founder Mr. Groll—Mr. Beck stops in a cavernous construction bay. It holds a machine destined for a Japanese-owned car factory located in the American South. The machine is a "stacker," a device used to take the stamped metal parts out of a press and stack them for traveling to an auto assembly line. It typically sells for more than $1.5 million.

Mr. Beck points to one of the six metal legs that prop up the vast mechanism. Until a year ago, each of those legs consisted of 32 pieces that took more than 30 hours to cut and machine into shape. Now, the company has redesigned the legs so that they require just 12 pieces that take two hours to cut.

Mr. Beck says he doesn't know why the original design of the legs was so complicated. The old design was simply used for so long that nobody thought to question it. That is, until the current crunch.

So far, the production overhaul and redesign efforts together have chopped 20% off the machines' production costs. Mr. Beck figures he can shave off another 10% once he reviews other parts of the machines and makes similar step-saving modifications.

Software Foray

At the same time, Mr. Beck is developing new software that allows customers to track such things as the productivity of a particular machine on a manufacturing line and pinpoint exactly where a problem is when a line breaks down. In the past, a maintenance technician would have had to dig out smudged drawings and could have spent an hour just figuring out where the problem lay. But the new software quickly flags the source of the problem and displays a digital rendering of it on a computer screen.

Automatic Feed just got its first order, valued at between $750,000 and $1 million, to supply the software to an entire automotive stamping plant, the section of a car factory where metal parts are pressed into shape. The company also is talking to auto makers about a similar software system for painting, assembly and machining departments. It figures the software could be modified for use in any sort of highly automated factory, such as a bottling plant.

Mr. Beck, who hopes to turn the software into a $5 million business in the next two years, says it has a "very, very good margin," because the company need only adapt it for different applications, rather than start from scratch.

Such innovations are especially critical now. While there are signs the worst may be over for U.S. manufacturing—with inventories going down and orders going up—the strong dollar is expected to remain a handicap. Some manufacturers worry it will make it tough for them to pull out of the recession. And if, as seems likely, the U.S. emerges from recession before the world's other major economies, the dollar could go even higher.

Benefits of Strength

Some economists argue the benefits of a strong dollar far outweigh the negatives. A strong dollar helps bolster stock and bond prices, for instance, and helps keep inflation at bay by holding down import prices. It isn't so much that manufacturers are being hurt by the strong dollar, says Edwin Truman, a senior fellow at the Institute for International Economics in Washington. "They're just not getting any of the benefits of the economy's natural recuperative processes," he says.

For Dormont Manufacturing, it's clear that the way it sells its flexible metal hoses will never be the same. The company, whose hoses are often used by fast-food restaurants to connect gas lines to deep fryers, has cut prices in Europe by between 10% and 15% simply to hold on to that market share. Though it has resisted laying off employees, it has cut costs at its factory in Export by introducing more efficient production methods.

Its most fundamental shift has been embracing salemanship. In the past, the company had employees whose sole job was to receive incoming calls from customers and jotting down orders. Now their job is to call customers, especially the smaller, often ignored ones, and ask what they need and how Dormont can do a better job serving them.

The company's 10 roving salespeople have gone through extensive training to create a uniform system for developing leads and figuring out ways to sell more to longtime customers. "You've got to really start to understand customer needs and do a better job," says Evan Segal, Dormont's president.

Because it encourages manufacturers to shift jobs abroad, economists say that the fallout from the strong dollar may still be evident once the U.S. economy recovers. In the case of Angell Manufacturing, the company that opened the German joint venture, jobs that might have otherwise boosted the local Lebanon, Ky., economy are being added in the lakeside German resort town of Lindau. The new German operation employs about 70. However, the company's pact with its German partner gives Angell some flexibility. If the dollar plunges in the future, for instance, it envisions the possibility of shifting work back to the U.S.

The goal, says Mr. Anglin, Angell's CEO, is to be prepared no matter which way the dollar goes. His company and others can't necessarily count on help from Washington.

Though it has met recently with manufacturing and labor groups to discuss complaints about the strong dollar, the Bush administration has insisted that market forces should determine the dollar's value. During a television interview in June, for example, Treasury Secretary Paul O'Neill put the issue this way: "The great ones [companies] don't worry about a weaker dollar or a stronger dollar."

Online Currency Failed To Make Sense

By Julie Mitchell
Investor's Business Daily

Online currency seemed like a good idea. It could be used to shop at Web sites without having to fill out credit card information and worry about security.

All you had to do was find a site that accepted the currency, shop for an item and enter an account number. The retailer would then deduct the purchase from your online currency account.

But in recent months, three major providers of online currency—Flooz.com, Beenz.com and CyberCash—have shut down or were acquired. The concept of online currency is essentially dead.

What went wrong? Well, the souring economy didn't help. Flooz.com was said to have been in merger talks with several companies, but was unable to find a suitable partner. It shut down in August without any warning to its customers.

Spill The 'Beenz'

Beenz.com gave customers exactly 10 days to use up their online money, or beenz, and then closed its offices in August as well. CyberCash filed for bankruptcy in April.

Many speculate that fraud had something to do with online currency's demise. Stolen credit card numbers were reportedly used online to buy Flooz currency. A ring of credit card thieves in Russia and the Philippines were said to be using Flooz as a way to launder money.

Others point to the fact that credit cards are simply easier to use than online currency. Credit cards have the advantage of being universally accepted by retailers.

And since some online currencies were not convertible back into real money, consumers had to spend the dollars online at specific sites to get the value for their money.

Michael Ahern, chief executive of GiftCertificates.com Inc., says there was no need for online currency.

'New Form Of Money'

"In this country, everyone has a credit card, and we're all comfortable using them," he said. "Online currency was like teaching people to use a whole new form of money."

GiftCertificates.com and others take a different approach. They offer gift certificates—in physical form or via e-mail—for employee incentives, customer loyalty programs, marketing efforts and gifts.

Online currency may have disappeared, but online gift certificates are going strong. They can be bought from sites like giftcertificates.com and webcertificate.com. Or you can go directly to sites from retailers such as Amazon.com and Eddie Bauer.

GiftCertificates.com

Founded in 1997, GiftCertificates.com represents more than 600 merchants, including Chanel, Neiman Marcus, Crate & Barrel and travel-related businesses such as hotels, airlines and restaurant chains.

Visitors to giftcertificates.com select a dollar quantity for a gift certificate and chose a retailer. Then they decide whether to mail or e-mail the certificate to the recipient.

Businesses that want to use gift certificates as part of an incentive program can provide recipients with a flexible SuperCertificate. It can be incorporated into their company-branded program.

Recipients can redeem their SuperCertificate for a merchant gift certificate of their choice by going to GiftCertificates.com's Web site or calling a toll-free number.

Despite the recent downturn, corporate incentives are on the rise, says Ahern. Companies are spending more than $22 billion annually on loyalty and incentive rewards.

"The weak economy has actually helped our business," he said. "With budget cuts, managers are looking for a way to reward employees."

"A $100 SuperCertificate lets recipients choose what they want and is better than a cash incentive," Ahern said.

Webcertificate.com offers gift certificates that can be used to buy anything at any U.S. retailer that accepts MasterCard. The certificates are available on the Web and are sent via e-mail to the recipient.

The e-mail contains a "Giftlink," which takes the recipient to a personal Webcertificate page. There's a gift ID number to use to redeem the gift.

Webcertificate shoppers can view a "shopbar" at the bottom of their screen that displays their account information. They can cut and paste the information from the bar onto a retailer's checkout form.

Travel And Toys

Microsoft Corp.'s Passport e-commerce service allows consumers to use a single sign-in name and electronic wallet at participating sites—including merchants in the travel, office supplies, furniture and toys categories.

That reduces the amount of information consumers need to remember or retype. The Passport service ensures security.

Online coupons also are on the rise. A 2001 survey by the New York marketing firm CyberDialogue found that 14.9 million U.S. adults downloaded online coupons in a three-month period.

"Online Currency Failed to Make Sense," *Investor's Business Daily*, October 18, 2001, p. A10. Reprinted by permission.

Afghan Connection

Taliban Banned TV But Collected Profits On Smuggled Sonys

Big Manufacturers Decry Illicit Traffic to Pakistan But Do Little to Stop It

Mr. Khan's Trips to Karkhano

By Daniel Pearl and Steve Stecklow
Staff Reporters of The Wall Street Journal

PESHAWAR, Pakistan—During their five years in power in Afghanistan, the Taliban raged against modern culture and values. But the regime profited from traffic in Sony televisions, Gillette shaving cream and Marlboro cigarettes, among other products.

None of these consumer goods from the West and Asia are made in Afghanistan, and under the Taliban government, they didn't have much of a market there. Watching television, for instance, was banned.

But for decades, whoever has run Afghanistan has exacted tolls on smugglers who ship foreign-made goods through the country and then illegally move the merchandise over the border to Pakistan. The products end up in places such as Peshawar's sprawling Karkhano market, where vendors' shelves are packed with cartons of smuggled Marlboro and Dunhill cigarettes and sidewalk carts offer bright Korean fabrics. Stacks of mud-stained cartons of Sony Trinitron televisions line courtyard after courtyard.

By smuggling these items through Afghanistan, traders evade Pakistan's stiff taxes and duties on foreign goods. This allows consumers at Karkhano and other markets to enjoy large discounts compared to legally imported products.

Boosting Sales

Smuggling also effectively boosts Western and Asian manufacturers' sales volume by allowing goods to be retailed at lower prices in Pakistan, a poor nation overall, but one with 140 million inhabitants and a substantial consumer class. The manufacturers all condemn smuggling but say they can't stop it once products leave their direct control. But a close look at the behavior of one

major manufacturer, Sony Corp., reveals that some company representatives appear to have tolerated smuggling as part of Sony's marketing strategy in the region.

The fees the Taliban collected on shipments of goods manufactured by Sony and other foreign companies provided one of that harsh regime's biggest sources of earnings. A United Nations study released last year estimated that "unofficial" exports from Afghanistan to Pakistan in 2000 totaled $941 million, with merchandise worth another $139 million moving illegally from Afghanistan to Iran. The U.N. estimated the Taliban's annual take at $36 million. The World Bank, in a 1999 report, said it was $75 million.

The prospect of exacting similar tolls on the smuggling business helps explain why the Taliban's successors are now wrestling for control over Kandahar, Jalalabad and other cities that are important transit points on smuggling routes. U.S. bombing and poor security have discouraged smuggling for the last three months, but it is expected to resume as relative calm returns.

Employment Opportunity

Beyond providing potential revenue to those in charge, smuggling offers employment to poor inhabitants of tribal areas along the Afghan border. That is one reason Pakistan—eager for stability in that area—has made only feeble attempts to compel vendors at Karkhano to pay taxes.

Smuggling economics are simple: A smuggled 21-inch Sony Wega TV typically costs the equivalent of about $400 in Pakistan. The same legally imported television costs the equivalent of $440, after duties and taxes. Sony receives the same payment—about $220—from the distributor either way. Manufacturers thus have little financial incentive to crack down on smuggling.

During most of the 1990s, Sony imported few TVs through legal channels into Pakistan and assembled no sets locally, according to Sony Gulf FZE, Sony Corp.'s wholly owned subsidiary and sales office in Dubai, United Arab Emirates. But that doesn't mean Sonys were unavailable. The Pakistan Electronics Manufacturers Association, a trade group that includes local TV assemblers hurt by sales of smuggled goods, found in a 1996 survey that 500,000 televisions were smuggled into the country that year. At least 70%, or 350,000, of them were Sonys, the survey found.

Today, Sony TVs remain one of the most prominent consumer-electronics products in Pakistani smuggled-goods markets. Sony Gulf's authorized distributor in Dubai sells sets to traders who often ship them to the Iranian port of Bandar Abbas. From there, some of the goods head northeast to the Afghan border near Herat, then southeast on the highway to Kandahar, on to Jalalabad, and then typically enter Pakistan illegally along the Khyber Pass near Peshawar.

Twice a month, Khalid M. Khan, a manager with Sony Gulf, visits the Karkhano market in Peshawar, which is widely known as a major retail center for smuggled goods. He says he makes the trips merely to see which models are popular and should be supplied legally by the local assembly plant in Pakistan that Sony opened in 1999. Mr. Khan acknowledges, though, that none of the locally made Sonys are sold in Karkhano. All of the TVs he sees changing hands here have been smuggled from Afghanistan, he says.

Dealers in the Karkhano market who acknowledge they sell smuggled TVs say that for years they have routinely ordered Sony products from the traders in Dubai who obtain the goods from the authorized Sony distributor there, Jumbo Electronics Co. One of the Karkhano dealers, Abdul Basir Khan, manager of Muslim Electronics, says Sony Gulf's Khalid Khan (no relation) "doesn't come here to book orders, but he gives ideas." For instance, the Sony Gulf man points out that "'such-and-such model is available,'" Abdul Basir Khan says. The Muslim Electronics shop is filled with Sony Trinitron TVs and has a large Sony sign above the door. "Khalid usually presses us hard to dispose [of inventory] as quickly as possible," Abdul Basir Khan says.

No Apology

For his part, Khalid Khan makes no apology for telling black-market dealers here that certain Sony models are available in Dubai or Singapore. "There is no harm" in this encouragement, he says. "They are making our brand popular in the country."

But he denies promoting smuggling in any way. He says that when Sony Gulf discovers traders selling through unauthorized channels, it threatens to punish them. The company has fined one trader and briefly cut off another one, he says. Smuggling hurts sales of the Sony televisions assembled in Pakistan, he says. But, he adds, smuggling is "beyond our control."

Ram Modak, a spokesman for Sony Gulf, also denies his company has knowingly shipped any goods intended for Pakistan through Afghanistan. He says, "Sony Gulf is not aware of the routes the [Dubai-based traders] use for their shipments to Pakistan." Kei Sakaguchi, a spokesman at Sony's headquarters in Tokyo, says the parent corporation has nothing to add to Mr. Modak's comments.

Vishesh L. Bhatia, director of Jumbo Electronics, says his company isn't allowed by Sony Gulf to sell goods directly in Pakistan, and it often can't control what traders do. "Duty barriers always encourage smuggling," he notes.

Minoru Kubota, Japan's ambassador to Pakistan from 1997 through early 2000, says he heard complaints from Pakistani businessmen during that period about the smuggling of Japanese goods. But he says the smuggling issue "is a business matter," not a

(Cont.)

concern of governments. "If trade shrinks, it will not benefit anyone," he adds.

Smugglers have operated across the Afghan-Pakistani border since Pakistan became independent in 1947. In the 1980s, huge amounts of U.S. money flooded the region, as the Central Intelligence Agency used Pakistani proxies to fund the mujahedeen resistance to Afghanistan's Soviet-backed government. Smuggling of electronics, tires, crockery and textiles gave some mujahedeen commanders a way to enrich themselves and keep supporters employed. For its part, "the government of Pakistan encouraged people to invest in this business," even supplying telephone and electricity connections for the Karkhano market, recalls Rafique Shinwari, a longtime distributor of smuggled goods in Peshawar who says he now imports only legally.

Shipping TVs

In 1994, after the Soviets had left Afghanistan and the country was divided among rival commanders, Abdul Haq, an ex-mujahedeen Afghan leader living in Peshawar, approached Sony Gulf about distributing TVs in Afghanistan. Sony Gulf's Khalid Khan says he negotiated a deal under which Mr. Haq's company, Khyber-Afghan International, began sending televisions by his family's airline from Dubai to Jalalabad, in eastern Afghanistan. "Whatever he did [with the TVs] inside Afghanistan, we don't know," Mr. Khan says.

Black-market dealers in Pakistan say Mr. Haq's family was prominent in the cross-border television trade in the mid-1990s. Mr. Haq was killed in October trying to organize anti-Taliban forces. His nephew, Abdul-rahim Zalmai, says, "The family itself was not involved by any means," in smuggling. But he says that traders in Jalalabad who bought TVs from his uncle may have smuggled them into Pakistan.

Pakistani officials say they haven't cracked down aggressively on smuggling markets such as Karkhano. "We have been working over the last two or three years to start curtailing smuggling," says Abdul Razak Dawood, Pakistan's commerce minister, but "through economic means rather than coercion."

Pakistan has been reducing import duties to diminish the price advantage of smuggled products. It has also ended duty-free access through the Pakistani port of Karachi for Afghanistan-bound goods, such as TVs, that often end up being smuggled back into Pakistan. Smugglers responded to the new obstacle in Karachi, however, simply by shipping through Iran and then across Afghanistan.

Traversing Afghanistan is by no means a simple trip. During the country's civil war in the early 1990s, various mujahedeen set up more than a dozen checkpoints along the country's major roads. Truckers had to pay small fees at each stop, and sometimes had their whole cargo expropriated by fighters or roving bandits.

The Taliban first gained prominence in Afghanistan in 1994 by eliminating most of the highway checkpoints and robberies. Afghan traders based in Dubai and Singapore poured money into the Taliban's coffers, as the regime extended its control from Herat to Jalalabad and enforced more orderly transportation, according to Pakistani officials who were also assisting the Taliban at the time.

Simplified Fees

After conquering Kabul in 1996, the Taliban simplified the fees for passage through Afghanistan, exacting a single payment determined by weight and other factors. For example, the Taliban sometimes imposed fees equivalent to roughly five-to-10 cents a kilogram, regardless of the merchandise, says one Dubai-based freight forwarder. "These guys didn't want to use calculators," he says.

The 1999 World Bank study estimated that televisions valued at $367 million were smuggled into Pakistan from Afghanistan in 1997.

Traders say they quickly adjusted to the Taliban's spiritually motivated rules. To get around the ban on packages with depictions of humans or living animals, traders put boxes in larger, blank cartons or simply reminded Taliban authorities that the packages were moving on to Pakistan.

The smuggling of American-made goods was hindered in July 1999, when former President Clinton signed an antiterrorism executive order prohibiting U.S. companies from exporting any goods, except for humanitarian aid, to Afghanistan. But Pakistani traders say they still could obtain products smuggled from Afghanistan—such as Gillette shaving cream, Head & Shoulders shampoo and Marlboro cigarettes—if the goods came from distributors outside of the U.S.

Manufacturers of these goods say they discourage any smuggling but can't always control it in distant lands. "It is obviously something we don't sponsor or endorse," says Eric Kraus, a spokesman for Gillette Co. Linda Ulrey, a spokeswoman for Procter & Gamble Co., maker of Head & Shoulders,

The Afghan Connection

Collecting payments from smugglers has provided critical revenue to the Taliban and earlier Afghan rulers. Smugglers move televisions, cigarettes and other consumer goods manufactured by Western and Asian companies through Afghanistan and over the border for sale in Pakistan, avoiding Pakistani taxes and duties.

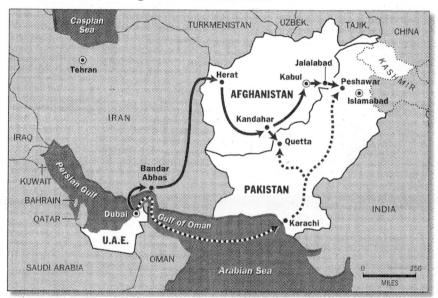

Traders in Dubai ship goods to Karachi, which then move by truck to Peshawar or Quetta and then over the border into Afghanistan. Then, the goods are taken by pack animal back into Pakistan, where they are sold tax- and duty-free at retail.

A second route goes through Bandar Abbas, Iran, into Afghanistan and then over the border to markets in Quetta or Peshawar.

174

(Cont.)

says the company lacks specific information about smuggling through Afghanistan.

A spokesman for Philip Morris Cos., which makes Marlboros, says the company can't comment because it doesn't do any business in Afghanistan. British American Tobacco PLC, maker of Dunhill cigarettes, says in a written statement that it doesn't condone or encourage smuggling.

Dubai's emergence as a major trading hub has helped fuel the expansion of smuggling through Afghanistan. In the mid-1990s, many large U.S., Japanese and European consumer-goods manufacturers opened operations that brought products through the duty-free zone of Jebel Ali, along the Dubai coast. Official Dubai customs records show that such "re-exports" from Dubai to Afghanistan jumped 79%, to $819 million, in 1996, the year the Taliban took over, compared with 1995.

Much of this trading relies on the illegal hawala currency-exchange system. (Hawala means "change" in Arabic.) Black-market consumer-electronics dealers in Pakistan say that after they place orders with traders in Dubai, they pay for the goods by giving Pakistani rupees to a hawala dealer in Peshawar. The hawala dealer telephones a counterpart in Dubai, who hands over United Arab Emirates dirhams to a consumer-electronics trader in Dubai. The hawala dealers settle their accounts later, splitting the commission.

Most of the victims of Afghan smuggling receive benefits as well. The Pakistani government has lost tax revenues, but border tribes engaged in smuggling are less likely to resort to kidnapping or drug-running. Authorized Pakistani dealers of foreign goods lose sales to black-market competition, but in the capital of Islamabad, many such dealers stock smuggled and legally imported goods on the same shelves.

The biggest losers have been local manufacturers that have assembled TVs but found their products consistently undercut by smuggled goods. Several local-assembly factories stopped production in the mid-1990s.

These difficulties prompted the Pakistan Electronics Manufacturers Association to conduct its 1996 survey. The trade group found that for every TV legally imported or assembled locally, more than two were smuggled in.

Sarfrazuddin, the association's chairman, who goes by one name, says he subsequently showed Sony officials and Japanese diplomats copies of documents indicating that in 1997 Sony Gulf was promoting service guarantees that retailers could offer to buyers in Pakistan. Since at the time Sony TVs were "neither being manufactured in Pakistan nor being imported" legally, "we wonder how the guarantees" could be offered, he wrote in a July 1997 letter to the Japanese Embassy in Islamabad, Pakistan.

Faiz Rahim Khan, chief executive of Data Electronics, a Lahore, Pakistan-based company that provided service under Sony Gulf's guarantees in Pakistan until 1999, says the Sony unit routinely reimbursed his firm for repairs on TVs sold in the Middle East and used in Pakistan. "How it got there was not our concern," he says.

Sony Gulf's Mr. Modak confirms the company had an agreement in the 1990s with Data Electronics to repair Sony products in Pakistan. He also says Sony Gulf's authorized Dubai distributor, Jumbo Electronics, has offered warranties on Sony products that are good in Pakistan. He adds that Sony Gulf didn't make the Pakistan warranties available to Dubai-based traders who bought products from Jumbo.

In 1999, Sony began assembling televisions in Pakistan, contracting with a Pakistani-Korean joint-venture company. Tahir Arshad, the venture's finance manager, says smuggling of Sony TVs has been reduced in recent years. Still, the local-assembly plant is running at only half capacity, and the venture's officials are worried about whether their contract will be renewed this year. Sony Gulf declines to comment on whether it will renew the contract.

Televisions are legal again in Afghanistan, and if Sony closes down local production in Pakistan, it "can still sell" in Afghanistan, says Mr. Arshad. In fact, the late Abdul Haq's brother, Haji Abdul Qadir, is back in power in Jalalabad as provincial governor, and he is trying to revive the family's Dubai-Jalalabad air-cargo service.

Khalid Khan of Sony Gulf says he has begun scouting for authorized Sony dealers to operate in Afghanistan. One place he intends to recruit is in Peshawar, although he says that any TVs imported into Afghanistan would be sold to Afghan buyers, not smuggled into neighboring countries. Mr. Modak, the Sony Gulf spokesman, says it hasn't authorized Mr. Khan to do this recruiting.

Some dealers of smuggled goods in Karkhano say they are eager to be recruited. "If we manage to work from Afghanistan, we can export to Russia, to Iran, to other neighboring countries"—if possible, without paying taxes and duties, says Muslim Electronics's Abdul Basir Khan. "We will have a much greater market."

Peter Landers in Tokyo contributed to this article.

Marketing Strategies: Planning, Implementation, and Control

KODAK IS THE PICTURE OF DIGITAL SUCCESS
But can the fast-selling EasyShare alter its profit outlook?

Digital cameras were in demand this Christmas, flying off the shelves along with Microsoft Corp.'s Xbox game consoles and low-cost DVD players. And the supreme hot seller? No, it wasn't Nikon or Canon that came out ahead. Instead, the hit product was from perennial also-ran Eastman Kodak Co. Thanks to its new digital offerings, struggling Kodak was suddenly looking awfully sharp. At Best Buy, Wal-Mart, and countless other stores across the country, Kodak's EasyShare digital cameras, introduced on Apr. 23, were often sold out well before Dec. 25. Says Kodak Chairman Daniel A. Carp: "We'll stay in the game long-term with [EasyShare]."

While the final numbers on 2001 aren't in, EasyShare sales clearly boosted Kodak's market standing. In a December survey of 90 major retailers by Salomon Smith Barney, 50% listed Kodak as their best-selling digital camera, compared with 29% in June. Second-ranked Olympus was a best seller at only about 35% of stores in the December survey, followed by Fuji and Sony. If the trend holds, Kodak will surely gain swiftly on Sony, which had 25% of the digital market in 2001, compared to Kodak's 14% share, according to International Data Corp.

The Kodak digital cameras—there are five in the product line, ranging from about $200 to $400—are a hit because they help resolve significant problems that have plagued digital camera owners. These include difficulty downloading images and short battery life.

The timing couldn't have been better. Kodak hasn't had a big hit in a long time—and never has it needed one more than now. The company relies heavily on sales of traditional film to consumers, a business that has been hit hard by both the recession and September 11,

as well as the shift to digital photography. Consumers last year cut back sharply on the use of traditional film—by as much as 5%, according to Goldman, Sachs & Co. In recent weeks, analysts have been steadily dropping Kodak's 2001 profits estimates, to just $667 million, down more than 54% from the prior year, according to UBS Warburg analyst Benjamin A. Reitzes. Now at $29, Kodak's stock is 41% off its high last June.

Having a hot new product line will help—though only so much. Digital cameras accounted for just $500 million of Kodak's estimated $13.1 billion in sales in 2001. That compares with $2.6 billion for the declining film business, according to Warburg's Reitzes. As a result, he contends, digital is chipping away at sales of traditional cameras, film, and photo processing services, but isn't yet boosting the bottom line much. What's more, as sales of digital cameras soar, the prices they command are plummeting. As a whole, camera makers sold nearly 9 million units in 2001, almost triple the number they unloaded in 1999. But the average price per camera has fallen to just under $300, from around $460 two years ago.

It is also unclear whether Kodak can successfully leverage the popularity of its digital cameras into higher margin ancillary lines. Kodak is eyeing future profits from photo-quality inkjet paper and the company's Ofoto.com online photo sharing and printing service. With 2 million members, Ofoto—one of three photo printing services featured in Microsoft's new XP operating system—is now growing 12% a month.

The home photo paper business may be tougher to crack. Right now, only 15% to 20% of digital images are ever printed. Kodak is banking that EasyShare's simplicity could boost demand for home printing,

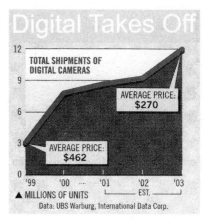

thus spurring sales of high-margin paper. But that in turn could eat into Kodak's existing sales of paper to printing labs.

Kodak has avoided the intensely competitive home printer market. Instead, it's pushing printing kiosks in retail stores such as CVS and Kmart. Customers can get their own prints by feeding a CD-ROM or memory card into some 24,000 kiosks that Kodak claims have been profitable since 2000. Add it all up, and as big a success as Kodak's EasyShare cameras are, they may not be enough. Keeping the momentum going—and the profits rolling in—will be no easy task.

By Geoffrey Smith and Faith Keenan in Boston

'Hog' Maker Gets (Financial) Motor Running

By MARILYN ALVA
Investor's Business Daily

Recessions don't faze Spuck Bennett, even though conventional wisdom says they should. After all, he sells high-ticket, discretionary products.

Bennett is a dealer for Harley-Davidson Inc. The century-old motorcycle company, renowned for its heavyweight "hogs," prides itself on being different.

True to form, Bennett's business cruised along even after Sept. 11.

"I've seen no difference . . . as far as sales," he said.

He figures sales at his flagship store in Seaford, Del., were up more than 12% for the year.

One thing did change, though. In December, like other Harley dealers, he started selling Harley's new custom cruiser, the liquid-cooled V-Rod, aimed at a younger crowd.

Suggested price: $17,000. The home office was to ship Bennett eight of the models, but his initial orders totaled 22.

That's nothing new for Harley, which specializes in heavy, air-cooled motorcycles sold to 1,300 dealers from Nebraska to Japan.

Harley officials have long claimed their business is recession-proof, and financials usually back them up. In last year's fourth quarter—a dismal period for many businesses—Harley's sales accelerated 18.3% from the year before to $894.4 million.

Earnings? They blasted ahead nearly 27% to 39 cents a share.

What's the secret?

"It's just like fine wine," said Bennett, who opened his third shop last April on Maryland's eastern shore. "If you have a Harley that's 5 or 10 years old, it's worth almost as much as you paid for it."

That high resale value, along with low interest rates, has made it relatively painless for customers to trade up to new bikes that cost $10,000 to $20,000.

"You would think demand would be a problem in a slow economy (with) a discretionary product, but it hasn't been," said analyst David Cumberland of Robert W. Baird & Co.

History shows the motorcycle industry doesn't follow the crowd even in the best of circumstances.

"It's an industry that's driven by its own cycle, no pun intended," said analyst Rick Fradin of William Blair & Co. "It doesn't seem to track very closely with the economy."

Harley is the leading motorcycle brand in the U.S., though its market share has slipped over the past few years from nearly 50% to about 45%. Its closest rival, Honda Motor Co., commands about a 20% share.

Leaving The Recession In Its Dust

Growth may be slowing some, but Harley-Davidson is still pumping out numbers that leave many recession-weary companies behind

Annual production

	Units	Year-over-year change
1997	132,285	11.4%
1998	150,818	14.0
1999	177,187	17.5
2000	204,592	15.5
2001	234,461	14.6
2002e	258,432	10.2
2003e	289,444	12.0

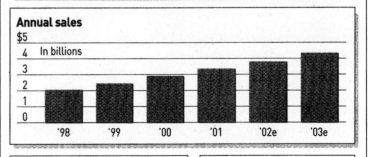

Annual sales

Annual earnings per share

Product mix
Sportster 21.5%
Touring 27.6%
Custom 50.9%

Sources: Company reports, Robert W. Baird & Co., First Call

"We've been capacity-constrained," said James Ziemer, Harley's chief financial officer. "The market is growing faster than our production."

Outside the U.S., Harley's biggest single market is Japan. It's had a tougher time in Europe, where sport bikes are more popular and Honda leads. Harley has lately reduced shipment growth to Europe in favor of the U.S., where margins are better anyway.

Because demand for bikes in the U.S. almost always outstrips supply, Harley's in an enviable spot, analysts say. That helps keep prices high and discounts to a minimum.

Harley could probably sell 30% more motorcycles in a year, Fradin says. "But they couldn't keep the quality up."

And quality has been Chief Executive Jeffrey Bleustein's mantra since taking over the helm in 1997.

Company officials plan a 10% increase in production this year to 258,000 units. But that increase is less than last year's 14.6%.

Earnings growth is heading down, too, analysts figure. Analysts polled by First Call see Harley's earnings this year hitting $1.66 a share. That's 16% above a year ago, when year-over-year earnings were up 27%.

Is there a slowdown on the horizon? Company execs don't see it.

"In a backdrop of 9-11, a recession and what's going on in worldwide economies, I'll tack that record up against most other companies," said Ziemer.

Harley's upcoming 100th anniversary should spark heightened interest in 2003-model products, watchers say. The year-long celebration begins in July.

Dealers already see strong demand for anniversary bikes, even though birthday models haven't yet been disclosed.

"Harley riders have such a strong relationship with the company and the bike, many will want to buy a 2003 bike even if it doesn't have any special insignia on it," said Cumberland.

And while earnings growth might be slowing, he notes the growth is coming up against increasingly tough comparisons.

"As the company grows larger, it's not as easy to put up 25%-type earnings growth," he said. "That said, 2002 and 2003 will be very good years for Harley."

Meanwhile, the firm has begun to attract a younger customer than its typical baby-boomer devotee, whose average age is 46.

Several dealers were asking—and getting—premium prices of up to 30% on the new V-Rod, industry sources say.

"One of my competitors is selling them at $29,000," Bennett said .

Harley shipped just 1,700 V-Rods in the fourth quarter, but plans to send out more than 10,000 this year.

The new Firebolt XB9R, a sports bike, also is expected to spark sales among younger customers. It's slated to hit the market by late March.

Harley is gearing up to bring new riders, including women, into the fold through a new Riders Edge motorcycle training program as well.

"Within a couple of years it will be available at enough dealers to make a difference," said Cumberland. "They're definitely taking steps today that should pay off in the long term."

"Harley-Davidson: 'Hog' Maker Gets (Financial) Motor Running," *Investor's Business Daily*, January 28, 2002. Reprinted by permission.

purchases through local wine stories. Others skirted the rules entirely. Many lobbied—most unsuccessfully—to overturn the laws in state legislatures.

Wine.com, based in Napa, Calif., was typical of the online wine stores, and for a while led the pack. Launched in 1995 by wine experts Peter Granoff and Robert Olson, who called the Web site Virtual Vineyards, the goal was to revolutionize wine shopping by giving consumers direct access to small wineries and high-end limited-production wines not always available though regional distributors.

With $50 million in funding, the company operated like an interstate wine broker, linking customers to suppliers. However, in order to make sales legal the company had to pay high handling fees to wholesalers and local retailers who functioned like fulfillment agents. Those costs were passed on to Wine.com's consumers.

One problem: The company never got enough customers to make the business profitable. Another: Like many Internet companies, Wine.com bought into the build-it-and-they-will come philosophy of the boom, hiring hundreds of employees and burning up capital on advertising.

"It was very difficult for them to aggregate orders in a meaningful way—they had big empty trucks shipping orders all over the country," says Mark Swartzberg, a New York-based analyst for Dutch bank ABN Amro. "They couldn't get critical mass to make the orders meaningful for the retailer or the wholesaler."

Yet another problem: Wine.com was not licensed as a winery, wholesaler or retailer, so it became enmeshed in court battles over whether its approach was legal. "The laws then were not in place for that kind of a success story," says Steve Gross, an analyst with the Wine Institute. The company filed for Chapter 11 bankruptcy protection in the spring of 2001.

San Francisco-based Wineshopper.com took a slightly different approach.

With $46 million in funding from Silicon Valley venture firm Kleiner Perkins Caufield & Byers and Amazon.com Inc., the company also followed a fulfillment model but focused on building a wine-distribution locator database, with the idea of partnering with the Wine & Spirit Wholesalers of America.

Its goal was to build a national inventory of wines on the Web, much like an online book catalog. The problem was many of the wholesalers didn't have the technological infrastructure or the will to participate. High customer-acquisition costs prompted the company to merge in August 2000 with Wine.com.

EVineyard.com, meanwhile, took a more painstaking approach. With $20 million in private equity, the company moved state by state to get licensed as a retailer. It operates basically like a virtual retailer with a virtual inventory, buying wine from wholesalers only when it is ordered, then passing it through packing warehouses before shipping via United Parcel Service.

The hitch, however, is that because the company is in essence a "retailer," it can only offer the wines made available by its regional distributors. "They've filled a niche, but not all of the niche," says Mr. Gross. "You can get product online but the choice still is limited."

Mr. Lauter says, however, that his company serves 77% of the premium wine-drinking market because it operates in 27 states, shipping intrastate as well.

"It took a long time," Mr. Lauter says. "In New York, it took us 10 months. In New Jersey, you cannot get a new license, you have to purchase an existing license and then have a physical presence no more than 100 yards away from the license you bought." To comply with the proximity rule, in New Jersey and 11 other states the company leased packing warehouses along existing wholesaler delivery routes.

The company operates like a retailer, with margins of 25% to 30%, Mr. Lauter says. With only 60 full-time employees, he says, fourth-quarter numbers will show the company turned a profit in December.

In April 2001 eVineyard.com paid $9 million in cash and stock to defunct Wine.com for its domain name, customer list, Web site and other intellectual capital and changed the site's name to Wine.com by eVineyard.

While eVineyard benefited from the demise of its rivals, industry observers like Jeremy Benson, a wine marketing executive in Napa, Calif., say the company did have a better business model. "EVineyard partly benefited from the implosion of the other two," Mr. Benson says. "Wine.com had a tremendous burn rate going on. They had a massive capital investment and spent it quickly." In contrast, he adds, "eVineyard started as a modest investment and didn't bet the farm that there would be an increase in online buyers."

EVineyard's cautionary approach also scored points with the industry's key middlemen. "EVineyard was evolutionary, whereas others were revolutionary," says Edward Maletis, chief executive of Columbia Distributing Co., a Pacific Northwest distributor based in Portland, Ore. "The other guys took a more bullish approach to being able to change the traditional way of how wine gets from the producer into the hands of the consumer. Some wholesalers were rubbed the wrong way."

Mr. Totty is a news editor for The Wall Street Journal Reports based in San Francisco. Ms. Grimes is a deputy chief of The Wall Street Journal's San Francisco bureau.

85

If at First You Don't Succeed...

Some retailers are finding success in industries long thought off-limits to e-commerce

By Michael Totty and Ann Grimes

Are some businesses just not cut out for the Internet?

It certainly seems that way. Consider furniture, which has witnessed the high-profile flameouts of Furniture.com and Living.com, among others. Or groceries, which suffered through the money-burning failure of Webvan Group Inc. and a host of lesser competitors.

These weren't just well-publicized flops of individual companies. Many retail experts saw them as signs that some sectors were doomed to be e-commerce disappointments. Consumers, it was said, won't buy a new sofa or dining-room table without touching the materials and testing the comfort. Online grocers won't be able to crack the brutal economics of food sales. Wine, another e-tail letdown, will never navigate the minefield of state alcoholic-beverage rules.

This conventional wisdom could still prove correct. But despite the dismal history, some retailers are finding ways to crack even the toughest e-commerce cases. They're doing so by avoiding the mistakes of the earlier wave of online-only wrecks and by closely tying their Internet operations with real-world stores and distributors. In most cases, they're also thinking small—in stark contrast with the New Economy hubris of e-tail start-ups—by limiting online sales to a few items or markets.

"It's premature to say these categories don't work," says Mohan Sawhney, professor of e-commerce and technology at Northwestern University's Kellogg School of Management. "The people who emerge from this will emerge stronger and smarter and will emerge as hybrids," combining online and physical stores.

Here's a look at three retail categories—groceries, furniture and wine—and how some companies are finding glimmers of success in these supposedly hopeless sectors.

Groceries

When Louis Borders launched **Webvan** in 1999, it seemed that the start-up may have finally figured out the online grocery puzzle. The company, based in Foster City, Calif., offered free delivery for bigger orders, eliminating one source of customer resistance. It promised to deliver within a 30-minute window, so customers didn't have to hang around the house all afternoon waiting for their orders.

What happened next wasn't pretty: After tearing through $830 million in start-up and IPO funds, the company sought Chapter 11 bankruptcy protection in July and began liquidating its assets. Other online grocers—Streamline.com, HomeRuns.com and ShopLink.com—have joined Webvan in the ash heap of dot-com history.

There are plenty of reasons for the failures, and they point to lingering obstacles for anyone trying to take the grocery business to the Internet. But the flops also offer a road map for companies still trying to make a go of it.

"I think we're getting our second wind," says Robert Rubin, a research director at Forrester Research Inc., in Cambridge, Mass. "The first wave failed as businesses but proved there's a value proposition for consumers. Now it's up to the traditional grocers to execute."

One problem with the first round, Mr. Rubin says, is that buying groceries online requires consumers to make a big change in the way they shop for basic household goods. As a result, the number of households that regularly purchased groceries over the Internet increased far more slowly than promoters had originally expected, to an estimated 5 million in 2001 from 3.7 million in 1999.

In most places, says Ken Cassar, a senior researcher at research firm Jupiter Media Metrix in New York, "going to the grocery store isn't as terrible an experience as companies like Webvan had hoped."

Another problem was price. Online grocers were competing with their storebound competitors by promising to be more convenient, but most consumers were more interested in price, and the online stores weren't any cheaper.

A Forrester survey last year of those who had bought groceries online but stopped found that nearly half said they could find better prices at stores.

This customer resistance led to expensive and devastating solutions. To build up a base of customers from scratch, the newcomers had to spend heavily on advertising and other marketing. Webvan, for instance, spent 25% to 35% of its revenue on advertising, according to its financial statements, compared with an average of about 1% spent by traditional grocers.

Then there were the expensive distribution centers. Webvan officials argued in the company's early stages that the centers, which could handle up to 8,000 orders a day—many times more than a traditional warehouse—would give it a big cost advantage over its bricks-and-mortar competitors. But it never gained the sales volume to take full advantage of the efficiencies, and so its gross margins trailed those of large traditional grocers.

Yet even as the grocery dot-coms fell away, traditional chains have been moving to build up their own online services. That's because grocers increasingly face competition from restaurants, discounters and specialty stores, and the Internet is one way to increase overall sales. And though the online market is small, consumers who are willing to buy groceries online represent the premium customers that companies are most loath to lose.

This time, though, e-grocers are avoiding the world-conquering ambitions of the failures and are proceeding cautiously, taking full advantage of their existing distribution and marketing channels and treating online grocery sales as a niche market.

One path is being taken by Dutch grocery chain **Royal Ahold NV,** which owns the Stop & Shop and Giant chains on the East Coast. In 2000, Ahold bought a majority stake in Peapod Inc., the oldest of the online groceries (last year it purchased the balance of Peapod shares) and proceeded to scale back Peapod's online ambitions.

For Ahold, the purchase "was a way to get into the e-commerce game in groceries without starting from scratch," a Peapod spokeswoman says.

The new owners shut down operations in Dallas, Houston and Austin, Texas; Columbus, Ohio; and San Francisco. Last summer, the owners also eliminated free deliveries.

Now, Peapod offers a scaled-down assortment of the most commonly purchased items, delivered from either its own in-store "warerooms"—areas set aside in existing stores—or distribution centers specially designed to package items for home delivery (as opposed to Stop & Shop's warehouses, which are set up to handle pallet-size delivery to stores). Its target market is busy families, and to encourage shoppers to place larger orders, it charges $9.95 for deliveries of up to $75, with a minimum $50 order, and $4.95 for orders over $75.

With an average order of $132, the service is posting operating profits—excluding marketing costs and some corporate overhead—in one of its five markets, and Peapod officials say the company is "on track with its profitability goals"; before it was taken over by Ahold, the company had projected to show operating profits by the end of 2002. And unlike Webvan, which envisioned expanding to 26 markets in two years, Peapod is taking it slow. "Right now we're focused on current markets," says Andrew Parkinson, Peapod's co-founder and now chief financial officer. "We'll expand when we can do so profitably in each market."

Safeway Inc., a Pleasanton, Calif., grocery chain, is taking a different approach, using a model refined by British grocer **Tesco** PLC, which last June invested more

Looking for a Foot in the Door

Traffic at selected e-commerce sites. Numbers represent the average number of total unique U.S. visitors per month within the quarter. Figures are in thousands.

FOOD & BEVERAGE	4Q '00	1Q '01	2Q '01	3Q '01	4Q '01
Wine.com	1,043	940	358	161	218
Food.com	583	300	263	170	185
Hickoryfarms.com	531	112	186	238	495
Netgrocer.com	886	264	155	151	154
Omahasteaks.com	646	740	992	508	841
Peapod.com	107	106	117	100	98
Webvan.com	231	679	553	NA	NA
FURNITURE & APPLIANCES					
Furniturefan.com	310	769	764	553	490
Furniturefind.com	146	651	507	396	437
Crateandbarrel.com	330	262	300	298	373
Potterybarn.com	279	278	283	327	381
MAJOR ONLINE RETAIL BENCHMARK					
Amazon.com	23,960	27,100	29,636	31,926	43,204

Source: ComScore Networks

Average monthly sales 2001 (in millions)

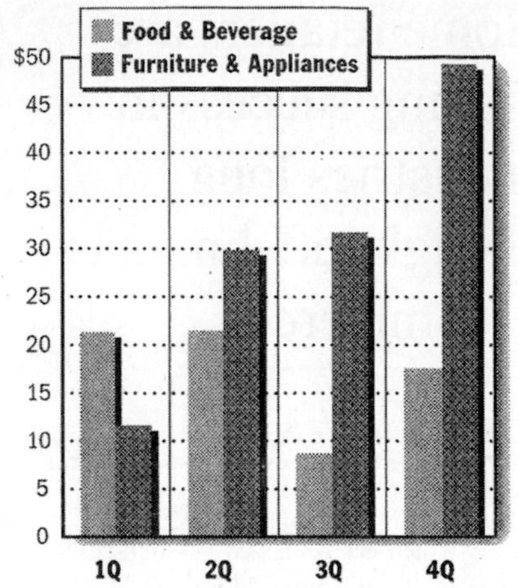

than $22 million in Safeway's online venture, GroceryWorks.com.

In the venture, which started operating last month in Portland, Ore., and Vancouver, Wash., Safeway will avoid expensive centralized distribution centers and instead fill customer orders from existing store inventories.

Using a special shopping cart developed by Tesco with a computer screen that displays a customer's order and shows where in the store ordered items can be found, Safeway says that it can fill orders at a fraction of the cost of using a centralized warehouse. Further, it only needs to invest in new trucks and hire more grocery pickers as demand for the business grows—avoiding the heavy investment costs Webvan incurred with its build-it-and-they-will-come approach.

"The cost of [filling orders] in the store is minimal compared to the warehouse model," says Deborah Lambert, a Safeway spokeswoman.

This "store-pick" model isn't new—it was used and later abandoned by Peapod. Though it holds down the cost of filling orders, Peapod found that as the service grew, its pickers overwhelmed the store aisles. It also led to too many orders going unfilled because items were out of stock and the site couldn't display actual store inventories.

Ms. Lambert says Tesco's technology will help avoid those problems. When a customer places an order, it is automatically routed to a computer in the nearest store, where the order will be filled. Problems with out-of-stock items are avoided because customers can order only items that are in the store's inventory. And she says the company can schedule pickers to work at off-peak hours to sidestep the inconvenience of congested aisles.

Forrester's Mr. Rubin says he prefers Peapod's approach to filling orders, since it's better able to grow without interfering with store operations. But he faults both companies for missing one of the key lessons of the earlier failures: charging for delivery, especially on the high-dollar orders that can make the service pay off. (Safeway charges a flat $9.95 for each delivery.) "By charging for orders over $100," he says, "you're creating a barrier for the customers you want."

Furniture

Selling furniture over the Internet makes the online grocery business look easy.

Few consumers, skeptics insist, will ever want to buy a sofa, chair or dining table without first touching the item and testing it for comfort. "Furniture is a product that consumers need to touch, to feel and to see," says Margaret Whelan, a furniture-industry analyst at UBS Warburg in New York.

Of course, that didn't stop a handful of start-ups from launching home-furnishing e-tail sites. Living.com, based in Austin, Texas, as well as Furniture.com of Framingham, Mass., and at least a half-dozen others plunged into the online furniture business on the notion that they could offer better selection and customer service than the highly fragmented bricks-and-mortar furniture business.

High-powered Internet tools went a long way toward overcoming the touch-and-feel problem. Furniture.com's site enabled browsers to design floor plans combining their existing furniture and items on the site. GoodHome.com used technology that allowed shoppers to alter the appearance of a mocked-up room by changing wallpaper or upholstery. (The San Rafael, Calif., company stopped selling furniture in January 2001 and morphed into a Web site-imaging-technology concern called Scene 7.)

But getting consumers willing to buy wasn't enough. Living.com shut down in August 2000 and is being liquidated in Chapter 11 bankruptcy proceedings. Furniture.com followed a few months later.

Part of the problem was that brand-name furniture manufacturers generally shunned the sites, not wanting to alienate their traditional retail outlets. In addition, delivery problems plagued the online stores. Lisa Poulin, the court-appointed trustee in Living.com's bankruptcy proceeding, says there are "mounds" of disputes and customer complaints over products that were delivered damaged or late.

Where traditional furniture stores can mark down and resell damaged or refused merchandise, the Internet companies didn't have an easy way to move returned pieces. Jerry Epperson, a furniture analyst in Richmond, Va., estimates returns for the online companies represented as much as 35% of sales.

So here's the surprising news: Online furniture sales hit $211 million in the last quarter of 2001 compared with $154 million in the year-earlier period, according to Forrester. Part of the increase came from the sale of furniture at online auctions, such as eBay Inc.'s, where the number of furniture listings doubled in the past year. Further, furniture sales, offline and on, increased in the

wake of the Sept. 11 attacks, as shoppers focused more of their spending on the home.

But part of the increase also can be traced to the fact that some retailers are finding success in selling furniture online.

One group, including Houston's **Gallery Furniture, BeHome.com** in Olathe, Kan., and **FurnitureFind.com** in Buchanan, Mich., grew out of mainly regional furniture stores that try to cater to online shoppers from all over the U.S.

FurnitureFind, which according to ComScore Networks Inc., a Reston, Va., market-research firm, averaged almost a half-million visitors a month in last year's fourth quarter, has its roots in a family-owned furniture retailer, Bookout's Furniture, based in southwestern Michigan. Bookout's put up a Web site in 1996 to provide information about its stores but soon found itself flooded with requests from shoppers looking to buy pieces online. By late that year, it began taking orders.

In early 2000, the company was acquired by GoodHome.com, which had hoped to combine its Web technology and FurnitureFind's relationships with manufacturers. But by the end of the year, GoodHome decided to get out of the furniture business to focus on its technology, and FurnitureFind's founders bought back the company. Since then, the site has booked more than $10 million in sales and is "cash-flow positive," says Stephen Antisdel, FurnitureFind's chief executive.

The site, which offers more than 10,000 items from a "master list" of more than 100,000, maintains no inventory, eliminating one costly mistake of the furniture dot-coms. Items aren't built until an order comes in—"just like Dell Computer," says Mr. Antisdel, who is a nephew of Bookout's founder. With an Internet business, he adds, "since you don't have to stock a showroom, what is the point of filling a warehouse?"

To work around the touch-and-feel problem, FurnitureFind sends swatches of materials to anyone who asks for one. And it maintains a call center staffed seven days a week with about a dozen customer-service reps, who train in the local Bookout stores to gain knowledge about furnishings, materials and styles. More than 90% of all sales involve at least one call to customer service.

FurnitureFind also keeps a close eye on deliveries, relying on partnerships with several furniture-moving companies to make sure that items are delivered and set up without damage. As a result, returns are kept at an extremely low 3% of sales, Mr. Antisdel says. The returns that do come in can be sold at the local Bookout outlet store. And it offers free delivery on purchases over $1,400, helping to prevent shopping-cart sticker shock and drive up average sales—which, not coincidentally, are just above $1,400.

The site lacks the kind of fancy technological features, like three-dimensional and design-a-room views, found at Living.com and others. "When we looked at all that cool stuff, we found it didn't translate into meaningful customer benefit," Mr. Antisdel says.

Still, the company is savvy about taking advantage of Internet technology in its marketing. It pays a sponsorship fee so that it is one of the top results when a browser searches for "furniture" at the Yahoo Inc. Web site.

"Anybody can build a Web page," Mr. Antisdel says. "Unless you figure out how this particular [online] world works and how to use this environment, you won't be able to build a viable business online."

For specialty home-furnishing retailers like **Crate & Barrel,** Northbrook, Ill., and **Williams-Sonoma** Inc.'s Pottery Barn unit, the formula is a little different: They offer only a relatively small number of pieces online, complementing their existing store and catalog sales.

Pottery Barn, for instance, lists fewer than 1,000 different pieces online—far fewer than the number of items typically available at a traditional furniture retailer. This means that it ends up selling large numbers of a single item, allowing its manufacturers to stockpile enough frames and other components to turn around orders quickly—and to keep many of the most popular items in stock.

"Many times, on our most popular items, the next day after it's ordered it's going on a truck," says Patrick Connolly, chief marketing officer at San Francisco-based Williams-Sonoma.

Pottery Barn began offering furniture through its catalog in 1994 and moved online in 2000. To get around the touch-and-feel problem, it depicts the furnishings in lavish "lifestyle" settings, in contrast with the warehouse settings of many big bricks-and-mortar furniture retailers. "The customer . . . says, 'My whole life would change if I owned that couch,'" Mr. Connolly says. "It more than makes up for the fact that you're not sitting in it."

The company doesn't disclose online sales. But, Mr. Connolly says, "furniture sales online are good for us."

Wine

Compared with groceries and furniture, wine should have been a snap to sell online. It's easy and relatively inexpensive to ship, and the fragmented retail wine market would seem to be ripe for competition from a national online retailer that could offer thousands of vintages.

It didn't turn out that way, though. In the heady days of dot-com mania, there were nearly a dozen online wine-selling start-ups, including Wine.com, Wineshopper.com and Winebuyer.com. All are now defunct, leaving Wine.com by eVineyard as one of the few survivors.

What happened? It turned out that wine selling was one of the toughest markets for online sellers to break into. A thicket of arcane regulations and laws, designed to support a three-tier distribution system of suppliers, state wholesalers and local retailers, have essentially blocked many Internet entrepreneurs' dreams of cheaper, faster, direct-to-consumer shipping. Blinded by visions of the borderless Internet, most of the newcomers failed to find a profitable way around the rules before their start-up funds ran out.

So, how did eVineyard survive? The company, based in Portland, Ore., expanded slowly, and it methodically complied with the tangle of laws. "It's the tortoise-and-the-hare story," says Brett Lauter, **eVineyard's** vice president and chief marketing officer. "This time last year, if you talked to the analysts, they didn't give us a chance."

Wine is a big business, and online sales still promise to be a key market. There are now about 2,100 U.S. wineries, up from 377 about 30 years ago, and annual sales hover in the $45 billion range. Internet wine sales are expected to account for 5% to 10% of retail wine sales by 2005, according to Salomon Smith Barney.

In general, the current regulatory system requires any company involved in the sale of alcoholic beverages to be licensed by the state as a producer (winery), a wholesaler/distributor or retailer. Generally, wine is purchased from the winery by the licensed wholesaler, which transports it to a particular state, where it is sold to licensed retailers, bars, restaurants, hotels or wine shops. This distribution system dates back to the end of Prohibition in the 1930s and was designed to prevent the consolidation of power that organized crime had over alcohol production and distribution. Supporters say the laws help keep online sales from siphoning off needed state sales taxes and make it harder to sell alcohol to minors.

Twenty-four states, plus the District of Co-lumbia, allow some form of direct interstat shipping between wineries and consumer Thirteen of these are "reciprocity states" t allow interstate shipments, but several st require various permits and conditions fo livery. The balance prohibit direct shippi

The peculiarities are confounding instance, according to the Wine Insti public-policy group in San Francisc cannot be sold in containers larger t gallon in Florida. In New York and states, consumers can't buy wine i stores. In Colorado, half-bottles c illegal. Oklahoma prohibits wir Labor Day, Independence Day Day, Thanksgiving and Christm ta, Missouri, Washington and W mit consumers to receive two a year directly from out-o some other states allow two Minnesota and Utah prohi of orders via the Internet. A

"It gets pretty insane,"

Initially, some wine e- the rules by devising elal methods to comply—fo

86

Europe Presenting Challenges For AOL

FEWER MINUTES SPENT ONLINE

AND THE COUNTRIES DIFFER IN WHAT TYPE OF CONTENT THEY WANT TO SEE ON THE WEB

By Doug Tsuruoka
Investor's Business Daily

Now for the hard part.

It was easy for AOL Time Warner Inc. to cough up $7 billion to buy Bertelsmann AG's 49.5% stake in its European Internet unit, AOL Europe.

The buyback announced Jan. 7 satisfies a condition set by European regulators in clearing America Online's merger with Time Warner last year. It's also a smart move for the company, analysts say, since Europe's a hot Internet growth area.

The number of new subscribers at AOL Europe jumped 40% to 5.5 million last year.

But the ride may get rougher. The world's biggest media company faces a pitched battle for new subscribers and markets in Europe, analysts say. And AOL Europe may not be profitable for some time.

"It's not going to be a walkover for AOL Time Warner in Europe," said Eric Kintz, an e-commerce expert for the consulting firm Roland Berger & Partner LLC. "You have strong local telecom companies that provide Internet services. They know their markets and have brand trust and customer relationships."

AOL's 5.5 million European users are a small fraction of the more than 60 million Internet subscribers in Europe. And the company still has to prove its online business model works in Europe.

Rivals include T-Online, an Internet service provider with 7.5 million members that's owned by German phone company Deutsche Telekom AG. There's also Wanadoo in France, with 2.3 million members. It's owned by France Telecom.

Tactics that worked for AOL in the U.S. may not work in Europe. Why? Europeans spend less time on the Net than Americans.

That's because they pay more to connect to online services, thanks to Europe's costly and tightly regulated phone markets.

While most U.S. consumers pay a flat monthly rate of $10 to $30 for unlimited Net usage, Europeans pay high fees to local telecom firms to access the Net on a minute-by-minute basis.

Culture, Language Gaps

That's the chief reason why only one in four Europeans surf the Net for more than a half-hour a day, says research firm International Data Corp. That compares with over 70 minutes per day of Internet use for the average U.S. AOL subscriber.

European firms also spend less money on online ads than U.S. users. Firms in Western Europe spent $1.5 billion on online ads in 2001, says researcher Jupiter Media Metrix. That compares with $7.3 billion for firms in North America.

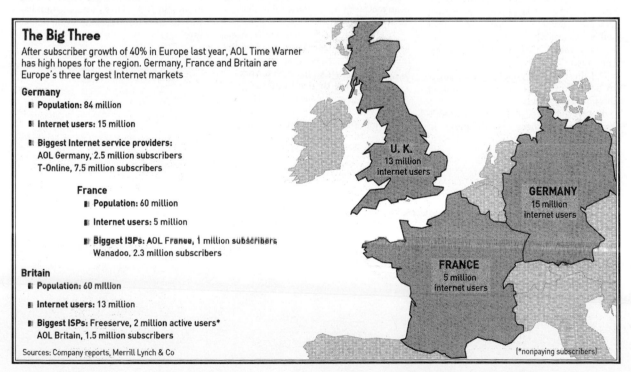

The Big Three

After subscriber growth of 40% in Europe last year, AOL Time Warner has high hopes for the region. Germany, France and Britain are Europe's three largest Internet markets

Germany
- Population: 84 million
- Internet users: 15 million
- Biggest Internet service providers:
  AOL Germany, 2.5 million subscribers
  T-Online, 7.5 million subscribers

France
- Population: 60 million
- Internet users: 5 million
- Biggest ISPs: AOL France, 1 million subscribers
  Wanadoo, 2.3 million subscribers

Britain
- Population: 60 million
- Internet users: 13 million
- Biggest ISPs: Freeserve, 2 million active users*
  AOL Britain, 1.5 million subscribers

Sources: Company reports, Merrill Lynch & Co

U.K. 13 million internet users

GERMANY 15 million internet users

FRANCE 5 million internet users

[*nonpaying subscribers]

(Cont.)

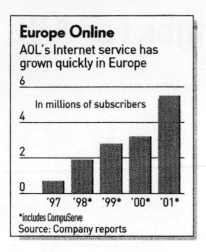

Europe Online
AOL's Internet service has grown quickly in Europe

In millions of subscribers

'97 '98* '99* '00* '01*

*includes CompuServe
Source: Company reports

Europe, unlike the U.S., also is stymied by big cultural and language gaps. French and German Internet users prefer different Web site features and content. That tends to stunt the spread of uniform Net technology across Europe.

"It would be a mistake to view Europe as a single market for the Internet," said Barry Parr, an Internet media consultant in San Francisco. "The market won't jell as quickly or as smoothly as the U.S."

More consumers in Europe access the Net through wireless phones rather than personal computers. That could hurt AOL's service, which is designed mainly for PCs rather than wireless devices, Kintz says.

All these factors could make it harder for AOL Time Warner to whip up cash in Europe from Net services.

Robert Pittman, AOL Time Warner's chief operating officer, says the pluses in Europe outweigh the minuses.

The company's ability to offer attractive Internet tech to consumers will keep its subscriber rolls growing, he says. He expects foreign markets like Europe to pick up the slack as dial-up subscriber growth in the U.S. slows.

"AOL Europe will be the foundation for the AOL Time Warner marketing machine in Europe," Pittman said in a conference call with analysts.

Another plus: The bursting of the dot-com bubble swept away many small ISPs in Europe, which were competing against AOL by offering free Internet access.

AOL Europe is the second biggest online service in Europe. It was launched five years ago as a 50-50 joint venture with Bertelsmann, the German media giant.

AOL Europe is the largest ISP in Britain with 1.5 million members. It's second in Germany, behind T-Online, with 2.5 million members. It's second behind Wanadoo in France with nearly 1 million members.

Pittman said last week the slow growth of Internet access in Europe gives the company room to expand.

Household penetration for the Internet in Europe ranges from less than 30% in some countries to less than 40% in others, AOL officials say. That compares with nearly 60% of U.S. households that use the Internet.

"AOL Time Warner has shown it can make good on growth trajectories like this," said Scott Kessler, an analyst with Standard & Poor's Corp. in New York.

Acquiring British Publisher

Pittman also wants to make AOL Europe the keystone for cross-marketing AOL Time Warner's products in Europe.

That means using the online service to hawk products like the European editions of Time Inc.'s magazines and Warner Bros. movies like "Harry Potter."

AOL also is in the process of acquiring IPC Media, Britain's leading magazine publisher, as part of its European push. The idea is to promote subscriptions to AOL Europe in British magazines.

Pittman wants international business to contribute 30% to AOL Time Warner's revenue by 2005. It currently makes up 17% of its estimated 2001 sales of $38 billion.

Others question AOL Time Warner's strategy in Europe.

They say it's spending too much to buy out Bertelsmann. It's paying nearly twice the market value for Bertelsmann's stake. The stiff price is a payback to Bertelsmann, which paid most of the operating costs for AOL Europe.

Still, each AOL Europe subscriber is worth less than half of a U.S. subscriber, says Merrill Lynch & Co. analyst Jessica Reif Cohen. That's because Europeans use the Internet in less cash-generating ways.

With this in mind, the Bertelsmann stake was worth only about $3 billion, not nearly $7 billion, Cohen says.

AOL Europe also is expected to post a loss of $600 million on revenue of $800 million in 2001. That shows the unit has a way to go before breaking even, analysts say.

"Europe Presenting Challenges for AOL," *Investor's Business Daily*, January 23, 2002. Reprinted by permission.

87

How Big Blue Plays D

On Paul Horn's watch, IBM Research has translated science into products better than any other corporate lab. But the way Horn juggles researchers and resources might be the most impressive discovery.

By: William J. Holstein

Bell Labs invented the transistor, the laser, and Unix, but it never invented a way for its parent, Ma Bell, to cash in. Xerox (*XRX*) PARC presented the world with laser printers, Ethernet computer networking, and the point-and-click interface; the world capitalized on the technology.

Lucent (*LU*), Hewlett-Packard (*HP*), and Eastman Kodak (*EK*) also employ brilliant scientists who win patents for big discoveries. But like the other storied R&D operations in corporate America, they have succeeded far better at R than at D. "We invented everything and developed nothing," laments Xerox PARC's founder, Jack Goldman.

Then there's IBM Research. With eight labs in six countries and a budget of roughly $5.6 billion for research, design, and engineering, it stands as the largest nongovernmental R&D shop in the world. Last year it filed for 2,886 U.S. patents, more than any other company for the eighth year in a row. Among the pure science now under way in IBM's labs are carbon nano-tubes that could shrink computers to the realm of "smart dust," and the Blue Gene project, which plans to build a computing system 500 times more powerful than any before to study proteins in human genes. And that doesn't include the most sweeping initiative of all: to change the architecture of computing itself with "autonomic" systems that self-heal and self-manage.

But what really makes IBM (*IBM*) stand out from its private-sector competitors is its success at converting cool science into cold cash. Fully a third of the patents that IBM won last year have been sold or commercialized in some form—breathtakingly fast for an organization of IBM's size. IBM's semiconductor division earned roughly $3.7 billion last year selling innovations from the labs, and the parent company collected some $1.7 billion by licensing its know-how to others. "This is a new golden age for IBM Research," chairman Louis Gerstner gushed to analysts in May.

Which is saying something, actually. A decade ago, IBM Research was organized more like a university lab,

with departments devoted to, say, materials or mechanical engineering. Researchers were rewarded for their papers and awards, not for commercial innovation. The company had discussed breaking up the labs or even shutting them down, and when Gerstner arrived in 1993, he found the operation defensive and dispirited. But while Gerstner was hardly a technologist, he believed in R&D. So he boosted funding, and in 1996 he handpicked Paul Horn—who had been running IBM's Almaden Research Center in San Jose—to take charge of IBM's entire research operation.

More than any other individual, Horn deserves credit for having turned the place around. A former physics professor turned tech developer, Horn pulled it off not by winning more patents or hiring more Ph.D.s, but by creatively managing the resources at his disposal and formalizing and deepening the labs' ties with the mother ship and its giant divisions. With his gray beard and small ponytail, he looks more like a Hollywood mogul than anyone's image of a corporate executive, let alone one from IBM. But he is a man with a mission. "Everything we do—our organization, our financial model, our measurement system, the feedback we give to people—it's all about flowing technology into the marketplace," he says.

One of IBM Research's key innovations is a funding model that enlists the business divisions as partners with the labs. Here's how it works: IBM Research draws a base budget from the corporation. It spends half of it on exploratory research, but it keeps the rest in reserve to match funding from a business unit. In a typical project, a third of the money comes from a lab's base budget, a third from the business divisions interested in the project, and a third from the lab's "reserves" for the most commercially viable projects. "That stimulates the right behavior," Horn says.

The evolution of TransNote, a new digital handwriting device based on the ThinkPad laptop, shows how the model can work. The concept arose in 1995 at the famous Thomas J. Watson Research Center in New York, and percolated in a series of e-mails and meetings between

(Cont.)

the New York lab rats and their counterparts in the North Carolina-based personal computing division, which designs ThinkPads. The teams put together a prototype that proved the idea would work. By the summer of 1999, the PC business division had put up its money, and that tipped the balance. The lab kicked in its "reserve," and TransNote made its debut in February to rave reviews.

How to mobilize more than 3,000 researchers over three continents presents another management challenge. Xerox's R&D brains, for example, are still headquartered near Stanford University, while the company's business units remain on the East Coast. "Xerox PARC was very isolated from the rest of Xerox, people-wise and agenda-wise," Horn says. He avoids the problem at Big Blue by moving key researchers around in lockstep with each project's development phase.

To Horn, division of labor is just as important as communication. In fact, they're related: Horn hires people from a range of different disciplines to spark cross-fertilization. In the case of TransNote, specialists in software architecture, user interface and user experience, electrical hardware, electronic ink, and packaging were all involved. Horn also bases his employees' compensation at least in part on their ability to market ideas, not just publish or patent them. He ties bonus pay and stock options to midterm goals in the marketplace as well as long-term ones in basic research.

Once researchers generate an idea with market potential, Horn's system encourages them to track it from the lab to store shelves. That underscores another Horn management dictum: Avoid technological "handoffs" at all costs. With TransNote, researchers gradually ceded control of the project to the ThinkPad folks, but remained involved up through the manufacturing process. "We try to keep the team together as we move into development,"

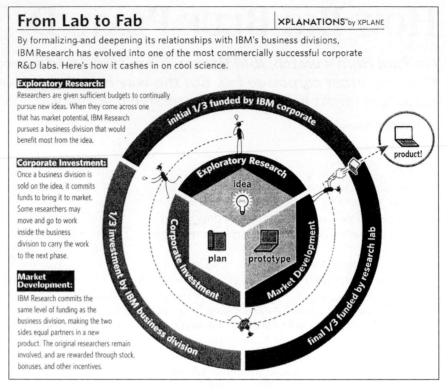

From Lab to Fab   XPLANATIONS™ by XPLANE

By formalizing and deepening its relationships with IBM's business divisions, IBM Research has evolved into one of the most commercially successful corporate R&D labs. Here's how it cashes in on cool science.

Exploratory Research:
Researchers are given sufficient budgets to continually pursue new ideas. When they come across one that has market potential, IBM Research pursues a business division that would benefit most from the idea.

Corporate Investment:
Once a business division is sold on the idea, it commits funds to bring it to market. Some researchers may move and go to work inside the business division to carry the work to the next phase.

Market Development:
IBM Research commits the same level of funding as the business division, making the two sides equal partners in a new product. The original researchers remain involved, and are rewarded through stock, bonuses, and other incentives.

initial 1/3 funded by IBM corporate

1/3 investment by IBM business division

final 1/3 funded by research lab

Exploratory Research

Corporate Investment

Market Development

idea

plan

prototype

product!

Horn explains. "I like to think of a baseball team. Some players come and go, but the team culture stays the same." To build even tighter linkages between the labs and the business units, IBM makes it easy for researchers to job-hop between the labs and their partner divisions. Horn calls this his "research diaspora," and says it was key to making TransNote happen. Says one of TransNote's lead engineers, John Karidis: "There is just no other way to have the contacts and the understanding of the different things going on in research."

Horn's way isn't the only way to keep a company at the edge of technological innovation. Cisco and Intel, for example, have traditionally relied on acquisitions of smaller, nimbler competitors with engineering departments that fit well with the larger enterprise. But IBM isn't Cisco, and Horn sees a healthy R&D lab as essential to keeping Big Blue's technological juices flowing. "To guarantee longevity, you've got to be vital," he says. "If IBM Research went away, IBM would die. So we're not going away."

"How Big Blue Plays D," *Business 2.0,* August/September 2001, pp. 152–154. © 2001 Time Inc. Reprinted by permission.

Mickey Mouse, Nike Give Advice On Air Security

BY STEPHEN POWER

Staff Reporter of THE WALL STREET JOURNAL

WASHINGTON—Hate the wait at airport security checkpoints? Would it be any easier if a talking robot entertained you?

The federal government may soon find out. In one of the more unusual government-industry partnerships in recent years, the Bush administration has turned to **Walt Disney** Co., among other consumer-friendly corporations, for help with easing travel delays as it creates the agency in charge of security at the nation's airports.

Disney has lent a manager from its Orlando theme parks to study how the new Transportation Security Administration might reduce waiting times at security checkpoints—or at least make the lines more tolerable. One concept that already has the agency's attention is Disney's "Fast Pass" system, which helps theme-park visitors avoid long waits at rides.

Another tool for managing cranky travelers is video: In Orlando, at Disney-MGM Studios, vistors waiting to get into a Muppet attraction watch tapes of Kermit the Frog on TV monitors. At the Magic Kingdom, visitors to the ExtraTerrorestrial Alien Encounter attraction are entertained by a talking robot before the show. At some rides, the company uses simple toys, like blocks, to help parents keep small children busy and happy during the wait. "That could be handy" at airports, a Disney spokeswoman says.

The govenment has also turned to **Nike** Inc. The athletic-apparel maker offered up advice on "branding"—specifically, how the fledgling security agency can help cultivate an elite image, akin to the one enjoyed by the Secret Service. Nike also provided pointers on how to liven up training for the roughly 30,000 airport screeners the agency must hire by November. "They make their training fun," a Transportation Department official says of Nike. " We haven't used that word a lot since Sept 11."

Marriott International Inc. and **FedEx** Corp. are suggesting ways to measure screeners' performance. And **Intel** Corp. has lent an engineer to advise on equipment-related purchases.

Last week, airlines began screening checked luggage for explosives, using hand searches, bomb-sniffing dogs, bag-matching and other methods. By the end of the year, all the nation's airports must have sophisticated explosive-detection machines in place. The strict new measures are certain to bring delays, but federal officials say they can learn a lot from Disney and others about minimizing disruption.

The benefits of Disney's Fast Pass—convenience, efficiency—are similar to those of government-issued identification cards, an idea the airlines favor. With Fast Pass, Disney issues a card to a visitor, who brings it to a crowded ride and inserts it into a nearby computer. The computer prints out a pass assigning a time window during which the guest can return and enter on an express queue, with little or no wait. Under the proposed ID card system, frequent fliers who submitted to a detailed background check would get cards that they would show to move through security checkpoints more quickly.

Perhaps it isn't surprising that the administration of the first MBA president would turn to big corporations for advice. Mr. Bush and many Republican leaders initially fought efforts to federalize airport screeners, preferring instead to keep the task in private hands while enhancing federal standards.

There aren't any airlines on the list of corporations lending executives to the new security agency. There was just one air carrier offering training pointers in a recent Transportation Department workshop: **El Al Israel Airlines,** known for its thorough security procedures. Other attendees included **Bank of America** Corp.; **Fluor** Corp.; **PricewaterhouseCoopers; Electronic Data Systems** Corp.; and **Cisco Systems** Inc.

The agency is "bringing in the best people we can from the private sector," says James P. Mitchell, the Transportation Security Administration's spokesman. But "when we get into companies we regulate, that's different."

Participants in the so-called private-sector senior advisor program are on loan to the new agency for the next few months. Employers pay their salaries. The government pays for travel and for out-of-pocket expenses not to exceed $6,000 a month.

The executives must promise not to work on matters "that are reasonably anticipated to have a direct and predictable effect" on their employers. The restrictions don't preclude their employers from bidding on contracts that the security agency is now offering, such as the ones for training airport screeners, unless the employee "has worked personally and substantially" on designing that contract.

Best Call Centers Stress Training, Track Results To Gauge Success

By J. Bonasia
Investor's Business Daily

When the Justice Department needed help with phone calls after the Sept. 11 attack, it sought Wisconsin Energy.

The utility had six hours to prep a call center. And in two days it took 14,000 calls.

The department chose the company because it runs one of the best call centers. Joan Shafer, head of the center, says good customer care depends on planning and preparation.

"The goal is to make it easy for the customer by making it easy" for the front-line staff, she said.

Kathy Hardy, research director for the Society of Consumer Affairs Professionals, says "best practices" vary based on company goals and needs. Most centers have expanded hours and contact options, including e-mail and fax.

"Giving customer choices is a huge trend," she said.

Forrester Research says national retailers spend about $13.3 million just on software and consulting to launch a center. Large regional banks spend $17.6 million.

Classroom Time

Shafer manages 240 agents, plus support. Her 24-hour unit handles 2.5 million calls a year on orders, billing and outages.

Its efforts start with training. New staffers spend 34 days in a class and 10 with a mentor. They get monthly coaching on scripts and business process changes.

The training stresses manners—"100% courtesy," Shafer said.

Call centers must manage schedules to maintain needed staffing. Shafer's managers watch call queues. Agents shift to clerical tasks or projects when calls ebb. And volume is tracked over time to stay on top of trends.

"Calls come in randomly but predictably," Shafer said.

Technology is another factor in call center success. Most centers use an interactive voice response system. They take calls and provide a menu of options.

An automated system routes calls. Agents check scripts and customer histories on their PCs.

Gauging Success

Perhaps the most crucial practice is setting standards to gauge success. Costs per call vary widely, but experts say normal calls cost $5 to $12 to resolve. Complex calls for health or financial data can run $15 to $25 or more.

Shafer's team strives to pick up 80% of calls within 30 seconds, and finish in less than six minutes.

"But we encourage people to take the time needed to complete a call satisfactorily," she added.

Similar standards apply at GlaxoSmithKline. It runs one of its industry's largest call centers in Research Triangle Park, N.C.

"These are very difficult calls when someone is ill, or diagnosed with a disease, or trying to learn how a new drug works," said Lu McLeod, head of customer response. "That kind of anxiety requires a whole different level of sensitivity and urgency."

McLeod says mergers in the 1990s increased Glaxo's product line and strained call center capacity. It joined several centers into one four years ago.

The center handles consumers and care providers. It also serves as Glaxo's human resource hub.

Agents specialize by subject, not by type of customer.

"We don't segment customers by profitability because our philosophy is that all customers are created equal," McLeod said.

'Once And Done'

Glaxo has 80 agents for 12 hours each weekday and emergency pager service. It handles 960,000 contacts a year, 90% by phone.

Glaxo uses Gallup polling to gauge results. Gallup found 75% of callers were extremely or very satisfied in the second quarter.

Agents try to boost customer satisfaction through "once-and-done" service, meaning customers are not sent elsewhere 80% of the time. And they strive to resolve calls in two to five minutes.

Speed is crucial, but McLeod says many centers err on this side. "If you focus only on reaching a specific number of calls per day, that gives you less quality," she said. "It's better to get a balance."

Another mistake is not rewarding agents. Those at utilities and in health care average $13 an hour. Yearly turnover runs 8% to 58%.

McLeod holds events for morale. Peers also name a rep of the month and a manager of the quarter.

"We make it a point to commend (staffers) for their hard work, both one-on-one and in group settings," McLeod said. "We also give out prizes like movie tickets."

Like Glaxo, General Mills provides call center services to stores and shoppers. Some 100 agents work with stores to manage orders, promotions and logistics. Each retailer has a rep.

The crew fields 800,000 contacts from shoppers a year. Each food brand has its own toll-free number, says Jeff Hagen, head of consumer services. That way his staff knows if a call is about Cheerios or Bisquick.

All staffers can answer questions on all products. Two-thirds of calls involve requests for recipes. Agents access product data, recipes, even package types.

Call center staff are trained in the Betty Crocker kitchens to better understand cooking and baking.

"Best Call Centers Stress Training, Track Results to Gauge Success," *Investor's Business Daily*, October 17, 2001. Reprinted by permission.

LET'S GET BACK TO BASICS, FOLKS!
Many companies' e-biz strategies used to be jumbled messes. Now, they're getting focused

During the Internet boom, the Web philosophy of many companies could be summed up in one sentence: Let a thousand Web sites bloom. Today, though, under the weight of a deteriorating economy, Corporate America is applying some weed killer to its digital gardens.

Companies short on patience and shorter on cash are stepping back and trying to figure out what has worked and what hasn't in the online world. Out are all the willy-nilly Web sites started up by department heads and individual staffers for projects that didn't advance the company's overarching goals. Forget experimental Web projects that have not yet shown a return on investment. Wave goodbye to glitzy marketing sites where the trappings were so gaudy that a Web surfer couldn't find a simple search button.

Instead, executives are demanding to see proof of future returns before deciding to keep projects going. Top management wants Web initiatives tied directly to core business goals, such as better relations with customers and more emphasis on brand-building. "People are going back to two things: What is the strategic rationale for getting into this, and what is the return on investment?" says Tim Byrne, a vice-president at Mercer Management Consulting.

Three companies have spent considerable time figuring this out. Their sagas hold lessons for any business now struggling to untangle its snarl of Web sites.

CITIGROUP. Few companies blew more money trying to build independent Web divisions than Citigroup, parent company of Citibank, Salomon Smith Barney, and Travelers Insurance. In 1997, it launched e-Citi with high hopes and a big task. E-Citi's job was to keep all of Citigroup on its toes— partly by competing with the very bank, credit-card company, and other businesses that made Citigroup a $230 billion giant. There was to be an e-Citi bank called Citi f/i and a financial portal called Finance.com. The maverick unit soon had 1,600 employees and more than 100 U.S. Web sites. The idea: Cannibalize your business before someone else did.

The only thing e-Citi gobbled was money. Citigroup's Web effort lost over $1 billion between 1998 and 2000. In online banking, for example, Citigroup was so determined to make Citi f/i an independent operation that customers of the online bank couldn't use Citibank branches. That turned off depositors. The online bank drew 30,000 accounts, vs. 146 million for the rest of Citigroup's banking operation. By March, 2000, word came down from Citigroup Chairman Sandy Weill: Web initiatives must be part of the existing business, not self-appointed upstarts trying to overturn them. "At the beginning of 2000, people were dreaming that you could take e-Citi public," says Deryck C. Maughan, Citigroup's vice-chairman. "I looked

very carefully [and asked], could it make a profit? Not in our lifetime."

Still, Citigroup wanted to keep ideas flowing and innovation humming. So last year, the company formed an Internet Operating Group of top execs to help Citigroup units share Web technology and to ensure that they all have a common look and feel. Innovation is still bubbling along: Citibank is making a big play in the online-payments business with its C2It service, which lets consumers e-mail money to each other for a 1% commission.

A year later, the results are easy to see. The number of online customers are up 80% because Citibank and Citi's credit-card operations are pushing Web services themselves,

Untangling the Web

In the rush to the Net, many companies let departments throw up Web sites with little regard for how they would help the overall business. Now they're trying to untangle their Net initiatives and get them focused on their core business. Here's a sampling:

	THE OLD WAY	THE NEW WAY
Citigroup	In 1997, Citicorp set up e-Citi as an incubator to come up with Web businesses. E-Citi spent $1.1 billion and launched an Internet-only bank called Citi f/i, which landed only 30,000 customers and created tension with other bank units.	A Corporate Internet Operating Group oversees Net strategy, with e-Citi providing technical support. Now Citi has 38 U.S. sites, down from over 100. Citigroup says moving its back-office functions online will save $1 billion-plus next year.
Ryder System	Separate divisions put up 10 Web sites for everything from selling used tractor-trailers to emergency road-side service. But many didn't link to the corporate site, ryder.com. And its shipment-tracking service was buried 10 clicks deep into the ryder.com site.	All the company's Web sites are now linked to ryder.com. A redesign helps customers locate their shipments within two clicks. Now Ryder uses the Web to coordinate its picking, packing, and shipping for customers.
Deere & Co.	Managers launched 13 Web initiatives, serving markets that generated little revenue. Deere makes most of its profits selling new construction equipment, yet it had three sites for used equipment.	The company merged the Web sites into deere.com. Now customers can buy new or used equipment, seek service or repairs—or even use the Web site to configure their own gear, a first for Deere.

instead of leaving that mostly to e-Citi. Citigroup now serves 10 million customers online. E-Citi has been scaled back to 100 people, who implement projects the operating groups propose. The 100 Web sites have been trimmed to 38. The reported loss for online efforts in the first half of this year was down 41%, to $67 million, from $114 million a year ago. And counting savings from moving procurement, human resources, and other back-office functions online, Citigroup says Web technologies will cut $1 billion off annual costs by next year. "I promise you, we are going to be saving a lot more than we are spending," Maughan pledges. Now, Citigroup has a chance of seeing profits from its Web efforts in Maughan's lifetime.

RYDER SYSTEM, INC. Almost daily, Ryder System executives want to curse those yellow trucks. You know them—the can't-miss-'em rental vans. Ryder sold that business five years ago to concentrate on leasing commercial trucks and handling the transportation and logistics needs of other firms. But the company still gets regular queries—many via e-mail—about moving vans.

At least one Ryder executive thinks of the yellow trucks as a beacon in the night. John Wormwood, the company's director of e-commerce solutions, credits them with alerting Ryder to its Web muddle: It was consumers seeking to rent a van who pointed out what a mess the site was. "We got feedback from [would-be renters] saying 'the Web site is unusable, difficult to navigate,'" says Wormwood.

About 10 sites had sprung up, some without a link to Ryder.com, the corporate site that explains the company's business. Although Ryder sells used tractor-trailers, for instance, buying them online required a visit to usedtrucks.ryder.com. "It was really a patchwork quilt of navigation, colors, and styles," says Wormwood.

Ryder needed to unravel the threads. In late 1999, it created an e-commerce group, including staff from all its major divisions. They agreed that Ryder needed a common look and produced a style guide to lay out where logos, photos, and text should go on all Ryder Web pages.

A renewed focus on customers, and on making it a snap for them to use the Web, has driven the $5.3 billion company's e-strategy ever since. In a year when many companies are cutting their tech budgets, Ryder upped its spending 15%, to $100 million. Of that, $500,000 went toward a Web-site makeover this year. Before the redesign, it took 10 clicks to track a shipment. Since the new site was launched in July, the function is just one click from Ryder's home page. Before, there was no search mechanism. There is today.

These and other improvements have helped Ryder attract new customers, including Northrop Grumman. The defense contractor hopes to cut its transportation costs by taking advantage of better rates Ryder gets through bulk buys of cargo space. Northrop is pleased that it can electronically track the shipments every step of the way, so that it can adjust to any possible snafus. "We're able to pull out a lot of manual processes that sometimes introduce errors," says T.W. Scott, director of supply-chain management systems. And when parts arrive at a Northrop factory, you can be sure they won't be traveling in a yellow truck.

DEERE & CO. When the e-commerce craze hit in the mid-1990s, managers at equipment-maker Deere & Co. motored onto the Internet like everyone else. The 13 major Web initiatives that just one division put up, though, were narrowly focused, with overlapping missions. Three sites focused on used equipment alone: one to list it, one to sell it through an online marketplace, and one to support used-equipment dealers. The sites targeted Deere's largely Web-allergic dealers, not customers who bought Deere products and might save time by locating parts or seeking repair know-how online.

Two years ago, with the sites developing little traction, Deere figured there had to be a better way. So it hired consultants to help organize its site and advise the company on overall Net strategy. By the end of 2000, a plan was in place: The $13 billion company would create an e-business group to oversee Web initiatives for its financing arm and its equipment divisions targeting farmers, consumers, and construction companies. Deere would create one Web site with areas for each customer group, and it would enable customers to search for parts or information about equipment online. The site offers "a new set of tools that will be applied to everyone's day-to-day business," says Kirk Siefkas, Deere's chief information officer.

By centralizing everything at deere.com, the company not only controls its corporate image but also makes life easier for its 4,000 independent dealers and their customers. Consider the case of Brent Mellergaard, president of Circle Lazy H. Inc., a farm in Ellensburg, Wash. In the past, if he needed a new part for a machine, he would simply eyeball it and tell the local dealer what he thought he needed. Mistakes would happen, and he might lose time in the field by having to reorder the part. In April, Deere gave farmers access to JDParts at deere.com. Now Mellergaard can check the parts online, find a clear drawing, description, and stock number, and be sure that he is ordering what he needs. "There are a lot of parts that it helps with," he says. "It's hard to tell them apart sometimes."

Deere aims to make life easier for buyers of heavy equipment as well. It plans to roll out online tools that let customers configure their own backhoe loaders, combines, lawn mowers, or other machinery. They no longer have to flip through several-inch-thick catalogs or negotiate with dealers, saving everyone time.

What does Deere get out of all this? It hopes customers will stick with the company because it's easy to do business with. That, in the long run, is likely to prove more valuable than trying to make money through a used-equipment marketplace.

By Faith Keenan and Timothy J. Mullaney

91

THE NET AS A LIFELINE

A tough economic environment makes the Web even more important for companies attempting to cut costs, generate new revenues, and better serve customers

As America stood still in the wake of the September 11 attacks, casino and hotel operator Harrah's Entertainment Inc. faced a sharp downturn in business. The country was in no mood for a party, and few people were willing to hop a flight to Las Vegas. Occupancy rates at Harrah's flagship hotel soon dropped by more than 25%. So on Sept. 14, Harrah's launched a small counteroffensive: The company sent out targeted e-mails to thousands of customers it thought might want to take a trip to the tables and slots. The gambit worked, helping to fill nearly 4,000 rooms that otherwise would have gone empty. By Sept. 30, the hotel was back near 100% occupancy. "We were able to get our message out immediately over the Internet," says Harrah's Chairman Philip G. Satre.

The key to Harrah's success: This summer, the company linked its database of 24 million gamblers to its Web site and e-mail marketing system. A year ago, Harrah's wouldn't have been able to seize the day. It has long known who the highest rollers are, based on its records of customer habits: Many avid gamblers participate in a rewards program that allows the company to track their playing, using cards that can be plugged into slot machines or presented to pit bosses. Until this summer, though, reaching those players with targeted pitches required bulk mailings via snail mail. Now, when a customer clicks to Harrah's Web site from an e-mailed pitch, the company knows how much the player spends and can offer a tailored deal. The customer can then immediately book the room and a flight to get there, and reserve a seat for a show.

Harrah's beat the house odds. The September 11 attacks instantly made the toughest economic environment in a decade even worse. But for companies such as Harrah's that have spent the time and the money to beef up their Internet capabilities, the sting may not be as bad. With its innovative marketing, Harrah's rebounded more quickly after September 11 than other big casinos in Vegas, says Bear Stearns & Co. analyst Jason N. Ader.

Suddenly, the Internet has become a lifeline. Companies in a sales squeeze are looking to the Net as a tool for cutting costs, generating new revenue streams, trimming inventories, and serving customers and employees more efficiently. Sure, this was happening before the attacks. Today, though, those efforts are no longer just an advantage—they're urgent.

Still, jittery executives only want to fund projects that promise to pay off fast. With the military on the move in Afghanistan, consumer confidence flagging, and further terrorist attacks an ever-present threat, corporations fear the economy may be heading into a recession. So they are carefully choosing the Net projects they go ahead with based on hard-nosed calculations of return on investment. Vague Web initiatives that cost millions to simply build the brand are out, the residue of giddier dot-com days. "There's going to be a search for more short-term payback," says Hal Sirkin, e-commerce practice leader at Boston Consulting Group. "People are still thinking how to reinvent the company, but they may not take the big leaps that they would have a few months ago."

The projects getting the green light are those with proven track records for delivering results. Companies are putting human resources and customer service online so they can reduce the number of call-center employees. They're pressing ahead with supply-chain management initiatives—although often in smaller pieces than two years ago. And they're moving all aspects of purchasing to the Web, allowing them to slash internal costs or wring deeper discounts from suppliers. DuPont expects to save $400 million a year buying supplies online. The initiative's total cost: just $15 million over three years. And the British arm of laboratory equipment distributor Fisher Scientific International Inc. is investing less than $50,000 in an online network that zaps invoices directly into the accounting systems of customers and suppliers. The project should pay for itself in six months, and within two years should cut 80% of the $370,000 Fisher spends annually to process bills from suppliers.

The key is putting the money in the right place. While spending on Net initiatives isn't climbing as fast as it did a year ago, it's still going to rise by 9% over the next 12 months, according to AMR Research Inc. Granted, that's down from a predicted 11% increase before September 11, but better than the 3.7% increase in overall spending on technology Deutsche Banc Alex. Brown is expecting. The areas being funded? Supply-chain projects are now expected to grow by 9%, AMR says. Customer-focused initiatives, such as projects that let clients help themselves to info online, are going to see 6% growth. Product-development programs will grow by 5%. Indeed, most managers are keeping the Internet faith: An Accenture Ltd. study this summer found 57% of 840 execs worldwide say e-commerce initiatives are fundamental to their company's survival.

What might endanger that survival is too much emphasis on short-term results. With the economy slipping into a recession, key longer-range projects could be put on hold. Most at risk: Squishier initiatives that don't show an immediate ROI, says Erik Brynjolfsson, co-director of the Center for e-Business at Massachusetts Institute of Technology. One example: knowledge management projects, which help companies better tap into and share the information their employees possess. "Firms that focus too much on cost savings may miss out on the productivity gains down the road," says Brynjolfsson.

Getting those gains requires more than just a technology fix. Simply grafting computers and software onto existing business processes will do little to give a company the productivity boost the Web-savviest companies are seeing. The real payoff comes when companies change the way they interact with customers and suppliers, organize their factories, and move products around the world. PC giant Dell Computer Corp. has been honing its Web operations for years, so today it knows what parts it has and what it's going to need as orders stream in. Dell can do this because it requires key suppliers to be linked over the Web. The Net makes all of this work faster, but long ago Dell built its entire business around super-tight integration with both customers and suppliers. "The Web expanded Dell's capabilities, but much of the architecture of its success was in place before the Net," says David C. Mowery, a professor at the Haas

Web Smart for a Changed World

As corporate profits fall and companies adapt to a more sober reality in the wake of the September 11 attacks, spending on e-business initiatives is getting more focused—with a renewed emphasis on projects that promise a quick return. Internet outlays are expected to rise by 9% this year, compared with 3.7% for tech spending overall. Here's what's still getting funded.

WINNING CUSTOMERS

The problem: For years, Casino operator Harrah's has had a database of customers it woos with cheap hotel rooms. But getting promotions out meant using snail-mail. The info wasn't connected to the Web, so it was hard to craft timely offers.

The solution: Harrah's linked the database to its Web site, allowing customers to go online and book rooms at discount prices based on their past spending habits.

The payoff: After September 11, occupancy at Harrah's flagship Las Vegas hotel fell by 25%. The chain sent e-mails with bargain offers, filling 4,000 rooms that otherwise would have stayed empty and bringing the hotel back to near-100% occupancy by Sept. 30.

SMART PROCUREMENT

The problem: With the chemical industry in a slump and DuPont's earnings expected to slide by half this year, the company needed to cut costs.

The solution: One $15 million initiative will streamline DuPont's purchasing of everything from software to sulphur dioxide. The project eliminates faxes and purchase orders, moving procurement online, where employees can order goods from suppliers that sell to DuPont at a discount.

The payoff: The company has cut procurement costs by $200 million—a 5% reduction—this year, and expects another $200 million in annual savings by 2003. Now, a typical order is processed in one day instead of five.

PAPERLESS PROCESS

The problem: Getting results of building inspections in Miami-Dade County was too slow. Inspectors schlepped to construction sites with pen and paper, then submitted reports to data-entry clerks. Results were available 48 hours later.

The solution: Today, inspectors fill out their reports on a wireless hand-held computer, then zap them off to a Web site where they're posted minutes later for builders to see.

The payoff: The county estimates the $880,000 project saves at least $175,000 in payroll and other expenses annually and frees the data-entry clerks to field inquiries about permits and other matters.

DIGITIZING DEALERS

The problem: Dealers for office furniture maker Herman Miller had to phone company reps to track orders, get shipping dates, or product information—waiting up to a week to make final arrangements.

The solution: This summer, Miller completed a $1 million project that links it to its 400 dealers via the Web, giving them easy access to info.

The payoff: Dealers say it helps them better serve customers by giving them instant access to order and shipping info without having to call. The company says facilitating access by dealers will encourage them to recommend its products over those of other makers.

TUNING UP PRODUCTION

The problem: Mexican steelmaker Hylsa's Bar & Rod Div. needed to improve customer satisfaction and lower inventory costs at its two plants.

The solution: Hylsa spent $800,000 on software, computers, and consulting to automate the process of planning production, managing inventories, and scheduling deliveries.

The payoff: The new system helped improve on-time deliveries from 70% to 88%, and boosted inventory turns—a measure of efficiency—from 2.2 to 2.8 times monthly. Next, the division plans to hook up electronically with its suppliers to coordinate production schedules.

PEOPLE POWER

The problem: Bank of America was spending nearly $100 million annually on human resources paperwork such as enrollment for its retirement programs. Simple changes often required weeks to complete.

The solution: The company moved those programs to the Web. Managers now log on to record promotions and raises. And all 140,000 employees can change doctors, monitor retirement accounts, and submit travel expenses online.

The payoff: The bank is saving with the system. Some processes, such as benefits enrollment, now take just minutes to process because they're done online. That's down from months under the old system.

Data: AMR Research, Deutsche Banc Alex. Brown, Company reports, BusinessWeek

School of Business at the University of California at Berkeley.

Dell's Web smarts allowed it to react quickly after September 11. While its efficiency put Dell at risk as borders were closed and air travel was shut down, it also helped the company make it through the disaster without a hitch. When the attacks began, Dell instantly sized up its operations and figured out where supplies might be disrupted. It quickly ramped up production in factories in Europe and Asia and filled orders from there. And with the Web giving it a real-time view into orders pending, it prioritized orders and filled the most important first. At the same time, Dell salespeople were able to look online to see the configurations that could be assembled and shipped quickly despite the disruption—and then steer customers accordingly. "The company with the most efficient supply chain was able to weather this the best," says Dell Chairman Michael S. Dell.

Indeed, companies that lost computers in the attacks were asking for thousands of replacements. The upshot: Dell expects a profit of $410 million for its third quarter ending Nov. 2, while competitors Compaq Computer Corp. and Gateway Inc. have told Wall Street to expect losses. Compaq was unable to ship $300 million worth of computers due to supply-chain disruptions after the attack.

Other companies are more fully embracing the Web. Copier maker Ricoh Co., for example, had long planned a gala sales meeting for more than 3,000 customers on Sept. 12 at the Jacob K. Javits Convention Center in New York City. The event, headlined by former Vice-Presidents Al Gore and Bob Dole, was designed to show off Ricoh gear and unveil a new online service for storing and sharing documents via the Web. As the terrorist attacks unfolded less than 24 hours before the gathering was scheduled to start, Ricoh quickly cancelled the meeting. The event is now likely to be rescheduled for next year, but Ricoh didn't want to wait that long to introduce the new service, called Document Mall.

Instead, Ricoh turned to the Web. The company plans to go ahead with the launch using a collaboration service called WebEx, which lets people see and talk to each other while sharing files online. This fall, 6,000 Ricoh salespeople and customers will be invited to Web seminars on Document Mall. Ricoh estimates it will save at least $60,000 in travel expenses, as well as countless employee-hours of flying and trundling through airports—while keeping skittish workers closer to home in these troubled times. "It's much more productive for us to do the rollout this way," says Isabel Kaplan, Ricoh's head of e-business marketing.

These days there's a lot less experimentation in Web projects. For example, two years ago Otis Elevator Co. thought it could goose its revenues by placing screens linked to the Web in elevator cars. These would present a constant feed of news—liberally salted with ads. Problem was, during the Internet boom years Otis faced upstarts with oodles of venture-capital funding that were giving away similar screen systems for free, making up the difference in ad sales. "The business model doesn't work with free screens," says Ron Beaver, Otis' vice-president for information systems. A year ago, Otis jettisoned the initiative.

You might think that was the end of Otis spending another penny on Internet projects. Wrong. This year, it more than doubled its Internet budget and expects a 50% increase in 2002. The bulk of the new money will go to an effort linking Otis with its suppliers and customers via the Web to streamline the way parts move in and out of its factories. Beaver estimates that half the elevator parts Otis sends out to construction sites arrive before they're needed, and end up sitting around for weeks or months, meaning the company carries them as inventory much longer than necessary. The new Web system should help the company better monitor whether a cable, a cab, or a carton of call buttons is ready to ship, because it will be in constant contact with its suppliers. And with progress reports available online, Otis will know what stage the builder has reached and when it's ready for each part.

Otis also is tapping the Net to slash repair bills. The company has a system that allows technicians at 10 centers around the globe to monitor elevators via a Net link. When a door sticks or the car doesn't stop at floor level, the elevator zips off a signal alerting Otis to send someone to fix it. Today, some 20% of elevators Otis maintains worldwide use the system—a number it hopes to nearly double by the end of next year. The payoff is huge: Since Otis no longer has to dispatch repair staff as often to check for problems, elevators with remote monitoring require only one-third the number of visits as those without the system. That has helped Otis keep its North American repair staff steady while increasing the number of elevators it services by 10%, to 120,000, over the last year.

These days, Web projects must be no-brainers. The payoff from some simple initiatives such as moving procurement online can be so huge you wonder why they didn't happen years ago. At DuPont, for example, purchasing on the Web has cut the cost of buying supplies by $200 million—a 5% reduction in the first year of the $15 million project. Better yet, the chemical giant expects another $200 million in annual savings by 2003—numbers that sound pretty good at DuPont, where analysts expect to see profits slide by half this year. Before the system was in place, employees ordered supplies, such as pipe fittings and lab chemicals, using phone calls, faxes, or by simply running out and picking stuff up. Now, employees log onto a Web site to buy virtually everything. DuPont can better control what gets bought—and can funnel orders to vendors who promise price breaks.

Corporate chieftains are figuring out that the Net can help them better weather tough times. No doubt, the terrorist attacks made a bad situation worse. But economic turmoil also creates opportunities for those who place their chips on the right numbers. The smart money is betting that getting Web smart is like having an ace in the hole.

By David Rocks
Contributing: Andrew Park, Aixa M. Pascual, Darnell Little, and Jeanette Brown

"The Net as a Lifeline," pp. EB16–EB23. Reprinted from the October 29, 2001 issue of *Business Week E.Biz* by special permission, copyright © 2001 by The McGraw-Hill Companies, Inc.

Priced to Move

Retailers Try to Get Leg Up on Markdowns With New Software

ShopKo, Used to Slashing Items Repeatedly, Finds Making Fewer Cuts Pays

Cleaning Up on Fleece Vests

By Amy Merrick
Staff Reporter of The Wall Street Journal

It's one of the great nail-biter decisions of retailing: just when to hit the markdown panic button.

Discount chain ShopKo Stores Inc. got nervous this spring, as shopper after shopper shunned its stretchy nylon track pants. They had a comfortable elastic waist. They had bright, contrasting stripes down the sides. But they simply weren't budging at their original price of $16.99.

ShopKo didn't want to resort to its strategy of years past: whittle the price a bit here and there, then chop it methodically once a month—to $9.99, then $7.99, then $3.99. Instead, it took only two measured swipes, marking them down to $10.79 on average in early May, then to $9.75 a month later. And it held firm there. With the new pricing plan, ShopKo sold out the last 12,500 pairs during the three-month clearance period, for a gross profit margin of 31%—nearly double its forecast.

Airplane Seats and Bikinis

It wasn't a random decision. ShopKo is one of a handful of retailers, including J.C. Penney Co., L.L. Bean Inc., Liz Claiborne Inc. and Gymboree Corp., trying to perfect the science of the markdown. They have been experimenting with sophisticated new software programs to test principles similar to "yield management," which airlines mastered years ago to eke out the maximum profit from every seat. Like a seat on a particular flight, an item such as a bikini is in demand for a limited time; as the end of the season approaches, its value to customers plummets. A big challenge: trying to outfox customers who have been more willing to wait and wait for a bargain.

Using number-crunching consultants, armed with mathematical models pioneered by think-tank researchers and astrophysicists, the stores analyze historical sales data to pinpoint just how long to hold out before they need to cut a price—and by just how much.

Their progress marks a new step in a growing trend toward highly flexible prices—for everything from mortgages to eBay merchandise. Instead of taking a one-price-fits-all approach, buyers and sellers are increasingly meeting in customized marketplaces transformed by technology.

With exploding competition from discounters and specialty stores, markdowns are soaring, making them a decisive issue in retailing. Marked-down goods, which accounted for just 8% of department-store sales three decades ago, have climbed to around 20%, according to the National Retail Federation.

Retailers hate markdowns. Discount an item too late, and stores are stuck with truckloads of inventory. Too early, and they lose profits as people snap up items thrown on the bargain table prematurely. Last month, Gap Inc. said its profit margins on June sales fell well below its internal forecast after it was forced to take deeper-than-expected markdowns on a mountain of merchandise, from Gap T-shirts to Old Navy shorts. And last week, Neiman Marcus Group Inc. cited steeper-than-planned markdowns for the second time in as many months in estimating a loss for its fiscal fourth quarter, ended July 28.

Retailing Wild Card

"You can intelligently and consistently predict a lot of other components of your business," says Steve Raish, chief information officer of J.C. Penney. But "markdowns—in particular seasonal markdowns—are one of the least predictable elements."

The technology, still fairly new and untested, requires detailed and accurate sales data to work well. And even if the new software programs can help crack the markdown riddle, they can't solve other problems, such as poorly chosen merchandise or a weak economy. "This is not the savior to the profitability of the company. This is just one more tool in the tool chest," says William Podany, the 55-year-old president and chief executive of ShopKo, based in Green Bay, Wis.

End-of-season sales—held two or three times a year—first came into vogue in the 1950s, as an easy way to clear inventory and free up cash. In the 1960s, department stores began adding back-to-school sales to draw in customers as the summer tailed off.

But as discounters improved their apparel selections over the years, department stores have found themselves constantly staging sales to stay competitive. "They don't even name sales anymore, because it would have to be called the 'June 13 sale,' followed by the 'June 14 sale,'" says Erik

Gordon, a marketing professor at the University of Florida's Warrington College of Business.

Much of the attention on markdowns in recent years has been regulatory, as state attorneys general charged numerous retailers with deceiving consumers by raising prices and then offering a discount off the inflated price. In some cases, investigators could not find any evidence that the goods had ever been sold at the so-called "original" price. Just last month, Kmart Corp. responded to a complaint from the Jewelry Advertising Review Program, a coalition of local Better Business Bureaus, which contended that Kmart was claiming to sell its jewelry at discounts from "original prices" that were not frequently offered. Without admitting wrongdoing, Kmart said it had changed its jewelry pricing to sell its jewelry at regular prices for at least 183 days each year.

ShopKo, a chain of 141 stores that likens itself to Target Corp.'s discount stores, began hunting for a technical edge early last year. The 39-year-old retailer, which also operates Pamida, a 229-store chain of small mostly rural discount stores, was facing a difficult year in 2000, which ultimately ended with disappointing sales of $3.5 billion and a $15.8 million loss. It subsequently had to cut jobs, close some stores and put remodeling and expansion plans on hold.

As part of its effort to get a handle on the business, it turned to Spotlight Solutions Inc., a Mason, Ohio, start-up that is one of the leaders in the markdown-software field. Spotlight's software uses mathematical models created by researchers such as Dr. Dale Achabal, a bespectacled professor who acts as an adviser to the company and sits on its board.

Trained in marketing and regional economics, Dr. Achabal in 1980 co-founded the Retail Management Institute at Santa Clara University, a private Jesuit school in California. He currently directs the institute, which includes the Retail Workbench, a corporate-sponsored think tank.

Inside the Mission-style building that houses the university's business school, researchers pow-wow with retail executives about common complaints: managing inventory, measuring advertising effectiveness and improving their supply chains. In one current project, Santa Clara researchers are analyzing consumer-preference data to help retailers create the best possible product assortments.

In the early 1990s, retailers complained that they were overwhelmed by all the sales results bar-code technology was vacuuming up, Dr. Achabal says. "They had more data, but they didn't have better information to make decisions," he says. So he and others began working on computer programs that would make sense of this mass of data. In 1993, Target installed an early system based on his research.

Impressed with that work, Shopko set up a pilot project last August to test the software, called Markdown Optimizer. Some forecasts from the Spotlight software proved to be dead-on. It correctly predicted that sales of boys' fleece vests would peak in mid-August. So instead of taking its typical markdowns of 10% or 20% again and again, ShopKo followed the software's recommendation of taking a single 20% markdown in November, according to Spotlight. It made a 30.2% gross profit margin on the vests during the three-month clearance period—a huge improvement over the previous year, Spotlight analysis shows.

By Feb. 1, the end of the pilot project, sales for the roughly 300 products in the test—everything from sheets to lotion to baby bottles—were 14% higher than a year earlier. By contrast, ShopKo's overall same-store sales during the fourth quarter were flat. More important, its gross profit margin percentage rose 24% for the test merchandise. And ShopKo figures it sold 13% more of each product at regular price than it would have in the past.

'Seasonal Demand Curve'

Behind the surprising gains: pricing analysis similar to that developed by the airlines, which can calculate with great precision just how many seats to hold open at premium fares for last-minute passengers and how many to sell ahead of time at lower prices. By analyzing several years' worth of sales data from similar items, Spotlight's retail software estimates a "seasonal demand curve" for each new product.

Sometimes resembling a jagged peak, other times a smooth wave, the curve predicts how many units would sell each week at various prices. For merchandise with short-term appeal—the bikini, for example—sales typically climb for several weeks, spike, then trail down until the "outdate," or the date a retailer wants to sell out of the item. The software also uses sales history to predict how sensitive customer demand will be to price changes, what economists call "price elasticity."

To create its new markdown program, ShopKo fed three years' worth of sales data from each store into Spotlight's computers, which suggested markdown prices based on how quickly the product category was expected to sell in each of the company's six store groups. The system uses the data to calibrate a system of mathematical models that incorporate such factors as price elasticity and the number of weeks until the outdate. It then solves equations to determine the most profitable price cuts for each product.

Software, however, can't predict unexpected events such as a major snowstorm or a surprise sale at a rival store. So it "learns" during the season, according to the developers of the programs, adjusting recommendations weekly based on new sales data.

"There will always be things you don't expect," says Scott Friend, president and chief executive of ProfitLogic, a Cambridge, Mass.-based competitor of Spotlight that draws heavily from the talent pool at Harvard University and the Massachusetts Institute of Technology. But because the software systems start with more precise forecasts and adjust their recommendations to early sales results, he adds, "on average, we are a lot more accurate" than past practices.

Before Spotlight, ShopKo was drowning in sales data. To determine which items were stagnating on shelves, store buyers had to sift through stacks of weekly reports with overall sales of each product. The reports also listed inventory levels and how many weeks remained until the outdate. With thousands of different products selling in more than 100 stores, overwhelmed buyers had to plan most markdowns before each season began. They revised their plans twice a month, marking down an item at the same time across all stores.

That chain-wide approach, common to many retailers, often sacrifices goods that could have sold at full price in some stores, and ends up leaving too much merchandise unsold in others. Another common practice is to chip away at price tags, with lots of small discounts. Dr. Achabal's research concluded that a combination of two markdowns will never be as profitable as a single markdown. Arriving early enough to tempt customers, the first markdown gives the greatest boost to profits, and extra price cuts simply add profit-eroding labor costs.

Before recruiting Spotlight, ShopKo had tried shifting its markdown dates. At one point, it carried some leftover merchandise into the next year, a practice it has abandoned. For the most stubborn clearance merchandise, it even offered an extra 25% off. "That created a lot of traffic, but it was terribly hurtful to our gross margin performance," says Mr. Podany, the ShopKo chief executive. "I'm going on my 33rd year in the business, and I've never mastered this."

Within a few weeks of starting to review forecasts in the pilot project in October, employees saw surprising recommendations. In its high-volume "superstores," for example, the average first markdown suggested by the program was 25.7%. In the lowest-volume stores, it was 46.3%—nearly twice as much. Says Paul Burrows, ShopKo's chief information officer, "We never would have been able to tackle that manually."

But, right out of the box, the software hit some bumps. On baby bottles, for example, the program called for an immediate 90% markdown. Thinking the discount too steep, ShopKo tried it in just a few stores. There, the bottles sold out far too quickly—within several days. "People who didn't even have babies were buying baby bottles," jokes Mr. Burrows. ShopKo says that pricing move was an anomaly, caused by a quirk in the selling pattern to which the system needed more time to adjust. It has since ironed out the problem by setting a 50% cap on first markdowns.

Cutting Labor Costs

Smarter markdowns also saved labor costs. ShopKo has calculated that it costs 18 cents to change the price on a single garment tag, and 24 cents to revise a shelf label. Whenever it lowers prices, clerks scurry through the stores in the early morning, wielding "price guns" that spit out brightly colored stickers with a new price. Before using the software, ShopKo frequently marked down products three or four times. Now, it often does it only once or twice.

Mr. Podany is waiting for a full year of data to pass final judgment on the new method. But the retailer is moving ahead with plans to use it throughout its stores by this fall, and it even hopes to eventually create a separate markdown schedule for every location.

On many items, the variation can be just pennies. But on more expensive merchandise, the program may suggest widely different markdowns in the same town. On a recent day in Green Bay, for example, one gas grill cost $189.99, or full price, at the ShopKo in the Bay Park Square mall. At a store across the Fox River, just a 20-minute drive away, the grill cost $121.59.

ShopKo is counting on shoppers to gravitate to the most convenient locations. It doesn't expect many customers to trudge from one store to another to compare markdowns. "I just don't have the time," says Connie Smith, a paper-mill operator leaving a ShopKo store in Menasha, Wis., recently. During the pilot test, ShopKo surveyed its store employees and found that customers didn't seem to notice—or care about—different markdowns at nearby stores.

Ethical Marketing in a Consumer-Oriented World: Appraisal and Challenges

Help Is on the Way For People Who Hate Spam, Telemarketing

By Thomas E. Weber

When it comes to intrusive advertising, many consumers would like the option to simply be left alone. Now regulators want to make it easier to say "no thanks" to both unwanted telemarketing calls and junk e-mail. Unfortunately for spam haters, stemming the flood of e-mail will probably prove much more difficult than stopping annoying phone calls.

First, the good news about telemarketing. The Federal Trade Commission is seeking comment on a proposal for a national "do not call" registry, a database of consumers who don't want to get telemarketers' calls. Consumers could call a toll-free number to add their numbers to the list. Once a number was there, it would be illegal for a telemarketer to call it.

Individual marketers already maintain do-not-call lists, and many states have do-not-call programs. In New York, for instance, consumers can sign up at www.nynocall.com. But the FTC plan would cover all 50 states with a one-stop number.

Not surprisingly, telemarketers don't like the idea. As the Direct Marketing Association points out—with some merit—tougher restrictions on marketing risk treading on free-speech rights. The group also argues that the FTC's plan isn't needed because the association already maintains a do-not-call registry that members are required to abide by.

However, to get on the association's do-not-call list, consumers must either submit a request in writing or pay $5 to register online. That's too complicated. More to the point, marketers who violate government-backed do-not-call lists face fines and injunctions, while those who violate the association's "telephone preference service" face only possible expulsion from the group. The FTC is looking for comments on its proposal, so visit www.ftc.gov if you want to weigh in.

If only there were a "do not e-mail" list. Unfortunately, while the do-not-call concept has proved effective in the world of phone calls, it has been all but useless on the Internet. The first rule of combating spam is: never click on an e-mail's "unsubscribe" link or follow any instructions that promise to remove you from a list. Unscrupulous spammers use those responses to verify that they've reached a real live person instead of an abandoned mailbox.

That's a shame, because mainstream marketers will typically respect "remove me" requests. Yet the endless ranks of spammers pitching pornography, diet schemes and sure-fire investments have trained savvy Net users to shun unsubscribe options. Unlike telemarketing, which requires call centers and warm bodies to reach masses of consumers, spamming is so cheap and easy that dishonest e-mail marketers have run rampant.

Even when an e-mail appears to come from a trustworthy source, consumers need to be wary. Last week I got a message that appeared to be from the makers of the popular Norton Utilities software packages. In the "From:" field, the e-mail claimed to be from "Norton SystemWorks 2002," and the pitch offered me more than $300 of Norton software for the absurdly low price of $29.99.

When I looked more closely, though, I found that the actual address for "Norton SystemWorks 2002" was "postmaster@dlb-direct.com." And in tiny print at the bottom, the message explained that "you have signed up to receive offers from dlbDirect.com" or one of its partners.

Oh, really? I tried phoning dlbDirect.com to inquire exactly when and with whom I had signed up. I got an answering machine. Then I did a little bit of Internet detective work and found the dlbDirect domain name and another phone number, which led me to a company called Trancos in Redwood City, Calif. More voicemail. I'm still waiting for someone to return one of the messages I left.

Next I called Symantec, maker of the Norton software line. A spokeswoman there told me that—surprise!—the e-mail definitely hadn't been sent on Symantec's behalf. Furthermore, she said, such bargain offers often turn out to be unauthorized copies, not legitimate software. "If you get an e-mail that says 90% off, you really should question that," she said. "Some things are just way too good to be true."

An experience like that underscores the need for consumers to know whom they're dealing with. A new program from TRUSTe, a privacy group backed by the technology industry, and ePrivacy Group, a consulting concern, should help. The program, called Trusted Sender, will place a forge-proof seal of approval on commercial e-mail from legitimate marketers.

Meanwhile, the Direct Marketing Association just released new e-mail guidelines for its members. Among other things, the guidelines require marketers to give e-mail recipients a link or notice they can use to opt out of future online solicitations. Some privacy advocates would prefer that consumers instead opt in to receive commercial e-mail, but at least this is a step in the right direction.

Finally, the FTC now says it will aggressively pursue spammers who use deceptive practices, including the use of fake opt-out notices. None of these approaches will eliminate junk e-mail, but together they could help differentiate mainstream marketers from purveyors of shady spam. That will let consumers opt out of mailing lists from companies that will respect their choice—and hopefully make indiscriminate spamming less attractive.

Web Ads Growing Intrusive

POP-UPS AIM TO DISRUPT

By Doug Tsuruoka
Investor's Business Daily

Everybody's seen them. You click to a Web page and begin reading an item like a film review. Suddenly an ad bloops onto your screen out of nowhere.

The ad blocks the text with a pitch for credit cards or online gambling. It takes an extra mouse click to make it go away.

These pop-ups aren't new. Plenty of advertisers use them. But there's been a blitz of such ads lately. And they're getting bigger, flashier and more disruptive.

"As the downturn drives companies to seek revenue by all available means, it's not surprising to see ads like these emerge into the consumer mainstream," said Panos Anastassiadis, chief executive of Cyveillance Inc., a firm that tracks the Internet.

The most intrusive pop-ups cover the entire screen. They hawk things like movies and use effects such as images that fade in and out.

Others flash their messages across the screen for several seconds before disappearing. There's nothing you can do to make them go away before then.

Among the Web sites featuring them: search engine Yahoo Inc., the Los Angeles Times' latimes.com and entertainment trade paper Daily Variety's variety.com.

Cyveillance estimates that 30% of the Internet's top 100 Web sites use intrusive ads. That's up sharply from six months ago, when analysts say 15% to 20% of sites used them.

Some say this shows how desperate the online ad industry is. With ad revenue slipping, advertisers and Web publishers are going all-out to get a rise out of consumers. Banner ads, which disappear from screens unless you click on them, aren't selling well. Hence the stress on developing ads that consumers can't ignore.

'Banners Are Irrelevant'

Jim Nail, an analyst at Forrester Research Inc., says marketers dislike banners because they have bad click-through rates—a key measure of an ad's success with consumers.

"Banners are irrelevant," Nail said. "They don't grab consumer attention."

Many pop-ups use technology that triggers them as soon as a surfer hits a Web site. They tap into a browser's JavaScript functions, HTML programming codes and Flash animation features to play their interactive effects.

The most common pop-up uses a technology called spawning. It launches a window containing an ad on your screen as soon as you enter a site.

Cyveillance found that spawning was one of the top 10 techniques used by Internet advertisers to expose Web surfers to unsolicited ads.

Another technique is called mousetrapping. It prevents users from backing out or exiting a Web page while the ad's running.

About 5.2% of all sites on the Internet use mousetrapping, according to Cyveillance.

Intrusive ads have another purpose. By making users wait or use extra clicks, Web sites running the ads can raise their visit-time statistics. Higher rankings help attract more advertisers.

Pop-ups aren't the only in-your-face ads these days.

Another is the so-called shoshkele ad. It has animated images that float across your screen when you click onto a Web site. An example is an owl from the recent "Harry Potter" movie. It flew across the screen of anyone who visited the home page of online service about.com recently.

Then there's the pop-under ad. The ad opens on the Web page under your browser and appears on the screen as soon as the browser is closed.

One of the best-known of this type is an ad for the tiny wireless video camera from Seattle-based X10 Wireless Technology Inc.

The X10 ads, which use women models, raised eyebrows when they hit the Web six months ago. They've since

Top Tactics

Online merchants have a number of ideas to lure Web surfers to their sites

1. Spawning: Launches a new browser window when Web surfers arrive at a site, or when they leave one.

2. Mousetrapping: Disables the user's ability to go back, exit or close while viewing a page.

3. Invisible seeding: Uses a hidden source code to get an ad to pop up in search engine traffic even though it has nothing to do with what consumers are looking for.

4. Unauthorized software downloads: Invades a consumer's privacy by leaving behind software on the computer that contains embedded advertising or tracking capabilities.

5. Spoof pages: Pages placed on a Web site to attract search engine traffic for higher rankings. These pages can contain selected words, brands, slogans or references to personalities like movie stars. These tactics which draw traffic from consumers who may be searching for information on an altogether different subject.

6. Typo-piracy and cyber-squatting: Web sites that play word games by using misspellings and derivations of a popular brand to divert traffic to their site. It is not uncommon to see thousands of derivations of popular brand names in registered domain names.

7. Changing home pages or favorites: Unauthorized substitution of a new home page setting or changes to a user's "favorites" list while they are visiting a Web site. Approximately 1.4% of sites on the Internet engage in one of these two intrusive tactics.

8. Visible seeding: Mixing ad slogans and mention of popular brands with proprietary content on a site to raise search engine rankings. Placing a brand name in the title bar at the top of a window would be one such example.

9. Mislabeling links: False labeling of hyperlinks that send the shopper to an unintended destination.

10. Framing: The shoppers think they have clicked out of a site, but they haven't. Users are kept on the original site while viewing the content of another, through the original site's window. This way, the original site can increase ad revenue via higher visit time statistics.

(Cont.)

been upstaged by more disruptive ads.

The new ads have lots of critics. Some consumers have started online clubs and chat rooms with names like "Pop-ups Must Die" to rage against them.

Some tech firms also have found a niche by selling software that filters out pop-ups and other types of unsolicited ads.

The software does this by stopping the ad from running before it has time to download on your screen.

One frequent complaint about pop-up and similar ads is that they steal bandwidth by taking up space in a computer's pipeline to the Web. This clogs the downloading of other data from the Net, and can lead to system crashes.

Intrusive ads may irk some. But Joe Apprendi, executive vice president of Eyeblaster Inc., says they're the wave of the future.

Eyeblaster is an Internet platform provider that lets advertisers visit its site and design pop-ups and other ads. Advertisers then take these ads to Web publishers, which run them.

Like TV Commercials

Apprendi thinks full-page, pop-up ads that run on screens for 10 or 15 seconds will become the norm now that old-fashioned banner ads have failed.

Consumers also will be forced to watch them as part of the trade-off for visiting an otherwise free Web site, such as Yahoo or about.com.

"Online advertising is going to resemble the commercial breaks you have on TV, though the ads will be of much shorter duration," Apprendi said.

He says Web publishers and advertisers will be drawn to these ads because they're one of the few workable ways to grab consumer attention.

Consumers will get used to the new format the same way they got used to TV commercials, he says.

"Using a full-page ad also means you have more screen to deliver engaging and entertaining ad content," Apprendi said.

Greg Stuart, chief executive of the Interactive Advertising Bureau, a trade group, says consumers shouldn't fret about Net ads becoming too intrusive.

Web publishers are still trying to find a balance between meeting the needs of marketers and consumers. Eventually, he says, that balance will be found.

"Web publishers won't run amok with these ads because they'd lose their audience," Stuart said.

"Web Ads Growing Intrusive," *Investor's Business Daily*, January 9, 2002. Reprinted by permission.

95

Peek-a-Boo, I See You—Clearly

Slumping Eyeglass Business Sets Its Sights on Toddlers; Better for Vision or Profits?

By Nancy Ann Jeffrey

Staff Reporter of The Wall Street Journal

Mallory Tivey used to hate her glasses so much she actually avoided putting them on in the morning. Now, she's so happy with the frames, she slips them on first thing—even before asking her mother for her sippy cup.

"She looks adorable," says Kelly Tivey of her two-year-old daughter, who got her wire specs a few months ago.

The $16 billion-a-year optical industry has set its sights on a new market: tots. With sales to adults slumping, eyeglass companies have stepped up marketing efforts not only to youngsters, but to toddlers and babies. Kids as young as one can now get everything from "Tiny Tot" frames by Fisher-Price to grown-up-looking copper models from OshKosh B'Gosh. A pitchman for Disney's kiddie frames? One-eyed Mike, the ugly but popular star of "Monsters, Inc." And business is doing well, with makers reporting sales increases of 10% to 25% in the past two years.

But do tykes really need glasses? Makers say eye problems in kids tend to get overlooked, and along with many optometrists, they're pushing for state-mandated eye exams for youngsters. But many doctors say the problem is nowhere near as big as manufacturers and optometrists claim, and that only a fraction of the youngest kids need glasses. They point out that many prescriptions often treat mild farsightedness, which is normal in young children and often lessens over time. And then there's the pocketbook issue: The flood of fancy, name-brand frames coming on the market can cost triple generic ones.

"It sounds more to me like a marketing scheme than a public health plan," says James Sprague, a pediatric ophthalmologist in McLean, Va.

Still, the pitch is catching on with parents across the country. For Jacquie Samsel of Roseville, Calif., all it took was the memory of being razzed as "four-eyes" for wearing "cat-eye" frames as a kid. After first getting her son Austin pretty plain glasses when he was just 14 months old, Mrs. Samsel has moved up the fashion chain in recent years. Her latest pick? A pair of $200 wire frames that make Austin look "like the boy from 'Jerry Maguire,'" says the homemaker.

In Falls Church, Va., Don Hammer merely wanted to satisfy his fashion-conscious five-year-old, Kathryn Ellen. When the doctor announced she needed glasses to correct a lazy eye and farsightedness, the kindergartener insisted on a pair of blue, octagonal frames from Esprit. "They're very elegant," says Mr. Hammer of the $250 specs.

Back in the mid-to-late '90s when the optical business was growing at a healthy clip, no one was very interested in kids' glasses, which made up less than 10% of the market. Usually, only children with serious eye problems saw eye doctors, and then only after a pediatrician or a parent noticed something amiss. But with business down 4% last year, and adults buying new glasses only every two years (it used to be every 16 months in the early '90s), the industry needed some help.

Courting the Little People

Their solution? Go after littler people. This spring, Nouveau Eyewear plans to send hundreds of doctors and optical shops copies of the coming book "Magenta Gets Glasses," about how the "Blue's Clues" character got her eyes checked. The Kenmark Group, which makes Hush Puppies' "Pups" line, is giving away stuffed animals to snag kids' loyalties. And then there's ClearVision Optical, makers of the "Tiny Tot" specs: In the past two years, the firm has seen sales of Fisher-Price glasses for infants to four-year-olds rise 15%.

Experts say the moves are well-timed to coincide with an expanding kid population and their parents' obsession with designer logos. Not only do fashion glasses cost between $150 and $300 a pop, but growing tots can need replacement frames as often as three times a year. "It's a very lucrative market if we can catch a young child," says David Friedfeld, president of the company that makes Fisher-Price glasses.

But how can doctors even tell if kids too small to read have vision problems? Creatively. Glen Steele, an optometrist in Memphis, Tenn., moves Mom and Dad around the exam room and watches to see if baby's eyes follow. Jim Rooney, an optician in St. Louis, entertains little customers with a Mickey Mouse hand puppet while he adjusts their frames. And when Wendy James of Canton, Texas, recently brought her 2 1/2-year-old quadruplets to have their eyes checked (three wear glasses), the doctor turned on a dancing Santa Claus figure to attract the focus of his little patients.

Performing Better in School

Advocates for mandatory eye exams, largely optometrists and eyeglass makers, say such tactics help catch problems early and ensure normal development. "When a child gets frustrated in the classroom, he doesn't do well," says Joel Zaba, an optometrist in Virginia Beach, Va. And the

Specs for Toddlers

Eyeglass outfits are stepping up their efforts to court younger and younger kids, including one- and two-year olds. Here are some of today's choices (lenses not included).

NAME/MANUFACTURER	AGE	PRICE	COMMENT
Barbie Rem	girls four to 10	$75 to $90	Only one Barbie doll has glasses, but the company is pushing a dozen styles.
Disney Marchon	infant to 9	$90 to $110	The models are plain or have small Mickey Mouse icons at the temples.
Fisher-Price ClearVision	infant to 8	$90 to $129	Frames are among the higher priced on the market. Infant styles have flexible ear coils to keep frames on heads.
Hush Puppies Pups Kenmark	four to 12	$98	The company makes glasses for both kids and adults, but the kids' "Pups" models are doing best, with sales having doubled in four years.
Osh Kosh B'Gosh Logo of the Americas	one to eight	$99	After company redesigned collection for a more adult look about a year ago, sales grew 10%.
Sesame Street Zyloware	two to eight	$80 to $120	While other companies are going more sophisticated, the company has put Elmo, rubber ducks and musical notes on its frames.

movement is picking up steam: Kentucky has passed a law requiring parents to have their preschoolers' eyes checked by a specialist before entering public school, and optometrists are pushing for similar laws in at least six other states.

But some experts complain that having a specialist check little kids' eyes is unnecessary, since most pediatricians do that anyway. What's more, though they don't think the wrong glasses would hurt a child's vision, some doctors say getting a prescription too early can cause headaches in a small number of cases.

Using a special eye instrument, ophthalmologist Steven J. Lichtenstein of Louisville, Ky., examined 123 pre-schoolers last year and says he found only two who had problems, both of which had already been flagged by their own doctors. He also says he recently saw a family of five kids, all of whom were wearing spectacles prescribed elsewhere. In his opinion, four didn't need glasses, and the fifth had been given the wrong prescription. "I'm making money on this, and I don't agree with it," says Dr. Lichtenstein.

Indeed, even some manufacturers concede that glasses could be overprescribed to increase profits. But "doctors are the ones prescribing," says Mr. Friedfeld, of ClearVision Optical. For him, that means that doctors—not eyeglass makers—are the responsible party. "I only make the eyewear," says Mr. Friedfeld.

Not that any of that matters to three-year-old Sarah Demsky. The trend-conscious tyke in Chesterfield, Mo., has been bugging her mom, Jamie, for glasses ever since her two best friends started wearing them recently. Mrs. Demsky tried consoling her daughter with a new pair of $5 kiddie sunglasses, but that just hasn't done the trick. "You can't reason with a three-year-old," sighs Mrs. Demsky.

Mixed Messages in Blues Singer's Ads Dismay Fans

B.B. King Pitches Burger King And a Device for Diabetics; 'I'm Just Trying to Be Real'

BY RACHEL ZIMMERMAN

Two matters weigh heavily on B.B. King: the balance of his bank account and his battle with the bulge.

"I'm still too fat," says the 76-year-old blues legend, a diabetic who struggles to control his weight. "Some people eat to live, I live to eat." On the topic of cash, Mr. King, the great grandson of former slaves, is even more blunt: "It's against my nature to turn down money."

So it's not surprising that Mr. King has made his share of product pitches over the years, building a business empire that exploits his outsized personality and stretches far beyond guitar-plucking. What is now raising concern among some of his fans is the seemingly mixed message that some of those pitches convey.

In addition to a new **Nextel Communications** Inc. commercial, Mr. King has become a salesman for diabetes products, vouching for a novel blood-sugar test kit by LifeScan Inc., a unit of **Johnson & Johnson,** and he was the featured performer at the American Diabetes Association's annual black-tie banquet last June. But at the same time, he's promoting the latest sandwiches from Burger King, including the King Supreme, a cholesterol and sodium-laden double beef patty with American cheese, half an ounce of "saucier sauce worth singing about" and "more beef than the Big Mac," according to the ad.

"I don't say 'eat it all,'" Mr. King says, speaking from a hotel in New Orleans before one of his 200 planned performances this year. "You can eat some now, some later, and some much later."

Mr. King's personal manager, Floyd Lieberman, says he sees no problem with the multiple messages: "It's an ad. We don't swear that we eat this product," Mr. Lieberman says. "You think Bill Cosby walks around eating Jell-O all the time?"

Still, just a few years ago, Mr. King probably wouldn't have touched a Whopper for any amount of money. "I haven't eaten meat since almost 10 years ago when I watched a TV show about the slaughter of chickens and cows," Mr. King wrote in his 1996 autobiography, "Blues All Around Me." But even then his no-red-meat-eating philosophy didn't limit his advertising plugs. "When Dave of Wendy's restaurants asked me to do a commercial, I agreed," Mr. King wrote. "I've always liked selling products, and I tell folks that if I did eat meat, I'd go to Wendy's."

As for Burger King, the company says that despite his past asceticism, Mr. King is now a burger lover. "He eats our product and he enjoys it," says company spokesman Rob Doughty. "It's a great connection—and a great name."

OK, so maybe Mr. King has earned the right to sell whatever he wants. Raised by cotton pickers on a plantation near Itta Bena on the Mississippi Delta, he recounts the "hungry days" of his childhood, when his family was forced to eat white people's discards: Pigs' brains and feet were transformed into hog-head cheese and hog-head salad.

Who, then, can begrudge him his desire to pursue the dream of B.B King Inc.? Jason Silverio, for one, and a chorus of other fans. "Why did he do a Burger King commercial?" asks Mr. Silverio in a Jan. 16 posting on the official B.B. King Web site. "I am very disappointed that such a legend would sell his image (i.e., soul) to such a terrible company. Does he really need the money?"

Maybe not, but "when they pay you $2 million to $3 million for a half an hour of work," it's "hard to turn down," says Mr. Lieberman, Mr. King's manager. "It's a wonderful thing for a black man, a great blues star, to be making this kind of money."

Money—the lack of it and the wonder of making it—has been a leitmotif in Mr. King's life. He once dreamed of a corporate conglomerate that included clothes, food and clubs. In his autobiography, he had visions of B.B. King guitar strings, B.B. King casual clothing and B.B. King barbecue sauce, B.B.

King salad dressing and B.B. King bean spreads. "We're even thinking about B.B. King frozen catfish," he wrote.

But so far, only his blues clubs and the merchandise sold there, including B.B. King lighters and bumper stickers, have made it onto the market. Today, there are five club venues: two at the Foxwoods Casino in Connecticut and one each in Los Angeles, Memphis and midtown Manhattan, where Mayor Mike Bloomberg threw his victory party in November.

Some advertisers say privately that they wish Mr. King's message was a bit more consistent, but none seems on the verge of severing ties. "LifeScan continues to be pleased with its association with B.B. King," the company says in a statement about the ads that are part of its national print and television campaign. "Not only does he have diabetes and use our One Touch Ultra product, but his personal situation highlights one of the product's key features, the option to perform less painful testing on the arm instead of the fingertips."

Jerry Franz, a spokesman for the American Diabetes Association, says several people at the association were struck by the King Supreme ads. "I don't know why Mr. King has made the decision he did," he says. He adds that eating a burger once in a while as a treat in no way violates some core health principle among America's 16 million diabetics, but he adds that some choices make more sense than others: "You might want to have one of the smaller burgers and a diet Coke," he notes.

As for Mr. King, he laughs off accusations of inconsistency and says that while he has never claimed to be pure, he does aspire to be honest. "I'm not trying to give mixed information," he says. "I'm just trying to be real. People have to eat, and you can't just live on salads."

Blues legend and diabetic B.B. King pitches breakfast sandwiches and burgers in ads for **Burger King**

Doctor Group Defies South Africa AIDS Policy

Importing Brazilian Generics To Expand Treatment, Physicians Risk Lawsuit

BY MARK SCHOOFS

Staff Reporter of THE WALL STREET JOURNAL

Doctors Without Borders, the Nobel-Prize winning humanitarian group, has defied South African patent law by importing inexpensive generic AIDS drugs manufactured in Brazil for use in a township clinic outside of Capetown.

The group, joined by local AIDS activists in Johannesburg, called on the South African government yesterday to open the way for much wider use of generic drugs in that AIDS-ravaged nation.

By importing the cheaper generic drugs, "we could be sued for patent infringement," acknowledged Toby Kasper, a spokesman for Doctors Without Borders. But noting that the Brazilian imports cost about half the price of the same medicines made by Western pharmaceutical companies, he added, "We are not going to stand for a situation where we would be able to treat twice as many patients as we could by using only patented drugs. As medical professionals, it is our obligation to put the lives of our patients first."

About 50 patients, all in the Khayelitsha township outside of Capetown, have been taking the Brazilian generic medicines for about one month. But Doctors Without Borders, better known by its French acronym MSF, announced the imports only yesterday at a news conference in Johannesburg. For MSF and AIDS activists, the Brazilian drugs mark the latest move in a protracted campaign to make life-prolonging medications accessible in poor countries, where AIDS and other epidemics take their greatest toll.

Under public pressure, large pharmaceutical companies such as **Bristol-Myers Squibb** Co. and **Merck** & Co., have steadily dropped their prices in recent years, only to be undercut by generics from India, Thailand and Brazil.

The two companies that hold patents on the medicines MSF imported from Brazil—**GlaxoSmithKline** PLC and **Boehringer Ingelheim** GmbH—said they are observing the situation but don't have immediate plans to take legal action, which would almost certainly bring down a hail of bad publicity. "You don't tilt against windmills," said Kevin McKenna, a spokesman for Boehringer Ingelheim South Africa.

Peter Moore, who runs GSK's South Africa office, said he was surprised at MSF's action because Glaxo has entered into an agreement with a South African generics producer, **Aspen Pharmacare** Ltd., to manufacture some of GSK's AIDS drugs. Aspen's generics, however, aren't yet available, because the company is still in the process of obtaining South African regulatory approval for such drugs.

As for Boehringer, it offers its AIDS drug nevirapine in South Africa for a discounted price of about $1.06 a day. The Brazilian manufacturer, FarManguinhos, sold the drug to MSF for about 59 cents a day. "Maybe—maybe—we can't compete with Brazil," said Mr. McKenna of Boehringer. He said that his company couldn't sell nevirapine, which it markets under the name Viramune, for much less than its current price. But he added that the company would continue its charitable program of offering the drug free of charge for use in pregnant women, where the drug slashes the chance of transmitting the AIDS virus to the baby.

In its latest action, MSF is aiming only part of its fire at multinational pharmaceutical companies. The activists are also targeting South Africa's government, which is widely perceived to be obstructing the use of AIDS drugs, called antiretrovirals.

The South African Department of Health responded to MSF's action by saying it would dispatch investigators to see whether MSF is in compliance with the country's medical regulatory rules. If MSF is found to have violated the law, the imported drugs "will be confiscated," said department of health spokesman Sibani Mngadi. However, MSF received a formal authorization from the South African equivalent of the U.S. Food and Drug Administration, the Medicines Control Council, to use the drugs in a research program. MSF said it also received a customs waiver allowing the drugs to be imported, and stated that it would welcome a visit by health-department investigators.

The response of the government appears certain to intensify the stand-off between it and AIDS activists. Against overwhelming scientific evidence, President Thabo Mbeki has questioned whether HIV actually causes AIDS, and recently he has gone against his country's own public-health authorities and questioned whether AIDS is really the leading cause of death in South Africa. The South African Department of Health estimates that 4.7 million South Africans, or about a quarter of the country's adults, are infected with HIV.

Mr. Mbeki has also questioned the safety and efficacy of the AIDS drug cocktails. AIDS doctors and activists recently took the South African government to court to force it to make the drugs available to pregnant mothers, to prevent the transmission of the virus to their babies. The government lost that case, but has appealed.

The government's increasingly isolated stand on AIDS has brought intense criticism from within the country. The Congress of South African Trade Unions, the nation's largest labor organization, participated in yesterday's MSF news conference. COSATU has been especially critical of the government, because it wants its many infected members to be able to obtain treatment.

Increasingly, ordinary South Africans are demanding access to AIDS medicines, creating a potential rift between the ruling African National Congress, which overturned apartheid, and the country's majority population of blacks, who are most heavily affected by the AIDS epidemic. Twenty-five-year-old Matthew Damane was sick with AIDS last June, when he entered the MSF program. Now he is working as an AIDS counselor, and was one of four activists to visit Brazil and bring back the generic medicines. "I want everyone who has HIV to be treated," he said.

Cheaper Treatment

Daily cost of AIDS drugs

AZT/3TC combination

GlaxoSmithKline (Proprietary company)
$2.00*

FarManguinhos (Brazilian generic)
$0.96

Nevirapine

Boehringer Ingelheim (Proprietary company)
$1.06*

FarManguinhos (Brazilian generic)
$0.59

*Special discount price
Sources: GlaxoSmithKline, Boehringer Ingelheim, Doctors Without Borders

Friendly Watchdog

Federal Regulator Often Helps Banks Fighting Consumers

Dependent on Lenders' Fees, OCC Takes Their Side Against Local, State Laws

Defending Uniform Rules

By Jess Bravin and Paul Beckett
Staff Reporters of The Wall Street Journal

When a federal appeals court in San Francisco took up the issue of automated-teller-machine fees earlier this month, it sparked the latest round in the battle between big banks and customers.

Sticking up for consumers were the cities of San Francisco and Santa Monica. They had banned certain ATM fees, after customers complained about being gouged when they use ATMs belonging to banks other than their own. Defending the fees were California's two largest banks—Bank of America Corp. and Wells Fargo & Co.— which had won at trial.

Also in the courtroom: the Office of the Comptroller of the Currency, the federal banking regulator. But in this case—as in more than a dozen others in recent years— the OCC wasn't there to check the economic power of banking titans. Instead, the regulator was helping the nationally chartered banks defend their fees. The appeals court is expected to rule in coming months.

Many federal regulators have a clear mandate to put consumers first. The Securities and Exchange Commission, for example, refers to itself as "the investor's advocate."

It's less clearcut for the federal banking watchdog. Time and again, the U.S. agency that bank customers might assume is on their side has lined up with banks to fight state and local measures that purport to aid consumers.

In addition to the ATM-fees case in California, the OCC recently has supported banks in their effort to kill a ban in Texas on certain check-cashing fees. In Pennsylvania and Rhode Island, the OCC has weighed in on the side of giant FleetBoston Financial Corp. against consumer allegations of improper increases in credit-card rates. And in Michigan, the federal agency has even

supported a push by banks making auto loans to curb a state law aimed at unscrupulous car dealers.

The OCC's solicitousness toward the businesses it oversees stems in part from its need to compete for their loyalty. In an uncommon arrangement, banks can choose either a state or federal regulator, and the selection has financial consequences: The OCC and state banking departments subsist entirely on fees paid by the institutions they regulate.

The competition, though discreet, can get intense. As consolidation has swept the industry, the OCC's once-mighty position has slipped. Since 1990, as the number of U.S. banks dropped 31%, to 8,300, the number regulated by the OCC dropped 45%, to about 2,230. It still regulates the bulk of the banking industry as measured by assets, but consolidation has made the agency increasingly dependent on a few big players. Third-ranking Bank of America, based in Charlotte, N.C., now pays $40 million a year to the OCC in fees, or the equivalent of 10% of the agency's annual $400 million budget.

The OCC promises federally chartered banks the predictability of a uniform set of rules, rather than the burden of complying with varying state standards. A further attraction is the likelihood that the agency will support its banks in court against aggressive state regulators. State banking authorities typically offer the competing enticement of lower examination fees.

The OCC, an arm of the Treasury Department with 2,900 employees, maintains that it safeguards customers by enforcing federal consumer-protection laws and by securing the overall health of the national banking system. But the agency's chief, John D. Hawke Jr., says that state efforts to stick up for bank customers often threaten to undermine the right of national banks under federal law to operate and charge fees as they see fit.

The OCC's siding with banks in court fights "may operate in some cases to the disadvantage of consumers," says Mr. Hawke, a 68-year-old lawyer who in private practice represented both state- and federally chartered banks. But his agency "can't pick and choose whether a [state] law or action is good or bad" for consumers. If it cramps banks' freedom to operate in the eyes of the OCC, it must go, he says.

History helps explain the OCC's stance. It was founded during the Civil War to oversee newly created national banks that were formed to circulate a national currency and finance the Union's military campaign. With strong backing from the federal courts, the OCC still interprets the National Bank Act of 1863 as authorizing it to oppose any state or municipal attempt to interfere with the ability of nationally chartered banks to engage in "the business of banking." When the agency goes to court, it also invokes a provision in the U.S. Constitution stating

that federal law prevails in conflicts with state law.

Frustrated consumers say the upshot is that the OCC favors the industry that pays its bills. "The individual bank customer is just no equal of the large banking institutions," says David Buda, an attorney in Fort Lee, N.J., who has complained unsuccessfully to the OCC about increases in the interest rate on his FleetBoston credit card. If "your only avenue is to complain to the comptroller of the currency, then all you're going to get is a form letter saying, 'We can't help you,'" Mr. Buda adds.

Other federal regulators operate differently. The SEC budget comes from fees from securities exchanges and publicly traded companies. But unlike banks, those companies don't have a choice of regulator, so the SEC isn't competing for their loyalty. About 12% of the Food and Drug Administration's budget comes from industry fees. The Federal Trade Commission is funded by taxpayers.

During tough economic times, the bank-regulatory setup comes under a brighter spotlight. Consumers find it harder to keep up financially. Banks, faced with rising loan losses, seek additional revenue with moves such as fee hikes on credit cards— making it that much more likely that consumers will seek help from the federal bank regulator.

Mr. Hawke, who was appointed by President Clinton in 1998 to a five-year term, says he spends time both looking out for consumers and seeking to defend his regulatory turf. In 1999, he introduced a 12-minute video the OCC distributes to banks called "The Value of the National Bank Charter." In it, he describes "how the OCC and a national charter can help banking organizations achieve their goals."

Personal Appeals

Sometimes, he makes personal appeals. In August 1999, when state-chartered AmSouth Bancorp of Birmingham, Ala., was in the process of buying OCC-chartered First American Corp. of Nashville, Tenn., Mr. Hawke flew to visit C. Dowd Ritter, AmSouth's chief executive. After exchanging pleasantries, Mr. Hawke reached into his briefcase to show Mr. Ritter a copy of a federal bank charter issued in 1884 to one of AmSouth's predecessor banks.

"This is something I thought you would like to see," Mr. Hawke said, according to Stephen Yoder, AmSouth's general counsel, who attended the meeting. "We have something in Washington that is part of your history."

Despite the imaginative appeal, AmSouth rebuffed Mr. Hawke, retaining its Alabama state charter after the merger. The bank says it already had a good relationship with its state regulator.

Mr. Hawke, who confirms the account,

(Cont.)

says that losing market share "is a matter of concern to us." But he stresses the OCC takes seriously its responsibility to protect consumers. He occasionally makes speeches chastising bankers for such practices as selling confidential customer information to telemarketing firms. And the agency enforces about a dozen federal consumer laws, including the Truth in Lending and Fair Credit Reporting Acts. Typically, the OCC enforces compliance with those laws during its routine bank examinations, agency spokesman Robert Garsson says.

Earlier this month, as the result of an examination, the OCC ordered Eagle National Bank, a small institution in Upper Darby, Pa., to get out of the business of funding so-called payday loans. These are high-interest loans repayable on the borrower's next payday and viewed by many regulators as exploitative. The OCC said it acted because Eagle's lack of oversight of the loans had placed its financial viability at risk.

In a separate case 18 months ago, the agency joined a civil probe initiated by the San Francisco district attorney into allegations that Providian Financial Corp., a San Francisco credit-card issuer, had misled customers about interest rates on credit cards. Providian allegedly promised card holders they wouldn't have to pay an annual fee when the company in fact imposed a mandatory $156 annual charge for "credit protection." Without admitting wrongdoing, Providian agreed to pay $300 million to purported victims, plus a $5.5 million penalty to San Francisco. Mr. Hawke calls the case a landmark exercise of the OCC's authority to ban deceptive practices.

Still, he doesn't apologize for using the OCC's power to override state and local laws designed to protect consumers. Enjoying this aid provides an incentive for banks to sign up with the OCC, he says. "It is one of the advantages of a national charter, and I'm not the least bit ashamed to promote it." His counterparts at the SEC, FTC or FDA don't have a comparable turf-related incentive to advertise their ability to knock down state and local consumer-protection laws.

State banking regulators often engage in their own efforts to lure banks. The Kansas banking commissioner, for instance, promises on his official Web site that state-chartered banks will have greater ability "to lobby [the] state legislature for changes in laws and regulations." Commissioner Franklin Nelson explains in an interview that his department is next door to the statehouse and can help bank officials and their lobbyists reach lawmakers. The OCC can't offer such access, he says.

State regulators also aren't shy about pointing out that national banks pay as much as 2.5 times the annual examination fees charged to state banks. The fees are determined by bank size. A small bank, with $500 million in assets, would typically have to pay

$43,000 under a state charter, compared with $113,000 under a federal charter, according to OCC estimates.

OCC Impact

It is the OCC's ability to help override state laws that has the biggest impact on consumers. The OCC's involvement in the California ATM case began in 1999, when Bank of America and Wells Fargo, which together control more than 60% of the ATMs in the state, asked a federal judge in San Francisco to void that city's and Santa Monica's bans on some fees, which generate about $6 million annually for the two banks. The OCC, in separate legal papers, said "the public interest" favored allowing banks to charge noncustomers more for using their ATMs. Otherwise, the OCC argued, the banks would lack the incentive to operate large numbers of ATMs in areas where they don't have many customers.

"That's flat-out wrong," Santa Monica Mayor Michael Feinstein responds in an interview. "We are closer to that consumer than the OCC is," he adds. And, on balance, he says, consumers want lower fees, even in the face of bank threats to deny noncustomers any access to their ATMs.

Mr. Hawke suggests that angry customers do as he says he does: walk a few extra blocks to find a no-fee ATM.

A federal judge in 2000 agreed with the OCC's argument and blocked the municipal ATM-fee restrictions, prompting this month's hearing before a three-judge panel of the Ninth U.S. Circuit Court of Appeals. Opposing the OCC in that case, officials from California, New York and seven other states filed papers siding with the cities.

The OCC came to the defense of the same pair of big banks, among others, last year in Texas. The legislature there had recently passed a law that effectively prevented a bank from charging noncustomers a fee for cashing certain kinds of checks. Four big banks that operate in the state, including Wells Fargo, levy the fees, which typically range from $3 to $5 per check. Bank of America is planning to do the same. The four that currently charge the fees account for 40% of bank deposits in the state and generate a total of $5.2 million a year from the fees, according to court papers.

Before the new law was scheduled to take effect Sept. 1, Wells Fargo, Bank of America and Bank One Corp. of Chicago, which also holds a federal charter, asked the OCC if they had to obey the law. The OCC said they didn't. The agency weighed in with a "friend of the court" brief in U.S. district court in Austin, arguing that the National Bank Act permits national banks to charge whatever fees they deem appropriate for their services. In December, Judge James R. Nowlin agreed.

The Texas Banking Department is appealing the decision. "Texas passed a consumer-protection law that was duly enacted

and should apply," says state Banking Commissioner Randall James.

The OCC even has backed its banks trying to knock down regulations that cover other companies they do business with outside of the banking industry.

In Michigan, the state Motor Vehicle Sales Finance Act, passed in 1950, requires that auto dealers fully disclose installment-payment terms. It also limits document-preparation fees to $40 and restricts the conditions under which a car can be repossessed. The statute applies only to dealers who sell cars through installment plans. It doesn't apply to banks.

But National City Bank, a unit of Cleveland's National City Corp., and Huntington National Bank, owned by Huntington Bancshares Inc. of Columbus, Ohio, sought in administrative proceedings to make the dealers who market their car loans exempt from the law. Michigan's commissioner of financial and insurance services, Frank Fitzgerald, ruled in January 2000 that car dealers who teamed with national banks were still covered.

'We Had to Do Something'

"We had to do something to get by that," says Daniel W. Morton, Huntington National's vice president and senior counsel. So the two banks asked the OCC for an opinion saying the state law was trumped by the National Bank Act. Commissioner Fitzgerald filed an objection, arguing that it would be "absurd" if the OCC could kill a state law aimed at nonbanking businesses.

In May, the OCC found otherwise, concluding that Michigan's law "frustrates the [banks'] ability to exercise their lending authority" and therefore shouldn't be enforced against car dealers marketing loans made by OCC-chartered banks. Michigan isn't contesting the ruling. The state doesn't think it can beat the OCC in federal court, says Mr. Fitzgerald.

Mr. Garsson, the OCC spokesman, says that consumers obtaining car loans funded by national banks—such as those in the Michigan case—would be covered by federal consumer protections that the OCC enforces.

In the FleetBoston case, the OCC received hundreds of letters from customers in 2000, complaining that the federally chartered bank had increased interest rates on its credit cards after allegedly promising a "fixed" rate. In response, the OCC sent customers letters saying it couldn't help. Federal law "recognizes banks' ability to change the terms of credit card account agreements," as long as the change is disclosed, the OCC said in a typical letter sent to a complaining customer on March 23, 2000. "If you wish to pursue further remedy to your complaint, we can only suggest that you contact private legal counsel regarding any additional remedies," the OCC added.

In October 2000, several customers filed

(Cont.)

suit, seeking class-action status and accusing FleetBoston of deceptive practices under Rhode Island state law. A Rhode Island state judge in Providence ruled in April that the case could proceed. But the OCC stepped in to help FleetBoston. The OCC argued in a friend-of-the-court brief that the state law on which the suit was based doesn't apply to FleetBoston because the OCC can take action against unfair and deceptive practices, as it did in the Providian case—although the agency hadn't done so regarding FleetBoston.

Justice Judith Colenback Savage of Rhode Island Superior Court rejected the OCC's argument last April, a decision the state's Supreme Court declined to review. The case was then consolidated with a similar suit filed by a separate group of disgruntled FleetBoston customers before another Rhode Island judge.

In December, the new judge, Michael Silverstein, handed the OCC a victory. He ruled that FleetBoston couldn't be sued under the state's deceptive-practices law. Such a suit would call into question the OCC's "very foundational authority to regulate national banks," the judge ruled. At a hearing last week, FleetBoston sought to have the suit dismissed on those grounds. A decision is expected by the end of March.

Evasive Maneuvers

Detroit Again Tries To Dodge Pressures For a 'Greener' Fleet

Oil Fears Since Sept. 11 Add Urgency to Latest Round Of Gas-Mileage Politics

'Supercars' and Fuel Cells

By Jeffrey Ball

Staff Reporter of The Wall Street Journal

DETROIT—For years the Big Three U.S. auto makers have dodged any increase in the federal fuel-economy standards their vehicles must meet. Now, amid growing concern in Washington over U.S. dependence on Mideast oil after Sept. 11, the car companies are running out of wiggle room.

So how are auto executives dealing with the looming threat of stiffer Corporate Average Fuel Economy rules? They're trumpeting a futuristic technological crusade they hope will earn them green points—and big subsidies—from Washington today. And they are still trying to maneuver, if no longer to block a CAFE increase, at least to structure it so it hurts them less and their Japanese competitors more.

It's a questionable strategy on both counts. Two of the Big Three—Ford Motor Co. and DaimlerChrysler AG's Chrysler unit—now are mired in red ink, and General Motors Corp. is only barely in the black. If they succeed in staving off a government requirement to make their most profitable vehicles substantially more environmentally friendly and technologically sophisticated, the companies probably won't soon make that change on their own. The Big Three's failure to innovate has repeatedly helped their foreign rivals. That's how Detroit lost its dominance in passenger cars in the 1970s and 1980s, and since the early 1990s, the same thing has been happening with the cash cows known collectively as "light trucks": sport-utility vehicles, pickup trucks and minivans.

Betting on Fuel Cells

The other danger is that Detroit's bet on a new technology, fuel cells, could take years to pan out, while its Japanese competitors capitalize on their existing edge and pull

away. Earlier this month, the Bush administration announced it was launching a program to subsidize fuel-cell research over several decades. The new push replaces a similar Clinton-era subsidy that spent $1.5 billion over nearly a decade to get the Big Three to produce hybrid electric "supercars" getting 80 miles to the gallon. In the end, they never left the lab. Meanwhile, Japan's Honda Motor Co. and Toyota Motor Corp. have begun selling their own hybrid cars and are preparing to put another generation of them on the road.

The CAFE rules were established by Congress in 1975 and implemented a few years later to reduce U.S. oil consumption in the wake of the Arab oil embargo. They apply to all manufacturers who sell cars or light trucks in the U.S. The rules divide the U.S. auto fleet into two groups: passenger cars and light trucks. They require a major manufacturer's fleet of cars each model year to average 27.5 miles per gallon, and its fleet of light trucks to average 20.7 mpg.

The difference seemed logical a generation ago, when light trucks were still relatively specialized vehicles. But today, they account for about half of all new-vehicle sales in the U.S. Their surging popularity, combined with their lower fuel economy, has pulled down the average fuel economy of the country's total new-vehicle fleet to its lowest level in two decades. That has sparked increasingly loud demands from environmentalists that the government close what they dub the rule's "SUV loophole."

Light trucks were among the hottest sellers when auto makers rolled out free financing in the wake of the Sept. 11 attacks. They accounted for 56% of all sales in December, according to Autodata Corp., an industry research firm. But the terrorist attacks also added urgency to the calls for less-thirsty cars and light trucks. Together, cars and light trucks consume about 41% of the oil used in the U.S. economy.

A Toehold for Japan

The Big Three blame the CAFE standards for giving Japanese auto makers a toehold in the U.S. market. Honda and Toyota already were making small cars for a home market that demanded fuel economy, and the CAFE standards ended up constraining the Big Three's ability to keep cranking out the big vehicles they had been selling Americans for years. Over the past decade, the Japanese manufacturers have followed the Big Three into trucks, and many of their biggest SUVs and pickups get no better mileage than the comparably sized models from the Big Three. But the biggest and thirstiest trucks still represent a smaller portion of the Japanese auto makers' total truck lineups than is the case with the Big Three.

The upshot is that the Big Three are running up against the CAFE ceiling. Most Japanese auto makers aren't. What scares the

Big Three is that, if the CAFE standard is raised, they would have to spend big to redesign their trucks to make them more fuel-efficient while the Japanese could grab more U.S. market share with their existing SUVs and pickups.

Detroit's efforts to minimize the pain of any CAFE increase are complicated by the blurring of lines that once defined domestic and foreign vehicles. Today, Japanese and European auto makers have factories on U.S. soil that employ thousands of Americans, and that gives them clout in Washington. Meanwhile, Chrysler has a German owner, Ford has acquired a passel of foreign luxury brands, and GM this month joined the Japan Automobile Manufacturers Association. The main auto-industry trade group in Washington, the Alliance of Automobile Manufacturers, represents 13 auto makers.

Getting the 13 to agree on any political issue is difficult, and nowhere more so than on what shape a CAFE increase should take. "There is going to be an increase in CAFE," says a DaimlerChrysler official. "You can pretty much design one that brings you a competitive advantage. But your competitive advantage is someone else's competitive disadvantage." And that, he adds, isn't "politically tenable."

One option would be simply to raise the current 20.7 mpg light-truck CAFE standard and require every major auto maker to retool its fleet to meet it by a certain date. But, given the prevalence of big trucks in their fleets, that would hit the Big Three hard.

On the Line

In the 2001 model year, Daimler-Chrysler's light-truck fleet registered an average fuel economy right at the limit: 20.7 mpg, according to preliminary figures from the National Highway Traffic Safety Administration, the agency that oversees compliance with the rule. GM's and Ford's fleets actually fell below the standard, to 20.5 mpg, though under CAFE's byzantine credit system, both manufacturers will be able to apply future- and prior-year credits to that number so they don't technically violate the standard.

By contrast, Honda's 2001 light-truck fuel-economy rating was 24.9 mpg. For Toyota the number was 22.1 mpg. Unlike Honda, Toyota builds pickup trucks and very large SUVs.

CAFE appears to be less of an issue for European car makers. Bayerische Motoren Werke AG, DaimlerChrysler's Mercedes-Benz unit, Porsche AG and their brethren have been violating the CAFE standard for years and paying the resulting federal fines as a cost of doing business. BMW, for example, paid $13.1 million in CAFE fines in 2000 for its 1999 models.

One alternative idea for toughening CAFE has been discussed for years as a way to avoid hurting the Big Three. It would require all major auto makers, regardless of their current

GM's "Autonomy" concept car. *It's the chassis of a car designed to run on hydrogen-powered fuel cells, and it has plug-in sockets for various futuristic bodies.*

It's Not Easy Being Green

The Big Three auto makers are still in the slow lane compared with their major Japanese competitors when it comes to fuel economy. Detroit's light trucks remain barely within range of the government's Corporate Average Fuel Economy, or CAFE, standards. Charts show fuel-economy performance of each manufacturer's light trucks for each model year, in miles per gallon.

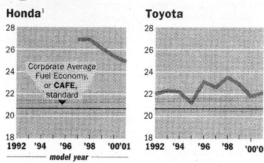

Honda[1]

Toyota

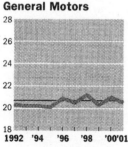

General Motors

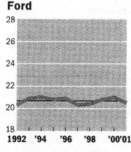

Ford

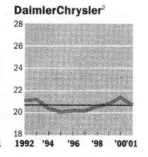

DaimlerChrysler[2]

[1]Government statistics don't include Honda light trucks before 1997.
[2]Chrysler only before 1999 model year.

Source: National Highway Traffic Safety Administration

But the cracks within the industry were apparent at a hearing last Thursday before the Senate Commerce Committee, which is expected within the next two weeks to recommend some sort of CAFE increase. Sen. John Kerry, a Massachusetts Democrat, who has made clear he supports an increase in the CAFE rule, noted that a National Academy of Sciences panel that studied the issue last year concluded that auto makers could make "significant" improvements in the fuel economy of their vehicles. Although the panel cautioned that its conclusions weren't recommendations for a specific CAFE increase, John DeCicco, a senior fellow with the advocacy group Environmental Defense, calculates that the panel's study suggests auto makers could feasibly boost the fuel economy of their combined car and truck fleets to about 32 mpg over 10 to 15 years from about 24 mpg today.

Greg Dana, the auto alliance's vice president for environmental affairs, testified that the alliance doesn't want Congress to do anything about CAFE. It wants the issue handled by the Bush administration's NHTSA, which also is studying the issue. The alliance says that's because NHTSA is better able than Congress to consider the complex technical issues of CAFE without being swayed by political emotions. Critics of the industry see a different motive. They note that throughout the late 1990s, when NHTSA was part of the Clinton administration and Congress was controlled by Republicans, the auto industry successfully lobbied Congress to pass annual provisions barring NHTSA from considering any CAFE increase. Only last year did the industry pull back and let the freeze expire.

'Sort of Silly?'

When, in last Thursday's hearing, Sen. Kerry asked the alliance's Mr. Dana how much auto makers could improve the fuel economy of their vehicles, Mr. Dana declined to answer. "Do you think the industry could do 1 mpg over 10 years?" Sen. Kerry asked. Mr. Dana demurred, saying he wasn't a technical expert. Responded Mr. Kerry: "Don't you think that renders you sort of silly?"

But the representative from Honda, the one big auto company that doesn't belong to the alliance, was more expansive. "There's a lot that can be done" to improve automotive fuel economy, even just by tweaking the century-old internal-combustion engine, said John Gorman, the Honda official, though he too stressed that any CAFE increase should be phased in over several years.

Honda also distanced itself from an argument long made by many other auto makers that requiring light trucks to get better fuel economy will make them less safe because it will force manufacturers to make them smaller and lighter. Honda, whose lineup is generally lighter and smaller than the Big Three's, said it recently hired a consultant to

CAFE levels, to boost them by the same percentage over a set period.

It's as if a high-school teacher told the C students they all had to become B students—but at the same time the B students also had to become A students. That would lock in the Big Three's ability to keep producing a fleet that is less fuel-efficient than their Japanese competitors[1].

It also probably would amount to a cost penalty for the Japanese manufacturers. They already have invested more than Detroit in fuel-efficient technologies, so they would have to resort to more-esoteric technologies to maintain their lead.

The United Auto Workers, which represents workers at the Big Three but not yet at U.S. plants wholly owned by Japanese auto makers, endorsed a percentage CAFE increase in testimony before the Senate Commerce Committee last month, saying that as long as it's small enough to be "technically feasible and economically practicable," it "could be achieved without job dislocation or disparate impacts on manufacturers."

Similarly, officials from at least some of the Big Three auto makers say privately that they prefer the percentage model. But they won't say so publicly. One reason is their fear that if they endorsed any kind of CAFE increase, they'd lose control of the political debate and be hit with a big one. Another reason is that doing so would expose publicly a rift that exists privately between the Big Three and other members of the automotive alliance, particularly Toyota.

study the issue, and that the preliminary conclusion is that reducing the weight of an average vehicle by 100 pounds has a "very small and not statistically significant" effect on the number of traffic deaths.

In the end, the discord among auto makers probably will doom the chances of a straight percentage increase in CAFE, say executives of both the Big Three and the Japanese, particularly since the Japanese manufacturers dislike it, and they have factories of their own in politically key states. "The word has come back from Senate offices that that's not going to fly," says a U.S. auto executive.

Another possibility is replacing the CAFE rule's distinction between cars and light trucks with a more complicated system that sets fuel-economy standards for vehicles depending on their weight. That would allow a manufacturer to build, say, as many big SUVs as it could sell, though it would be required to make those SUVs go somewhat farther on a gallon of gas.

This approach has critics, too. Chief among them are environmentalists, who note that it could be as ripe as the current system for manipulation. An auto maker, they argue, might be able to avoid improving the fuel efficiency of a vehicle in a particular classification by adding more features to it,

thus making it heavier and shifting it to a classification with a less-stringent CAFE requirement.

Before Sept. 11, proponents of a CAFE increase were basically limited to environmental activists and their political supporters. Since the terrorist attacks, however, the voices calling for a CAFE increase have broadened to include those whose focus isn't protecting the planet, but reducing U.S. consumption of Mideast oil in the name of national security.

The auto industry's answer is the fuel cell. The holy grail of clean-car technologies, the fuel cell in its ideal form combines pure hydrogen with oxygen from the air to produce electricity that can power a vehicle's four wheels while producing only water as exhaust. One big practical problem is cost. Another is how to get pure hydrogen to thousands of filling stations. But even using conventional fuel as a hydrogen source, the fuel cell likely would produce less carbon-dioxide exhaust than an internal-combustion engine.

Although it's a longshot, the auto industry argues the fuel cell is the only technology with real potential to significantly cut the nation's long-term demand for oil. At the Detroit auto show earlier this month, GM Chief Executive Rick Wagoner rolled out the

"Autonomy," a mockup of a chassis for a fuel-cell-powered car that he said could end up "largely removing the automobile from the environmental equation."

Two days later in Detroit, Energy Secretary Spencer Abraham announced Freedom Car, a Bush administration program to subsidize fuel-cell research. Freedom Car will help the nation "invent our way to energy independence," said Mr. Abraham, a former U.S. senator from Michigan.

To Sen. Carl Levin, a Michigan Democrat sitting in the front row at Mr. Abraham's announcement, all the talk about fuel cells has near-term political value. It should help persuade lawmakers anxious to reduce U.S. dependence on Mideast oil to subsidize the Big Three's long-term research rather than saddling the industry with big increases in CAFE requirements now. "The more you focus on mandates," Mr. Levin said, "you are going to detract from your effort to make a leap ahead."